15015094

D1564042

The Theory of Epistemic Rationality

THE THEORY OF EPISTEMIC RATIONALITY

Richard Foley

Harvard University Press
*Cambridge, Massachusetts
and London, England   1987*

Library of Congress Cataloging-in-Publication Data

Foley, Richard.
   The theory of epistemic rationality.

   Bibliography: p.
   Includes index.
   1. Knowledge, Theory of. I. Title.
BD161.F57   1987   121'.6   86-31963
ISBN 0-674-88276-8 (alk. paper)

To Holly, with love

PREFACE

This book was motivated by an apparently simple question, one that had been of interest to me since my days as a graduate student— namely, under what conditions is it rational for an individual to believe a claim? When six or seven years ago I began once again to think seriously about this question, I found a bewildering variety of answers in the literature. It is not unusual, of course, for philosophers to disagree, but it struck me that the disagreements over this question were more fundamental than in other areas of philosophy. It was as if the disputants were offering answers to different questions. Philosophers of science, for example, seemed to be answering a different sort of question than were traditional epistemologists, who in turn seemed to be answering a different sort of question than, say, reliabilists. As I continued to think about the notion of rational belief, this initial impression persisted, and it is what accounts for the concern in this work with meta-issues as well as first-level issues; I am concerned not only with defending a particular theory of epistemic rationality but also with describing what sort of question such a theory should be trying to answer.

In preparing this book, I made use of previously published material. Section 3.1 is based on "What's Wrong with Reliabilism?" *The Monist* 68 (1985), 188–202. I first discussed many of the themes of chapter 4 in "Epistemic Luck and the Purely Epistemic," *American Philosophical Quarterly* 21 (1984), and sections 6.2–6.3 incorporate material from "Epistemic Conservatism," *Philosophical Studies* 43 (1983), 165–182.

There are many people whose influence on this work should be acknowledged. First, I would like to thank my parents simply for

being the kind of people they are. It is my hope that this book reflects at least in an imperfect way the standards of honesty and fair-
mindedness that they taught me. Among philosophers my deepest
debt is to Richard Fumerton, who is as good a philosophic critic as
there is anywhere and who has been my good friend since we were
graduate students together. I have learned an enormous amount of
philosophy from him over the years, much of which has found its
way into this book. Peter Klein also had a great influence on this
book. Peter read with his characteristic care the first half of the manuscript while I was visiting at Rutgers during the fall semester of 1985–
86. Both the book and my way of thinking about epistemology im-
proved dramatically as a result of his constant prodding. The spring
before my visit at Rutgers, I received similar prodding from my col-
leagues at Notre Dame and in particular from Mike DePaul, Aron
Edidin, and Al Plantinga. We met weekly during that spring and
during a good part of the summer, discussing various sections of the
manuscript. I regard those discussions and the spirit of helpfulness
and good humor with which they were conducted as the epitome of
collegiality. Ernie LePore also deserves special thanks, both for his
unwavering friendship and for his equally unwavering questions. He
is not an epistemologist, but he has as active a mind as anyone I have
ever met. The result, when doing philosophy, is a barrage of questions,
questions that forced me to think much more deeply about what I as
an epistemologist was trying to do. William Alston and Richard Feldman were the referees of the manuscript, and they too should be
mentioned, first for their generous evaluations of the work and second
for the particular care with which they prepared their comments.
Almost all of the changes that they recommended, substantive as well
as stylistic, were incorporated into the book. I also wish to thank
Lindsay Waters, General Editor at Harvard University Press, for being
the paradigm of a good editor—supportive, informative, and always
straightforward.

There are groups as well as individuals to whom I am indebted.
Graduate students at Notre Dame and at Rutgers have read the manuscript, and some notes upon which sections of the manuscript were
modeled were the basis for part of a graduate seminar I gave at the
University of Iowa the year before I began writing the manuscript. In
addition, I have given lectures loosely based on portions of the manuscript to the philosophy departments at Notre Dame, the University
of Illinois at Chicago, and Rutgers, as well as to the philosophy of
science course held at the Inter-University Centre in Dubrovnik. I
received useful comments from each of these groups. I want also to

offer special thanks to Professors Martin Benjamin, Richard Momeyer, and Carl Hedman who first sparked my interest in philosophy, and to the Department of Philosophy at Brown, where I was a graduate student. It was there that I learned about the care and precision with which good philosophy is done. I was especially influenced by Professors Dan Brock, Roderick Chisholm, John Ladd, Phil Quinn and Ernie Sosa. A long list of contemporary epistemologists whose works have deeply influenced me would include (in addition to those already mentioned), Robert Audi, Fred Dretske, Roderick Firth, Alvin Goldman, Keith Lehrer, Robert Nozick, John Pollock, and of course many others as well. My disagreements with many of these philosophers will be obvious, but I have never failed to learn a great deal from studying their work.

Finally, thanks also are due to the secretary of the Philosophy Department at Notre Dame, Ryan Welsh; the Assistant Chairman, Montey Holloway; and the Dean of Arts and Letters, Mike Loux. Each has done a great deal to make my job as chairman bearable and at times even enjoyable, and each, more times than I can remember, covered for me when I was secluded in my office during the mornings, working on the manuscript and refusing to answer my phone. Ryan in particular had her patience tried to the limit as I presented her with one set of revisions after another, each time assuring her that these were the last.

CONTENTS

The Theory of Epistemic Rationality

INTRODUCTION

What is epistemology? This question is no easier to answer than comparable questions about other branches of philosophy. No doubt an interesting and perhaps even coherent story can be told concerning why all of the following philosophers have been regarded as doing epistemology: Democritus, Plato, Aristotle, Epicurus, Zeno, Plotinus, Augustine, Aquinas, Ockham, Descartes, Malebranche, Spinoza, Leibniz, Locke, Berkeley, Hume, Reid, Kant, Mill, Hegel, Bradley, Husserl, James, Peirce, Dewey, Moore, Russell, Lewis, Wittgenstein, Carnap, Ryle, Quine, and Chisholm. Even so, it would not be surprising to find that the projects of these philosophers, including the parts that are most apt to be deemed epistemological, are different in important ways. On the contrary, it would be surprising if they were not different; it would be surprising, for example, if Quine's epistemology were not a somewhat different kind of account—one that is put forth as an answer to a different question—than that found in, say, Aquinas, and in turn it would be surprising if Aquinas' epistemology were not a somewhat different kind of account than that found in Descartes'. Many different kinds of work, sometimes only subtly different but sometimes almost startlingly different, can be done under the name of epistemology.

I mention this for a reason. This book is presented as one in epistemology, and yet some of the notions most closely associated with epistemology are pretty much ignored. I say little about the notion of justification and little about the notion of warrant, nor do I devote much effort to discussing the notion of knowledge. What I do say quite a lot about is the notion of epistemic rationality. I try to describe in some detail what is involved in it being epistemically rational for someone to believe some claim (whether or not he in fact believes it).

Of course, it may well be that once this notion is understood, it can be used to help us understand other epistemic notions—justification, warrant, knowledge, evidence, and information, as well as others. Indeed, I will make a number of suggestions concerning how this might be done. Be this as it may, this is first and foremost a work that is concerned not with knowledge or justification or warrant or some other epistemic notion but rather with epistemic rationality. In particular, it is a work in which I seek to articulate a general conception of epistemic rationality; in so doing, I try to identify the kind of rationality that is the subject of *the* theory of epistemic rationality (hence the title). I also propose *a* theory of epistemic rationality— that is, a specific account of this kind of rationality.

Why might one be interested in such an account? A full answer to this question cannot be given before articulating a general conception of epistemic rationality, but at least a preliminary answer can be sketched now. One might be interested in such an account because one is interested in understanding what it is rational for an individual to believe insofar as he has the goal of having true beliefs and not having false beliefs. It is natural for anyone with such interests to be interested in understanding epistemic rationality.

However, insofar as our interest in epistemic rationality is motivated by such a concern, it is at least tempting to adopt a conception of epistemic rationality that I will be at considerable pains to disavow, a conception implying that in doing epistemology one is to describe rules (or principles, or methods) of belief acquisition whose use ensures that we will not be fooled, or at least not frequently fooled, into believing what is false. The idea, in other words, is to look for rules (principles, methods) of belief acquisition that if followed will guarantee that our beliefs are mostly true.

The efforts of epistemologists who have found this conception attractive have met with little success. The rules (principles, methods) of rational belief acquisition they have proposed have tended to be vulnerable to the following trilemma: Either they are insufficiently strict, in which case they fail to rule out the possibility that even if we are epistemically rational we might fall into massive error, or they have skeptical implications, in that they imply that little of what we believe is epistemically rational for us to believe, or they are not sufficiently fundamental, in that the rules make epistemic rationality a function of what is true without providing more fundamental criteria to distinguish what is true from what is false (for example, "it is epistemically rational to believe those claims that reliable rules of belief acquisition recommend"). Indeed, the failure of the efforts of such epistemologists has prompted in some quarters a deep pessimism about epistemology; it has prompted the view that perhaps it is best to abandon epistemology altogether.

In contrast to such pessimism, my approach recommends that it is not epistemology that is to be abandoned, but rather a certain traditional and pervasive conception of epistemology, a conception that insists upon an excessively intimate link between what is epistemically rational and what is true. The present work properly can be viewed as an extended defense of a conception of epistemic rationality and of the epistemological enterprise that is very different from this traditional conception.

EPISTEMIC RATIONALITY

1.1 The Theory of Epistemic Rationality

Suppose a group of people wanted by means of argument to reach agreement concerning what they believe, and suppose in addition they wanted their agreement to be relatively stable. What kind of arguments would be of help to such people in seeking this kind of consensus? Arguments that are sound—arguments that have true premises and a truth preserving form—might be of only little help, since perhaps not every person in the group would recognize them to be sound. The same can be said of arguments that are "inductively sound"—arguments that are likely to be truth preserving and that in addition have true premises. But arguments that merely are believed by all to be sound (either deductively or inductively) might not be of much help either, since they might not generate a stable consensus; it might be that if the members of the group were to reflect for a moment on these arguments, they would come to believe that they are not sound after all. What is needed is not so much arguments that are sound or arguments that are merely believed by the people involved to be sound but arguments that are genuinely uncontroversial for them, in the sense that they would regard the arguments as sound were they to be reflective. The idea, more exactly, would be to look for arguments such that were the people involved to be reflective, they would think that these arguments are likely to be truth preserving and in addition they would think that there is no good reason to be suspicious of their premises. This constitutes an outline of what might be called "the theory of persuasive argument."

The theory of epistemic rationality, I suggest, is in important ways analogous to the theory of persuasive argument. The most important difference is that the theory of epistemic rationality is a first-person theory and that as such it attempts to describe not the propositions[1] of whose truth two or more persons who are seeking agreement via argument should believe. Rather, it seeks to describe what an individual person should believe insofar as he wants now to have true beliefs and now not to have false beliefs. Even so, one way of thinking about the theory of epistemic rationality is to think of it as a theory of first-person persuasive argument. In particular, I will claim that an adequate theory of epistemic rationality, roughly speaking, implies that it is epistemically rational for an individual to be persuaded of the truth of just those propositions that are the conclusions of arguments that he would regard as likely to be truth preserving were he to be reflective and that in addition have premises that he would uncover no good reason to be suspicious of were he to be reflective. The idea, in other words, is that a proposition is epistemically rational for a person just if using premises that are uncontroversial for him he can argue for the proposition in a way that is uncontroversial for him.

To arrive at this view of epistemic rationality, one need not rely on an analogy with persuasive argument. The same kind of view can be developed in a deeper way by appealing to an Aristotelian conception of rationality and to what distinguishes epistemic rationality from other kinds of rationality.

By an Aristotelian conception of rationality, I mean one that is goal-oriented, one that understands rationality in terms of a person carefully deliberating about how to pursue his goals effectively and then acting accordingly. However, since it can be rational for a person to do something even though he does not take the time to deliberate about how to achieve his goals and even though he does not in fact do this something, we need to broaden this initial idea somewhat. In particular, let us broaden it by thinking of rationality in terms of what a person would have to do in order to pursue his goals in a way that he would believe to be effective, were he to be carefully reflective. According to this conception, from the fact that a person merely believes, perhaps without much thought, that something constitutes an effective means to his goals, it does not follow that it is rational for him to bring about that something. After all, he might believe that Y is an effective means to his goals and yet were he to be even a little reflective he might be disposed to change his mind. It might be that on reflection he himself would conclude that it would be a mistake to bring about Y. Likewise, from the fact that a person is pursuing his goals in a way that actually is effective, it does not follow that it is rational for him to pursue his goals in this way. Y might in fact be an effective means to a person's goals even though from his perspective there is nothing to indicate this. If so, it need not be rational for him to bring about Y, even though by hypothesis it effectively would secure his goals.

Thus, according to an Aristotelian conception, rationality is best understood in terms of a person pursuing his goals in a way he would believe to be effective were he to take time to reflect carefully on the question of how best to pursue them.[2] In particular, if a person has a goal X and if he on careful reflection would believe Y to be an effective means to X, then, all else being equal, it is rational for him to bring about Y. Of course, in most cases all else is not equal. Perhaps on reflection this person would believe that although Y is an effective means to X, Z is an even more effective means to X. Or perhaps he would believe that although Y is likely to be an effective means to X, there is a small but real chance of Y bringing about not X but rather something disastrous. Or he may have other goals and it may be that on reflection he would believe that something other than Y would do the best overall job of satisfying these goals. In these and other similar cases, it may very well not be rational in the final analysis for him to bring about Y, despite the fact that he on careful reflection would believe Y to be an effective means to X.

On the other hand, if on careful reflection a person S would believe that Y is an effective means to his goal X and if all else is equal—if none of these complicating factors obtain—then it is rational for S to bring about Y. Of course, the claim that it is rational for S to bring about Y will be of little interest if Y is a trivial means to X. For example, the claim will be of little interest if Y is the state of affairs of being that which will cause X to occur or the state of affairs of being that which an omniscient being would try to bring about were he in S's position and wanted X. Regardless of his particular situation, S can know, and know a priori, that such states of affairs are effective means to X. He can know this just because they in a trivial, empty way guarantee that X will occur. Thus, S can know a priori that bringing about something that causes X, or something that an omniscient being who wanted X would try to bring about were he in S's position, is an effective means to X, and yet have no concrete idea of what in fact would bring about X.

To rule out these uninteresting claims, let us say that the form rationality takes in the simplest of cases is as follows: A person has a goal X, on careful reflection he would believe Y to be an effective and nontrivial means to X, and he brings about Y. Under these conditions, the person has brought about what it is rational for him to bring about.

Does this way of thinking about rationality suggest that the goals of an individual are not themselves susceptible to rational evaluation? Does it suggest, in other words, that it cannot be irrational for an individual to have a goal X? No; given his other goals, it might very well be irrational for him to have X as a goal, since X might interfere systematically with his other goals. What this way of thinking about rationality does preclude is the possibility of an individual's goals being coherent, in the sense that there are no systematic conflicts among them, and at the same time being thoroughly irrational. So, if we imagine an individual with coherent albeit perverted goals, this way of thinking about rationality may not allow us to say that it is irrational for the individual to have these goals. Remember, however, that not every failure is a failure of rationality, a failure that results from the individual not being sufficiently rational. Some failures are failures of character, of not caring for the right things. Thus, even if we cannot always say of an individual with perverted goals that it is irrational for him to have those goals, we still can say what is far worse; we can say that he has perverted goals.

It is important to notice also that this way of thinking about rationality allows a natural distinction between what is rational if all of a person's goals are taken into consideration and what is rational if only a subset of a person's goals are taken into consideration. Indeed, it allows a natural way to introduce talk of different kinds of rationality. For example, if a certain subset of a person's goals are grouped together as goals of kind K and if on careful reflection he would believe that Y is an effective means to goals of this sort, then in the simplest of cases—in cases where all else is equal—it is rational in sense K for him to bring about Y. If the goals that are related to a person's material well-being and physical comfort are grouped together as prudential goals and if on careful reflection he would believe Y is an effective means to goals of this sort, then all else being equal it is rational in a prudential sense for him to bring about Y.

These very general remarks about the nature of rationality and about different kinds of rationality are relevant to the theory of epistemic rationality because they can be applied to beliefs as well as to actions. Thus, if a person has goals of kind K and if on careful reflection he would believe that having beliefs of a certain sort is an effective means to these goals, then, all else being equal, it is rational in sense K for him to have such beliefs. What this suggests, in turn, is that if we are interested in identifying a distinctly epistemic kind of rationality, it is necessary to identify a distinctly epistemic goal. What might such a goal be? I suggest that we take it to be what epistemologists have often said it to be, now to believe those propositions that are true and now not to believe those propositions that are false. Or perhaps better, we can take this to be the goal with respect to those propositions that an individual can understand. In any event, the epistemic goal is not a goal that is concerned with believing propositions that will serve one well with respect to one's practical concerns (since it might be the case that now believing a falsehood, even a proposition that is obviously false, would serve these practical concerns). Likewise the epistemic goal is not a goal that is concerned with believing propositions that will serve one well with respect to one's believing truths in a few years or in a few weeks or even in a few moments (since again it might be the case that believing a falsehood, even a proposition that is obviously false, would serve this concern). Rather, the epistemic goal is concerned with *now* believing those propositions that are true and *now* not believing those propositions that are false. If a person has this goal and if on careful reflection he would believe Y to be an effective means to this goal, then, all else being equal, it is rational (in an epistemic sense) for him to bring about Y. This is the most general form that epistemic rationality takes.

What, then, might a person on careful reflection believe to be an effective means to his epistemic goal? Since the goal here is a present-tense goal—the goal is now to have true beliefs and now not to have false beliefs[3]—the question of what on careful reflection S would believe to be an effective means to the goal reduces to the question of what S would believe to be an effective "direct" means. We are not to imagine S being concerned with what would bring about his having true beliefs and not having false beliefs in the future, even the near future. So the way to think about something being an effective means to this present-tense goal is to construe "means" in a somewhat extended sense, so that something can be a means to a goal by effectively satisfying the goal (and not just by being causally efficacious in bringing about the goal). Accordingly, if on reflection S would believe that having beliefs of a certain kind would effectively satisfy his epistemic goal of now having true beliefs and now not having false beliefs, then on reflection he would believe that having such beliefs is an effective means, in the stipulated sense, to this present-tense goal. Remember, however, that the means here cannot be trivial. It is, for example, of little interest to know that S on reflection would believe that having true beliefs is an effective way to satisfy his epistemic goal.

With this clarification in hand, I return to the question: What might a person on careful reflection believe to be an effective means to his epistemic goal? This depends upon the person. Consider the most extreme cases first. If on careful reflection a person S would believe that he is infallible (and hence that all of his beliefs are true) and if in addition he would believe that he is omniscient (and hence that every truth is believed by him, or at least every truth that he is capable of understanding), then on careful reflection he would believe that the most effective means to his epistemic goal is to believe precisely what he now believes.

At the other extreme is the radical skeptic, who on careful reflection would believe that no means is any better than any other means as a way of achieving his epistemic goal. On careful reflection he would think that the means by which most of us come to believe what we do—perception, memory, and the like—are no more likely to generate true beliefs and to discourage false beliefs than would deciding what to believe on the basis of what the ouija board says or on the basis of a flip of a coin. Moreover, on careful reflection he would think that no other means holds out any better prospects for achieving his epistemic goal. Since there is nothing that such a person on careful reflection would take to be an effective means to his epistemic goal, there is nothing that is epistemically rational for such a person.[4]

Between these two extremes, the optimistic and the pessimistic, is the middle ground, which is occupied by all (or almost all) human beings. Any remotely normal person on careful reflection would not believe that the conservative strategy of believing all and only that which he now believes is an effective means (or at least the most effective means) to his epistemic goal. He would believe there are ways to improve upon what he now believes. He would not be a radical skeptic either. On reflection he would think that some proposals concerning how to achieve his epistemic goal are likely to be effective and others are not. For example, he presumably thinks, and on reflection would continue to think, that with respect to the goal of now believing truths and now not believing falsehoods, believing the conclusions of certain arguments is appropriate and believing the conclusions of certain other arguments is not. In particular, he presumably thinks, and on reflection would continue to think, that certain arguments have unsuspicious premises that can be used to argue for their conclusions in a way that is likely to be truth preserving while other arguments do not. If so, the former arguments are uncontroversial for him while the latter arguments are not. Thus it is epistemically rational for him to believe the conclusions of the former sort of arguments, while it need not be epistemically rational for him to believe the conclusions of the latter sort. It is *rational,* all else being equal, for such a person to believe the conclusions of the former arguments because he on careful reflection would believe this to be an effective means to one of his goals, and it is *epistemically rational* for the person to believe these conclusions because the goal to which he would believe this to be an effective means is the epistemic one of now believing truths and now not believing falsehoods.

So, if on careful reflection a person would uncover no good reason to be suspicious of the premises of an argument and if, in addition, on careful reflection he would think that if the premises are true the conclusion is likely to be true, then he would think that, all else being equal, believing the conclusion of the argument is an effective means to his epistemic goal.[5] Thus, it is epistemically rational for him to believe the conclusion.

This conception of epistemic rationality is just the one that is reached when the theory of epistemic rationality is interpreted to be the theory of first-person persuasive argument: It is epistemically rational for a person to believe the conclusions of arguments that are uncontroversial for him—those that would be persuasive for him were he appropriately reflective.

Of course, people can and do have goals other than the epistemic one of now believing truths and now not believing falsehoods. Likewise people can and do think that acquiring certain kinds of beliefs will help them realize these nonepistemic goals. Accordingly, just as it can be epistemically rational for someone to believe something, so too it can be rational in various nonepistemic senses for someone to believe something. For example, if a person S has goals concerning his material well-being and physical comfort, and if on careful reflection he would think that believing favorable things about himself is an effective means to these goals (because, say, having such beliefs will build his self-confidence, which in turn will make him more likely to secure these goals), then, all else being equal, it is rational in a prudential sense for him to have such beliefs. Similarly, if S has the goal of having true beliefs in the long run and if on careful reflection he would think that the regular use of belief-acquisition method M is an effective means to his having true beliefs in the long run, then, all else being equal, it is rational in this truth-in-the-long-run sense for him to have those beliefs that method M recommends. However, neither of these senses of rational belief, important though they may be, is a genuinely epistemic sense of rational belief. This is illustrated by the fact that it can be rational in either of these senses for a person to believe p even though from his perspective p is obviously false, that is, even though not*p* is the conclusion of an argument that is uncontroversial for him. This in turn is possible because the goal that makes it rational in these senses for the person to believe *p* is not the goal of his now having true beliefs and now not having false beliefs. It is this goal that distinguishes epistemic rationality from other kinds of rationality that can be ascribed to beliefs.

Because people can have various kinds of goals, there can be various senses in which it is rational for a person to believe something. These senses of rational belief can conflict. It can be rational with respect to the epistemic goal for a person to believe *p* and rational with respect to some nonepistemic goal for him not to believe *p*. Concerning such conflicts the theory of epistemic rationality is altogether silent. It does not imply that epistemic considerations always take precedence over nonepistemic considerations in determining what it is rational for *S* to believe. It does not even imply that they ever take precedence. The theory of epistemic rationality seeks only to describe what it is rational for a person to believe insofar as he has the goal of now believing truths and now not believing falsehoods. It implies nothing about what it is rational for him to believe when securing this goal precludes his securing other goals. What it is rational for an individual to believe when such goals conflict is not within the province of the theory of *epistemically rational belief*. Rather, it is within the province of the theory of *rational belief*. The theory of rational belief seeks to describe what it is rational for a person to believe, all things being considered— that is, when all his goals (epistemic, prudential, and the like) are taken into account. The theory of epistemically rational belief is but a part of the theory of rational belief. (For further discussion, see sec. 2.8 and chap. 5.)

Consider the opposite kind of problem, not the problem of *S* having goals that conflict with his epistemic goal but rather the problem of his lacking the epistemic goal. Might not *S* lack the goal of now believing truths and now not believing falsehoods? Perhaps not. Perhaps this is impossible, at least if the notion of a goal is understood in a suitably broad sense. After all, the vast majority of us are intrinsically curious about the world; we intrinsically want to have true beliefs. And presumably, even if some people do not intrinsically want or need to have true beliefs and not to have false beliefs, they still regard it as important to have such beliefs. In order to have a better chance of obtaining something they do want or need for its own sake, they think that it is important now to have true beliefs and now not to have false beliefs. And insofar as they do think this, it can be regarded as one of their goals.[6]

However, suppose somehow it is possible for there to be a person *S* who does not intrinsically want or need to have true beliefs and not to have false beliefs and who also does not think it is important in an instrumental sense to have such beliefs. For such a person, would the theory of epistemic rationality once again be silent? That is, would it imply that because such a person lacks the epistemic goal, nothing is epistemically demanded of him?

Not necessarily, since there is perhaps a sense in which X can be a goal for someone although he neither wants it nor needs it nor regards it as important. Perhaps, for example, it is morally required for *S* to be concerned with having true beliefs and not having false beliefs, and perhaps an acceptable account of what it is to have a goal would imply that whatever is morally required of *S* is a goal of *S* (whether or not he wants or needs it).

On the other hand, if *S* does not in any of these senses or in any other sense have the goal of now having true beliefs and now not having false beliefs—and, as I have said, this may be impossible— then, strictly speaking, nothing is epistemically rational or irrational for him. He has no epistemic goal, and so it is trivial that nothing can be an effective means to his epistemic goal. Even so, a secondary kind of epistemic evaluation of *S* and his beliefs can be useful and altogether appropriate. Specifically, it might be useful and altogether appropriate to evaluate *S* and his beliefs as if he did have the epistemic goal. That is, we might still find occasions to evaluate *S* and his beliefs with respect to what would be rational for him to believe were he to have the epistemic goal. Of course, given that *S* in fact does not have this goal, we normally cannot expect such evaluations to move *S* in any way. We cannot, for example, expect *S* to be motivated to develop intellectual habits that encourage his believing that which would be epistemically rational for him were he to have the epistemic goal. However, this does not affect the point. Whether or not *S* has the goal of now having true beliefs and now not having false beliefs, it can be perfectly appropriate for us to evaluate his beliefs as if he did. It can be perfectly appropriate for us to evaluate his beliefs from an epistemic point of view.[7]

Is it also appropriate for us to make such evaluations even if *S* lacks control over his beliefs? More exactly, does saying that from an epistemic point of view it is epistemically rational for a person *S* to believe the conclusions of arguments that are uncontroversial for him presuppose that *S* either now has or did have some kind of control over what he believes? I will argue in chapter 5 that although people ordinarily do have at least some kind of indirect control over what they believe, the answer to this question nonetheless is no. It can be epistemically rational for a person *S* to believe even that which, given his circumstances or given his limitations as a believer, he cannot believe. It also can be epistemically rational for *S* to believe that which, given his circumstances, or given his limitations as a believer, he cannot help but believe. Of course, in such cases *S* should not be blamed or praised for believing what he does. In cases where a proposition that he cannot believe is epistemically rational for him, he should not be blamed for not believing it; and in cases where he cannot help but believe what is epistemically rational for him, he should not be praised for believing it.

So, to say that a person believes something that is not epistemically rational for him or to say that he fails to believe something that is epistemically rational for him is not to say that he has not been as good an epistemic agent as he might have been.[8] To say that a proposition is epistemically rational for a person is to say only that there is an argument for it that is uncontroversial for him. It is not to say that he has control over whether he believes it or not.[9]

However, at least with respect to each particular proposition that is epistemically rational for an individual, this usually is a moot point. We may have only limited control over what we believe, so that we cannot believe at will just anything, but it ordinarily is the case that a person is able in an indirect way to get himself to believe a proposition *p* that is epistemically rational for him. He can do so by engaging in reflection of an appropriate sort, reflection that would make him aware of an uncontroversial argument for *p*. For if he becomes aware of such an argument and becomes convinced that it is a good argument, he normally will come to believe *p*.[10]

On the other hand, even if each particular proposition that is epistemically rational for an individual *S* is such that *S* is able to believe it, he may very well be unable to believe all the propositions that are epistemically rational for him. The entire set of propositions that are epistemically rational for him may be simply too large for it to be feasible for him to believe every member of this set. For example, any proposition that is epistemically rational for *S* will imply in relatively obvious ways a huge number of other propositions, many, if not most, of which are likely to be epistemically rational for *S* (since many, if not most, will be conclusions of arguments that *S* on reflection would take to be good arguments). Yet *S* may be unable to believe all of these propositions simultaneously, even if he can believe each one individually. Even so, this is irrelevant for the theory of epistemic rationality; it is irrelevant because even if *S* cannot believe all of these propositions, by hypothesis each of these propositions is "worthy" of belief with respect to the epistemic goal. Accordingly, it would be ideal to believe each and every one of these propositions. Of course, given that this ideal for him cannot be met, it is natural to ask which of these propositions it is rational for S to believe. But once again, this is a question that the theory of epistemic rationality cannot possibly answer. The answer to this question lies not within the sphere of the theory of epistemically rational belief but rather within the sphere of the theory of rational belief. It is a question to be decided on the basis of which of these propositions are the most important for S to believe—important, say, from the standpoint of being pragmatically useful or from the standpoint of guiding inquiry so that one's chances of acquiring truths (or at least important truths) in the future are enhanced.

What I am claiming is that it is epistemically rational for a person to believe a proposition just if there is a way of arguing for the proposition that is uncontroversial for him. To claim this, however, is to provide only the barest outline of a general conception of epistemic rationality. So far, I only have briefly described this general conception—I have not yet argued for it, nor have I yet said how I think it is best to fill in the details. In particular, given this general conception, two major questions need to be addressed: What exactly is it for the premises of an argument to be uncontroversial for a person, and what exactly is it for the premises of an argument to support its conclusion in a way that is uncontroversial for a person? I have already suggested, in broad terms, the answers to these questions. An argument has uncontroversial premises for a person just if careful reflection would reveal to him no good reason to be suspicious of their truth, and the premises of an argument support its conclusion in a way that is uncontroversial for a person just if he would think that the argument is likely to be truth preserving were he to be carefully reflective. However, not just any kind of careful reflection will do here. It needs to be reflection of an appropriate idealized kind. So I will have to try to describe in detail this appropriate, idealized kind of reflection. Then it will be easier to return to the general conception of epistemic rationality to see what there is to be said in favor of it, and what advantages it has over the approaches taken by other epistemologists, including traditional foundationalists, coherentists, and reliabilists. Part of the attractiveness of my approach will derive from the plausibility of the criteria of epistemic rationality it encourages us to adopt; another part will derive from the fact that although these criteria differ significantly from those proposed by traditional foundationalists, coherentists, reliabilists, and others, my approach provides a framework for understanding and appreciating these other accounts. It provides, in effect, a way of giving proper recognition to the worries and considerations that prompt these other accounts.

The hope is that the general conception of epistemic rationality not only will help generate plausible criteria of epistemic rationality but also will provide a way of thinking about epistemic rationality that will allow the insights of other approaches to be preserved; it will allow us to see what is right about traditional foundationalism, coherentism, reliabilism, and so on. If these hopes are realized, this itself will constitute as good an argument as there can be for the general conception. The best way to defend the general conception is to show that the way that it recommends thinking about questions of rational belief provides more understanding and clarity than any other way.

1.2   *Arguments That Are Sufficiently Likely to Be Truth Preserving*

A proposition is epistemically rational for an individual, I have suggested, just if the proposition is the conclusion of an argument that is uncontroversial for him—an argument that has uncontroversial premises used in an uncontroversial way to support its conclusion. What is it for an argument's premises to support its conclusion in a way that is uncontroversial for an individual? It is for the argument to be such that were the individual in question to be carefully reflective, he would think that it is sufficiently likely to be truth preserving. For the moment, ignore the question of what kind of careful reflection in which we are to imagine the person engaging, and ignore also the question of what "sufficiently likely" means here. I will return to both questions shortly. Bracketing these questions, the rough idea is that an argument's premises can be used to argue for its conclusion in a way that is uncontroversial for an individual S just if on reflection S would believe that most possible situations in which the argument's premises are true are situations in which the argument's conclusion is true. Thus, one way in which an argument can be uncontroversial for S is by being such that S on reflection would believe that it is impossible for its conclusion to be false if its premises are true. For the sake of simplicity, we can say in such cases that S on reflection would believe that the premises imply the conclusion, as long as this is not taken to suggest that S has anything like a philosophical view about what it is for one proposition to imply another. It need not be supposed, for example, that S knows anything about the theory of implication. It need only be supposed that he has some notion, perhaps rough, of certain pairs of propositions being related in such a way that any possible situation in which the first is true is a situation in which the second is true as well.

Not all arguments that are uncontroversial for an individual *S* have premises that *S* on reflection would believe imply their conclusions. Some uncontroversial arguments are such that *S* on reflection would believe that although their conclusions need not be true in all possible situations in which their premises are true, their conclusions are true in a sufficiently great percentage of possible situations in which their premises are true. Or at least, their conclusions are true in a sufficiently great percentage of relevant possible situations in which their premises are true. (What constitutes a relevant situation will be discussed shortly.) Of such arguments, we can say that *S* on reflection would believe that their premises make probable, or make likely, their conclusions. But again, saying this is simply a matter of convenience. The only presupposition here is that *S* has some notion, perhaps rough, of certain pairs of propositions being related in such a way that most relevant possible situations in which the first is true are situations in which the second is true as well.[11]

So the premises of an argument can be used to argue for its conclusion in a way that is uncontroversial for an individual *S* just if, roughly, on reflection *S* would think that the argument is sufficiently likely to be truth preserving. And for *S* on reflection to think that an argument is sufficiently likely to be truth preserving is for him on reflection to think that a sufficiently great percentage of relevant possible situations in which its premises are true are situations in which its conclusion also is true. However, this is only a rough formulation; it implies that any argument whose premise *S* on reflection would take to imply its conclusion is an argument whose premises support its conclusion in a way that is uncontroversial for *S* (since he on reflection would believe of any such argument that its conclusion is true in all possible situations in which its premises are true). However, this is not quite right; there are exceptions. The exceptions are arguments with conclusions that *S* on reflection would take to be necessarily true or with premises whose conjunction *S* on reflection would take to be necessarily false. *S* on reflection would believe of such arguments that their premises imply their conclusions, but not every such argument need be uncontroversial for him. Such an argument will be uncontroversial for *S* only if he on reflection would take its premises to be relevant to its conclusion. However, for the moment, ignore these kinds of arguments; I will return to them shortly. Then, with respect to arguments whose premises S on reflection would take to imply these conclusions, it can be said as a rule of thumb that it is epistemically rational for S to believe these conclusions insofar as the premises of these arguments are uncontroversial for him. The conclusions of such arguments are propositions he can argue for in a way that is uncontroversial for him using premises that are uncontroversial for him.

But things are not quite as simple for arguments whose premises S on reflection would take not to imply but to make sufficiently probable their conclusions. The complication is that S on reflection would think that even if the premises of such arguments are true, believing their conclusions involves at least some risk of believing a falsehood. As a result, these arguments are defeasible for S in a way in which arguments whose premises he takes to imply their conclusions are not. Accordingly, it need not be epistemically rational for S to believe the conclusions of such arguments even when their premises are uncontroversial for him. Suppose, for example, that the argument $(e^1, e^2, \ldots e^n;$ thus, $p)$ is such an argument. Then it need not be epistemically rational for S to believe p even if $e^1, e^2, \ldots e^n$ are uncontroversial for him, since the support these latter propositions give p can be overridden; it can be overridden by his having defeating information.

Only some of the arguments that are uncontroversial for S are such that on reflection he would think it is impossible for their conclusions to be false if their premises are true. Correspondingly, only some of the arguments that are uncontroversial for him are such that he is epistemically committed to believing their conclusions if their premises are uncontroversial for him. Nevertheless, something analogous is true for these other arguments: S is epistemically committed to believe their conclusions if their premises are uncontroversial for him and if in addition all else is equal.

This is an important point, since it places a restriction upon what arguments are uncontroversial for S. For example, suppose S believes that almost all fire engines are red. Nonetheless, S on reflection need not believe that in a sufficiently large percentage of relevant possible situations in which something is a fire engine chosen at random, it also is red. After all, there are many possible situations in which most fire engines are not red. On the other hand, if S is like the rest of us, he presumably would believe on reflection that in a sufficiently large percentage of possible situations in which something is a fire engine chosen at random and in which almost all fire engines are red, the thing in question also is red. If so, the argument (X is a fire engine chosen at random; almost all fire engines are red; thus, X is red) is likely to be uncontroversial for S even if the argument (X is a fire engine chosen at random; thus, X is red) is not. But then, if the premises of the former argument are uncontroversial for him and if all else is equal, the conclusion that X is red is epistemically rational for him. He can argue for this conclusion using premises that are uncontroversial for him in a way that is uncontroversial for him. However, this need not be so for the latter argument; its conclusion need not be epistemically rational for him even if its premise is uncontroversial for him and all else is equal.

The point here becomes clearer when it is understood what "all else being equal" means. What it means is that there is no defeating proposition that is uncontroversial for the person S.[12] A proposition d is a defeater of an argument for S if adding d to the premises of the argument results in a new argument that does not even prima facie support its conclusion. So, suppose the argument ($e^1, e^2, \ldots e^n$; thus, p) is uncontroversial for S even though S would not think that its conclusion is implied by its premises. Suppose, in other words, he believes p is true in a sufficiently high percentage of relevant possible situations in which the propositions $e^1, e^2, \ldots e^n$ are true. Proposition d, then, is a defeater of this argument for S if the argument ($e^1, e^2, \ldots e^n, d$; thus, p) is not in this way uncontroversial for S. In particular, it is a defeater if S on reflection would believe that p is not true in a sufficiently high percentage of relevant possible situations in which $e^1, e^2, \ldots e^n$ and d are true.[13]

Thus, if the argument ($e^1, e^2, \ldots e^n$; thus, p) is uncontroversial for S, S on reflection would believe that p is true in a sufficiently high percentage of relevant situations in which e^1, e^2, and e^n are true. Accordingly, from an epistemic point of view, there is a presumption in favor of S's believing p if $e^1, e^2, \ldots e^n$ are uncontroversial for him. What this means, in turn, is that in such situations it is epistemically rational for him to believe p as long as all else is equal—as long as there is no defeater proposition that is uncontroversial for him.

To return to the earlier example, even if S believes that in fact almost all fire engines are red, the argument (X is a fire engine chosen at random; thus, X is red) need not be uncontroversial for S. For he on reflection might very well believe that there is a significantly large percentage of relevant possible situations in which most fire engines are not red. And if so, the information that something is a fire engine does not by itself provide him with any kind of presumption at all, even a defeasible one, that it is red. Thus, it need not be epistemically rational for him to believe that the thing is red even if it is uncontroversial for him that the thing is a fire engine and even if in addition he has no other information about its color. On the other hand, the argument (X is a fire engine chosen at random; almost all fire engines are red; thus, X is red) presumably is not like this. It presumably is uncontroversial for *S*. Consequently, if its premises are uncontroversial for him and if he has no other relevant information (and hence no relevant defeating information), its conclusion is epistemically rational for him.

However, an important question arises with respect to arguments such as this one that does not arise with respect to arguments whose premises *S* takes to imply their conclusions. How likely must *S* on reflection believe the conclusion of such an argument to be, given the truth of its premises, in order for the argument to be uncontroversial for him? That is, in order for such an argument to be uncontroversial for *S*, what percentage of the relevant possible situations in which its premises are true must be situations in which the conclusion is true, according to *S* on reflection? No doubt the percentage has to be at least fifty (otherwise *S* on reflection would think that believing the conclusion is less likely to satisfy his epistemic goal than believing the conclusion's negation), and it is plausible to think it has to be significantly greater than fifty (otherwise *S* on reflection might believe that neither believing the conclusion nor believing its negation would be sufficiently likely to satisfy his epistemic goal). But this still leaves the question of how much greater than fifty the percentage must be. With arguments whose premises *S* on reflection would take to imply their conclusion, this question poses no problem, since *S* on reflection believes it is impossible for the conclusion to be false given that the premises are true. Thus, he on reflection believes that the premises support the conclusion as strongly as is possible. In all situations in which the premises are true the conclusion is true. However, with other arguments the situation is different, since *S* on reflection believes it is possible for their conclusions to be false even if their premises are true. So with them there is a problem—how likely *S* on reflection must believe the conclusion of an argument to be (given that its premises are true) if the argument is to be uncontroversial for him.

This problem can also be expressed in terms of *S*'s epistemic goal, his goal of now believing truths and now not believing falsehoods. The two aspects of this goal tend to pull *S* in opposite directions. One of the aspects, believing truths, encourages him to believe the conclusion of an argument, in order to prevent his failing to believe a truth. The other, not believing falsehoods, discourages him from believing the conclusion of the argument, in order to prevent his believing a falsehood. The question, then, is how these two aspects of the epistemic goal ought to be weighted in deciding whether the argument is sufficiently likely to be truth preserving. Should they be weighted equally, or should preference be given to one of them?

When the problem is expressed in this way, it again is clear that with respect to arguments whose premises S on reflection would take to imply their conclusions, there is no difficulty. With respect to them, S on reflection would believe that on the assumption that their premises are true, he is certain to believe truths if he believes their conclusions. However, with other arguments the case is different. He believes that even on the assumption that the premises of these arguments are true, it is not certain that by believing their conclusions he will be believing truth. For such arguments it is important to know how small S takes the risk of error to be, if the argument is to be uncontroversial for him.

There is no general, quantitative answer to this question. It is not possible, for example, to stipulate that if a person S believes that the conclusion of an argument has an 80 percent, or 90 percent, or an even higher chance of being true, given that its premises are true, then the argument is uncontroversial for him. This is not possible for two reasons. First, for many (and perhaps even most) arguments that S considers, he may have in mind no such numerical estimate of how likely it is that the conclusion is true, given that its premises are true. Indeed, he might even be at a loss as to how to go about trying to make such an estimate. Nevertheless, some such arguments S might find unproblematic; that is, some such arguments might be uncontroversial for him.

For example, suppose S considers the argument (I seem to remember my being at the zoo last Saturday, my memory seems to be generally accurate—there seem to be no large gaps in my memory nor any glaring inconsistencies in what I seem to remember; thus, I was at the zoo last Saturday). Or suppose he considers the argument (I seem to see a cat on the mat, there seem to be no perceptual cues indicating that my visual equipment is not now reliable; thus, there is a cat on the mat), or the argument (I do not remember ever having seen a nonblack crow, I do not remember anyone else telling me that they have seen a nonblack crow nor do I remember anything else that would indicate there are nonblack crows; I do remember seeing lots of black crows; thus, most crows are black). It is hard to see how S, at least if he is at all like most of us, would calculate in precise numerical terms the likelihood of the conclusions of such arguments being true, given that their premises are true. How would S approach the problem of calculating these likelihoods? How would he start? How, for example, would he begin thinking about what precise percentage of the relevant possible situations in which he seems to see a cat on the mat and in which his vision seems to him to be in good working order are situations in which he actually does see a cat on the mat? What would make him think, for example, that 70 percent of such situations are situations in which he sees a cat, or that 90 percent of such situations are like this, or that some other percentage of the situations are like this?

If *S* is like most of us, he would have no idea of how to begin making such calculations. However, this need not mean that he thinks arguments of the above sort are bad arguments. To the contrary, he might very well think that they obviously are good arguments. But if so, what arguments are uncontroversial for a person *S* is not something that can always be specified quantitatively, in terms of how likely he believes the conclusion to be, given the truth of its premises. Rather, an argument can be uncontroversial for a person *S* even though he neither is prepared nor on reflection would be prepared to specify quantitatively exactly how likely the conclusion of the argument is, given that its premises are true. Were he pressed he might be prepared to conclude that the likelihood is very high, or perhaps even overwhelming, but he need not be prepared to say in numerical terms what "very high" or "overwhelming" means. Accordingly, we must be content with saying that such an argument is uncontroversial for *S* just if *S* on reflection would believe the conclusion is true in a sufficiently high percentage of possible situations in which its premises are true, where "sufficiently high" cannot be reduced to some specific percentage.

But suppose I am wrong about this. Suppose, contrary to what I am claiming, that a normal person *S* is such that for most, or even all, arguments that he is capable of considering, he either does have or would have on reflection an estimate in numerical terms of how likely its conclusion is, given that its premises are true. Moreover, suppose we had a list of these estimates. This still would not tell us what arguments are uncontroversial for *S*. What arguments are uncontroversial for *S* is also a function of what attitudes *S* on reflection would have toward epistemic risks, and this is not something that we impose upon him. He on reflection must decide for himself whether in his search now to have true beliefs and now not to have false beliefs, it would be appropriate for him to believe the conclusion of an argument whose premises he believes make the conclusion likely to a certain degree. He must decide, that is, whether or not the conclusion would be true in a high enough percentage of relevant situations in which the premises are true to make the risk of believing a falsehood in such situations an acceptably low risk, insofar as he wants to believe truths and not to believe falsehoods. If on careful reflection he would decide that the risk of his believing a falsehood would not be too great, then on the assumption that the argument's premises are uncontroversial for him and all else is equal, his believing the conclusion is rational from an epistemic point of view.

So even if for each argument he is capable of considering, S generates, or would on reflection be prepared to generate, a numerical estimate of how likely its conclusion is, given the truth of its premises, this alone is not sufficient to produce a list of arguments that are uncontroversial for S. It also is necessary to know how S, on careful reflection, would weight the possibility of believing a truth against the risk of believing a falsehood. There is no need for this weighting to be constant. For certain kinds of arguments, perhaps arguments concerning highly theoretical matters, S on reflection might take a relatively daring attitude toward the risk of believing a falsehood. For other kinds of arguments, perhaps arguments concerning the truth of his perceptual beliefs or memory beliefs, he might take a relatively conservative attitude.

Just as we do not impose upon S an attitude toward epistemic risks, so too we do not impose upon him a view about what kinds of possible situations are relevant to a determination of whether the premises of an argument make its conclusion sufficiently probable. What situations are relevant is determined by what S himself on reflection would think about the likelihood of various situations. If he on reflection would regard a situation as sufficiently likely to occur as to be of concern when deciding whether believing the conclusion of the argument is an acceptable epistemic risk, the situation is relevant. Otherwise it is not.

How then are we to imagine S deciding whether a possible situation in which the premises of an argument are true is probable enough to be of concern in assessing the truth-preservingness of the argument? We are to imagine S making the decision on the basis of his current beliefs and, in particular, on the basis of his various general beliefs about the world—beliefs about the laws of nature, about what kinds of entities there are, and so forth. These beliefs in effect function as a kind of anchor, preventing situations that S regards as too distant from his current situation from being of concern when deciding whether believing the conclusion of an argument is an acceptable epistemic risk. In particular, for most arguments the relevant range of possible situations for assessing its truth-preservingness will include only situations in which at least many of these general beliefs are true; these ordinarily will be the situations that *S*, on reflection, would take to be of concern in deciding whether or not his believing the argument's conclusion is likely to be an effective way for him to satisfy his epistemic goal. By contrast, possible situations in which the premises of the argument are true but which *S* takes to be highly unrealistic (say, because the laws of nature are radically different from what *S* takes them to be or because he is under the control of an evil demon) are unlikely to be relevant; *S* is unlikely to think that such situations are relevant to the question of whether insofar as he is interested in now having true beliefs and now not having false beliefs, it is a good idea, all else being equal, for him to believe the conclusion of this argument. And this in turn is so because *S* on reflection would believe that these situations are so highly unlikely to obtain. They are, he would think, too bizarre and too far removed from any situation that is likely to occur to be of any concern.

There are, however, some complications. Suppose, for example, that the premises of an argument conflict in an obvious way with a number of *S*'s general beliefs about, for example, the laws of nature and what kinds of entities there are.[14] Such arguments are unlikely to be of much use in determining what is epistemically rational for *S*, since the premises of such arguments will not be uncontroversial for him. Nonetheless, it is instructive to note what situations are relevant for the assessment of the truth-preservingness of such arguments. In particular, it is instructive to note that for such arguments, the relevant range of possible situations cannot include situations in which the general beliefs with which the premises conflict are true. On reflection, *S* would think that none of the situations in which these general beliefs are true are situations in which the premises of the argument are also true. So what possible situations are relevant for purposes of evaluating the truth-preservingness of this argument? The relevant range of possible situations is determined in the same way as for other arguments. It is determined by what *S*, on reflection, would think about the likelihood of various possible situations in which the premises of the argument are true. The only difference is that here even the most probable of these situations are those that *S*, on reflection, would regard as improbable; they are situations that he on reflection would regard as being distant situations, far removed from anything that is likely to happen. For example, the range of relevant close possible situations here might consist of those situations in which the premises of the argument are true (and hence in which his general beliefs that conflict with these premises are false) but in which his other general beliefs are true. Such situations, albeit improbable, might well be what *S*, on reflection, would take to be the least improbable of those possible situations in which the premises of the argument are true. Accordingly, it may well be that *S*, on reflection, would regard such an argument as one that is sufficiently likely to be truth preserving. For, although he, on reflection, would regard the argument's premises as being improbable, he nonetheless might think that if he were to find himself in a situation in which these premises were true, believing the conclusion of the argument would be an effective way (all else being equal) of satisfying his epistemic goal. He might think, in other words, that in the unlikely event that these premises were true, it would be likely that the conclusion is true as well.

Something like the reverse is true of arguments whose conclusions imply in an obvious way the truth of one or more of those general, background beliefs that *S*, on reflection, ordinarily might be disposed to use in deciding what situations are relevant for assessing the truth-preservingness of other arguments. The general beliefs whose truth the conclusion obviously implies presumably would not be used by *S*, on reflection, to determine what situations are sufficiently probable to be relevant for assessing such an argument, since the argument itself is at least in part concerned with the probability of such beliefs. Indeed, if *S* were to use these beliefs to determine what situations are relevant, it might very well turn out to be trivial that the conclusion is true in most relevant situations in which the premises are true (if, say, the conclusion just is the claim that these general beliefs are true). Rather, for such an argument, *S*, on reflection, is likely to determine the relevant range of situations by appealing to his other general beliefs, those whose truth the conclusion does not imply. A situation will be regarded as irrelevant, then, just in case relative to these other general beliefs, *S*, on reflection, would regard it as so improbable as to be not worth worrying about in reaching a decision about the truth-preservingness of the argument in question.

The most general and most important point here, however, is that for such arguments, as with all others, what counts as a situation that is relevant to the assessment of the truth-preservingness of the argument is something that an individual is to decide for himself on reflection. He himself must decide whether a possible situation in which the premises of the argument are true is so unlikely as not to be relevant to the question of whether the premises of the argument make sufficiently probable its conclusion—that is, sufficiently probable to make believing it (all else being equal) an acceptable epistemic risk were its premises to be true. In imagining S making such decisions, we imagine him doing so against a backdrop of his other beliefs. Which of his beliefs S would appeal to in order to make such decisions will be relative to the argument he is considering. If an individual S is like most of the rest of us, in making such decisions about ordinary arguments he is likely to appeal to very general beliefs that he has— say, about the laws of nature or what kinds of entities there are. These beliefs act as a constraint on the possible situations that S, on reflection, would deem as relevant for deciding whether the premises of the argument make probable its conclusion. They determine in effect how distant a possible situation can be from what S takes to be the actual one and still be relevant. Accordingly, situations in which laws of nature constantly change or are radically different from what S takes them to be or in which there are no entities of a kind S takes there to be (for example, no physical objects) are unlikely to be situations that are relevantly close; S on reflection is unlikely to think that such situations are relevant for deciding whether the premises of an argument make probable its conclusion.

On the other hand, situations that are so close as to be almost identical with what S takes to be the actual situation are unlikely to be the only situations that are relevantly close. Rather, on reflection S is likely to think that a number of situations that in broad outline are similar to the actual situation are relevant for assessing the argument (providing they are situations in which the premises of the argument are true). Indeed, if S were to think that the only relevant situations are ones almost identical with what he takes to be the actual situation, it would follow trivially that on reflection he would think that all arguments whose premises and conclusions are true are arguments whose premises make probable their conclusions. But as a matter of fact, any relatively normal person, on reflection, is unlikely to think this. Rather, a relatively normal person is likely to think that some arguments with true premises and true conclusions are such that believing their conclusions is not in general an effective way of satisfying his epistemic goal in situations in which their premises are true.[15]

So if an individual S is like most of the rest of us, he is not likely to regard as relevant for an assessment of most ordinary arguments only those situations that are almost identical with what he takes to be the actual situation. Nor is he likely to regard as relevant those situations that are not even broadly similar to what he takes to be the actual situation; not every possible situation in which the premises of an argument are true, no matter how improbable the situation, is likely to be a situation that S regards as relevant. The only situations likely to be relevant to an assessment of the truth-preservingness of most ordinary arguments are those that the individual S, on reflection, would not regard as vastly improbable. Even so, this does not mean that all such situations are likely to be relevant. It does not mean that an individual S is likely to regard as relevant all possible situations in which the premises of an argument are true and which are, in broad outline, not drastically different from what he takes to be the actual situation. On the contrary, many such situations, perhaps most, are likely to be regarded by S as irrelevant. Suppose, for example, S considers the argument (I seem to see a cat on the mat, there seem to be no perceptual cues indicating that my visual equipment is not reliable; thus, I see a cat on the mat). Notice that there may well be uncountably many possible situations in which the premises of this argument are true and its conclusion false. There even may be uncountably many such situations that S would not regard as being drastically different from the actual situation. But from this it does not follow that there are uncountably many *relevant* possible situations of this sort. Suppose that S imagines a relatively close situation in which the premises of this argument are true but its conclusion is false; suppose, for example, that he imagines a situation in which the premises of the argument are true but in which he mistakes some other kind of small animal for a cat. There may well be uncountably many variations of this situation—a situation in which S mistakes a dog that weighs exactly 10.00 pounds for a cat, a situation in which S mistakes a dog that weighs 10.01 pounds for a cat, a situation in which he mistakes a raccoon that weighs 10.02 pounds for a cat and in which there are exactly 158,345 aardvarks on earth, and so on. To be sure, these are distinct situations, but they need not be regarded by S as distinct *relevant* situations. And they presumably would not be, at least if S here is like most of the rest of us. For if he is, he would not take the precise weight of the animal on the mat to be a relevant factor in judging whether the above argument is likely to be truth preserving. Although the approximate weight of the animal on the mat may be relevant, it does not matter whether the animal weighs exactly 10.00 pounds or 10.01 pounds. A fortiori it does not matter how many aardvarks there are on earth.

The point here, most generally expressed, is that when we imagine S considering various possible situations in an effort to decide whether an argument is sufficiently likely to be truth preserving, we need not imagine him considering maximally specific situations. In effect, we need not imagine him considering various possible worlds, where a possible world, for present purposes, can be thought of as a special kind of possible situation, one that is defined by a maximally consistent set of propositions. Indeed, we not only need not imagine S considering maximally specific situations, we need not even imagine that the situations he considers are highly specific; they need not be situations that are defined by a very large set of (what S takes to be) consistent propositions. Instead, the situations that we imagine S considering can be relatively broad; they can be situations that are defined by a relatively small set of (what S takes to be) consistent propositions.

So, although there may well be uncountably many possible situations that would make the premises of the above argument true and that in addition in broad outline resemble what S takes to be the actual situation, not all of these situations (and certainly not an uncountably large number of them) need be situations that S, on reflection, would regard as being relevant for an assessment of the truth-preservingness of the argument. Not all of them, in other words, need be such that S, on reflection, would think that they are relevant for determining whether believing the conclusion of the argument is an acceptable epistemic risk if its premises are true. Indeed, just as a general rule it is safe to assume that S here would regard as irrelevant possible situations that he takes to be radically unlike the actual situation (for example, a situation in which the laws of nature are radically different from what he takes them to be), so too as a general rule it is safe to assume that he would regard as irrelevant possible situations that contain highly specific or gratuitous details (such as situations defined by the precise weight of the animal on the mat or situations defined by the number of aardvarks, where the argument in question has nothing to do with aardvarks).

This is not to say, however, that it is altogether impossible for an individual S, on reflection, to regard as relevant for the assessment of most ordinary arguments all possible situations in which the premises of these arguments are true. Suppose that S, on reflection, would think this. What then? Then there are likely to be fewer arguments whose premises support their conclusions in a way that is uncontroversial for him. In the most extreme case, he may even be a skeptic, one who thinks almost no argument (or at least no nondeductive argument) is sufficiently likely to be truth preserving).[16]

Fortunately, it is presumably safe to assume that few, and perhaps no, people are like this. Few of us, and perhaps none of us, on reflection would think of most arguments that each and every possible situation in which their premises are true is to be treated as relevant for assessing whether these arguments are sufficiently likely to be truth preserving, sufficiently likely to make believing their conclusions an acceptable epistemic risk. Likewise, few of us would think that the only situations that are relevant for assessing the likely truth-preservingness of most ordinary arguments are situations that are almost identical in every detail with what we take to be the present situation. All, or at least almost all, of us presumably fall somewhere between these two extremes.

But whether or not this is so, the important theoretical point is that in general an argument has premises that support its conclusion in a way that is uncontroversial for an individual S just if S, on reflection, would think that its conclusion is true in a sufficiently great percentage of relevant possible situations in which its premises are true. However, there are exceptions—arguments whose conclusions S, on reflection, would take to be necessarily true and arguments whose premises are such that S, on reflection, would take their conjunction to be necessarily false. If the conclusion of an argument is a proposition that S, on reflection, would regard as necessarily true, then S, on reflection, would think that it is impossible for its premises to be true and its conclusion false. And he would think this regardless of what these premises are, even if they are propositions that he would take to be altogether irrelevant to the conclusion. Similarly, if he, on reflection, would think that the conjunction of the premises is necessarily false, he would think that it is impossible for these premises to be true and the conclusion false, and he would think this regardless of what the conclusion is. Since S, on reflection, might think that the premises of these kinds of arguments are irrelevant to their conclusions, such arguments need not be uncontroversial for him, even though by hypothesis he does think that it is the case that there are no possible situations in which their premises are true and their conclusions false. Arguments of these kinds require a special treatment.

For arguments whose premises are such that S, on reflection, would regard their conjunction as necessarily false, the treatment is straightforward. Let us stipulate that an argument can be uncontroversial for an individual S only if he, on reflection, would think that there are possible situations in which all of its premises are true. This is a prerequisite of an argument being uncontroversial for him. Accordingly, no argument with premises whose conjunction S, on reflection, would regard as necessarily false can be uncontroversial for S. And this is so despite the fact that by hypothesis he, on reflection, would think that the premises of such arguments imply their conclusions.[17]

However, matters cannot be so straightforward for arguments whose conclusions an individual *S*, on reflection, would regard as necessarily true. Some but not all of these arguments will be uncontroversial for *S;* some but not all, in other words, will have premises that can help make their conclusions epistemically rational for *S*. To distinguish those that are uncontroversial for *S* from those that are not, let us say that in order for the premises of such arguments to support their conclusions in a way that is uncontroversial for *S*, it must be the case that *S*, on reflection, would think that these premises are positively relevant to the conclusion. With ordinary arguments, this requirement is automatically satisfied if *S*, on reflection, would think that the conclusion of the argument is true in most relevant possible situations in which its premises are true. But for arguments with conclusions that *S*, on reflection, would take to be necessarily true, this special requirement is needed. The way to think about this special require-ment is in terms of *S*, on reflection, bracketing his conviction that the conclusion is necessarily true, in order to concentrate upon the relation between the premises and the conclusion. More specifically, if the argument is to be uncontroversial for him, it must be the case that on reflection he would think that its premises can be used to show why it is impossible for the conclusion to be false. Or alternatively, it must be the case that he on reflection would think that the premises provide him with good "inductive" support for the necessary truth of the conclusion. Consider each of these cases in turn.

To help illustrate the first, contrast the argument (all right triangles have a ninety-degree angle; all equilateral triangles are equiangular; thus, no right triangle is equilateral) with the argument (if it rained yesterday, then either it rained or it snowed yesterday; $2 + 2 = 4$; thus, no right triangle is equilateral). Suppose that *S* believes, and would continue to believe on reflection, that the premises as well as the conclusion of each of these arguments are necessarily true. Since on reflection he would regard the conclusion of each argument as necessarily true, he would think that the premises of each argument imply its conclusion. But if *S* is at all like the rest of us, he, on reflection, would think that only the first of these arguments has premises that are relevant to the claim that no right triangle is equilateral. And in particular, on reflection he presumably would think of the first ar-gument but not of the second that its premises if jointly understood could be used to provide him with an understanding of why it is impossible for the conclusion to be false.[18] He presumably would think, in other words, that understanding the information contained in the conjunction of the premises is enough to allow him to see why the conclusion has to be true and that, accordingly, there is in this sense a kind of internal connection between the truth of the premises of the first argument and the truth of the proposition that no right triangle is equilateral. On the other hand, he presumably would not think this of the second argument; rather, he presumably would think that its premises are at best only externally connected with the truth of this proposition; although the premises imply this proposition, there is no way of using them (without assuming the necessary truth of the proposition) to show why it cannot be false.[19]

Arguments whose premises and conclusions are both such that S, on reflection, would regard them as necessarily true are uncontroversial for S only if he, on reflection, would think that their premises could be used to provide him with an understanding of why the conclusion cannot be false. Moreover, this same requirement applies to arguments whose premises and conclusions are such that S, on reflection, would regard them as necessarily true *if true at all* (where this leaves open the possibility that even on reflection S may not be sure whether they are necessarily true).

What about arguments whose premises S, on reflection, would regard as being necessarily true? And what about arguments with premises that S, on reflection, would regard as either necessarily true or necessarily false (although even on reflection he might not be sure which)? Consider, for example, an inductive argument for Goldbach's conjecture.[20] Suppose S has tried very hard to find an even number greater than two that is not the sum of two primes but that he has failed to do so. Moreover, suppose he is aware that numerous other mathematicians also have tried to find such a number but that they too have failed to do so. Then, even if S cannot prove that every even number greater than two is the sum of two primes, he is likely to have an inductive argument for this claim that on reflection he would regard as a very good argument. But unlike other inductive arguments, his thinking that this argument is a good one cannot be a matter of his thinking that the conclusion is true in most relevant situations in which the premises are true. After all, by hypothesis he, on reflection, would think that Goldbach's conjecture is either necessarily true or necessarily false. So, on reflection he would think that either the conclusion is true in all possible situations in which the premises are true or that it is true in no possible situation in which the premises are true. And even after ideal reflection, he may not be sure which is the case. Moreover, there is a problem here even if we grant that although S on reflection is not likely to be able to *prove* that Goldbach's conjecture is true, he (presumably like many of the rest of us) on reflection nonetheless would *believe* that it is necessarily true. For then, even with respect to what he, on reflection, would regard as bad inductive arguments for Goldbach's conjecture—for example, an argument based on an examination of just a couple of even numbers, say the number 4 and the number 8—he would think that the conclusion is true in all possible situations in which the premises are true. So here once again, S's thinking that he has a good argument for Goldbach's conjecture cannot be a matter of his thinking that in most situations in which the premises of the argument are true the conclusion also is true.

What then is it for him, on reflection, to think that his argument for Goldbach's conjecture is a good one? It is for him on reflection to think that the argument is a kind of argument that is likely to have a true conclusion. Of course, any argument will be an instance of countless different kinds of arguments. But just as we left it up to S himself, on reflection, to decide what situations are relevant for determining the likely truth-preservingness of ordinary arguments, so too let us leave it up to S, on reflection, to decide what arguments are relevant for an assessment of his argument concerning Goldbach's conjecture. The idea, then, is for S to consider relevantly similar arguments, where he is the judge of what counts as a relevantly similar argument, for other conclusions that, like Goldbach's conjecture, are either necessarily true or necessarily false. For example, he would be likely to consider possible arguments for various other mathematical claims, arguments the truth of whose premises he would not take to be so unlikely as to make them irrelevant to an assessment of the argument, and whose premises in addition contain inductive support for their conclusions that is comparable to the massive inductive support he takes himself to have for Goldbach's conjecture. He then is to ask himself if the conclusions of most such arguments are true. If, as is likely to be the case, he, on reflection, would think that a sufficiently great percentage of the conclusions of these relevantly similar arguments are true, then his argument for Goldbach's conjecture is uncontroversial for him; it is a kind of inductive argument that he, on reflection, would think is sufficiently likely to have a true conclusion.[21] On the other hand, on reflection he is unlikely to think this of other arguments for Goldbach's conjecture—for example, inductive arguments based on an examination of just a couple of even numbers greater than two. But if so, these arguments are not uncontroversial for him, and they are not uncontroversial for him even if on reflection he would believe that their premises imply their conclusions.

Unlike arguments whose premises and conclusions S, on reflection, would take to be contingent, arguments whose conclusions S, on reflection, would take to be necessarily true do not automatically become uncontroversial for him by virtue of the fact that on reflection he would believe that their conclusions are true in a sufficiently great percentage of possible situations in which their premises are true. For unlike arguments of the former kind, he, on reflection, might believe this of an argument of the latter kind even if he also, on reflection, would believe that its premises are altogether irrelevant to its conclusion. (Nevertheless, for the sake of simplicity, in what follows I will ordinarily characterize uncontroversial arguments as those that the individual, on reflection, would believe to be sufficiently likely to be truth preserving.)

A final word of warning. My remarks about S's attitudes toward epistemic risks, about what kinds of possible situations an individual S, on reflection, is likely to regard as relevant for assessing an argument, and about arguments whose conclusions S, on reflection, would regard as necessarily true should not be taken as implying that S has a whole battery of sophisticated epistemic concepts. Thus, for example, in saying that S's attitudes toward epistemic risks as well as his views about what counts as a relevant possible situation are crucial in determining what arguments are uncontroversial for him, I do not mean to say that S, on reflection, would have some sophisticated way of determining what is an appropriate attitude toward epistemic risk and what is a relevant possible situation. Indeed, as I hinted earlier, in order for an argument to be uncontroversial for him S need not have any very sophisticated epistemic concepts at all. For most arguments he need only be sophisticated enough to be able to decide whether the conclusion of the argument would be true in enough of the relevant (not vastly improbable) possible situations in which the argument's premises are true to make believing it a good epistemic bet—a good epistemic bet in a situation in which its premises are true. And for arguments with conclusions that he, on reflection, would regard as necessarily true, he need only be sophisticated enough to be able to decide whether the premises are relevant to the conclusion, where this is a matter of deciding either that most relevantly similar arguments have true conclusions or that the information in the premises is sufficient to allow him to understand why the conclusion cannot possibly be false.[22] Even so, we can represent his decisions about these matters in terms of certain, relatively sophisticated epistemic notions. For example, with respect to ordinary arguments, we can represent S's decision as manifesting S's way of weighting the two aspects of his epistemic goals, believing truths and not believing falsehoods, and as manifesting what possible situations he regards as relevant to an assessment of whether the argument's premises make sufficiently probable its conclusion.[23] Most important, we can take it also as manifesting whether the argument has premises that support its conclusion in a way that is uncontroversial for him.

1.3   Believing on Reflection That an Argument Is Sufficiently Likely to Be Truth Preserving

Arguments that are uncontroversial for a person, I have said, are arguments that on careful reflection he would regard as sufficiently likely to be truth preserving. But in what kind of careful reflection are we to imagine a person engaging? The answer is: Reflection that reveals the person's own deepest epistemic standards. This answer, of course, merely pushes the question back a step. The question now becomes: What kind of reflection reveals a person's own deepest epistemic standards? The answer is: Sufficient reflection from an epistemic point of view.

I will have more to say shortly about what is involved in being sufficiently reflective, but first consider what is involved in reflection from an epistemic point of view. To reflect from an epistemic point of view is to reflect upon an argument solely with the idea of deciding whether the inference recommended by the argument is sufficiently likely to be truth preserving.[24] It is to reflect solely with the idea of deciding whether or not the conclusion of the argument is true in a sufficiently great percentage of relevant possible situations in which its premises are true, sufficiently great to make believing the conclusion an acceptable risk (with respect to the epistemic goal of now believing truths and now not believing falsehoods). Nevertheless, in imagining a person engaging in such reflection, we need not imagine him reflecting only on the argument in question. In particular, we need not imagine him reflecting only on various possible situations in which the argument's premises are true in an effort to decide whether its conclusion is true in a sufficiently great percentage of these situations that are relevant. Rather, we can imagine him reflecting on any consideration at all that he might think important to the epistemic assessment of the argument. So, for example, he might reflect upon other arguments, in order to compare and contrast the argument in question with these arguments. Presumably, the more similar the argument in question is to other arguments that he thinks are sufficiently likely to be truth preserving, the better the chances are that he will approve of it. Correspondingly, the more similar the argument is to other arguments that he thinks are not sufficiently likely to be truth preserving, the worse the chances are that he will approve of it. He also might reflect upon various abstract argument schemas and then evaluate the argument in question against what he is inclined to think of these schemas. However, all these reflections take place against the backdrop of his trying to decide whether the argument in question is sufficiently likely to be truth preserving.

In imagining a person reflecting upon an argument, we are to imagine him deliberating over any consideration—whether these be other arguments, argument schemas, or whatever—that he deems relevant to the question of whether the argument is sufficiently likely to be truth preserving. Were he to engage in such reflection, conflicts might very well emerge. Some of the considerations upon which he deliberates might suggest to him that the argument is sufficiently likely to be truth preserving; other considerations might suggest to him that this is not so. For example, it may be that on reflection he would become convinced that the argument in question is relevantly similar to some other argument about which he is suspicious. Nevertheless, he may also be strongly inclined to think that the argument in question is highly likely to be truth preserving. In the case of such a conflict, we are to imagine him correcting the conflict in the way that seems best to him from an epistemic point of view. For example, he might upon further reflection conclude that although at first glance the two arguments seem very similar, in fact they are not. He might find some feature of the argument in question that distinguishes it from similar-looking arguments of which he is inclined to disapprove. Or he might resolve the conflict more straightforwardly, by altering his initial judgment of the argument in question or his initial judgment of the argument he thinks is relevantly similar to it. Thus, in some such cases he might be sufficiently confident of his initial judgment concerning the argument in question that he would be prepared, on reflection, to alter his initial judgment concerning the argument he thinks is relevantly similar. Other times just the opposite might occur; he would alter his initial judgment concerning the argument in question rather than alter his judgment about the truth-preservingness of the argument that seems relevantly similar. Regardless of which is the case, the point is that we are to imagine how, given his present dispositions and given the epistemic goal of his now believing truths and now not believing falsehoods, he would decide such conflicts were he to be sufficiently careful in his reflections. If upon being sufficiently reflec-

tive, the argument in question seems to him to be one that is sufficiently likely to be truth preserving—sufficiently likely to make believing its conclusion an acceptable risk in situations in which its
premises are true—then the argument reflects his own deepest epistemic standards.

What, then, constitutes *S*'s being "sufficiently reflective"? How
much reflection is required before his opinion of an argument is in-
dicative of his own deepest epistemic standards? Is it enough for him
to reflect for a few minutes, or for a few hours, or for a few days, or
what?

The answer is that strictly speaking there is no limit. We imagine
him reflecting until his view stabilizes, until further reflection would
not alter his opinion of the argument in question. This by definition
is the point at which the person is not susceptible to further self-
criticism. It is by definition the point at which had the person reflected
still more, he would not have charged himself with being mistaken
in his earlier evaluation of the argument. If at this point the person
would believe that the argument is sufficiently likely to be truth preserving, then the argument conforms to his own deepest epistemic
standards. Further reflection would not prompt him to think he was
mistaken in his assessment of the argument.

To determine whether an argument is genuinely uncontroversial
for an individual, we imagine him reflecting from an epistemic point
of view upon the argument in question and upon various other arguments and argument schemas and upon any other consideration
he, on reflection, would take to be relevant. Moreover, we do not
impose a limit on this reflection. In effect, we imagine him reflecting
until he has considered any proposal that might occur to him concerning how best to evaluate the argument. Or at least we imagine
him reflecting on such proposals until reflection on any other proposals would not alter his opinion of the argument in question. In
this way, the arguments that are uncontroversial for him are arguments that conform to his ideal epistemic standards, where his ideal
epistemic standards in turn are a function of what he now is disposed
to think about these arguments were he to be sufficiently reflective.
So, if an individual on reflection is disposed to think that the argument
is sufficiently likely to be truth preserving and if in addition he is so
disposed that further reflection would not change his mind about this,
then the argument conforms to his own deepest epistemic standards.
Accordingly, the premises of the argument support its conclusion in
a way that is uncontroversial for him.[25]

Given that the notion of an uncontroversial argument is understood in this idealized way, it may be difficult for the rest of us to know whether an argument is uncontroversial for a person *S*. Indeed, with respect to many arguments, it will be difficult for *S* to know this about himself. Moreover, these difficulties are not eased any by the fact that there is nothing in principle to prevent an argument from being un-controversial for *S* at one time but not at another.

However, difficulties of this sort should not be exaggerated. For many arguments, especially relatively simple ones, it will be clear that they are uncontroversial for *S*. It will be clear, in other words, that *S* thinks that they are sufficiently likely to be truth preserving and that further reflection would not alter *S*'s opinion of them. Further reflection might alter his opinion concerning the truth of one of the premises of such an argument, but that is not what is at issue here. What is at issue is whether further reflection would alter *S*'s opin-ion concerning whether the inference recommended by the argument is likely to be truth preserving, and at least for many simple argu-ments we can be confident that further reflection would not alter his opinion.

Moreover, for more complex arguments, if we can determine what *S*'s opinion of them would be were he to reflect carefully upon a relatively wide range of possible situations and a relatively large num-ber of similar arguments, we can be relatively confident that further reflection on slightly different arguments and situations would be unlikely to alter his opinion. So we need not try to determine exactly what might be *S*'s reactions to these other arguments and examples.

But might not there be arguments such that there is *no* point at which *S*'s opinion of them would be unswayed by further reflection? With continuing reflection *S*'s opinion of such arguments might os-cillate between acceptance and rejection. Or short of this, continuing reflection might result in continuing indecision on his part. Thus, *S* might be so disposed that no matter how much he reflected upon the argument, he would not arrive at a stable decision concerning whether the argument is sufficiently likely to be truth preserving.

Perhaps there are such arguments, arguments about which *S* would not reach a stable, final decision. Perhaps no matter how long he reflected he would be perplexed, not knowing what to conclude, or perhaps he would continue to change his mind. Such arguments might be complex enough or for some other reason confusing enough that *S* as he is now would not be able to reach a final decision concerning them no matter how long he were to reflect upon them. (Analogously, we could imagine presenting to a person a sentence such that no matter how much he reflected, he would not accept it as being grammatically well formed and likewise would not reject it as being grammatically ill formed; instead he would simply be perplexed, whether by its complexity or by some other feature.)

Arguments of this sort, about which a person *S* would not reach a stable decision no matter how long he were to reflect, are not uncontroversial for *S*. They do not conform to *S*'s own deepest epistemic standards. An argument meets *S*'s own epistemic standards just if he would regard it as sufficiently truth preserving were he sufficiently reflective. But by hypothesis, arguments about which, on reflection, he would reach no stable decision as well as arguments which, on reflection, he would reject outright fail to meet this standard. So from an epistemic viewpoint it need not be rational for him to believe the conclusions of such arguments even if all of their premises are uncontroversial for him and all else is equal.[26]

Arguments that are uncontroversial for *S*, I have claimed, are arguments that *S* would regard as sufficiently likely to be truth preserving were he to be sufficiently reflective. Suppose, however, that *S*'s reflections affect his opinions of arguments in some unusual way— via, say, an external source. Suppose, to take an extreme example, an evil scientist is prepared to alter *S*'s opinions of various arguments were *S* to reflect upon them. Suppose the scientist is able to do this by stimulating *S*'s brain in appropriate ways. If *S* were to reflect on considerations that he otherwise would regard as counting in favor of an argument A, the scientist would stimulate *S*'s brain in such a way that these considerations would no longer seem favorable to *S* and in this way would cause *S* to disapprove of A. Under these conditions, then, if *S* were to be reflective, he would disapprove of A. The scientist by being prepared to manipulate *S* ensures that this is so.

Does this then mean that argument A does not conform to *S*'s deepest epistemic standards? Does it mean that in a situation where argument A's premises are uncontroversial for *S* and all else is equal, A's conclusion might not be epistemically rational for him? Not necessarily, for the phrase "what *S* would believe were he to be sufficiently reflective" should be understood in such a way that it precludes *S* being manipulated in this way. In particular, this phrase should be understood in a way that ensures that *S*'s beliefs are self-generated. The situation in which we are to imagine *S*, in order to determine whether argument A conforms to his deepest epistemic standards, is not a situation in which there is an external source altering *S*'s beliefs or dispositions. Nor is it even a situation in which S is taught or shown that argument A is likely to be truth preserving. Perhaps he could be taught this. But even if he could, it does not follow that if left on his own to reflect he would have reached this conclusion. Rather, the situation in which we are to imagine S, in order to determine whether A conforms to his deepest epistemic standards, is one in which S as he is now with his present dispositions, habits, and inclinations, reflects upon argument A without any external source altering these dispositions, habits, and inclinations.

However, it is admittedly difficult to find an absolutely precise way to distinguish situations in which S as he is now (with his present dispositions), on reflection, would approve of an argument and situations in which S, on reflection, would approve of the argument, because such reflections would trigger some external event (such as the actions of an evil scientist) that in turn would alter what he is disposed to think of the argument. The problem here is the difficulty of finding an absolutely precise way to distinguish between a person having a disposition and his acquiring a disposition. It is especially difficult to distinguish situations in which a person has a secondary disposition—a disposition to acquire a new first-order disposition— from situations in which he acquires an altogether new first-order disposition. For instance, although S may be initially disposed, on reflection, to favor an argument A, it might be that his initial reflection on A and his initially favorable response to it normally would trigger further reflection that ultimately would lead him to disapprove of it. So, S here has a secondary disposition that would be triggered by and that would override his primary disposition (his initial inclination on reflection to approve of A). This sort of case, involving secondary dispositions, needs to be distinguished from cases in which his reflections are controlled by an external factor—the evil scientist sort of case. In the latter, the scientist is prepared to alter S's dispositions— perhaps both his first-order and his higher-level dispositions—if he reflects on considerations that otherwise would incline S to approve of A. In the former, any alteration in S's dispositions is self-generated, via his reflections triggering higher-level dispositions.

The two kinds of cases can be intuitively distinguished, but it may be difficult to find an altogether precise way of explicating the distinction. Nonetheless, in the vast majority of cases the distinction is clear enough, and even in problematic cases nonarbitrary decisions ordinarily can be made. For example, suppose we assume that the evil scientist already has tampered with S. Suppose he yesterday tampered with S's brain so that the reflection on A by S that otherwise (had the scientist not tampered) would have inclined *S* to approve of A will instead result in his disapproving of it. So, *today S* would disapprove of A were he to reflect sufficiently upon it. In this and similar situations a plausible case can be made for the claim that the tamperings of the scientist yesterday changed *S*'s epistemic standards. Before yesterday, given *S*'s dispositions, he, on reflection, would have approved of argument A, but the tamperings changed this. The tamperings have altered *S* in such a way, that, given the way he is now (that is, given no further tamperings), he on reflection is disposed to disapprove of A. Given the way he is now, it need not be epistemically rational for him to believe A's conclusion even if its premises are uncontroversial and all else is equal. This case, then, stands in contrast with the case discussed earlier, in which the scientist has in fact not tampered with *S* but is prepared to do so were he to be reflective. Since the scientist in the earlier case has not yet tampered with *S*, he has not yet altered *S*'s epistemic standards. Accordingly, in that case it is epistemically rational for *S* to believe A's conclusion, assuming that A's premises are uncontroversial for him and that all else is equal.[27]

1.4 Definition of "Tends to Make Epistemically Rational"

If the phrase "sufficiently reflective" is used to pick out the above-described process of ideal reflection from an epistemic point of view (where one is solely concerned with the truth-preservingness of the argument in question) and if the phrase "sufficiently likely to be truth preserving" is used in the way described above (where an argument is sufficiently likely to be truth preserving just if, given the truth of the premises, the conclusion is likely enough to make believing it worth the epistemic risk) and if the term "relevant" when applied to arguments whose conclusions an individual on reflection would regard as necessarily true if true at all is used in the way described above (where if such an argument has necessarily true premises, the premises are relevant to the conclusion just if the premises can be used to show why it is impossible for the conclusion to be false, and where if the argument has contingent premises, the premises are relevant to the conclusion just if the argument is a kind of "inductive" argument that is likely to have a true conclusion), then the following defines what it is for an argument to be such that its premises can be used to argue for its conclusion in a way that is uncontroversial for a person *S* at a time *t*:

Propositions e^1, e^2, ... e^n can be used to argue for proposition p in a way that is uncontroversial for S at t.	= df	If S at t were to be sufficiently reflective, then (i) he would believe that an argument with e^1, e^2, ... e^n as premises and p as its conclusion is sufficiently likely to be truth preserving, (ii) if he would believe that p is necessarily true if true at all, he also would believe that (e^1, e^2, ... e^n,) are relevant to p and (iii) he would not believe that (e^1 and e^2 ... and e^n) is necessarily false.

Or expressed more simply, we can say that given these conditions, propositions e^1, e^2, ... e^n tend to make p epistemically rational for S at t, where "tend to make epistemically rational" is defined in terms of the definition above:

Propositions e^1, e^2, ... e^n tend to make p epistemically rational for S at t.	= df	Propositions e^1, e^2, ... e^n can be used to argue for p in a way that is uncontroversial for S at t.

1.5   Epistemically Insecure Propositions

A proposition p is epistemically rational for an individual S just if using propositions that are uncontroversial for him he can argue for p in a way that is uncontroversial for him. What this means, in the terminology I have adopted, is that p is epistemically rational for S just if propositions that are uncontroversial for him tend to make p epistemically rational for him and there are no defeater propositions that are uncontroversial for him.

What is it for a proposition to be uncontroversial for an individual? As an initial characterization, we can say that a proposition is uncontroversial for an individual just in case the individual believes it with such confidence that nothing else he believes with comparable confidence gives him a reason to be suspicious of it. So, at a minimum the individual needs to be convinced of the proposition's truth if it is to be uncontroversial for him. He needs to believe it. This does not mean, however, that he needs to be explicitly considering the proposition. Five minutes ago I was not explicitly considering the proposition that I then was alive, but I then did believe this proposition. Propositions can be believed in either an occurrent or in a nonoccurrent sense.

However, believing a proposition, either occurrently or nonoccurrently, is not enough to make a proposition uncontroversial for an individual. In addition, it must be the case that the individual would uncover no good reason to be suspicious of the proposition's truth were he to engage in an appropriate kind of reflection. What is the appropriate kind of reflection? It is reflection upon the other propositions that he now believes and upon the arguments that are uncontroversial for him. The idea is that a proposition *p* that *S* believes is uncontroversial for him only if reflection upon his doxastic system and his epistemic standards would give him no good reason to be suspicious of *p*'s truth. How might *S*'s doxastic system and his epistemic standards provide him with a good reason to be suspicious of *p*? By providing him with the "materials" for an appropriate argument against *p*—an appropriate argument in terms of what else he believes and in terms of what arguments he would regard as sufficiently truth preserving were he to be reflective.

This explication can be made more precise by describing what constitutes an appropriate argument against a proposition *p*. But first something must be said about the strength with which an individual believes various propositions.

The strength with which a person believes a proposition is a matter of how confident he is of its truth. Some propositions he will believe with great confidence; others he will believe with considerably less confidence. Moreover, this is so for propositions he is explicitly considering as well as for those that he is not; five minutes ago I believed with great confidence the proposition that I then was alive, even though I was not then explicitly considering this proposition. It is sometimes claimed that the strength of a person's beliefs can be measured by engaging him in situations in which he bets on the truth of what he believes, with the odds he is willing to take determining how confident he is of that truth. However, whether or not this is so, the notion here is familiar enough; people believe certain propositions with greater confidence than they believe certain others.

The confidence with which an individual believes a proposition is relevant to the question of what propositions are uncontroversial for him, because the more confidently an individual believes a proposition the more likely it is that the proposition is uncontroversial for him.[28] This is not to say, however, that confidently believing a proposition is enough to make it uncontroversial. On the contrary, it is possible for a proposition p to be believed by an individual with great confidence and yet be controversial for him, since he might believe with equal or greater confidence other propositions that can be used in an uncontroversial way to argue against p. For example, suppose there are propositions e^1, e^2, . . . e^n, each of whose truth a person S feels as sure, or even more sure, than he does of p's truth, and suppose in addition that these propositions tend to make not$p$ epistemically rational for him. Consider the simplest cases of this sort. Suppose that S on reflection would believe (although perhaps he does not now believe) that these propositions imply not$p$. Under these conditions, proposition p is epistemically insecure for him, in the sense that given what he now believes and the confidence with which he believes it and given also his current epistemic standards (that is, given the arguments that are uncontroversial for him), he has a good reason to be suspicious of p.[29]

Situations that do not involve arguments with premises that S on reflection would take to imply their conclusions are somewhat more complicated. Suppose that propositions e^1, e^2, . . . e^n tend to make not$p$ epistemically rational for S but that he on reflection would believe that these propositions do not imply but rather only make sufficiently probable not$p$. Suppose further that he believes all these propositions with as much confidence as he believes p. Under these conditions, there is a presumption that p is controversial for him, since he has an argument against p that has premises he believes as confidently as p. There is only a presumption here, however, because the argument in question is not one whose premises he, on reflection, would take to imply its conclusion. So the premises of the argument give him a reason to be suspicious of the conclusion only if all else is equal. On the other hand, if we suppose that all else is equal—if we suppose that there is no convincing defeater proposition—then the proposition p is controversial for him.

What makes a proposition a convincing defeater of an argument that threatens to make p controversial? This question can be answered by distinguishing a *potential* defeater of such an argument from a *genuine* or *convincing* defeater of the argument. A proposition d is a potential defeater of an argument that threatens to make p controversial just if adding d to the premises of the original argument generates a new argument whose premises do not tend to make not$p$ epistemically rational. Thus, if the premises of the original argument are e^1, e^2, . . . e^n—if S on reflection would believe that not$p$ is true in a sufficiently high percentage of relevant possible situations in which propositions e^1, e^2, . . . e^n are true—then d is a potential defeater of this argument if S on reflection would believe that it is *not* the case that not$p$ is true in a sufficiently high percentage of relevant possible situations in which e^1, e^2, ... e^n and d are true.[30]

What makes d a genuine, or convincing, defeater? Think of the question in this way: Since an argument with not$p$ as its conclusion makes p controversial for S only if its least strongly believed premise is believed as strongly as p, a proposition d will be a convincing defeater of such an argument only if it is believed at least as strongly as the least strongly believed premise. In other words, the argument with not$p$ as its conclusion—the argument with premises e^1, e^2, ... e^n— will be defeated (preventing it from making p controversial) only if there is a potential defeater d that is believed by S at least as confidently as is some proposition in the set $(e^1, e^2, ... e^n)$.[31]

In addition, for d to be a convincing defeater of the argument, it must not beg the question against that argument. So, for example, the defeater d cannot be p itself. The fact that S believes p as confidently as some proposition in the set $(e^1, e^2, ... e^n)$ does not convincingly defeat the argument. Likewise, the argument cannot be convincingly defeated by the fact that S believes that p is probable. Assume for present purposes that the expression "p is probable" is elliptical for something like "p is probable given the total relevant available evidence."[32] Often an individual S will believe, albeit perhaps nonoccurrently, that p is probable if he believes p is true; believing p and believing that p is probable are in this way intimately linked.[33] So resorting to the proposition that p is probable to defeat the argument for not$p$ begs the question against the argument just as much as resorting to p itself. Accordingly, neither the proposition p nor the proposition that p is probable can be used to *convincingly* defeat the argument. Nor can a convincing defeater be a proposition that has the proposition p or the proposition that p is probable as part of its "content." This again would beg the question against the argument for not$p$. Moreover, the defeater cannot have as part of its content any "relevant" part of p's content. For example, propositions e^1, e^2, ... e^n may tend to make not$p$ epistemically rational because they tend to make epistemically rational the negation of a proposition p^1 that is part of p's content. If so, the argument against not$p$ cannot be defeated by a proposition d that has as part of its content this proposition p^1. Once more, this would beg the question.

These remarks can be made more precise by introducing a notion of entailment that is distinct from a broader notion of implication. A proposition p implies a proposition q just if it is impossible for q to be false if p is true. On the other hand, in order for p to entail q, the relation between p and q has to be not just "logically intimate" but also "conceptually intimate," so that the "content" of p includes the "content" of q. Let us say that a proposition p entails a proposition q just if p implies q, *and* necessarily whoever thinks p also thinks q, *and* necessarily whoever believes p also believes q and believes it with at least as much confidence as he believes p.[34] Thus, the proposition that it is raining implies but does not entail the proposition that it is either raining or snowing. A person can think (entertain) the first without thinking (entertaining) the second. Likewise, the proposition that Jones is thinking of a number that is the sum of two primes is not entailed by the proposition that either Jones is thinking of a number that is the sum of two primes or he is thinking of an even number greater than two. The first is implied by the second (assuming Goldbach's conjecture to be true), and necessarily whoever thinks the second thinks the first (since the first is a "component" of the second), but it presumably is not the case that whoever believes the second believes the first and with as much confidence. It presumably is possible to believe the second and yet either not see that it implies the first or be in doubt whether it implies the first. On the other hand, the proposition that it is cold and raining both implies and entails the proposition that it is raining. No one can think the first without thinking the second; no one can believe the first without believing the second; no one can believe the first with more confidence than he believes the second.

Given this notion of entailment, reconsider the question of what makes a proposition d a convincing defeater for S of an argument that threatens to make p controversial—an argument with premises $e^1, e^2, \ldots e^n$. We now can say that d is a convincing defeater just if (1) d is a potential defeater of the argument, (2) d is believed by S as confidently as some proposition in the set $(e^1, e^2, \ldots e^n)$, and (3) d does not "beg the question" against the argument $(e^1, e^2, \ldots e^n$; thus, not$p$), where d begs the question against this argument just if either (i) d entails the proposition p or (ii) d entails the proposition that p is probable or (iii) d entails some proposition p^1 such that p^1 is entailed by p and such that propositions $e^1, e^2, \ldots e^n$ tend to make notp^1 epistemically rational for S or (iv) not$d$ entails either the proposition not$p$ or the proposition that it is not the case that p is probable or some proposition notp^1, where p^1 is entailed by p and where $e^1, e^2, \ldots e^n$ tend to make notp^1 epistemically rational for S.

Consider an example to illustrate how these conditions work. Suppose S believes proposition p but that he also believes with the same confidence as p the proposition that Jones, who normally is highly reliable about these matters, says that not$p$ is true. Call this latter proposition e, and suppose that e tends to make not$p$ epistemically rational for S. Accordingly, the argument (e; thus, not$p$) threatens to make p controversial for S. We now want to know whether there is a convincing defeater of this argument. Is there a defeater that prevents this argument from making p controversial for S? The above conditions tell us that neither p itself nor the proposition that p is probable can be such a defeater, even though they are potential defeaters that may be believed by S as confidently as e. Since every proposition entails itself, conditions (3i) and (3ii) respectively preclude these propositions from being convincing defeaters. Likewise, condition (3i) rules out the possibility that the conjunctive proposition (p and $1 + 2 = 3$) is a convincing defeater. What about the disjunctive proposition (p or $1 + 2 = 4$)? This proposition is likely to be a potential defeater (since the second disjunct is necessarily false, the proposition is true just in case p is true) and yet neither (3i) nor (3ii) nor (3iii) rule it out as a convincing defeater. For example, (3i) does not rule it out, since this disjunctive proposition presumably does not entail p; it presumably is at least theoretically possible for one to believe $1 + 2 = 4$. But if so, it is possible to believe the disjunction (p or $1 + 2 = 4$) without believing p. Short of this, it presumably is possible for one to believe the disjunction more confidently than he believes p (since he might not be absolutely certain that $1 + 2 = 4$ is false). However, condition (3iv) *does* prevent this disjunction from being a convincing defeater, since the negation of the disjunction entails not$p$. By way of contrast, the proposition that Jones in this situation is not in a good position to judge the truth of p (say, because his vision is temporarily impaired) might very well be a convincing defeater of the argument for not$p$. It presumably is a potential defeater of the argument, thus satisfying condition (1). It might be believed by S as confidently as e, thus satisfying (2). And it does not seem to beg the question in any of the senses specified by (3).

Consider another example. Let p be the proposition that there are unicorns, and let e be the proposition that Jones, who normally is highly reliable about these matters, says that notp^1 is true, where p^1 is the proposition that there are animals with horselike heads and a single horn. Suppose that e tends to make not$p$ as well as notp^1 epistemically rational for S, and suppose that S believes e with the same confidence as he believes p. Accordingly, the argument (e; thus, not$p$) threatens to make p controversial for S. The above conditions— specifically condition (3iii)—tells us that p^1 cannot be a defeater that prevents this argument from making p controversial for S. It cannot be such a defeater even though it is a potential defeater that is believed by S as confidently as e. For p^1 is a proposition entailed by p and e tends to make its negation epistemically rational.

So, if propositions $(e^1, e^2, \ldots e^n)$ tend to make not$p$ epistemically rational for S and if these propositions are believed by S as confidently as p and if finally there is no convincing defeater proposition, where a convincing defeater is a proposition that satisfies conditions (1), (2), and (3), then the proposition p is controversial for S. It is controversial for him because given what he now believes and the strength with which he believes it and given also his epistemic standards (the arguments that are uncontroversial for him), he has a good reason to be suspicious of p. Propositions of whose truth he now feels as sure as he does of p's truth tend to make not$p$ epistemically rational for him and moreover there is no proposition of whose truth he feels equally sure that is a convincing defeater. Thus, the fact that there are such propositions $e^1, e^2, \ldots e^n$ makes the proposition p prima facie controversial for him, and the fact that there is no convincing defeating proposition indicates that there is nothing to override the prima facie controversial status that p has for S. Accordingly, p is controversial for S.[35]

Details aside, then, a proposition p is controversial for an individual S if there is an argument for not$p$ that he on reflection is likely to regard as truth preserving and that has premises that he believes as confidently as p. Under these conditions, his present doxastic system and his present deepest epistemic standards combine to give him a reason to be suspicious of p, preventing it from being uncontroversial for him. Moreover, the reason that makes p suspicious for him here is a reason that S himself would uncover were he to be ideally reflective about what he believes and about what arguments are likely to be truth preserving.[36]

The idea here is that in determining whether a proposition p is uncontroversial for an individual S, we begin by holding fixed his current doxastic system, asking whether, given what he currently believes, he has a reason to be suspicious of p. We do not, for example, imagine S reflecting directly upon what he believes with the purpose of deciding whether he has a good reason to be suspicious of those propositions that he believes. Were S to engage in such reflection, his belief system no doubt would be altered in various ways. He might cease to believe certain propositions, come to believe others, and believe still others with a different degree of confidence. However, this is irrelevant here. The idea here is not to determine whether S would have a reason to be suspicious of p, given his present epistemic standards and given what his doxastic system would be were he to reflect upon it in an effort to improve it or to correct it. Rather the idea is to determine whether *S* now has a reason to be suspicious of *p*, given his present epistemic standards and given his present doxastic system.[37]

So far, what I have claimed is that one way in which *S*'s epistemic standards and doxastic system can give him a reason to be suspicious of *p* is by providing him with an argument whose premises tend to make not*p* epistemically rational for him and in addition whose premises are believed by him as confidently as is *p*. This is sufficient to make *p* controversial for *S*. It is not necessary. Another way in which *p* can be controversial for *S*, given his epistemic standards and given his doxastic system, will be introduced shortly. According to this other way, even propositions that do not tend to make not*p* epistemically rational for *S* can play an important role in making *p* controversial for him. For example, suppose there are propositions that *S* believes as confidently as *p* but are such that *S*, on reflection, would think these propositions just barely miss making not*p* sufficiently probable. Therefore, these propositions do not tend to make not*p* epistemically rational for *S*. Accordingly, the requirement above—that there be no argument for not*p* whose premises *S* believes as confidently as *p*—is not violated in such a case. And yet intuitively it seems as if in such a case *S* might very well have a good reason to be suspicious of *p*, given his epistemic standards and his doxastic system. The requirement to be introduced shortly will explain how such propositions, those that cannot be used to argue for not*p*, can make *p* controversial for *S*.[38]

However, it is important to note first how the requirement above might be violated even in situations where at first glance it might not seem to be. Consider, for example, a situation in which there are propositions that tend to make not*p* epistemically rational for *S* but of whose truth *S* feels less sure (perhaps only slightly less sure) than he does of *p*'s truth. Suppose, for example, that propositions $e^1, e^2, \ldots e^n$ tend to make not*p* epistemically rational for *S* but that *S* believes one of these propositions—say, e^1—with a little less confidence than he believes *p*. Then strictly, according to the requirement above, these propositions do not make *p* controversial for *S*. But even so, closely related propositions might. In particular, if *S* believes e^1, he also is likely to believe (at least nonoccurrently) a proposition about the likelihood of e^1, and he might believe this proposition as confidently as *p*.[39] For instance, he might believe as confidently as *p* the proposition that e^1 is highly probable. Moreover, substituting this proposition for e^1 in the original argument might generate another argument whose premises tend to make not$p$ epistemically rational for S. If so, this argument will make p controversial for S (assuming there is no convincing defeater).[40]

Similarly, suppose S has a number of arguments with not$p$ as their conclusions but that each such argument contains a premise of whose truth he feels less sure than he does of p's truth. Might not the fact that he has so many (individually weak) arguments of this sort nonetheless make p controversial for him? Yes, for he might very well believe with as much confidence as he does p the proposition that at least one of these arguments is a good one, and this proposition in turn might itself be capable of being used to argue against p. Suppose, for example, that each of the following sets of propositions tends to make rational not$p$—the set $(e^1, e^2, \ldots e^n)$, the set $(f^1, f^2, \ldots f^n)$, and the set $(g^1, g^2, \ldots g^n)$—but that each set contains at least one premise that S believes less confidently than p. Nevertheless, S might very well believe the disjunction of these sets as confidently as p and this disjunction might tend to make not$p$ epistemically rational for S. If so, p once again will be controversial for S.

Thus, if either of these tactics—the tactic of "probabilifying" a weakly believed premise in an argument with not$p$ as its conclusion, and the tactic of disjoining the premises of several such arguments— or some other tactic—generates an undefeated argument with premises that S believes as confidently as he does p, then p is not uncontroversial for him. (Each of these tactics also can be used to generate convincing defeaters of an argument that threatens to make p controversial.) Unfortunately, there is one exception to this general rule (which I discuss in section 1.6), an exception that allows p to be uncontroversial for S even though there is an undefeated argument for not$p$ with premises that S believes as confidently as p.

1.6   Epistemic Basicality

One way of summarizing the discussion is to say that a proposition p is uncontroversial for an individual S only if it is "argument-proof" for him, in the sense that all possible arguments against it are implausible. In particular, all such arguments fail to give him a good reason to be suspicious of p, either because their premises do not tend to make not$p$ epistemically rational for him or because he feels less sure of the truth of one of their premises than he does of p's truth or because there is a convincing defeater of the argument.

However, there is an additional way in which S can have a good reason to be suspicious of a proposition p that he believes. He might have no good epistemic reason to think that p is likely to be true. For a proposition p to be genuinely uncontroversial for S—for it to be a proposition that he has no good reasons to be suspicious of, given what he believes and given his epistemic standards—it is not enough for him to lack an argument for not$p$. He must also have reasons in favor of p. For if S were to have no good reason to think that p is true (as well as no argument for not$p$), withholding judgment on p would be his best option. But then, p would be controversial for him; he would have a good reason to be suspicious of p by virtue of lacking a good reason for thinking that p is true.

So for p to be genuinely uncontroversial for S, he must have no good reason to be suspicious of p, given what he believes and given his epistemic standards. And in order to have no good reason to be suspicious of p, he must have a good reason to think that p is true, given what he believes and given his epistemic standards. How then might his beliefs and his epistemic standards give him such a reason? There is a seemingly obvious answer to this question, but it will be instructive to consider first some less obvious answers. For example, one possible answer is that if S cannot argue for not$p$ using propositions that he believes as confidently as p, then, given his beliefs and given his epistemic standards, he has no good reasons to think that not$p$ is true and this itself constitutes a reason to think that p is true.

A view of this sort amounts to an endorsement of arguments ad ignorantiam. It is an endorsement of the idea that a lack of reasons for not$p$ always constitutes a good reason for thinking that p is true. But of course, this is not so. Let p be the proposition that the beaches of Cape Cod have an even number of grains of sand on them. Presumably most of us lack reasons for thinking that p is true, but this does not imply that we have good reasons for thinking that not$p$ is true. It does not imply that we have good reasons for thinking that the beaches of Cape Cod do not have an even number of grains of sand on them.

What other answers might be given to our question, the question of what might give S a reason for thinking that p is true, where S believes p and where no other proposition that S believes with comparable confidence can be used to argue against p? Another possible answer is: simply the fact that he believes it. In other words, one answer is that whenever an individual believes a proposition p, regardless of what p is, he thereby acquires a reason for thinking that p is true.

But why is it at all plausible to think that simply by believing a proposition *p*, whatever the proposition *p* is, S inevitably acquires a reason for thinking that *p* is true? After all, people can believe some very odd propositions, and *p* here might be one of these. Moreover, S himself, on reflection, might very well think that the mere fact that he believes *p* is no indication that *p* is likely to be true.

Perhaps we should say that although mere belief is not enough to give a person a reason for thinking that what he believes is true, belief coupled with the fact that he has no argument against what he believes *is* sufficient to give him a reason. In particular, perhaps we should say that if an individual S believes *p and* if in addition nothing else that he believes with comparable confidence can be used to argue for not*p*, then he has a reason to think *p* is true.

But why is this suggestion any more plausible than the suggestion that mere belief always provides a reason for what is believed? Again it is worth remembering that people can have very odd beliefs, and sometimes these will be such that nothing else that is believed with comparable confidence can be used to argue against them. Indeed, people can even have momentary surges in the confidence with which they believe a proposition, coming to believe with tremendous confidence a proposition about which only moments earlier they had significant doubts and about which only moments later they again will have significant doubts. Moreover, these propositions might be such that if the person (as he is now) were to be reflective, he himself would agree that the mere fact that he believes them with great confidence is no indication that they are likely to be true. But if so, it is hard to see how such a surge in the confidence with which an individual believes a proposition *p* is enough in itself to give a person a reason for thinking that *p* is true, even if it is enough to ensure that no comparably believed propositions can be used to argue against *p*.[41]

Thus, we still lack a convincing answer to our question of how S's beliefs and epistemic standards might plausibly be thought to give him a reason for thinking that *p* is true, where *p* is a proposition that he believes and where in addition nothing that he believes with comparable confidence can be used to argue against *p*. However, as I suggested earlier, there is a seemingly obvious answer to this question. The other propositions that S believes might give S a reason for thinking that *p* is true. Suppose, in particular, that S believes propositions that tend to make *p* epistemically rational for him. Might he not then have a good reason for thinking that *p* is likely to be true? Accordingly, might not then *p* be genuinely uncontroversial for him? In other words, might not *p* be genuinely uncontroversial for S if, given what he believes and given his epistemic standards, there is a good argument for p as well as no good argument against p?

Unfortunately, answering yes to this question seems only to push our problem back a step. It is hard to see how other believed propositions can make p uncontroversial for S unless they themselves are uncontroversial for him. It is hard to see, that is, how these propositions can ensure that S has a reason to think p is true unless he has reasons to think they are true. But if so, we are faced with a second question: What gives S a reason to think these other believed propositions are true? Moreover, the answer to this question cannot simply be that they are believed with such confidence that they cannot be argued against using propositions that S believes with comparable confidence.

Of course, to answer this second question, one might try simply repeating the answer given to the original question. That is, one might try insisting that what makes these other believed propositions (the propositions that tend to make p epistemically rational) uncontroversial for S is still other believed propositions that tend to make them rational. And if questions are then raised about these latter propositions, the same sort of answer can be given about them, even though this may very well involve citing proposition p or one of the other believed propositions cited at an earlier "level."

However, at best this kind of reply is puzzling. It is puzzling to claim that by using otherwise suspicious propositions to argue for one another the suspicions attaching to each of these propositions somehow disappear. How can propositions that S otherwise would have no reason to think true be used to argue for one another in such a way that there are reasons to think that each is true? At first blush, this would seem to be the epistemic analogue of creation ex nihilo. Of course, the situation would be different if we could assume that some of the propositions that S believes are propositions that he has reason to think are true. Then the fact that these propositions tend to make epistemically rational others that he believes might plausibly be thought to give him a reason to think the latter are true as well. Unfortunately, in the present context we cannot simply assume that some of the propositions that S believes are propositions that he has reasons to think are true.

Thus, there might seem to be a dilemma here. We are looking for some way in which S's beliefs and epistemic standards can plausibly be said to give him a reason for thinking that p is true, where p is a proposition that he believes and where in addition p cannot be argued against using comparably believed propositions. But if we say that S

has a reason to believe p by virtue of believing other propositions that tend to make p epistemically rational, we seem only to push our problem back a step. For then we will want to know what gives S a reason for thinking that these other propositions are true. On the other hand, if the other propositions that he believes do not give him a reason to think p is true and if we are to find this reason for p in S's doxastic system and in his epistemic standards, then it apparently must be the very fact that he believes p that gives him this reason. Unfortunately, this at first glance does not seem plausible either. It does not seem plausible to say that the mere fact that he believes a proposition p, whatever p may be, gives S a reason for thinking that p is true.

Is there a way to avoid this dilemma? I think there is. We can do so by finding some consideration in S's doxastic system or in his epistemic standards that plausibly indicates that some, but not all, propositions are such that by believing them S acquires a reason to think that they are true. We can do so, in other words, by finding some consideration that can plausibly be taken to indicate that some but not all of S's beliefs tend to be self-justifying. Suppose, for example, that S's belief p is such a belief. Then his having a reason for thinking that p is true will not be dependent upon his believing any other proposition that tends to make p epistemically rational for him. So our problem of understanding what gives S a reason to think p is true is not pushed back a step to the problem of understanding what gives him a reason to regard as true some other proposition that he believes. Moreover, if we can find a consideration of the sort described, we also will not be committed to saying that just any proposition is such that by believing it S acquires a reason to think that it is true. Accordingly, we will have avoided both horns of the dilemma.

How then can we plausibly distinguish propositions such that S's believing them gives him a reason, albeit not necessarily an indefeasible reason, to think that they are true, from other propositions that S believes? We can do so by appealing to S's own epistemic standards. Suppose S's epistemic standards imply that his believing p is epistemically significant. Suppose, more exactly, that S, on reflection, would think that his believing p makes p sufficiently likely to be true. Suppose that the proposition that S believes p itself tends to make the proposition p epistemically rational for S. Then S's own epistemic standards imply that all else being equal p is sufficiently likely to be true when he believes p. Accordingly, S's own epistemic standards imply that this proposition p (as well as his belief p) has a special status for S. His own epistemic standards imply that the fact that he believes this proposition p is itself enough to make p sufficiently likely.

Are there any propositions like this: Are there any propositions such that S's believing them tends to make them epistemically rational for S? (This question is discussed in detail in chapter 2, especially the first two sections.) For now it will do simply to assert that if S is relatively normal, the answer would seem to be yes. For example, most people presumably think, and on reflection would continue to think, that most relevant possible situations in which they believe they are in pain are situations in which they in fact are in pain. Likewise, they presumably believe this of many of their other conscious psychological states as well. Accordingly, it is plausible to think that the proposition that they believe they are in such a state tends to make epistemically rational for them the proposition that they are in this state. Similarly, it is plausible to think that most people believe, and on reflection would continue to believe, that most relevant situations in which they believe that they see (or hear, touch, smell, taste, or remember) something are situations in which they in fact see (or hear, touch, smell, taste, or remember) this something. For example, it is plausible to think that most people believe, and on reflection would continue to believe, that most relevant possible situations in which they believe that they see a cat on the mat are situations in which they in fact see a cat on the mat. But if so, their believing they see a cat on the mat tends to make epistemically rational for them that they do see a cat on the mat.

In addition, the propositions that a person S believes, and on reflection would continue to believe, to be necessarily true are like this. Indeed, it trivially will be the case that S, on reflection, would think that propositions of this sort would be true in most situations in which he believes them. However, it is not trivial that he, on reflection, would think that his believing such a proposition is relevant to the truth of the proposition. Recall that if an argument with a conclusion that S, on reflection, would regard as necessarily true is to be uncontroversial for him, he, on reflection, must regard the premises as being relevant to the conclusion, where for arguments with premises that he, on reflection, would take to be necessarily true his thinking this is a matter of his thinking that the premises can be used to provide him with an understanding of why the conclusion cannot be false; and for other arguments, his thinking this is a matter of his thinking that the premises of the argument, albeit contingent, provide him with good inductive support for the necessary truth of the conclusion. Arguments of the form (S believes p; thus, p), where S, on reflection, would regard p as necessarily true, have a contingent premise, and hence resemble inductive arguments for conclusions that are necessarily true if true at all; they resemble, for example, an inductive argument for Goldbach's conjecture. Even so, let us assimilate such arguments to those whose premises an individual, on reflection, would regard as necessarily true, treating them as special and particularly "pure" instances of such arguments. In particular, let us insist that S's believing p tends to make p epistemically rational for him, where p is a proposition that he, on reflection, would take to be necessarily true, only if it is the case that, on reflection, he would think that understanding the proposition p is itself enough to provide him with an understanding of why p must be true. It must be the case, in other words, that S, on reflection, would think that p is in this way self-evident for him; he, on reflection, would think that all he needs to do in order to see why p cannot be false is to understand p. If S, on reflection, would think this of p, then his believing p is relevant to p for him; it gives him an epistemic reason in favor of p. For he cannot believe p without understanding p.

Are there any propositions about which S, on reflection, is likely to think this? Again the answer would seem to be yes, if S is relatively normal. Any relatively normal individual on reflection would be likely to think that any number of simple mathematical, logical, and analytical propositions are like this—for example, the proposition that $2 + 2 = 4$, the proposition that if it is either raining or snowing and if it is not cold enough to be snowing, then it is raining, the proposition that every square is a rectangle, and so on.[42] By way of contrast, a relatively normal individual S is not likely to think this of, say, Goldbach's conjecture. He is not likely to think, in other words, that understanding this proposition is itself enough to provide him with an understanding of why it cannot be false. And he is not likely to think this even if he, on reflection, would believe that Goldbach's conjecture is necessarily true.

So for these kinds of necessary propositions and for the former kinds of contingent propositions, and perhaps for other kinds of propositions as well, it is plausible to think that S's believing them tends to make them epistemically rational for him. Propositions of this sort are special for S. Unlike other propositions, he can have a reason for thinking such propositions are true even if no other proposition that he believes gives him this reason. The fact that he believes them is itself enough to give him such a reason. The fact that he believes them (his own epistemic standards imply) is itself enough to make them sufficiently likely to be true. In this sense, S's beliefs in these propositions tend to be self-justifying.

Suppose p is such a proposition for S. Then his believing p is enough to give him a reason for thinking that p is true. This is not to say, however, that S might not also have other reasons for thinking that p is true. He may very well have other reasons. It is only to say that he would have a reason to think that p is true even if he did not have these other reasons; his believing p is enough.

To illustrate this, consider a case that is likely to be confusing. Suppose that S believes p and that his believing p tends to make p epistemically rational for him. But suppose that in addition to believing the proposition p, S believes the proposition that he believes p. By hypothesis, this latter proposition (the proposition that he believes p) tends to make p epistemically rational for S. Thus, if we assume that S has a reason for believing this latter proposition, his believing it might give him a reason to believe p. Even so, his having a reason for p is not dependent upon his having this second-order belief. Even if he did not believe that he believes p, he would have a reason for thinking that p is true. Unlike most propositions, p is one that he can have a reason to regard as true even if no other proposition that he believes gives him this reason. His own deepest epistemic standards imply that p is special for him. His own epistemic standards imply that unlike most propositions that he believes, the mere fact that he believes p is enough to make p likely to be true. So, unlike most propositions that he believes, S can have a reason for thinking that p is true without having an argument for p, an argument whose premises he believes and whose premises tend to make rational for him its conclusion.

Of course, there is a sense, albeit an extended sense, in which S here has a reason to think that p is true only because there is a good argument for p. Namely, S has a reason to think p is true only because the argument (S believes p; thus, p) is one that conforms to his deepest epistemic standards—one that he, on reflection, would think is sufficiently likely to be truth preserving—and only because in addition he in fact believes p. However, the point is that this argument, unlike other arguments for p, can give S a reason to believe its conclusion even if he does not believe its premise. It is enough that the premise be true.

Alternatively, we perhaps could say (if it is not stretching the notion of argument too much) that S here has a special kind of argument for p, a kind of "zero-premise" argument for p. The argument perhaps can be represented as (——; thus, p), the idea being that in order to have a reason for p, S need not believe any premise; it is enough for him to believe the conclusion of this zero-premise argument.[43]

There may be yet other ways to interpret the claim I am making. But the key idea, however we interpret it, is that for a certain select set of propositions, S's own epistemic standards imply that there is a special relation between S's believing the proposition and the proposition being true, and this is enough to give S a reason for thinking that the proposition is true.

On the other hand, if a believed proposition p is not like this—if S's epistemic standards do not imply that it is special in this way—then S (all else being equal) has a reason to be suspicious of p. He (all else being equal) has a reason to be suspicious of p by virtue of the fact that (all else being equal) he has no reason to think that p is likely to be true. At least his believing p does not give him such a reason. For were he to be reflective, he himself would not think that p is true in a sufficiently large percentage of relevant possible situations in which he believes p. So his own deepest epistemic standards suggest that in situations where he believes p, there may well be (all else being equal) a significantly large risk of error.

Of course, all else may not be equal. He may have other information indicating that p is likely to be true. In particular, once we have identified a certain select set of propositions such that S's believing them is itself enough to give him a reason for thinking that they are true, we open the possibility that these propositions might provide S with a reason for thinking that other propositions that he believes, such as p, are likely to be true. For propositions belonging to this select set might tend to make p epistemically rational for S. However, if it is such propositions that give S a reason for thinking that p is true, p will lack an important kind of epistemic basicality that these other propositions possess. These other propositions merely by being believed acquire (all else being equal) a positive epistemic status for S; the fact that S believes these propositions gives him a reason to think them true. They need not be supported by other uncontroversial propositions to have this status. Proposition p by contrast is not like this.

But what difference does it make how a proposition becomes uncontroversial for him? If a proposition is believed by a person S and he has a good reason to think it true and has no good reason to be suspicious of it, is it not uncontroversial for him? Does it matter how a person comes to have a good reason for thinking it true? Does it matter whether this reason is generated by the fact that he believes *p* or by the fact that *p* is supported by other propositions that are uncontroversial for him?

It does matter, and it matters because the task here is to identify those propositions whose truth *S* uncontroversially can assume in order to argue for others, and because propositions that are uncontroversial simpliciter need not be uncontroversial when used as premises. In particular, propositions that are uncontroversial for a person— propositions that the person *S* has a good reason to think true and no good reason to be suspicious of—and that do not need to be supported by other uncontroversial propositions in order to have this status are uncontroversial for *S* to use as premises. They are epistemically basic for him. On the other hand, uncontroversial propositions that do need to be supported by other uncontroversial propositions in order to be uncontroversial themselves are not epistemically basic. Correspondingly, they might not be uncontroversial for *S* to use as premises. Using them as premises to argue for other propositions is problematic in a way in which using epistemically basic propositions is not.

The explanation for this is that there can be situations in which a person *S* has good evidence for a proposition *p* but in which *p* itself cannot properly be added to *S*'s evidence and used to argue for other propositions. The fact that a person has good evidence for a proposition that he believes and no good evidence against it is no guarantee that the proposition can be used properly as evidence for other propositions. It is no guarantee, in other words, that it is uncontroversial for him to use such a proposition as a premise in arguments for other propositions.

Suppose, for example, that *S* believes proposition *p* and that there is no argument against *p* that gives *S* a reason to be suspicious of *p*. Moreover, suppose he also has a good reason for thinking that *p* is likely to be true. Then *p* is uncontroversial for him. However, suppose that *S* has a reason for thinking *p* is likely to be true only because propositions e^1 and e^2, which tend to make *p* epistemically rational for him, are uncontroversial for him. Now imagine the following to be the case: Proposition *p* and another proposition that is uncontroversial for *S*—call it e^3—can be used to argue for proposition *q* but the propositions e^1, e^2, and e^3 cannot be used to argue for *q*. If proposition *p* simply by virtue of being uncontroversial can be uncontroversially assumed as a premise and used to argue for q, then by hypothesis S here will have an uncontroversial argument for q—the argument (p, e^3; thus, q). Intuitively, however, it seems that he need not have an uncontroversial argument for q. After all, S has a reason to think p is true only because e^1 and e^2 are uncontroversial for him, but these propositions (along with e^3) cannot be used to argue for q.

To make the case more concrete, let e^1 be the proposition that S remembers John saying a number (he remembers not which) between 1 and 16, let e^2 be the proposition that 75 percent of the numbers between 1 and 16 are between 1 and 12, let p be the proposition that John said a number between 1 and 12, let e^3 be the proposition that 75 percent of the numbers between 1 and 12 are between 1 and 9, and let q be the proposition that John said a number between 1 and 9. Suppose e^1, e^2, and e^3 are uncontroversial and basic for S. That is, suppose each of these propositions is such that it is believed by S, he has no plausible argument against it, and his believing it gives him a good reason to think it is true. On the other hand, suppose that p is uncontroversial for S but not basic for him. Specifically, suppose that S has a reason for thinking that p is true only because e^1 and e^2 tend to make p epistemically rational for him. Finally, suppose that e^3 and p tend to make q epistemically rational for S but that e^1, e^2, and e^3 do not tend to make q epistemically rational for S.

The point of this example is that if we grant that the proposition p by virtue of being uncontroversial simpliciter for S is also uncontroversial for S to use as a premise, then, all else being equal, S will have a good argument for q. Accordingly, all else being equal, q will be epistemically rational for S. Moreover, all else might very well be equal. Propositions e^1 and e^2, for example, need not be defeaters. If p and e^3 tend to make q epistemically rational, then presumably p, e^1, e^2, and e^3 also tend to make q epistemically rational. For, if the proposition p is true—if John in fact said a number between 1 and 12—then the propositions e^1 and e^2 are not particularly relevant for determining the likelihood of q. Of course, they would be relevant (in conjunction with e^3) if p's truth cannot be assumed. They would be relevant if S cannot properly assume that John said a number between 1 and 12. However, if this is not so—if p is proper to assume—S might very well have an argument that makes q epistemically rational for him.

This is counterintuitive. S here does not have an uncontroversial argument for q. He has a reason to think p is likely to be true only because e^1 and e^2 are uncontroversial for him. But given these propositions and e^3, q has only a slightly better than even chance of being true. So even if, relative to p and e^3, q has a relatively good chance of being true, S nonetheless lacks an uncontroversial argument for q. He lacks such an argument because, although p may be uncontroversial simpliciter for him, it is not uncontroversial for him to use it as a premise. He has a reason to be suspicious of using p as a premise to argue for other propositions, propositions such as q. The reason derives from the fact that p is not epistemically basic for him.

This is not to say that every proposition that is not epistemically basic will be like p here. Sometimes it will do no harm to add to one's evidence a proposition p that is uncontroversial but that is not epistemically basic. That is, sometimes it will do no harm to assume such a proposition p as a premise in an argument for another proposition q. Specifically, it will do no harm in those cases where the propositions that make p uncontroversial can themselves be used to argue for q. But then, the nonbasic proposition p is not needed to argue for q.

In cases where the propositions that make a nonbasic proposition such as p uncontroversial for S can themselves be used to argue for a proposition such as q, S need not *assume* p's truth—he need not use p as a premise—in order to argue for q. On the other hand, in cases where these propositions cannot be used to argue for q, there is a reason for S to be suspicious of assuming p's truth in order to argue for q. If the considerations that give him a reason to think p is likely to be true cannot themselves be used to argue for q, this gives him some reason to be suspicious of resorting to p to argue for q.

Accordingly, when a proposition p is uncontroversial for S only because it is made so by other propositions, it is controversial for S simply to assume its truth. The proposition can and should be argued for rather than simply assumed.[44]

Thus, propositions that are genuinely uncontroversial for S to use as premises are those that are not only uncontroversial simpliciter but also epistemically basic. They are, in other words, propositions that are believed by S with such confidence that nothing else he believes with comparable confidence can be used to argue against them and that in addition are such that S's believing them gives him a reason to think that they are likely to be true. They are epistemically basic as well as epistemically secure.

One additional condition has to be met in order for p to be uncontroversial for S to use as a premise. Not only must S's believing p give him a good reason for thinking that p is true, but also this reason must not be convincingly defeated. This additional condition is needed because S's believing p need not provide an indefeasible reason for p. Accordingly, if there is a convincing defeater, S in the final analysis may lack a good reason for thinking that p is likely to be true. And if he does lack such a reason, p will be controversial for him.

What kind of proposition would be a convincing defeater of the reason that S's believing p provides for p? It must be a potential defeater of the argument (S believes p; thus, p); it must be believed by S as confidently as he believes p; and in addition it must not itself be convincingly defeated. Thus, suppose d is as confidently believed by S as is p, and suppose in addition that d is a potential defeater of the above argument. Then p, all else being equal, is controversial for S. He has a reason to be suspicious of using p as a premise, unless there is a proposition d^1 that convincingly defeats d's defeater status— where d^1 convincingly defeats d's defeater status just in case (1) S believes d^1 as confidently as d, (2) the propositions (S believes p, d, d^1) tend to make p epistemically rational for S, (3) d^1 does not beg the question against d, where d^1 begs the question against d if either (i) d^1 entails the proposition p or (ii) d^1 entails the proposition that p is probable or (iii) d^1 entails some proposition p^1, where p entails p^1 and where d is a potential defeater of the argument (S believes p; thus, p^1) or (iv) notd^1 either entails not$p$ or entails the proposition that it is not the case that p is probable or entails some proposition notp^1, where p entails p^1 and where d is a potential defeater of the argument (S believes p, thus, p^1).[45]

Consider an example. Let p be the proposition that S sees a red ball in front of him. Suppose nothing else that S believes with as much confidence tends to make not$p$ epistemically rational for him, and suppose S, on reflection, would believe that the argument (S believes p; thus, p) is sufficiently likely to be truth preserving. Accordingly, his belief p tends to be self-justifying. Nevertheless, S might still have a reason to be suspicious of p. Suppose, for example, he believes as confidently as p the proposition that he has been given a hallucinatory drug that prompts about half of the people to whom it is given to have radically false but coherent perceptual beliefs. Call this proposition d. Proposition d, notice, presumably does not tend to make not$p$ epistemically rational for S, since it implies that the drug prompts only about half of the people to whom it is given to have hallucinations. Nevertheless, d presumably does give S a reason to be suspicious of p; it does this by defeating the reason he has for p, the reason that he has (all else being equal) by virtue of believing p. More exactly, it gives him a reason to be suspicious of p unless d's defeater status is itself convincingly defeated. For example, the proposition that S belongs to the half of the population for whom the drug in question does not produce hallucinations or the proposition that he has been given an antidote might be a convincing defeater of d, provided that S believes it as confidently as he does d.[46] On the other hand, p itself cannot convincingly defeat d—condition (3i) rules this out—nor can the proposition that p is probable—condition (3ii) precludes this. Similarly, the proposition that S sees something red in front of him cannot convincingly defeat d; condition (3iii) rules this out. And condition (3iv) prevents the disjunction (S sees a red ball or $1 + 2 = 4$) from convincingly defeating d.

Notice that intuitively the above proposition d gives S a reason to be suspicious of p, all else being equal, by virtue of giving him a reason for withholding judgment on p. In effect what the above restriction does is to allow what we intuitively would regard as reasons for *withholding* on a proposition p as well as what we intuitively would regard as reasons for disbelieving p to make p controversial for S. They can do so by defeating S's reason for thinking that p is true. In particular, they can do so by defeating the reason that S's believing p provides for p.

Consider another example. Suppose that S's belief p tends to be self-justifying but that S has an argument A for not$p$ with premises whose truth he feels as sure of as he does of p's truth. However, suppose also that S, on reflection, would think that this argument falls just barely short of being sufficiently truth preserving. So the premises of A do not tend to make not$p$ epistemically rational for him; they do not give him a good reason to think that not$p$ is true. Nonetheless, it seems as if these premises might be enough to keep p from being uncontroversial for S. The restriction above explains how; they might do so by virtue of defeating the reason that S's believing p, all else being equal, provides for p.[47]

One last wrinkle remains, one that concerns an exception referred to in section 1.5, an exception to the general rule that a proposition p is uncontroversial for S only if there is no argument for not$p$ whose premises S believes as confidently as he does p. It now is possible to see that not just any such argument will make p controversial for S. In particular, an argument will do so only if the conjunction of its premises is a potential defeater of the argument (S believes p; thus, p). In other words, it will do so only if the conjunction of its premises tends to defeat the reason that S's believing p tends to generate for p. Consider an example to illustrate why such a restriction is needed. Suppose that S believes with great confidence that he now sees a giraffe directly in front of him, and suppose that this belief tends to be self-justifying for him. Let this perceptual proposition be p. However, suppose S believes with equal confidence two other propositions, q and r, where q is the proposition that S is now standing on Wall Street and where r is the proposition that almost never are there giraffes on Wall Street. Suppose finally, as is not implausible, that q and r together tend to make rational for S the proposition that there is not now a giraffe on Wall Street, as well as the proposition that he does not now see a giraffe. So q and r here threaten to make p controversial for S. They are believed by S as confidently as p and they tend to make not$p$ rational for him. Moreover, there is no obvious defeater here. The proposition p itself cannot be a defeater, for example; it begs the question against q and r. Accordingly, it looks as if q and r here might very well make p controversial for S. Yet intuitively this does not seem right; it seems as if when S believes with great confidence that he sees a giraffe in front of him, this proposition might very well be uncontroversial for him even if he believes with equal confidence that he is in a situation in which, all else being equal, he is unlikely to see a giraffe. Or at least this would seem to be so unless S has some independent reason to be suspicious of his vision.

The way to handle this difficulty is to require that the premises of any argument that threatens to make p controversial for S, where S's belief p tends to be self-justifying for S, be such that their conjunction is a potential defeater of the argument (S believes p; thus, p).[48] In the giraffe case, the proposition (q and r) is unlikely to be a potential defeater of this argument; S, on reflection, is likely to think that his believing that he sees a giraffe makes it probable that he does see a giraffe even when he is in a situation in which, all else being equal, there are unlikely to be giraffes. And if so, p might be uncontroversial for S despite the fact that he believes q and r with as much confidence as p.[49]

1.7   *Propositions That Are Uncontroversial to Assume and Propositions That Are Epistemically Rational*

A proposition p is epistemically rational for an individual S just if he has a genuinely uncontroversial argument for p. S has a genuinely uncontroversial argument for p, in turn, just if propositions that are uncontroversial for him to assume as premises can be used to argue for p in a way that is uncontroversial for him. When can a set of propositions be used to argue for p in a way that is uncontroversial for S? When the propositions constitute the premises of an argument for p that S, on reflection, would regard as sufficiently likely to be

truth preserving. Under these conditions the propositions in question
tend to make p epistemically rational for S. When is it uncontroversial
for S to assume a proposition as a premise? When the proposition is
both epistemically secure and epistemically basic for S. What, then,
makes a proposition epistemically secure? A proposition p is epistemically secure (or uncontroversial simpliciter) for S just if he believes
p, there is no argument for not$p$ that gives him a good reason to be
suspicious of p, and there is a good reason for him to think that p is
likely to be true. Finally, if p is epistemically secure for S and if, in
addition, his believing p gives him a good (undefeated) reason for
thinking that p is likely to be true, then p is epistemically basic for S
as well as epistemically secure for him. It is, in other words, uncontroversial for him to assume p as a premise.[50]

More precisely, the following defines what it is for a set of propositions e^1, e^2, ... e^n to threaten to make p controversial for S; this
notion in turn can be used to define what it is for a proposition p to
be uncontroversial for S to assume:

Propositions e^1, e^2, ... e^n threaten to make p controversial for S at t.	= df	1. Propositions e^1, e^2, ... e^n tend to make not$p$ epistemically rational for S at t.
		2. Each proposition in the set (e^1, e^2, ... e^n) is believed by S with as much confidence as he believes p.
		3. If the argument (S believes p; thus, p) is an argument whose premise tends to make its conclusion epistemically rational for S at t, then the proposition (e^1 and e^2 ... and e^n) is a potential defeater of the argument for S at t.
It is uncontroversial for S at t to assume p.	= df	1. S at t believes p.
		2. If there are propositions e^1, e^2, ... e^n that threaten to make p controversial for S at t, then there is a proposition d such that (i) S believes d as confidently as at least one of

the propositions $e^1, e^2, \ldots e^n$, and (ii) d is a potential defeater for S at t of the argument ($e^1, e^2 \ldots e^n$; thus, not$p$), and (iii) d does not beg the question against this argument.

3. The proposition that S believes p tends to make p epistemically rational for S at t, and if there is a proposition d such that S believes d as confidently as p and d is a potential defeater for S at t of the argument (S believes p; thus, p), then there is a proposition d^1 such that (i) S believes d^1 as confidently as d, (ii) the propositions (S believes p, d, d^1) tend to make p epistemically rational for S at t, and (iii) d^1 does not beg the question against d.

This latter definition can be simplified by leaving unspecified the exact nature of convincing defeater propositions.[51]

It is uncontroversial for S at t to assume p.   = df   1. S at t believes p.

2. If there are propositions that threaten to make p controversial for S at t, then there is a convincing defeater proposition.

3. The proposition that S believes p tends to make p epistemically rational for S at t and there is no convincing defeater proposition.

These definitions express what it is for a proposition to be such that it is uncontroversial for S to use it as a premise. They in conjunction with the previous definition of "tends to make epistemically rational," which expresses what it is for propositions to be such that they can be used to argue for another proposition in a way that is uncontroversial for S, can be used to say what it is for a set of propositions to make epistemically rational another proposition for a person S (as opposed merely to *tend* to make the proposition epistemically rational):

Propositions $e^1, e^2, \ldots e^n$ make p epistemically rational for S at t.	= df	It is uncontroversial for S at t to assume $e^1, e^2, \ldots e^n$ respectively, and $e^1, e^2, \ldots e^n$ tend to make p epistemically rational for S at t, and there are no other propositions d^1, $d^2, \ldots d^n$ all of which are uncontroversial for S at t to assume and which in addition are such that $(d^1$ and $d^2 \ldots$ and $d^n)$ is a potential defeater for S at t of the argument $(e^1, e^2, \ldots e^n$, thus, p).

Alternatively, we can say that propositions $e^1, e^2, \ldots e^n$ make p epistemically rational for S at t just if these propositions tend to make p epistemically rational for S at t, they are all uncontroversial for S to assume, and all else is equal (that is, they are not defeated by any proposition that is uncontroversial for S at t to assume or any conjunction of such propositions).[52] In terms of this definition, the propositions that are epistemically rational can be identified:

It is epistemically rational for S at t to believe p.	= df	Either it is uncontroversial for S at t to assume p or there are propositions that make p epistemically rational for S at t.

Since every proposition (or at least every proposition that S understands) tends to make itself epistemically rational for S, this definition can be further simplified:

It is epistemically rational for S at t to believe p.	= df	There are propositions (or a proposition) that make p epistemically rational for S at t.

And then, the epistemic rationality of withholding judgment can be defined:

It is epistemically rational for S at t to withhold judgment on p.	= df	It is not epistemically rational for S at t to believe p, and it is not epistemically rational for S at t to believe not p.

These definitions provide the details that fill in the general conception of epistemic rationality I sketched at the beginning of this chapter, a conception that is motivated by an idealization of an Aristotelian conception of rationality. According to an Aristotelian conception, rationality is a function of an individual pursuing his goals in a way that he, on reflection, would take to be effective. Since epistemic rationality is concerned with the epistemic goal of now believing truths and now not believing falsehoods, the Aristotelian conception suggests that it is epistemically rational for an individual S to believe p just if he, on reflection, would think that believing p is an effective means to his epistemic goal. This in turn motivates the idea that p is epistemically rational for S just if he has an uncontroversial argument for p, an argument that he would regard as likely to be truth preserving were he to be appropriately reflective, and an argument whose premises he would uncover no good reasons to be suspicious of were he to be appropriately reflective. The definitions above constitute my suggestions concerning what kind of reflection is appropriate for characterizing epistemic rationality. With respect to the truth-preservingness of the argument, the suggestion is that it be ideal reflection from an epistemic point of view. If an argument is such that S would regard it as sufficiently likely to be truth preserving were he to be ideally reflective from an epistemic point of view, then the argument reflects S's deepest epistemic standards and its premises tend to make its conclusion epistemically rational for him. With respect to the premises of the argument, the suggestion is that the appropriate kind of reflection is reflection upon what else S believes and upon his deepest epistemic standards (that is, upon the arguments that he would regard as sufficiently truth preserving were he to be ideally reflective). In particular, if these premises are believed by S and in addition are such that (1) S would have no good reason to be suspicious of their truth were he to reflect upon what else he believes and upon the arguments that he on ideal reflection would take to be sufficiently truth preserving and (2) S on ideal reflection would think that his believing them makes them sufficiently likely to be true, then these premises are uncontroversial for him to assume as premises. Accordingly, on the assumption that there are no defeaters, these premises make the conclusion p epistemically rational for S.

The definitions above can be regarded as embodying the formal part of a theory of epistemic rationality—the theory proper. But there is also a substantive part of the theory generated from the theory proper together with plausible assumptions about our nature as believers. The substantive part of the theory seeks to articulate what kinds of propositions are likely to be epistemically rational for relatively normal people. This substantive part of the theory is one of the main concerns of chapter 2. The goal is for the substantive part of the theory to generate intuitively plausible results about what kinds of propositions are likely to be epistemically rational for us. But in addition to being intuitively plausible, there will be something else to recommend the results generated by the substantive part of the theory. These results are generated by plausible assumptions about our nature as believers and by a formal account of epistemic rationality that in turn is motivated by a plausible and a perfectly general conception of rationality, an Aristotelian conception.

2

SUBJECTIVE FOUNDATIONALISM

2.1   Subjective Foundationalism

A proposition p is epistemically rational for an individual S just if propositions that are uncontroversial for S to assume tend to make p epistemically rational for him and no other propositions that are uncontroversial for him to assume can be used to defeat the support that these propositions give p. The idea is that a proposition p is epistemically rational for a person just if either p is properly basic for him or p is made epistemically rational for him by other propositions that are properly basic for him.

Thus, the account of epistemic rationality I am defending can be construed as a foundationalist account, but it is a special kind—what might be called a "subjective foundationalist" account. It provides a subjective account of what is involved in a proposition being properly basic (being uncontroversial to assume) and of what is involved in these propositions supporting (tending to make epistemically rational) other propositions.

The definition of "it is uncontroversial for S to assume p," for example, emphasizes the subjective persuasiveness of p for S. It requires S to believe p and requires him to believe it with more confidence than he believes propositions that can be used to argue against it. In addition, p must be such that S, on reflection, would believe that in most relevant possible situations in which he believes p his belief would be true. By way of contrast there is nothing in the definition that requires p to be true and nothing that requires S to have some kind of privileged access to the truth of p.[1] Likewise, there is nothing in the definition to indicate that those propositions that are uncontroversial for a person to assume must be irrevisable, and nothing to indicate that the kind of propositions uncontroversial for one person cannot be significantly different from the kind of propositions uncontroversial for another person.

Even so, this is not to say that traditional foundationalist accounts are altogether wrong. It may be (see section 2.8) that traditional foundationalist accounts, or at least some such accounts, are not best construed as accounts of epistemic rationality. It may be that they are best understood as attempts to explicate a somewhat different notion. But if so, traditional foundationalism and subjective foundationalism are not competitors; they might both be right. However, for the time being suppose this is not so; suppose that traditional foundationalism is best construed as an account of epistemic rationality. Even granting this, traditional foundationalists may not be altogether wrong, in, for example, some of the ways they have of characterizing properly basic propositions. Thus, it is not wrong to suggest, as traditional foundationalists sometimes do, that properly basic propositions be thought of as those that there are no good reasons to doubt, or as those against which it is impossible to argue convincingly. A subjective foundationalist can accept these characterizations of properly basic propositions provided he gives them a subjective gloss, so that what there is a good reason to doubt and what can be convincingly argued against is a function of what a person believes, the strength with which he believes it, and the person's own deepest epistemic standards. Similarly, it is not wrong to claim, as traditional foundationalists do, that what characterizes properly basic propositions is that our beliefs about them are self-justifying, as long as it is understood that it is a person's own epistemic standards that make beliefs self-justifying for him—as long as it is understood that S's belief p tends to be self-justifying just if S's own epistemic standards imply that when he believes p, p is sufficiently likely to be true.

Moreover, traditional foundationalists may not be altogether wrong about what propositions are properly basic. They may not be wrong, for example, in claiming that propositions about one's own psychological states or at least certain sorts of one's own psychological states—what one is occurrently thinking or believing, what sense-experiences one is having, and so on—are among the strongest candidates for properly basic propositions. After all, such propositions are ones that most of us believe with great confidence, and they also are such that we have difficulty finding propositions that we believe with comparable confidence that can be used to argue against them. Moreover, presumably most of us, on reflection, would think that such propositions are likely to be true when we believe them to be true; we, on reflection, would think that in most relevant possible situations in which we believe such propositions our beliefs would be true.

Even if traditional foundationalists are wrong about our having a privileged access to the truth of propositions about our own psychological states, they need not be wrong about these propositions being properly basic. On the other hand, nothing I have said implies that they even are wrong about our having some kind of privileged access with respect to such propositions. Indeed, if we do have privileged access to the truth of propositions about our own psychological states, this might help in explaining why these propositions are properly basic for us. For if we do have privileged access to the truth of these propositions, this might help in explaining why we believe them with such great confidence. Moreover, it might help in explaining why we have so much trouble imagining how our beliefs about these propositions might be false. But in turn, it is these factors that make propositions about our own psychological states such good candidates for being properly basic. Insofar as we believe them with great confidence, it is likely that nothing else we believe with comparable confidence can be used to argue against them. And insofar as we have trouble imagining how such beliefs could be false, it is likely that we, on reflection, would think that in most relevant possible situations where we have such beliefs these beliefs would be true. But if so, our beliefs in these propositions will tend to be self-justifying for us, and the propositions themselves will tend to be properly basic for us.

Thus it is possible for a traditional foundationalist and a subjective foundationalist to agree that for many (or even all) people, many (or even all) of the propositions about their own conscious mental states are properly basic for them. Likewise, it is possible for them to agree that we have some kind of privileged access to the truth of such propositions. But even if they do agree on these things, they still will disagree, and disagree fundamentally, over the criterion of proper basicality. Traditional foundationalist accounts emphasize the truthfulness of properly basic propositions. According to such accounts, when a person believes a properly basic proposition, the belief is guaranteed to be true—perhaps because the person is "directly aware" of the truth of the proposition—and moreover without such a guarantee the believed proposition would not be properly basic. A subjective foundationalist, in contrast, emphasizes how psychologically convincing properly basic propositions are. The emphasis is upon a properly basic proposition being such that it is argument-proof for him (being such that no comparably believed propositions can be used to argue against it) and in addition being such that he, on reflection, would think that when he believes it the proposition is sufficiently likely to be true. On the other hand, if these conditions are not met, the proposition is not properly basic for the person, even if propositions of its kind are guaranteed to be true whenever they are believed by him—even if his beliefs about such propositions are infallible. Infallibility in and of itself is epistemically irrelevant; the mere fact that a person's beliefs about a certain kind of proposition are infallible does not make such propositions epistemically rational for him, much less properly basic for him. This becomes especially obvious if we imagine situations in which the person is altogether unaware (and on reflection would continue to be unaware) of his infallibility with respect to these propositions and in which he even has what he would consider to be a good argument against them. In these kinds of situations, the propositions in question are not properly basic for him even if his beliefs about them are infallible. They are not properly basic for him because they are not uncontroversial for him. Although *we* from our perspective may recognize that his beliefs with respect to these propositions are infallible, *he* from his perspective has a reason to be suspicious of them. So, they are not uncontroversial for *him* to assume. Of course, if we are able to convince him that his beliefs about these propositions are guaranteed to be true, this might change; he then might have no reason to be suspicious of them. But until this happens, they are not uncontroversial for him to assume; they are not properly basic for him.[2]

So, contrary to what is claimed by the traditional foundationalist, it is not so much an objective guarantee of truth as it is a subjective persuasiveness that makes a proposition properly basic for a person. No guarantee of truth will make a proposition properly basic if the proposition is not uncontroversial for the person, given his perspective, and correspondingly the lack of such a guarantee will not preclude a proposition from being properly basic if it is uncontroversial for him, given his perspective.

Similar points hold for what is not properly basic for a person. Subjective foundationalists and traditional foundationalists differ over what makes propositions that are not properly basic for an individual epistemically rational for him. Traditional foundationalist accounts imply that the support relation between basic and nonbasic propositions is to be understood objectively, in terms of the former either implying or making probable the latter. So, nonbasic propositions are epistemically rational for an individual just in case they are the conclusions of arguments whose premises are properly basic for the individual (which, according to the traditional foundationalist, are guaranteed to be true) and whose premises in fact make likely their conclusions. Subjective foundationalist accounts, by contrast, imply that properly basic propositions might make other propositions epistemically rational for an individual even if they do not in fact make these propositions likely. It is enough that the person, given ideal reflection, would be convinced that they make these propositions likely. Subjective foundationalist accounts also imply that even if propositions that are properly basic for a person do make some other proposition likely, it need not be the case that they tend to make this proposition epistemically rational for him. After all, it might be that no matter how much the person reflected he would not realize that these properly basic propositions make this other proposition likely. Nothing would convince him of this. But if so, then from his perspective there need be no reason to think that the proposition is likely to be true. Accordingly, it need not be epistemically rational for him to believe the proposition.

No argument that is in fact likely to be truth preserving will make a proposition epistemically rational for an individual if the argument is not uncontroversial for that individual, given his perspective, and correspondingly an argument that is uncontroversial for him, given his perspective, can make its conclusion epistemically rational for him even if in fact it is not likely to be truth preserving.

One way to illustrate these differences between traditional foundationalism and subjective foundationalism is by considering an extension of a traditional skeptical hypothesis—we are under the influence of an evil demon who without giving us any indication of his presence regularly deceives us about the external world and about the past. Extend this hypothesis by imagining not only that the demon exists in this world but also that he would exist in most close possible worlds. For the traditional foundationalist, this extension of the evil demon hypothesis—assuming it to be true—seems to preclude the possibility that our ordinary beliefs about the external world or about the past are epistemically rational. For according to the traditional foundationalist, propositions about the external world and about the past cannot be properly basic for us, since we do not have a special direct access to their truth. Thus, if they are to be epistemically rational for us, we must be able to argue for them using propositions that are properly basic for us. In particular, we must be able to argue for them using propositions about our current psychological states. But if there is such a demon, it is impossible for us to argue for most of the propositions we believe about the external world and about the past using as premises propositions about our own psychological states and to do so in a way that is likely to be truth preserving. The demon by hypothesis ensures that most such arguments are ones whose conclusions would be true only in a relatively small number of the close possible situations in which their premises are true. Accordingly, given traditional foundationalism, the lesson is that if unbeknownst to us there is such a demon, few if any of the propositions that we believe about the external world or about the past are epistemically rational for us.[3]

The subjective foundationalist, by way of contrast, need not draw a skeptical conclusion from such a hypothesis. Nothing in subjective foundationalism implies that if unbeknownst to us there is such a demon, then no proposition about the external world or the past is epistemically rational for us. Moreover, the subjective foundationalist is not committed to this skeptical conclusion even if he were to agree with the traditional foundationalist that these propositions can be epistemically rational only if they are made so by propositions about our own psychological states. The subjective foundationalist does not insist that nonbasic propositions are epistemically rational for an individual only if they can be argued for in a way that in fact is likely to be truth preserving. Instead, he insists that the arguments be such that were the individual to be sufficiently reflective he would regard them as likely to be truth preserving. Thus, if there is an evil demon who exists in most close possible worlds and gives us no indication of his presence, he might very well prevent us from having arguments whose premises make probable propositions about the external world and about the past, but he does not thereby automatically prevent us from having epistemically rational beliefs about the external world and about the past. Indeed, what propositions are epistemically rational for us is in no way affected by the mere presence or absence of such a demon. Of course, if we had some indication of the presence of such a demon, this would make a difference in what propositions are epistemically rational for us. But by hypothesis this is not the case. So the same propositions are epistemically rational for us whether or not there is such a demon; the same propositions are properly basic for us and the same propositions are made epistemically rational for us by these properly basic propositions.

Moreover, there is another and equally important difference here between subjective foundationalists and traditional foundationalists. Unlike the traditional foundationalist, the subjective foundationalist allows the possibility that propositions about the external world and the past can be epistemically rational for us even if they are not made so by propositions about our own psychological states. Such propositions might very well be properly basic for us—they might very well be uncontroversial for us to assume. Moreover, it is not just *possible* for such propositions to be properly basic for us. Rather, it is plausible to think that some such propositions in fact are properly basic for us. Consider, for example, the proposition that S remembers being at the zoo last Saturday and the proposition that S sees in front of him a cat on the mat. These propositions, the one about the past and the other about the external world, are propositions that S is likely to believe with great confidence (if he believes them at all). In addition, if the situation in which S believes these propositions is relatively normal, it is likely that nothing else S believes with comparable confidence can be used to argue against them. Finally, if S is like the rest of us, he may very well believe, and on reflection would continue to believe, that most relevant possible situations in which he believes such propositions are situations in which the propositions are true. That is, S's own epistemic standards may imply that these propositions are likely to be true in situations where he believes them to be true.[4] But if so, this proposition about the external world and this proposition about the past are likely to be properly basic for S.

Other such propositions about what we are seeing or hearing or tasting or touching or smelling or remembering may also be properly basic for us. This claim, of course, conflicts with the views of traditional foundationalists. However, this should not be surprising, since they have been obsessed with the search for foundational propositions that are absolutely certain. Once we give up the requirement that the only propositions whose truth we can properly assume (without argument) are propositions that are absolutely certain for us, we lose the rationale for denying that simple propositions about the past and the external world can be properly basic. To be sure, these are propositions about which we might be deceived. But this possibility, contrary to what is suggested by traditional foundationalists, no more prevents them from being properly basic for us than it prevents them from being epistemically rational for us.

Moreover, the most problematic part of the claim that propositions about the past and about the external world can be properly basic— the part that implies that our beliefs about such propositions tend to be self-justifying—is granted at least implicitly by a number of traditionally inclined foundationalists, those who are disposed to claim that the only properly basic, contingent propositions are propositions about our own psychological states. Roderick Chisholm, for example, says that if a person S "believes, without ground for doubt, that he is perceiving something to be F, then it is evident for S that he perceives something to be F." Similarly, he also says that "if S believes, without ground for doubt, that he remembers F, then it is beyond reasonable doubt that he does remember perceiving something to be F."[5] What Chisholm is granting here is that some propositions about what we are perceiving and remembering, all else being equal, acquire a favorable epistemic status for an individual simply by being believed by him. What this in effect means is that when we believe such propositions, our beliefs tend to be self-justifying; our believing such propositions is enough to give us a reason to think they are true provided that we have no grounds for doubt—that is, provided that nothing defeats the reason that our believing them generates.

If this is so, why would Chisholm and other like-minded foundationalists not admit that such propositions about the external world and about the past can be properly basic? There probably is no simple answer, but perhaps the closest we can come is this: Chisholm and other such foundationalists tend to think that properly basic propositions must be ones whose truth is guaranteed when we believe them. They think that if a proposition is not in this way guaranteed to be true, it needs to be defended; it cannot simply be assumed. Accordingly, if there were no propositions that are guaranteed to be true when we believe them, there would be a problem with a regress. Moreover, traditionally inclined foundationalists tend to think that properly basic propositions are ones that cannot be defended using other propositions. Properly basic propositions are in this sense epistemically independent from one another; they cannot be used to argue for one another. Thus, for example, if the belief that I now am having a visual experience of there being a red ball in front of me were not self-justifying, then (it is claimed) nothing else I believe could make this proposition epistemically rational for me.

Propositions about what we are perceiving and what we are remembering have neither of these characteristics. Our beliefs about them are not guaranteed to be true, and they often can be argued for using other propositions that are good candidates for being properly basic. Subjective foundationalism, however, rejects both of these requirements on proper basicality. According to a subjective foundationalist, propositions can be uncontroversial for an individual to assume—they can be properly basic for him—even if they are not guaranteed to be true when he believes them. It is enough if they are uncontroversial for him to use as premises. In particular, it is enough if nothing else he believes with comparable confidence can be used to argue against them and if in addition his own epistemic standards imply that his believing such propositions makes it likely that they are true. This is enough to stop a potential regress of reasons. Moreover, according to a subjective foundationalist, propositions that are properly basic might well be the conclusions of good arguments; properly basic propositions are to be thought of as propositions that need not be argued for, rather than as propositions that cannot be argued for. Although the proposition that *S* sees a cat on the mat and the proposition that he remembers being at the zoo last Saturday may well be propositions that *S* can argue for using other properly basic propositions (such as using propositions about his current psychological states—about, say, his visual experiences and about what he *seems* to remember), this does not preclude these propositions from being properly basic for him. It does not preclude their being uncontroversial for him to assume as premises of arguments.

What other kinds of propositions might be properly basic? In addition to propositions about our own conscious psychological states and propositions about what we see, touch, hear, remember, and so on, perhaps a few general propositions are also good candidates to be properly basic. For example, the proposition that there are material objects, the proposition that there are other people, the proposition that the world has a significant past (that is, that it did not come into existence just a moment ago), the proposition that nature is not fundamentally chaotic (for example, that there are stable regularities in nature), and perhaps others as well. Propositions of this sort are ones that almost all of us believe with great confidence. So, ordinarily nothing else we believe with comparable confidence can be used to argue against them. Moreover, it is not implausible to assume that at least many of us (and perhaps most of us), on reflection, would think that these propositions are true in a sufficiently great percentage of relevant possible situations in which we believe them to be true (see section 2.2). But if so, beliefs about such propositions tend to be self-justifying for many of us, just as beliefs about what we see, remember, and so on, and beliefs about our own conscious psychological states tend to be self-justifying for many of us.

By way of contrast, consider relatively specific *nonperceptual* beliefs about the external world and *nonmemory* beliefs about the past. Consider, for example, *S*'s belief that there is a cat on the mat and his belief that he was at the zoo last Saturday. These beliefs are less likely to be self-justifying than the corresponding belief that *S sees* a cat on the mat and that he *remembers* being at the zoo last Saturday, and this is so despite the fact that the former are more modest in content than the latter. For example, the proposition that there is a cat on the mat is entailed by the proposition that *S* sees a cat on the mat but not vice versa. So, whenever *S* believes the latter proposition, he believes the former as well, but not vice versa; and whenever the latter is true the former is true as well, but not vice versa. This might seem to indicate that a belief in the former is more likely to be self-justifying than a belief in the latter. But in fact, the reverse is the case. For notice, although there are situations in which *S*'s perceptual belief that he sees a cat on the mat is false but in which his nonperceptual belief that there is a cat on the mat is true, *S*, on reflection, is likely to regard such situations as being relatively improbable. For instance, think of a situation in which *S* is fooled by a highly realistic painting into believing that he sees a cat on a mat but in which there actually is a cat on a mat directly behind the painting (out of *S*'s sight). On the other hand, *S*, on reflection, is likely to think that it is not as improbable for there to be situations in which he lacks the perceptual belief that he sees a cat on the mat but in which he nonetheless believes falsely that there is a cat on the mat. For example, think of situations in which he has his eyes closed or in which he is concentrating on the document on his desk or in which he has his eyes fixed upon the ceiling but in which he nonetheless believes that there is a cat on the mat in front of him—say, because he has been told this by someone or because he remembers there being a cat on the mat or because he believes there almost always is a cat on the mat. If *S* here is like the rest of us, he presumably thinks, and would continue to think on reflection, that the chance of error in such situations is greater than the chance of error in situations where he believes he sees a cat on the mat. There is, as it were, more room for things to go wrong. But then, his belief that there is a cat on the mat might not be self-justifying. Moreover, it might not be self-justifying even in those situations in which he has a self-justifying perceptual belief that he sees a cat on the mat.[6]

The point can also be made more positively by explaining what it is about the perceptual proposition, that *S* sees a cat on the mat, that might incline *S*, on reflection, to think that it is likely to be true when he believes it. Notice, first, that this perceptual proposition entails not only that there is a cat on the mat but also that *S* is having an appropriate kind of visual experience. No doubt it is complicated business, given perceptual relativity, to describe what makes a visual experience the sort that is appropriate for seeing a cat. After all, what a cat looks like will depend on the perceptual conditions, one's perceptual equipment, and the cat itself. Nevertheless, the general idea is clear enough: Even if there is a cat on the mat and the individual believes that there is, normally he cannot be said to see a cat on the mat if his visual experiences are of the sort that most of us would have in a completely darkened room or if they are of the sort that most of us would have if we were in front of an elephant. These kinds of visual experiences (at least for beings like us) are not appropriate for seeing a cat on the mat. They are not cat-on-the-mat kinds of visual experiences. (The proposition that S sees a cat on the mat presumably entails not only that S is having a cat-on-the-mat kind of visual experience but also that S's having this experience is caused in an appropriate way by there being a cat on the mat; however, for the sake of simplicity this can be ignored in what follows.)

So when S believes that he sees a cat on the mat, he believes that there is a cat on the mat and that he is having a cat-on-the-mat kind of visual experience. Notice also that this latter proposition—that he is having a cat-on-the-mat kind of visual experience—is likely to be properly basic for S. He is likely to believe it with such confidence that nothing else he believes with comparable confidence can be used to argue against it, and his belief in it is likely to be self-justifying. In addition, if S is like the rest of us, it is likely that he, on reflection, would think that situations in which he both has a cat-on-the-mat visual experience and a belief that there is a cat on the mat are highly likely to be situations in which there is in fact a cat on the mat. By contrast, he on reflection might not think this of situations in which he simply has a cat-on-the-mat visual experience, since there is a relatively wide variety of ways of coming to have a nonveridical cat-on-the-mat visual experience—that is, of coming to have a cat-on-the-mat visual experience without there in fact being a cat on the mat. For example, S could place a highly realistic toy cat on the mat and generate this experience; he might see a movie of a cat on a mat; he might see a realistic painting of a cat on a mat; and so on. But, presumably most of these ways of coming to have a nonveridical cat-on-the-mat visual experience are such that S would not be fooled by them into believing that there is in fact a cat on the mat. Presumably most of them are such that S would be aware that he is having a nonveridical cat-on-the-mat visual experience. Some kind of perceptual cue would tip him off. When he is looking at a highly realistic painting of a cat on a mat or looking at a movie of a cat on a mat, the rest of his perceptual field will normally make him aware that there is not, in fact, a cat on the mat in front of him. For example, he normally will be perceptually aware of the frame of the painting or of the screen upon which the movie is being projected. As a result, his cat-on-the-mat visual experience will not fit in, it will not cohere with the rest of his visual experiences in a way that convinces him that there is in front of him, in fact, a cat on the mat. His visual field will not have a veridical cat-on-the-mat gestalt. Of course, it presumably is possible to have a thoroughly coherent and hence convincing hallucination of a cat on the mat (witness the clever evil demon who gives *S* no hint of the presence), but *S*, on reflection, is likely to think that most possible situations in which he has a nonveridical cat-on-the-mat visual experience either will be situations in which there is available to him some indication of the experience's nonveridicality (as with a highly realistic painting of a cat on a mat) or they will be situations that are so improbable as to be irrelevant for an assessment of arguments involving his perceptual beliefs (for example, evil demon situations and the like). But if so, it is not implausible to assume that although perhaps *S*, on reflection, would not believe that his having a cat-on-the-mat visual experience by itself makes it sufficiently probable that there is a cat on the mat (since there are many relevant situations in which he might have a nonveridical cat-on-the-mat experience), he would believe that his having a cat-on-the-mat visual experience and a belief that there is a cat on the mat makes it sufficiently probable that there is a cat on the mat (since there are relatively few relevant situations in which he would have a nonveridical cat-on-the-mat visual experience without also having some indication of its nonveridicality, an indication that would discourage his believing that there is a cat on the mat). But then, the proposition that *S* has both a cat-on-the-mat visual experience and a belief that there is a cat on the mat tends to make epistemically rational for *S* the proposition that there is a cat on the mat.

If so, we have at least a loose explanation for why *S*'s belief that he sees a cat on the mat is likely to be self-justifying. It is likely to be self-justifying because (1) for *S* to believe that he sees a cat on the mat is (at least roughly) for him to believe that he is having a cat-on-the-mat kind of visual experience and that there is a cat on the mat, and because (2) *S*, on reflection, would think that if he believes that he is having a cat-on-the-mat kind of visual experience, it is highly likely that he is having such an experience, and because (3) the proposition that *S* has both a cat-on-the-mat visual experience and a belief that there is a cat on the mat tends to make epistemically rational for *S* the proposition that there is a cat on the mat; as a result, it also tends to make epistemically rational for him the conjunctive proposition (that he is having a cat-on-the-mat visual experience and there is a cat on the mat)—that is, it tends to make epistemically rational for him the proposition that he sees a cat on the mat.[7]

By way of contrast, *S* can believe the nonperceptual proposition that there is a cat on the mat without believing the proposition that he is having a cat-on-the-mat kind of visual experience. Accordingly, the explanation for why it is plausible to think that *S*'s simple perceptual beliefs might tend to be self-justifying is not available for *S*'s simple nonperceptual beliefs about the external world. (Analogous points can be made with respect to why it is plausible to think that our simple memory beliefs but not our simple nonmemory beliefs about the past might tend to be self-justifying.)

Are there any other kinds of propositions that are good candidates for being properly basic? All of the above candidates are contingent propositions. What about propositions that an individual *S*, on reflection, would take to be necessarily true? Which of these kinds of propositions are likely to be properly basic?

Recall that if such a proposition *p* is to be properly basic for an individual *S* it is not enough for *S*, on reflection, to think that *p* is true in most possible situations in which he would believe *p*. For on reflection he would think that *p* is true in all possible situations whatsoever, regardless of whether he believes it or not. In addition, it must be the case that *S*, on reflection, would think that his believing *p* is relevant to *p*, where what this means is that on reflection he would think that his believing and hence understanding the proposition *p* is itself enough to provide him with an understanding of why it is impossible for *p* to be false. It thus must be the case that on reflection he would in this sense regard the proposition as self-evident (see section 1.6).

What kinds of propositions, then, are likely to be properly basic for *S* in this way? The best candidates are what *S*, on reflection, would take to be simple mathematical truths, simple logical truths, and simple conceptual truths. For example, if *S* is like the rest of us, the proposition that $1 + 2 = 3$, the proposition that if John is married either to Helen or to Ann and if he is not married to Ann, then he is married to Helen, the proposition that if a ball is blue all over, then it is not red all over, and numerous other similar propositions might be properly basic for him. By way of contrast, more complicated necessary truths (such as Goldbach's conjecture and Fermat's Last Theorem, assuming that they are necessarily true) are less likely to be properly basic for him, since it is less likely that, on reflection, *S* would think that understanding them is itself enough to provide him with an understanding of why they cannot be false. And in addition, even if a proposition is such that on reflection he would believe that understanding it is enough to provide him with an understanding of why it cannot be false, it cannot be properly basic for S if he in fact does not believe it (since only believed propositions can be properly basic).[8]

When a proposition p that S, on reflection, would take to be necessarily true is properly basic for S, it can be said to be properly basic a priori for him, since understanding the proposition, he, on reflection, would think, is itself sufficient to allow him to see why it cannot be false. In this respect, the properly basic a priori is different from the properly basic a posteriori. His believing a proposition of the latter kind—say, a proposition q—is epistemically significant for him because he, on reflection, would think that q is true in most possible situations in which he believes it to be true. But this cannot be what makes his believing a proposition of the former kind—say, a proposition p—epistemically significant for him. For p is a proposition that by hypothesis he, on reflection, would take to be true come what may, regardless of whether he believes it or not and regardless of what else may or may not be the case. Rather, believing p is epistemically significant for him because he, on reflection, would take there to be an internal connection between his believing p and p, a connection that he, on reflection, would think allows him to understand why p cannot be false simply by virtue of understanding p.[9]

In summary, the kinds of propositions that are the best candidates to be properly basic, given subjective foundationalism, are just the kinds of propositions that common sense tells us are generally the least problematic—propositions about our current, conscious psychological states (say, that I have a headache), simple perceptual propositions (say, that I see a cat on the mat), simple memory propositions (say, that I remember being at the zoo last Saturday), fundamental "general" propositions (for example, that there are material objects), and simple propositions that we on reflection would take to be necessarily true (for example, that $2 + 3 = 5$).

However, in saying that such propositions are good candidates to be properly basic, it is important to keep in mind that this claim, like all claims of epistemic rationality, is first and foremost a claim about the *proposition p* rather than a claim about an individual's *belief p*. Of course, the two kinds of claims are not altogether independent; to say that a proposition p is epistemically rational for S is just to say that p is epistemically rational for him to believe. But on the other hand, to say that S believes what is epistemically rational for him to believe is not to say that the considerations that make p rational for him are considerations that he is aware of, much less that they are considerations that prompt him to believe p. Likewise, to say that p

is properly basic for S is not to say that the considerations that make p properly basic for him are considerations that prompt him to believe p or even that they are considerations of which he is aware.

Consider a case to illustrate this. Suppose that S is not even vaguely aware of the good reasons he has for thinking that p is true. Suppose that although he believes that he has reasons for p, what he believes to be his reasons are such that were he to be ideally reflective he himself would regard them as patently silly. Perhaps, for example, an astrologer has assured him that p is true, and perhaps he believes for what he, on reflection, would think are silly reasons that this astrologer is reliable. Nevertheless, the proposition p by hypothesis is one that he has good epistemic reasons to believe. So in believing p he is believing what is epistemically rational for him. However, there is something left to be desired in the way that S believes p. In other words, although S cannot be epistemically criticized for believing p (since by hypothesis he has good epistemic reasons to believe it), he can be criticized for the way that he believes it (since he is not aware of what his good epistemic reason for it is). Expressed in terms of a distinction that I will discuss in more detail in section 4.2, we can say that although S's belief p here is propositionally rational, it is not doxastically rational.

This distinction is an important one for propositions that are properly basic as well as for propositions that are epistemically rational but not properly basic. Suppose, for example, that S believes p and that S, on reflection, would take p to be necessarily true. Suppose also that on reflection S would think that his understanding p is enough to provide him with an understanding of why it is impossible for p to be false. Then p is properly basic a priori for S. Nonetheless, S may not now think that p is necessarily true; even though by hypothesis he would think this, were he to be sufficiently reflective, he may not have reflected much about p.[10] Indeed, he may believe p for what he himself, on reflection, would regard as silly reasons. Suppose, for example, that an astrologer has told him that p is true, and that he believes for what he, on reflection, would take to be silly reasons that this astrologer is reliable. Even so, the *proposition* p still is one he has good epistemic reasons to believe. What can be criticized here is the way that S believes p. He is unaware of his real reasons for thinking that p is true. By hypothesis he would be convinced that p is necessarily true were he to reflect upon it and what it implies, but in fact he has not engaged in such reflection. Instead, he simply takes the astrologer's word that it is true. Accordingly, although his belief p is propositionally rational (since he believes a proposition that is epistemically rational for him to believe), it is not doxastically rational.[11]

So in claiming that a proposition *p* is properly basic for *S* (either properly basic a priori or properly basic a posteriori), I am not claiming that there can be nothing epistemically substandard about the way that *S* believes *p*. I am claiming only that given his deepest epistemic standards and given what else he believes, there is no good reason for him to be suspicious of using the *proposition p* as a premise. Analogously, in claiming that a proposition *q* that *S* believes is epistemically rational but not properly basic for him, I am not claiming that there can be nothing substandard about the way that he believes *q*. I am claiming only that given his deepest epistemic standards and given what is properly basic for him, there is a good argument for *q*.

2.2   *Logic, Probability Theory, and Metaphysics*

I have pointed out that many traditional foundationalist positions can be incorporated into a subjective foundationalist account of epistemic rationality if they are given an appropriate subjective twist. Other standard work in epistemology and related areas in a similar way can be given a subjective twist and incorporated into subjective foundationalism.

Consider, for example, work in deductive logic and on the probability calculus. There is no denying the value of such work, but there is a question of understanding what it is about such work that makes it significant from an epistemic point of view. The subjective foundationalist position I have been advocating suggests that its epistemic significance is likely to derive from its power to convince us were we to be sufficiently reflective. This is not to suggest that the rules of deduction and of the probability calculus should be construed subjectively. On the contrary, nothing I have said prevents one from placing as objective an intepretation as one prefers on such rules. Nothing I have said, for example, indicates the truth of any kind of "psychologism," which implies that the rules of deduction or of the probability calculus simply are summaries of how people are disposed to make inferences. Indeed, such views inevitably are implausible, and what makes them implausible is that they confuse considerations that broadly speaking are metaphysical with considerations that broadly speaking are epistemological. Whether *a* implies *b*, or makes probable *b*, is not dependent upon what we now believe, or upon what arguments we, with sufficient reflection, would regard as likely to be truth preserving, and is not dependent in any other straightforward way upon our present constitution. A proposition *a* can imply *b* even if upon sufficient reflection we would believe that the truth of one is unrelated to the truth of the other. Likewise, a proposition *b* may have a probability of, say, .9 given *a* even if we, on reflection, think they are unrelated. On the other hand, the fact (if it is one) that even with sufficient reflection we would not recognize the way in which *a*'s truth is related to *b*'s *is* significant epistemically. It indicates that although *a* implies or makes probable *b*, it does not tend to make *b* epistemically rational for us. Accordingly, it need not be epistemically rational for us to believe *b* even if *a* is properly basic. Indeed, it can be epistemically rational for us to believe not*b*. For insofar as we, on sufficient reflection, would be convinced that *a* implies or makes probable not*b* and insofar as *a* is uncontroversial for us to assume, it is epistemically rational for us, all else being equal, to believe not*b* rather than *b*. And this is so even if in fact it is the latter and not the former that is implied or made probable by *a*. After all, by believing *b* we would be believing the negation of what we on reflection would take *a* to support, and no further reflection would convince us that it is a mistake to think this.

However, cases of this sort presumably are the exception. It presumably is safe to assume that most arguments that are deductively valid (and that are not too complex for us to understand) would be regarded by most people as truth preserving, were they to be sufficiently reflective. Similarly, it presumably is safe to assume that if the probability calculus implies that the conclusion of an argument is highly probable, given its premises, then most people would regard the argument as likely to be truth preserving, were they sufficiently reflective. Indeed, the history of logic and probability theory suggests that this is so. Although there often has been disagreement about how to interpret the rules of deductive logic and the probability calculus, and disagreement about what set of axioms it is best to use to derive these rules, and disagreement as well with respect to the probability calculus about how to apply these rules to situations that do not closely resemble games of chance, there generally has been relatively little disagreement among the experts (that is, among those who reflect carefully on the question) concerning what the rules are. On the assumption that these experts are not too different from the rest of us (except that they have reflected much more seriously than we upon these rules), it is likely that most of the rest of us, were we sufficiently reflective, would approve of arguments that straightforwardly reflect these rules and would not approve of arguments that straightforwardly violate them. So, if a proposition *a* straightforwardly implies a proposition *b* or if the probability calculus straightforwardly implies that *b* is highly probable given *a,* then ordinarily the proposition *a* will tend to make *b* epistemically rational for us.

Thus, deductive and probabilistic relations between propositions can be construed in as objective a manner as one pleases. In particular, they can be construed so that their obtaining does not depend upon what we now think, believe, or feel. Likewise, they can be construed so that their obtaining does not depend upon what we would think, believe, or feel were we sufficiently reflective, and does not in any other way depend upon our present constitution. Indeed, it is our tendency to construe these relations objectively that in large part accounts for why we are so interested in knowing what they are. However, this should not be allowed to conceal the fact that the epistemic significance of such relations lies in our being capable of grasping them were we sufficiently reflective. Their epistemic significance, in other words, does depend upon our constitution. In particular, it depends upon our being such that most arguments whose premises straightforwardly imply their conclusions as well as most arguments whose premises, given the probability calculus, straightforwardly make probable their conclusions are arguments that we would regard as likely to be truth preserving, were we sufficiently reflective.[12]

Of course, all this is not to say that ordinary people either do know or even in a robust practical sense are capable of knowing in a detailed way the rules of deduction and the rules of probability. The needs and demands of everyday life are often too pressing to engage in the kind of lengthy reflection required to grasp these rules. Even so, this does not mean that these rules are not reflected in the deepest epistemic standards of ordinary people. It does not mean that the arguments they would accept, were they sufficiently reflective, do not in general conform to these rules. Accordingly, even if ordinary people do not know what these rules are, they still may be used to evaluate epistemically the beliefs of ordinary people.

This, then, is what accounts for the importance of studies in logic and probability theory for epistemology: Progress in these fields ordinarily represents progress in understanding our own deepest epistemic standards.

Work in other fields of philosophy also may be of relevance to epistemology, albeit perhaps not as directly as work in logic and probability theory. In particular, work in other fields may be of relevance to epistemology not so much because it helps disclose our own deepest epistemic standards but rather because it helps explain at least in some loose way why we have the standards that we do. For example, consider the philosophy of mind. I have assumed that most people think, and on reflection would continue to think, that when they believe they are in pain, it is probable that they in fact are in pain. And likewise, I have suggested that this is so for many other psychological states as well. But if this is so, work in the philosophy of mind may be of help in explaining why it is so, since the reason it is so may well have to do with the way we think about psychological states; it may well have to do with our concept of a psychological state, with what we take to be the nature of psychological states. For instance, perhaps part of our notion of a psychological state is of a state such that an individual who is in that state is disposed to be aware of it when he is introspective.[13] So a state that standardly is not introspectively available to an individual cannot be a psychological state of his. Or perhaps this is so at least for certain kinds of psychological states, such as pains, sense-experiences, and the like. But if this is so, there is a conceptual connection between, say, being in pain and believing that one is in pain, at least for beings such as we who are capable of believing that we are in pain. Perhaps it is not so for animals. The connection here (even if we concern ourselves only with humans) is perhaps not as tight as some have suggested; it perhaps is not the case that believing one is in pain implies that one is in fact in pain. Nonetheless, even a looser connection may be of some help in explaining why most of us, on reflection, would be inclined to think that our believing we are in pain makes it likely that we are in pain. For if the suggestion above is on the right track, our notion of a pain is in part a notion of a state that ordinarily is introspectively available to us. It ordinarily is not hidden from us; it tends to make itself known to us. Consequently, it is difficult for us to imagine situations in which our pains *are* regularly hidden from us, in the sense that we would remain unaware of them even if we were to be introspective. A fortiori, it is difficult for us to imagine situations of this sort that we would consider to be even remotely like our present situation. Rather, any such situation is likely to be one that we would regard as highly improbable, even bizarre. But then, we are unlikely to think that such situations are relevant for an assessment of whether our believing we are in pain makes it probable that we are in pain. Similarly, it is likely to be difficult for us to imagine situations (or at least situations that we would deem relevant) in which a state that is not a pain-state regularly prompts us in a direct way to believe we are in pain.[14] For insofar as a kind of state "functions" in this way, insofar as it is a kind of state that regularly prompts us in a direct way to believe we are in pain, it has one of the most important characteristics of a pain-state. Accordingly, we will be inclined to think that any situation in which something that is not pain functions in this painlike way is likely to be a highly unusual situation.

So our concept of pain may very well be such, and our concept of other psychological states also may be such, that it is not surprising that we on reflection would think that our believing that we are in such a state makes it likely that we are in fact in such a state. It is not surprising, in other words, that our deepest epistemic standards imply that our believing we are in such a state tends to make it epistemically rational for us that we are in that state. For there are conceptual pressures that encourage us to have such epistemic standards.

Of course, I do not pretend to have argued here that some psychological states should be understood in this way, such that there is a conceptual connection, albeit perhaps loose, between an individual being in that psychological state and his being aware that he is in that state. My aim here is not so much to do philosophy of mind as to illustrate how work in philosophy of mind might be of some help in explaining why we have the epistemic standards that I have assumed we in fact do have with respect to propositions about our own current psychological states. In particular, my aim is to illustrate how work in the philosophy of mind might be of some help in explaining why many such propositions are likely to be properly basic for us.

In an analogous way, other work in metaphysics also can be relevant to epistemology. Consider, for example, metaphysical issues involved in the perception of physical objects. One not unnatural way to think of physical objects is to think of them (at least in part) as objects that by their very nature tend to disclose themselves to beings such as us in perception. Suppose we say that a "tablelike" visual experience is one that is appropriate for our seeing a table. As I have admitted in section 2.1, it may be a delicate business, given perceptual relativity, to describe what phenomenological features a visual experience must have in order to be the sort of visual experience that is appropriate for seeing a table. What a table looks like to creatures with visual equipment of the sort we have will be a function of perceptual conditions and the table itself. Even so, some kinds of visual experiences clearly are tablelike visual experiences and most others just as clearly are not. Given this notion of a tablelike visual experience, we can make at least a bit less vague the idea that a physical object such as a table by its very nature tends to disclose itself to beings such as us in perception. A table, for example, can be thought of (at least in part) as something that by its nature tends to cause creatures with the kind of perceptual equipment we take ourselves to possess to have tablelike visual experiences when they are appropriately situated—when, for example, the table is in front of them, when their eyes are open, when there is good light, and so on. No doubt this way of putting the matter is still unacceptably vague, but the important point is that something like this way of thinking about physical objects has been attractive to a whole host of philosophers and that insofar as they are right in thinking of physical objects in this general way, there is a conceptual tie between something being a table and something having a tendency under normal conditions to cause creatures such as we to have tablelike visual experiences.[15] Presumably there might be such ties with our other senses as well; physical objects such as tables tend to cause creatures such as us to have certain characteristic sorts of tactile experiences under appropriate conditions, certain characteristic sorts of auditory experiences under appropriate conditions, and so on. In any event, views of this sort discourage the idea of there being situations in which something is a table but in which that something is systematically "hidden" from us, such that we have no perceptual access to it. They discourage this idea because they imply that the concept of a physical object is in part the concept of something to which creatures such as we standardly do have perceptual access. This is not necessarily to say that it is impossible for there to be situations in which there are physical objects to which we have no perceptual access. The conceptual tie between something being a physical object and that something disclosing itself to us in perceptual experience is perhaps not this intimate. But even if it is not, it may very well be sufficiently intimate to imply that any situation in which physical objects are systematically hidden from us has to be an extraordinary situation. For if a view of the above sort is right, physical objects necessarily have a tendency to make themselves known to creatures such as we. So it cannot be standard, given whatever the laws of nature are, for such objects to be hidden from us. Rather, if physical objects are to be systematically hidden from us, something extraordinary has to take place; some condition must interfere, or "defeat," this natural tendency of physical objects to disclose themselves to creatures such as we in sense-experience.

Something like the reverse also may be true. Any view of the above sort, which conceptually links the notion of something being a physical object and something having a tendency to be perceived by creatures such as we, also discourages the idea of there being situations in which many of the perceptual tests of something being, say, a table are passed and yet in which there is no table. Any "chunk" of space-time that passes a good many of these perceptual tests without generating negative perceptual evidence (that is, perceptual evidence indicating that there is no table there) has one of the most important characteristics of a chunk of space-time that in fact has a table in it. Accordingly, any situation in which there is a chunk of space-time without a table in it but that nonetheless passes many of these perceptual tests (without generating negative perceptual evidence) is likely to be an unusual situation. In particular, at best it is likely to be a situation that S, on reflection, would regard as improbable—for example, a situation in which someone has concocted an elaborate illusion of a table—and at worst it is likely to be a situation that S, on reflection, would regard as so radically improbable as to be irrelevant for an epistemic assessment of arguments involving his perceptual beliefs—for example, an evil demon situation or a brain-in-a-vat situation. But if this is so, it helps explain why such perceptual beliefs tend to be self-justifying for S and why the propositions so believed tend to be properly basic for him.[16]

Moreover, the idea of there being a conceptual link between physical objects and what creatures such as we have a tendency to perceive can be pressed from the other direction as well, from the direction of how we conceive of ourselves as well as from the direction of how we conceive of physical objects. What I have in mind here is that although we initially might be inclined to regard certain kinds of situations as situations in which we might be likely to have nonveridical perceptual experiences, further reflection might convince us that we could not be in such a situation; our nature precludes this. Imagine an extreme situation of this sort, one in which it is for some reason impossible for there to be physical objects. Suppose, for instance, that the laws of nature in this situation are significantly different from what we take them to be in the actual world and that these "funny" laws somehow preclude the possibility of there being ordinary physical objects. Situations of this sort are unlikely to be those that we, on reflection, would regard as being relevant to the question of whether our believing that we see a table makes it probable that we do see a table. This is so not only because we, on reflection, are likely to regard such situations as radically improbable. In addition, we, on reflection, might very well doubt whether *we* could be in such a situation. Perhaps, for example, *I* could not be in a situation in which there could not be physical objects. Perhaps it is plausible to think both that I necessarily am a human being and that there cannot be human beings in a world in which, given the laws of nature, there cannot be physical objects. But if so, although it initially might seem to me as if this is a kind of situation in which my perceptual equipment could radically mislead me, on reflection I might not think this at all.

Notice, moreover, that if there is this kind of conceptual link between physical objects and creatures such as we, it might be of some help in explaining not only why we, on reflection, would be inclined to think that our particular perceptual beliefs are likely to be true (say, my belief that I see a cat on the mat) but also why we, on reflection, would be inclined to think that certain, very general nonperceptual beliefs are likely to be true. Consider, for instance, the proposition that there are physical objects. If as a result of conceptual pressures of the above sort we, on reflection, would be inclined to think that it is impossible for us to be in a situation in which, given the laws of nature, there could not be physical objects, this will make it more difficult for us, on reflection, to imagine many possible situations in which we falsely believe that there are physical objects. And this in turn makes it more likely that the proposition that there are physical objects is properly basic for us.[17]

Again, the idea here is not so much to defend views of this sort as to illustrate how the answers we are inclined to give to questions about our nature and about the nature of physical objects might be of some help in explaining why we have the epistemic standards we do with respect to physical objects claims. In particular, the way we conceive of ourselves[18] and the way that we conceive of physical objects may fit together in certain ways that make it more difficult than it might seem at first thought to imagine situations in which we have radically false perceptual beliefs about the physical world. Roughly speaking, the idea is that our conceptions of ourselves may in part be a conception of creatures who have a tendency to be "physical object receptors" and that our conception of ordinary physical objects may in part be a conception of things that tend to be "human experience generators." These conceptions, in turn, exert a kind of pressure upon us, a kind of conceptual pressure that encourages us, on reflection, to think that unless something nonstandard or artificial or just plain weird happens, our simple perceptual beliefs are not likely to be false. But if on reflection we would think this, such beliefs will tend to be self-justifying for us.[19]

One final example is worth mentioning. Consider the so-called new riddle of induction. The old riddle of induction is concerned with the vindication of the inductive arguments that we commonly take for granted. What Nelson Goodman calls the new riddle concerns the search for a criterion that distinguishes what we take to be good inductive arguments from what we take to be bad inductive arguments.[20] Goodman and others argue that the criterion cannot be a matter of the form of inductive arguments, since the argument (every emerald I have ever seen is green; thus the next emerald I will see will be green) has the same form as the argument (every emerald I have ever seen is grue; thus, the next emerald I will see will be grue) and yet most of us are inclined to think that the first argument, all else being equal, is a good inductive argument while the second argument is not. Expressed in the terminology I have been using, Goodman's point is that the inductive argument concerning the greenness of emeralds reflect our deepest epistemic standards while the inductive argument concerning grueness does not, but that the explanation for this is unlikely to have anything to do with the formal properties of these two arguments.

But then what is the explanation for why we are inclined to think that the one argument is likely to be truth preserving while the other is not? Perhaps the explanation has to do with how we conceive the property that is being "projected," with what we take to be its "nature." One possible explanation, for example, invokes supervenience. Perhaps the property "green" by its very nature supervenes on nontemporal natural properties, where what this means (roughly) is that it is impossible for an object at two different times to have the same nontemporal natural properties and yet be different with respect to greenness at the two times; it cannot be green at the one time and not green at the other time. On the other hand, the property "grue" is not like this.

Of course, all this is extremely vague. Much more would have to be said, for example, about what a nontemporal natural property is. Moreover, even if some of the vagueness could be eliminated, none of this amounts to a vindication of our inductive practices; it does not provide an answer to the old riddle of induction. Nor does it even really explain why many of us think (assuming that we do think this) that the inductive argument involving the property green is likely to be truth preserving. What it does help explain is what perhaps should have been obvious all along. It helps explain why, given that we think inductions involving greenness are likely to be truth preserving, we are not equally tempted to think the same of inductions involving grueness.

This suggestion concerning the supervenience of the property green upon nontemporal natural properties is made in the same spirit as the other suggestions. The point is not so much that this suggestion is ultimately defensible but rather that it is the kind of suggestion that might be of some help in explaining why we have certain epistemic standards and why we lack others. Of course, all of these suggestions presuppose that we do in fact have the epistemic standards I have been assuming we have. In particular, what I have been assuming is that most relatively normal people, on reflection, would be prepared to trust most of their normal introspective, perceptual, and inductive practices. They, on reflection, would think that most of what they introspectively are inclined to believe about their own psychological states is likely to be true; they, on reflection, also would think that most of what they are perceptually inclined to believe is likely to be true; and likewise they, on reflection, would think that most of the simple inductive inferences they are inclined to make are likely to be truth perserving. I have taken this as a kind of datum. The point here has been to illustrate that certain kinds of philosophical investigations may be of some help in explaining why most ordinary people are like this. In particular, the suggestion has been that there may be deep conceptual reasons for why we have some of the epistemic standards that we do. The way we conceive of ourselves, or the way we conceive of physical objects, or the way we conceive of psychological states, or the way we conceive of certain color properties, may be of help in accounting for at least some of our epistemic standards. And in this way they also may be of help in making our own deepest epistemic standards seem less arbitrary, less accidental, and less mysterious to us than they otherwise might seem to be.

On the other hand, even if such explanations of our epistemic standards are not forthcoming, I take it as relatively uncontroversial that most of us do have (at least roughly) the kind of epistemic standards that I have suggested we have, standards implying that our simple introspective beliefs, our simple perceptual beliefs, our simple memory beliefs, our simple inductive beliefs, are likely to be true (and hence, implying also that such beliefs tend to be self-justifying). How to best explain why we have such standards is a separate issue.

However, what if contrary to what I have been assuming, our deepest epistemic standards are not like this? What if most of us, given sufficient reflection, would believe that our simple introspective beliefs, our simple perceptual beliefs, our simple memory beliefs, our simple inductive beliefs, are not sufficiently likely to be true, all else being equal? Then presumably relatively little of what we believe as a result of introspection, perception, memory, and induction, would be epistemically rational for us. Such propositions would not be properly basic for us, since our beliefs in these propositions would not be self-justifying. Moreover, they are unlikely to be made epistemically rational for us by other propositions that are properly basic, since if these propositions are not properly basic for us, it is unlikely that very many other propositions would be properly basic for us either. For these propositions are the best candidates to be properly basic. And even if there were other properly basic propositions, it need not be the case that these other propositions could be used to argue for our introspective beliefs, perceptual beliefs, and other such beliefs in a way that we, on reflection, would regard as sufficiently likely to be truth preserving. And so, if our deepest epistemic standards are not (at least roughly) as I have assumed them to be, most of our introspective, perceptual, memory, and inductive beliefs are likely to be epistemically irrational.

There is nothing in subjective foundationalism per se that implies that our simple introspective beliefs, our simple perceptual beliefs, and so on, are likely to be self-justifying for us. As a result, there is nothing in the theory proper that altogether rules out the possibility that the skeptic is right in claiming that little of what we believe as a result of introspection, perception, and so on, is epistemically rational for us. Nevertheless, this is unlikely to be the case for relatively normal people. Even if subjective foundationalism proper does not altogether rule out this skeptical possibility, the theory proper in conjunction with plausible assumptions about what would be believed by relatively normal people on reflection does make such a skepticism improbable. In particular, the theory proper in conjunction with these assumptions suggests that an individual's simple introspective beliefs, his simple perceptual beliefs, and so on, will tend to be self-justifying unless the deepest epistemic standards of this individual are very different from the deepest epistemic standards of most people. (See the discussion of "common-sensism" in section 2.4.)

2.3 Coherentism

According to the subjective foundationalist, the traditional foundationalist gets the structure of epistemic rationality right (distinguishing properly basic propositions from those that are epistemically rational but not properly basic), but much of the spirit of traditional foundationalism, with its emphasis on guarantees of truth, is misguided. With the coherentist, matters are reversed. According to the subjective foundationalist, the coherentist is mistaken about the structure of epistemic rationality, but there is much in its spirit, with its emphasis upon the person's actual doxastic situation, that is fundamentally correct.

For instance, one of the central doctrines of coherentism—perhaps the central doctrine—is expressed by the maxim "there is no exit from the circle of one's beliefs."[21] In part, this maxim is meant to express a negative doctrine; it is meant in a suggestive way to express the idea that traditional foundationalist views about privileged access are indefensible—that there is no privileged and immediate access to the truth of propositions about our own psychological states or to the truth of any other proposition. However, the maxim has a more positive side; it is meant to express the idea that what is rational for a person to believe always is a function of what else he believes. So, whether or not it is epistemically rational for a person to believe some proposition is not something that can be determined by looking at that belief, or that proposition, in isolation. It cannot be determined, for example, by establishing that the person has some sort of privileged access to its truth. Rather, one always needs to take into account the rest of his doxastic situation.

This is a doctrine that the subjective foundationalist also embraces. Given subjective foundationalism, one can never determine whether a proposition is epistemically rational without taking into account the rest of a person's doxastic situation. Moreover, this is so even for the propositions that are properly basic for him. According to subjective foundationalism, a proposition p is properly basic for an individual S only if he believes it with such confidence that nothing else he believes with equal confidence can be used to argue against it in a way that he, on reflection, would believe to be truth preserving.

There is, however, a stronger interpretation of the maxim that there is no exit from the circle of one's beliefs, an interpretation that most coherentists would endorse but one that a subjective foundationalist cannot accept. In particular, coherentists are likely to use this maxim to express the idea that only another belief can make a belief rational. Most coherentists will insist, in other words, that if an individual S is to have a reason in favor of a proposition p that he believes, then something else that he believes must provide him with that reason.[22] This is a claim that the subjective foundationalist cannot accept, since according to the subjective foundationalist some beliefs are self-justifying; there are some propositions such that S's believing them is enough to give him a reason to think that they are true.

But even here, the difference between subjective foundationalism and coherentism is not as great as might appear at first glance. For, according to the subjective foundationalist, even the notion of self-justification is to be understood in terms of what else an individual believes and what he would believe on sufficient reflection (where what he would believe on sufficient reflection need not be something that he now believes, even nonoccurrently). In particular, S's belief p is self-justifying only if he, on sufficient reflection, would believe that p is true in a sufficiently great percentage of relevant possible situations in which he believes p and only if in addition nothing else he believes with as much confidence as p is a defeater of this argument, unless it itself is defeated by yet something else that he believes.

So, although at first glance it may appear as if there is an enormous difference between the subjective foundationalist and the coherentist on this issue—with the subjective foundationalist claiming that some beliefs are self-justifying and the coherentist denying this—this first appearence is somewhat misleading. For, whether or not a belief p is self-justifying for an individual S is a matter of what else he believes and of what he would believe, on reflection, about the truth-preservingness of the argument (S believes p; thus, p). It is, in other words, a matter of S's doxastic system and his epistemic standards. Although the subjective foundationalist cannot accept the doctrine that an individual has an epistemic reason in favor of what he believes only if something else he believes gives him this reason, the subjective foundationalist does accept a very similar doctrine—the doctrine that an individual has an epistemic reason in favor of what he believes only if his doxastic situation and his deepest epistemic standards give him this reason, where his deepest epistemic standards consist of the set of arguments he would believe are sufficiently likely to be truth preserving, were he to be sufficiently reflective.

Seen in this light, it is plausible to think that in spirit subjective foundationalism is closer to coherentism than to traditional foundationalism. Then why regard it as a version of foundationalism? Because of the structural similarities. Subjective foundationalism, like traditional versions of foundationalism, implies that the collection of propositions that are epistemically rational for a person has a fundamentally different kind of structure than what is implied by coherentist accounts of epistemic rationality.[23] To put the point metaphorically, a subjective foundationalist account proposes a tiered structure, in which properly basic propositions make epistemically rational other propositions, while coherentist accounts propose a nontiered structure. All propositions that are epistemically rational are on the same level. There are no properly basic propositions. Instead, the set of propositions it is epistemically rational for a person to believe is determined by amending through a process of give and take an initial set of propositions (ordinarily a subset, proper or otherwise, of the propositions a person happens to believe) in order to achieve a maximum amount of mutual support, where a set of propositions mutually support one another just if each proposition in the set is adequately supported by the remaining propositions in the set.[24]

So, although there is much that subjective foundationalism shares in spirit with coherentism, there is this fundamental structural difference between the two kinds of accounts. Moreover, this structural difference has far-reaching consequences. By insisting that there are important differences between propositions that are epistemically rational, with some being properly basic and others not, subjective foundationalism altogether avoids a difficulty that plagues all coherentist accounts of epistemic rationality. In particular, by insisting on this distinction, the subjective foundationalist, like other foundationalists, is able to say that a proposition p is epistemically rational for an individual just in case it is adequately supported by the set of propositions that are properly basic for him—that is, just in case there are properly basic propositions that tend to make p epistemically rational for him and there are no properly basic propositions that are defeaters of the support that these propositions give to p. A coherentist, by contrast, insists that a proposition p is epistemically rational for an individual only if it is adequately supported by the set of propositions that are epistemically rational for him. Every proposition that is epistemically rational for him must be adequately supported by the totality of other propositions that are epistemically rational for him. Otherwise, the set of propositions that are epistemically rational for S would not be mutually supportive; they would not cohere. In this sense, every proposition that is epistemically rational for an individual is eligible to serve as a premise in an argument for or against any other proposition.[25] The implication of this, in turn, is that no proposition that is epistemically rational for S can be such that the other propositions that are epistemically rational for him constitute the premises of a good argument whose conclusion is the denial of the proposition in question. A fortiori the set of propositions that are epistemically rational for S cannot be mutually inconsistent in an obvious way, since a set of propositions that is mutually inconsistent in an obvious way will be such that the denial of any proposition in the set is the conclusion of an argument that S, on reflection, would recognize to be deductively valid and whose premises are the remaining members of the set. So any genuine coherentist position will imply that the set of propositions it is epistemically rational for a person to believe cannot be in an obvious way inconsistent; any such set could not be mutually supportive.

Why is there a restriction that the set of propositions be *obviously* inconsistent? Because there are various ways in which a coherentist can understand the notion of mutual support and not all of these ways imply that it is impossible for an inconsistent set of propositions to be mutually supportive. For example, instead of understanding mutual support in an objective manner, such that the propositions in a set are mutually supportive only if, say, each proposition in the set is implied or made probable by the remaining members, a coherentist might understand mutual support in a subjective manner, so that the propositions in a set are mutually supportive for an individual S just if he believes, or perhaps would believe on reflection, that each proposition in the set is implied or made probable by the remaining members.[26] And if a coherentist does understand mutual support in this subjective way, it will be possible for propositions that are in fact inconsistent to be mutually supportive for an individual S.

So a coherentist account of epistemic rationality need not rule out the possibility of it being epistemically rational for an individual to believe each member of an inconsistent set of propositions. Moreover, this is fortunate for the coherentist, since it seems as if *any* plausible account of epistemic rationality must allow for this possibility.[27] A set of propositions that contains a necessarily false proposition is inconsistent, since it is impossible for all the members of such a set to be true. And yet, it can be epistemically rational for someone to believe a necessarily false proposition. (Imagine a necessarily false mathematical claim that an individual S does not recognize to be necessarily false and that perhaps he would not recognize to be such even if he were reflective, and imagine that S believes this claim because he has been told by a reliable mathematician that it has been proven true.) Likewise, it presumably can be epistemically rational for S to believe each member of a set of propositions where unbeknownst to him and perhaps unbeknownst to everyone else there is a complicated deductive argument from some of the claims in the set to the denial of another. But then, despite the fact that the set of propositions is inconsistent, it might be epistemically rational for S to believe each member of the set. He might have overwhelming evidence for each member and have no reason at all to suspect that the set of them is inconsistent.

Thus, all accounts of epistemic rationality, if they are to be plausible, must allow at least the possibility of it being epistemically rational for an individual to believe each member of an inconsistent set of propositions.[28] However, part of what distinguishes coherentist accounts from other accounts of epistemic rationality is their insistence that it cannot be epistemically rational for a person to believe each member of a set of inconsistent propositions if it is obvious to the person that the set is inconsistent. For if it is obvious to the person that necessarily one member of the set is false, then the set of propositions cannot be mutually supportive. After all, the person realizes that with respect to any proposition p in the set, if the remaining propositions are assumed true, p must be false. He realizes, in other words, that there is a truth preserving argument for not$p$ that has as its premises the remaining propositions in the set. Accordingly, the set of propositions in question is not mutually supportive, and hence on a coherentist account it cannot be epistemically rational for the person to believe each and every member of the set.

The coherentist must say similar things about what might be called "nearly inconsistent" sets of propositions. A set of propositions is nearly inconsistent just if assuming that the other members of the set are true makes it highly improbable that the remaining member is true. Although the coherentist, as with inconsistent sets of propositions, can allow the possibility of it being epistemically rational for S to believe each member of a set of nearly inconsistent propositions, he cannot allow this possibility with respect to a set of propositions that in an obvious way is nearly inconsistent. More exactly, he cannot allow this if all else is equal—if there is no other proposition epistemically rational for S that defeats the near inconsistency. For if all else is equal, the set of propositions that are epistemically rational for S cannot be mutually supportive. There are propositions in the set whose negations can be argued for using other propositions in the set and no further propositions that defeat these arguments. Thus, the coherentist must deny that it could be epistemically rational for the person to believe each member of the set.

The coherentist position on both inconsistent and nearly inconsistent sets of propositions is untenable. It *is* possible for each proposition in an inconsistent or nearly inconsistent set of propositions to be epistemically rational for a person S even if he recognizes that the set is inconsistent. Consider lotterylike situations, for example. It can be epistemically rational for S to believe that one of the tickets in a lottery (he has no idea which) will win and also be epistemically rational for him to believe with respect to each of the individual tickets that it will not be a winner, even though he recognizes that not all of these propositions could be true. Suppose, for instance, that the lottery has a million tickets, or even a billion, and suppose moreover that the lottery is fair. Then S might realize that the chances that ticket number one will not win are very high. Indeed, in a billion-ticket lottery the chances are 999,999,999 to 1 that it will not win. So, S has very strong reasons for believing that ticket one will not win. But of course, he might have equally strong reasons for believing the proposition that ticket two will not win, and for believing the proposition that ticket three will not win, and so on for corresponding propositions about each of the other tickets. What this suggests is that each of these propositions might be epistemically rational for S. But if each of these propositions as well as the proposition that some ticket will win is epistemically rational for S and moreover if this is so despite S's realizing that not all of these propositions could be true, then each member of an obviously inconsistent set of propositions can be epistemically rational for S.

The usual argument against this being possible is a reductio. It is argued that if it is possible for each member of an obviously inconsistent set of propositions to be epistemically rational for S, it also is possible for explicitly contradictory propositions to be epistemically rational for S, and this is absurd. In particular, it is claimed that if it is epistemically rational for S to believe of each ticket that it will lose and to believe also that some ticket will win, then it must be epistemically rational for him to believe that some ticket will win as well as to believe that it is not the case that some ticket will win (that is, that no ticket will win). The former by hypothesis is epistemically rational, and the latter, it is claimed, has to be epistemically rational given that it is epistemically rational for S to believe that ticket one will not win, that ticket two will not win, and so on for each of the other tickets.

The problem with this purported reductio, however, is that from the fact that it is epistemically rational for S to believe that ticket one will not win, that ticket two will not win, and so on, it does not follow that it also is epistemically rational for him to believe that no ticket will win—that is, it does not follow that it is epistemically rational for him to believe the conjunction (ticket one will not win and ticket two will not win . . . and ticket n will not win). This *would* follow if it were granted, as a coherentist would, that every proposition it is epistemically rational for S to believe can be assumed as a premise and then used to argue for or against other propositions. In other words, the reductio would work if it were granted that each and every proposition that is epistemically rational for S can be used as evidence to evaluate any other proposition. But this is just what should be denied. Not every proposition for which one has good evidence can itself be used as evidence to argue for other propositions. Even if the propositions that ticket one will not win, that ticket two will not win, and so on, are epistemically rational, it does not follow that they can be assumed as premises in order to argue for the claim that no ticket will win.

The point can also be illustrated by appealing to other, more common sorts of cases. Suppose, for instance, that a person is convinced he is fallible. Suppose, in particular, he believes the proposition that the set $(p^1, p^2, \ldots p^n)$ is likely to contain at least one false proposition, where this is a set of propositions for which he believes he has strong evidence. If this proposition about set $(p^1, p^2, \ldots p^n)$ is itself added to the set, the resulting set of propositions is nearly inconsistent, and the person may very well recognize it to be such. Yet it might be epistemically rational for a person to believe each member of this set. Indeed, this is not just a bare possibility. Since it presumably is often epistemically rational for us to be fallibilists with respect to a set of propositions for which we have good evidence, it presumably is not even unusual for there to be sets of inconsistent, or at least nearly inconsistent, propositions each member of which it is epistemically rational for us to believe. However, this is just what the coherentists must say is impossible.

The coherentist's refusal to admit that it is even *possible* for each member of such a set of propositions to be epistemically rational is a direct consequence of his refusal to give a preferred status to any of the propositions that are epistemically rational for a person. Since none is given a preferred status, all are equally vulnerable to arguments that use as premises the remaining propositions that are epistemically rational for him. Accordingly, each proposition must be such that at a minimum the remaining ones do not support its denial. A fortiori each proposition must be such that its denial cannot be deduced in an obvious way from the remaining propositions.

The result, curiously enough, is that coherentist accounts, like traditional foundationalist accounts, require that a person be overly concerned with avoiding false beliefs. Like traditional foundationalist accounts, they in effect require that a person be obsessed with the avoidance of false beliefs, and in this way, again like traditional foundationalist accounts, they unwittingly encourage skepticism. The obsession of the traditional foundationalist is direct and obvious, especially with respect to the possibility of error in the foundations. With the coherentist the obsession is more hidden, but it is there nonetheless. In particular, coherentist accounts require that a person be obsessed with leaving open the possibility that everything that he believes is true. A person is epistemically forbidden to believe propositions that jointly and obviously imply, or even make probable, that one of them is false. So, according to the coherentist, in the lottery case it *cannot* be epistemically rational for a person to believe the proposition that ticket number one will lose, regardless of whether the lottery consists of a thousand tickets, a million tickets, or a billion tickets. In other words, it cannot be epistemically rational for S to believe this proposition regardless of whether its probability is .999, or .999999, or .99999999—regardless, that is, of whether he has stronger evidence for it than he does for most of the other propositions he believes.

This might seem counterintuitive but of little consequence as long as we concern ourselves only with lottery cases. However, as suggested above, the problem is that cases relevantly similar to a lottery case can be generated with many of the ordinary propositions that we believe, propositions that intuitively we are inclined to think are epistemically rational for us (since intuitively we think we have good evidence for them). More precisely, this is so providing that we assume (as is plausible to assume) that it often is epistemically rational for us to adopt a healthy fallibilism with respect to our beliefs about such propositions. The assumption, in other words, is that it is epistemically rational for us to believe that at least one such proposition (we know not which) is likely to be false. For if we do make this assumption, the coherentist's obsession will force him to say that, contrary to what intuitively seems to be the case, not all of these propositions can be epistemically rational for us. This in turn encourages skepticism almost as much as does the traditional foundationalist's obsession. The traditional foundationalist unwittingly encourages skepticism by making the standards of proper basicality so stringent that the skeptic plausibly can claim that little if anything satisfies these standards. The coherentist unwittingly encourages skepticism by insisting that in order for a proposition p to be epistemically rational it is not enough that it is highly likely to be true. In the million-ticket lottery, for example, it is not enough that the proposition that ticket number one will not be the winner has a .999999 chance of being true. Since every proposition that is epistemically rational for an individual can be used as a premise to argue for or against other propositions, it also has to be the case that no other propositions that are epistemically rational for the individual can be used to argue against p. But this allows the skeptic to claim plausibly that only those propositions about whose truth we are certain and a relatively small number of other propositions are likely to be epistemically rational for us. If a set of propositions about which we are not certain is large—as large, for example, as the set of propositions that we are inclined to think are now epistemically rational for us—it may very well be epistemically rational for the individual to believe that at least one is likely to be false. But then, according to the coherentist, not all can be epistemically rational.[29]

A subjective foundationalist avoids the counterintuitive results by identifying properly basic propositions, propositions whose truth he properly can take for granted. These propositions, then, are the propositions in terms of which other propositions are made epistemically rational. It cannot automatically be assumed that these latter propositions, which are epistemically rational but not properly basic, properly can be used as premises in arguments for or against other propositions. It cannot be assumed, in other words, that every proposition for which there is good evidence can itself be used as evidence. Accordingly, given subjective foundationalism it is possible for the set of propositions that it is epistemically rational for a person to believe to be in an obvious way inconsistent or nearly inconsistent. This is possible because every proposition in an inconsistent set of propositions might be adequately supported by the set of properly basic propositions—as seems to be so in the lottery case, for example.

Even so, it bears repeating that the subjective foundationalist and the coherentist adopt a very similar outlook in determining what it is rational for an individual to believe, an outlook that emphasizes the individual's current beliefs. The subjective foundationalist, however, insists that although a person's current beliefs (and what he would believe on reflection about the truth-preservingness of various arguments) determine what is epistemically rational for him, the set of propositions epistemically rational for him has just the sort of internal structure claimed by traditional foundationalists—the set consisting of propositions that are properly basic and propositions that are made epistemically rational by these properly basic propositions. In this sense, subjective foundationalism represents a marriage between traditional foundationalism and traditional coherentism. And unlike some marriages, it is a marriage that brings out the best in both parties.

2.4   Is Subjective Foundationalism Overly Permissive?

Is subjective foundationalism overly permissive? Does it make being epistemically rational too easy? After all, almost any proposition, no matter how bizarre it might seem to the rest of us, in principle could be properly basic for a person S. Likewise, almost any argument, no matter how bizarre, in principle could be one that S on reflection would regard as likely to be truth preserving.

Even so, this does not indicate that the account is overly permissive. It only indicates that what it is rational for a person S to believe from an epistemic point of view is not a function of my perspective and my epistemic standards, or your perspective and your epistemic standards, or an omniscient being's perspective and epistemic standards. Rather, it is a function of S's own perspective and epistemic standards. It is a function of what he believes and the confidence with which he believes it and the arguments he, on reflection, would find persuasive. But from the fact that epistemic rationality is so understood and from the fact that understanding epistemic rationality in this way allows at least the possibility that what is epistemically rational for S may seem bizarre to the rest of us, it in no way follows that being epistemically rational is easy.

On the contrary, given subjective foundationalism, it is no easy thing to be epistemically rational. It is no easy thing for a proposition to be properly basic and no easy thing for a proposition to be argued for in an acceptable way. Consider, for example, the former. Consider how difficult it is for propositions to be uncontroversial for a person S to assume—that is, to be properly basic for him. For one, such propositions cannot be inconsistent in an obvious way, unlike propositions that are epistemically rational but not properly basic. They cannot be such that S on reflection would realize that the negation of any member of the set is implied by the remaining members. For then any proposition in the set would be such that the rest of the propositions in the set would tend to make its negation epistemically rational for him. Thus at least one proposition in the set—the least confidently believed one—would not be properly basic, since there would be other propositions he believes as confidently that can be used to argue against it.

Likewise, in order for each member of a set of propositions to be properly basic, there cannot be propositions *outside* the set that S believes as confidently as he believes the least confidently believed member in the set and that when added to this set creates an obviously inconsistent set of propositions. For then, there again would be propositions that he believes as confidently as the least confidently believed member of the original set and that can be used to construct a good argument against it.

Analagous points hold for sets of propositions that are nearly inconsistent in an obvious way. Suppose a set of propositions is such that S, on reflection, would think that the other members of the set constitute the premises of a good nondeductive argument for the negation of the remaining member. Suppose, in addition, there is no convincing defeater of this argument. Then not all the propositions in the set can be properly basic for S. At least one proposition in the set—the least confidently believed one—must be such that propositions S believes as confidently as he believes it tend to make its negation epistemically rational for him, where there is no convincing defeater proposition.

Moreover, the same conclusion follows if there are propositions outside the set that S believes as confidently as the least confidently believed member and that when added to the set create a new set that in an obvious way is nearly inconsistent (again assuming that there are no convincing defeaters). Under these conditions, at least one proposition in the original set is not properly basic for S.

At first glance these might not seem to be especially strong restrictions upon proper basicality. But in fact they are. One way to appreciate this is to recall how easy it is to create inconsistency and near inconsistency. To any set of believed propositions, $e^1, e^2, \ldots e^n$, one need only add the proposition that at least one of the propositions in this set is false and the resulting set of propositions will be inconsistent. Similarly, if one adds the proposition that it is highly likely that at least one of the propositions in the set is false, the resulting set will be nearly inconsistent. Moreover, these resulting sets ordinarily will be inconsistent (or nearly inconsistent) in an obvious way—in a way that S would recognize were he to be reflective. So, if propositions $e^1, e^2, \ldots e^n$ are to be properly basic for S, it is not just that these propositions cannot themselves be inconsistent or nearly inconsistent in an obvious way. S also must feel sure enough of their truth that he is not tempted to believe with confidence that one of them is false, or even that one of them is highly likely to be false.

But might not this make the requirements of proper basicality *too* stringent? Consider any relatively large set of propositions that an individual S believes. Will S not be inclined to believe (at least nonoccurrently) of any such set of propositions that at least one is false? No; this need not be so. At least it ordinarily will not be so with respect to those propositions that I have suggested are likely to be the best candidates for proper basicality—propositions that are the objects of our simple introspective beliefs, our simple perceptual beliefs, our simple memory beliefs, and a few very general propositions such as the proposition that there are physical objects, the proposition that the world has had a significant past, and the like. If an individual *S* is relatively normal, he is not likely to believe of the set of such propositions that even one is false. And even if he does believe of this set that one is false, he is unlikely to believe this with anything like the confidence that he believes the individual propositions in this set. This is so even if the set of such propositions is large. For these propositions are ones that *S* is likely to believe with something approaching maximal confidence. He is likely to believe with something approaching maximal confidence propositions such as that he now has a headache, that he now sees a newspaper in front of him, that he spent the past weekend at the beach, that there are physical objects, and an enormous number of other such propositions. This is not to say, of course, that with respect to such propositions *S* thinks that there is no chance at all of their being false. But this does not matter; these propositions can be properly basic for *S* even if he feels less than absolutely sure of their truth. So, for example, if $(e^1, e^2, \ldots e^n)$ is the set of propositions that are properly basic for him, he can feel less than absolutely sure of these propositions. What *is* required is that he believe each with more confidence than he believes the proposition that one member of the set $(e^1, e^2, \ldots e^n)$ is likely to be false (unless there is a convincing defeater proposition). Otherwise, at least one proposition in the set will be such that there is an undefeated argument against it with premises he believes as confidently as he believes it. But there do seem to be sets of propositions that meet this requirement—sets composed of propositions that are objects of our simple introspective beliefs, our simple perceptual beliefs, and so on.[30]

Even so, if the set $(e^1, e^2, \ldots e^n)$ is the set of propositions properly basic for him and if there is no guarantee that these propositions are true, might not it be epistemically rational for *S* to believe that the set $(e^1, e^2, \ldots e^n)$ contains at least one falsehood? And if so, might not there be situations in which subjective foundationalism implies that propositions $e^1, e^2, \ldots e^n$ are properly basic for *S* only if *S* fails to believe or believes with little confidence a proposition that is epistemically rational for him?

No, since if *S* is at all like most of the rest of us, it cannot be epistemically rational for him to believe that $(e^1, e^2, \ldots e^n)$ contains a falsehood. This is so because if he is at all like most of the rest of us, he on reflection would regard conjunctive arguments as truth preserving. Or at least this is so for all but those conjunctive arguments that are too complicated for him to understand. Consider, for example, the conjunctive argument (*a, b;* thus (*a* and *b*)). All or at least almost all people, given sufficient reflection, would realize that if the premises of this argument are true, it is impossible for the conclusion to be false.

But given that a person S on reflection would regard conjunctive arguments as truth preserving and given that $(e^1, e^2, \ldots e^n)$ is the set of propositions that are properly basic for S and given finally that a conjunctive argument with these propositions as premises is not too complex for him to understand, it is epistemically rational for S to believe the conjunction $(e^1$ and $e^2 \ldots$ and $e^n)$. This proposition is the conclusion of an argument with properly basic premises that tend to make its conclusion epistemically rational for him. Accordingly, it is epistemically rational for S to believe of the set of propositions properly basic for him that it contains only truths.[31] Of course, like the other propositions it is epistemically rational for S to believe, this proposition need not in fact be believed by S and it need not in fact be true. He may very well not believe that $(e^1, e^2, \ldots e^n)$ contains only truths, and there may well be false propositions in the set $(e^1, e^2, \ldots e^n)$. But given that all of these propositions are properly basic for S, it is epistemically rational for him to believe that this is not so. It is epistemically rational for S to believe that all these propositions are true.

The point here also can be expressed negatively, in order to emphasize once again how difficult it is for propositions to be properly basic. In particular, it can be expressed by saying that only propositions that properly can be conjoined can be properly basic. Thus, if it is not epistemically rational for S to believe that the set $(e^1, e^2, \ldots e^n)$ contains only truths, not all the propositions in the set can be properly basic for him.[32]

Indeed, for the subjective foundationalist this is one of the important differences between propositions that are epistemically rational for a person S by virtue of being properly basic for him and propositions that are epistemically rational for him by virtue of being made so by propositions that are properly basic for him. It would not be at all surprising if it were *not* epistemically rational for S to believe of a set composed of the latter that it contained only truths, but this would be surprising for a set composed of the former. Correspondingly, it would not be at all surprising if a set of the latter were inconsistent or nearly inconsistent in an obvious way. On the other hand, it is impossible for a set of the former to be either. Likewise, it would not be at all surprising if a set of the latter could be made inconsistent or nearly inconsistent in an obvious way by the addition of a proposition that is believed by S as confidently as the least confidently believed member in the set, but again this is impossible for a set of the former.

All these differences are indications of how difficult it is for propositions to be epistemically rational for a person without his having a good argument for them. They are indications, in other words, that the requirements of proper basicality are significantly more stringent than the requirements of epistemic rationality.

Even so, might not there be a problem here? After all, does not any proposition whatsoever become a good candidate for being properly basic if S comes to believe it with something like maximum confidence? And is it not possible for S to come to believe with maximum confidence even relatively complex propositions, propositions that intuitively do not seem to be good candidates for being properly basic?

Yes, perhaps this is possible. But believing a proposition with something approaching maximum confidence is not enough to make a proposition properly basic. Relatively complex propositions are unlikely to be properly basic for us even if we believe them with such confidence that nothing else we believe with comparable confidence can be used to argue against them. Ordinarily, our beliefs concerning complex propositions will not be self-justifying.

Consider an extreme example. Suppose p is the proposition that every March 15 at exactly twelve noon Greenwich time the number of rabbits alive on earth is an even number greater than three million. Of course, this is not the kind of proposition that many of us are likely to believe at all, much less with confidence. It may not even be a proposition that many of us *can* believe with great confidence. But suppose that somehow a person S suddenly does come to believe p with great confidence. Even so, p is highly unlikely to be properly basic for S. Moreover, it is unlikely to be properly basic even if nothing else that S believes with comparable confidence tends to make not p epistemically rational for him. For p is a highly complex proposition. And presumably, if S is at all like the rest of us, he on reflection would not believe that the argument (S believes p; thus, p) is sufficiently likely to be truth preserving. The proposition p in this respect is different from propositions about, say, S's own current conscious psychological states. If he is at all like the rest of us, S would have some difficulty imagining ways in which his beliefs about his own current conscious psychological states might go wrong. However, he presumably would have no trouble imagining all sorts of ways (that is, all sorts of relevant situations) in which he might come to believe a proposition such as p when it is false. Indeed, if he is at all like the rest of us, he on reflection may very well be tempted to think that given simply the information that he believes it, a proposition such as p is about as likely to be false at it is to be true.

Moreover, even *if* we assume that for some reason S on reflection would be inclined to think that his believing p does make p sufficiently probable—even if we assume that his belief p tends to be self-justifying—p *still* is unlikely to be properly basic for him. For if S is at all like most of the rest of us, there is likely to be a convincing defeater of the support that his believing p tends to provide for p. This is so because if S is at all like the rest of us, something else that he believes with great confidence is likely to give him a reason for withholding on p. For example, perhaps he believes (at least nonoccurrently) that the only reliable way of determining the number of rabbits on earth is to count them and that neither he nor anyone else recently has counted all the rabbits on earth, and a fortiori perhaps he believes that no one on a recent March 15 has counted all the rabbits on earth. Moreover, perhaps he believes that any counting of three million or more rabbits would take a sufficient length of time that one couldn't be confident whether a previously counted rabbit had died before the count was completed, thus throwing off the count. Or perhaps he believes the proposition that there is at least a 50–50 chance of one of the above propositions being true. If S is at all like the rest of us, these and a huge number of other such propositions will be potential defeaters of the argument (S believes p; thus, p). But then, if S believes any of these propositions with as much confidence as p, p will not be properly basic for him. Moreover, any individual who is at all like most of us—in particular, any individual whose view of the world and of the ways creatures such as we can gather information about the world is at all similar to the view that most of us have—will believe propositions of this sort with great confidence. Accordingly, it is plausible to think that a complex "queer" proposition such as p could be properly basic only for an individual who is radically unlike most of us.

However, even if all this is admitted, might not there still be a problem with propositions that are *not* properly basic? In particular, might not it be too easy, given subjective foundationalism, for properly basic propositions to make epistemically rational other propositions? Might not it be too easy, for example, for a proposition about S's current psychological states to tend to make epistemically rational for S a proposition about the external world?

This much has to be admitted: Given subjective foundationalism, the arguments that make propositions epistemically rational need not be truth preserving. However, this does not mean that it is easy for one proposition to epistemically support another proposition. On the contrary, propositions e^1, e^2, . . . e^n tend to make another proposition p epistemically rational for S only if an argument with these propositions as premises and p as a conclusion reflects S's deepest epistemic standards—that is, only if S on reflection would think that such an argument is sufficiently likely to be truth preserving and only if in addition no further reflection would change his mind. So not just any argument that S regards as truth preserving after a moment or two of reflection will reflect S's deepest epistemic standards. Thus, for example, the proposition that S has a chair-in-front-of-him kind of visual gestalt (roughly, that he has a chair-in-front-of-him kind of visual experience and no visual experience of the sort that would incline him to believe that there is *not* a chair in front of him—no visual experiences of the sort he associates with, for instance, seeing a photograph of a chair) does not tend to make epistemically rational for S the proposition that there is a chair in front of him just because S in fact thinks the latter is likely to be true when the former is. It does so only if it is the case that were S to be ideally reflective he would still think this.

Of course, subjective foundationalism does allow for the possibility that this proposition—the proposition that S is having a chair-in-front-of-him kind of visual gestalt—might help make epistemically rational for him not the proposition that there is a chair in front of him but rather some radically different proposition. Indeed, there presumably is no limit to the propositions that could possibly be made epistemically rational for S by the proposition that he is having a chair-in-front-of-him kind of visual gestalt. This latter proposition, for example, might tend to make epistemically rational for him the proposition that there is a demon who is causing him to have such visual experiences or the proposition that his brain is in a vat where it is being stimulated to give him experiences of this sort. Or it might tend to make epistemically rational yet some other, even more bizarre proposition. But in fact, it is implausible to suppose that having a chair-in-front-of-him visual gestalt tends to make epistemically rational for S any such propositions, at least if he is at all like most of the rest of us. This is implausible not because it is likely that S has or even thinks that he has some way of conclusively proving that he is not under the influence of such a demon or that he is not a brain in a vat. Rather, this is implausible because if S is anything like most of the rest of us, he is strongly inclined to believe that there is a chair in front of him when he has a chair-in-front-of-him visual experience and when in addition the rest of his perceptual experiences cohere with it in the appropriate way. Under these conditions he finds it "natural" to have this belief, where "natural" here is used loosely to refer to a deep-seated and hence hard-to-avoid inclination—an inclination whose presence can be explained perhaps conceptually (by, for instance, the fact that the concept of a chair is in part the concept of something that tends to cause beings such as we to have chair-like visual experiences) or perhaps genetically (by, say, the fact that the processes of natural selection tend to favor our having such inclinations) or perhaps environmentally (by, say, the fact that when we are children we are trained to have such inclinations by our parents and by the rest of our culture) or perhaps by some combination of these factors. Moroever, if S is at all like most of the rest of us, he, on reflection, would not significantly question this "natural inclination." Various skeptical hypotheses about the origin of his perceptual experiences presumably would occur to him on reflection, but after taking these into account he presumably still would find it difficult not to think that trusting this natural inclination is likely to be an effective way of satisfying his epistemic goal. In other words, he would find it difficult not to think that in most relevant possible situations in which he has a chair-in-front-of-him visual experience along with appropriately coherent other perceptual experiences, there in fact is a chair in front of him.

Similarly, consider the proposition *p*, that in the past a beaker of water has eventually boiled when it has been heated over a powerful burner. Why is it plausible to think that this proposition tends to make epistemically rational for most of us the proposition *q*, that the water if heated would boil this time as well? Not because we have or on reflection would discover some argument that proves that nature is uniform, but rather because most of us are naturally inclined to make inferences that presuppose the uniformity of nature. As a result, we are naturally inclined to believe *q* when we believe *p*. Moreover, most of us on reflection would be willing to trust this natural inclination; we on reflection would think (even if we could not prove) that in most relevant possible situations in which we might find ourselves, relying on such inferences would be an effective way of satisfying our epistemic goal.

And why is it plausible to think that the proposition that all the emeralds we have seen have been green tends to make epistemically rational for us the proposition that the next emerald we see will also be green, while the proposition that all the emeralds we have seen have been grue does not tend to make epistemically rational for us that the next emerald we see will be grue? Not because we have or on reflection would discover some argument proving that arguments "projecting" greenness are truth preserving while analogous arguments "projecting" grueness are not, but rather because we find it natural to believe and to continue to believe on reflection that inductive arguments involving greenness are likely to be truth preserving while the corresponding arguments involving grueness are not.

In each of the examples above then, a proposition p tends to make epistemically rational for most of us another proposition q not because there is any guarantee that if the former is true the latter also is true, or at least is likely to be true. The explanation instead lies in the fact that most of us are inclined to believe the latter if we think that the former is true, and in the fact that on reflection we are inclined to trust this inclination. It lies, most simply, in our nature as believers and in our willingness on reflection to trust what that nature "recommends" to us.[33]

This appeal to our nature as believers is characteristic of subjective foundationalism. There is nothing in the formal part of the theory that guarantees that our simplest and most fundamental beliefs about the external world, the past, and the future are likely to be epistemically rational for us, but the formal part of the theory together with plausible assumptions about our nature as believers does imply that such beliefs are likely to be epistemically rational for us. Correspondingly, there is nothing in the formal part of the theory that prevents "queer" propositions—for example, the proposition that we are brains in a vat, the proposition that the earth and its inhabitants were created only five minutes ago—from being epistemically rational for us. But again, the formal part of the theory together with plausible assumptions about our nature as believers does imply that this is highly unlikely; together they imply that such propositions are likely to be epistemically rational only for beings very different from us.

In this admittedly nonstandard sense subjective foundationalism encourages a naturalization of epistemology. What is epistemically rational for us ordinarily is a function of our natural inclinations to make certain kinds of inferences and our willingness on reflection to trust these natural inclinations even if we cannot prove that this attitude of trust is likely to help secure our epistemic goal.

Even so, subjective foundationalism does not imply any kind of crass common-sensism, which makes epistemic rationality simply a reflection of our commonsense way of viewing the world. I have been claiming that, given subjective foundationalism and given our nature as believers, it is plausible to think that many of our everyday beliefs about the external world, the past, and the future are epistemically rational. But nothing I have said entirely rules out the possibility that most beliefs of most people are not epistemically rational. In other words, nothing I have said is incompatible with a skepticism that implies that little of what we believe is epistemically rational. Moreover, such a skepticism would not be ruled out even if most people were familiar with the requirements of epistemic rationality and tried as hard as they could to believe in accordance with these requirements. For even if they tried as hard as they could to be epistemically rational, nothing precludes the possibility of people making significant mistakes about what propositions are properly basic for them and about what arguments they, with sufficient reflection, would regard as truth preserving. Of course, we may very well think (and it may very well be epistemically rational for us to think) that if we take the time to reflect carefully, we will reduce the chances of making such mistakes. Even so, such reflection will never produce certainty. And insofar as we cannot be certain of what propositions are properly basic for us and what arguments we on reflection would regard as truth preserving, then so too we cannot be certain of what is epistemically rational for us. So, try as we may to be epistemically rational, we still will be susceptible to epistemic error—to believing propositions that are not epistemically rational and not believing propositions that are epistemically rational.[34]

Two lessons, then, are suggested by all this. First, the subjective foundationalist account of epistemic rationality, far from being overly permissive, is relatively strict. It makes escaping epistemic irrationality no easy task. It is no easy thing for a proposition to be properly basic for a person, and it is no easy thing for a proposition to be argued for in a way that conforms to a person's own deeper epistemic standards.

Second, the question of the adequacy of the general requirements of epistemic rationality needs to be separated from the question of whether the kinds of propositions that I have suggested are likely to be properly basic are in fact properly basic, and it needs also to be separated from the question of whether the kinds of arguments that I have suggested that most people on reflection would regard as truth preserving would in fact be regarded by them as truth preserving. In other words, the formal part of the theory, or subjective foundationalism proper, needs to be separated from what can be called the substantive part of the theory. Maybe I am right in suggesting that propositions about a believer's own psychological states and propositions about what he is perceiving or remembering are good candidates for being properly basic. And maybe I also am right in suggesting for most people the proposition that they are having a chair-in-front-of-them kind of visual gestalt tends to make epistemically rational for them the proposition that there is a chair in front of them. On the other hand, maybe I am mistaken. Maybe some of the kinds of propositions I have picked out as good candidates for being properly basic are not, but some other kinds are. And maybe no propositions about our own psychological states tend to make epistemically rational for us propositions about the external world. If we were to be sufficiently reflective, maybe we would not believe that our having a cat-on-the-mat visual experience and appropriately coherent other perceptual experiences makes probable that there in fact is a cat on the mat. And maybe—but just maybe—a general skepticism follows from my account, so that relatively little of what we believe is epistemically rational for us.

The point here is that none of these possibilities are incompatible with subjective foundationalism proper, not even skepticism is incompatible with it. I in fact believe that, given subjective foundationalism proper, much of what I believe is epistemically rational for me, and I believe as well that much of what many of the rest of you believe is epistemically rational for you. Moreover, I believe that, given subjective foundationalism proper, this belief of mine about the epistemic rationality of our beliefs is itself epistemically rational. But nothing in the subjective foundationalist account I am defending *implies* that what I believe about what propositions are epistemically rational for me and for you has to be true. So nothing in the account altogether rules out the possibility that the skeptic is right in claiming that little of what we now believe in fact is epistemically rational for us.

Similarly, nothing in the formal part of the theory altogether rules out the possibility that some proposition that seems altogether bizarre to the rest of us is epistemically rational, or even properly basic, for some other individual. Nothing in the formal part of the theory rules out the possibility that an individual might have beliefs and epistemic standards wildly different from those that most of us have. There *are*, however, constraints in addition to those imposed by the formal part of the theory that make this unlikely—constraints having to do, for example, with the concepts we use or having to do with the similarities in our genetical makeups and in our environments. These constraints shape our nature as believers, making it highly unlikely that the beliefs or the epistemic standards of different individuals will vary radically. Even so, these constraints do not altogether rule out the possibility that, given subjective foundationalism, what seems crazy or bizarre or outlandish to most of the rest of us might be epistemically rational for someone else.

Suppose, then, that there are such individuals. What is to be said about them? What is to be said is just what I have said—namely, that what is epistemically rational for them is crazy and bizarre and outlandish, and that insofar as they believe what is epistemically rational for them, they have crazy, bizarre, and outlandish beliefs. It is important to remember that not every failure is a failure of rationality, despite an inclination, especially among philosophers, to claim otherwise. In ethics, for example, there is a tradition that insists upon claiming that the problem with the egoist is a problem with his reason—a problem that is caused by his being irrational in some way—instead of a problem of character, a problem of his caring about the wrong things. In epistemology there is an analogous temptation—the temptation to think that one who has beliefs that are silly or outlandish must be epistemically irrational. It is tempting to think that it is not enough to point out that his way of looking at the world is fundamentally wrong-headed; rather, we must also be able to pin upon him the charge of irrationality. But as is the case in ethics, this is a temptation to be resisted; there are criticisms that we can make of an individual that are as damning as the criticism that he is irrational.[35]

2.5   *Second-level Arguments*

I have claimed that it is epistemically rational for a person to believe a proposition p just if there is an argument for p that is uncontroversial for him. However, an argument is uncontroversial only if its premises are properly basic, and might not it be relatively rare for a person to consider explicitly arguments that have properly basic propositions as their premises? Not necessarily; the subjective foundationalist, unlike the traditional foundationalist, allows lots of "ordinary" propositions to be properly basic for an individual, propositions about what he is perceiving, what he remembers, and the like. But even if it is rare for individuals to consider explicitly arguments with properly basic propositions as premises, this matters little for the theory of epistemic rationality, since in order for a proposition to be epistemically rational for an individual he need not be explictly aware of an argument that makes the proposition epistemically rational. There only has to be such an argument.

Indeed, it might not be feasible for a person to try to make himself explicitly aware of the arguments that make propositions epistemically rational for him, and moreover the person might very well realize this. In particular, he might realize that trying to formulate such arguments might be sufficiently time-consuming that it would make more difficult the satisfaction of his nonepistemic goals. And if so, relative to these nonepistemic goals it may very well be irrational for him to try to construct such arguments. In addition, since the arguments that make propositions epistemically rational for him might be relatively complex, any attempt to consider explicitly very many of them might also result in his making many epistemic mistakes; it might even lead to his believing a higher percentage of propositions that are epistemically irrational for him than otherwise. Or at least, it might be epistemically rational for S to believe that it would lead to this result and, accordingly, to believe also that epistemically he will be better off *not* trying to formulate explicitly the kind of arguments that are good candidates to make propositions epistemically rational for him. Rather, insofar as he is going to consider what arguments he has for a proposition, he will be better off considering various "short-cut" arguments—for example, arguments whose premises are not properly basic for him.

But this raises a question about these short-cut arguments. Do they have any epistemic significance? What role, if any, can they play in making a proposition epistemically rational for an individual? For convenience, suppose we say that first-level arguments are arguments with premises that are properly basic for S and with conclusions that are made epistemically rational for S by these premises, and suppose we say that other arguments are second-level arguments. Now suppose that in deliberating about some proposition p (or perhaps in arguing with someone else about p), S discovers what seems to be a plausible argument for p, and as a result he comes to believe p. However, suppose this argument is a second-level argument; suppose its premises are not properly basic for S. Is p epistemically rational for S? The answer is yes if S has a good first-level argument for p and no if he does not. Even so, this second-level argument can play an important role in making p epistemically rational for S.

Suppose, for example, that it is epistemically rational for S to believe that this second-level argument for p is a kind of argument that is likely to have a true conclusion. In other words, suppose S has a first-level argument indicating that certain kinds of second-level arguments are likely to yield true conclusions and that his present argument for p is such an argument. Then, all else being equal, it will be epistemically rational for him to believe the conclusion of this second-level argument. All else being equal it will be epistemically rational for him to believe p, since all else being equal S will have a good first-level argument for p. He will have this first-level argument for p in virtue of having a good first-level argument for the claim that the second-level argument he has for p is a kind of second-level argument that is likely to have a true conclusion. In this respect, second-level arguments can play an epistemic role analogous to that of testimony; just as S can have a good first-level argument for p in virtue of having a good first-level argument for the claim that R's testimony is reliable and R says that p, so too he can have a good first-level argument for p in virtue of having a good first-level argument for the claim that the second-level argument he has for p is "reliable" and it "says" that p.[36]

What kinds of considerations might make it epistemically rational for S to believe that a second-level argument is likely to have a true conclusion? Ordinarily it will be epistemically rational for S to believe this if it is epistemically rational for S to believe both that all of the premises of the argument are true and that the conclusion is highly likely to be true if these premises are true.[37] Moreover, any number of considerations might make it epistemically rational for S to believe this of an argument. In particular, any number of inductive considerations, based, say, on what S has seen, what he remembers, what he has been told, and so on, might make it epistemically rational for S to believe this of an argument.

The lesson here, then, is not just that ordinarily these second-level arguments, or "short-cut" arguments, out of practical necessity will be the arguments that we consider insofar as we in our everyday lives consider arguments at all; the lesson also is that from an epistemic point of view it is altogether appropriate to do so. It is appropriate to do so insofar as it is epistemically rational for us to believe that these second-level arguments are likely to have true conclusions.

Indeed, this is to understate the lesson. These second-level arguments are enormously important epistemic tools. To be sure, they are tools that are "created" by first-level arguments, but once created these tools can be used to argue for propositions that could not be defended by first-level arguments on their own. The idea is that the conclusions of first-level arguments provide the materials for the construction of good second-level arguments. They might do so, say, by providing us with data for the claim that there is a lawlike connection between the truth of certain propositions and the truth of some other proposition (or if not a lawlike connection, at least a highly reliable correlation). For instance, the conclusions of first-level arguments may provide us with data indicating that when propositions $e^1, e^2, \ldots e^n$ are true, proposition p is usually (or perhaps always) true. If so, then these first-level arguments in effect warrant the argument (e^1, e^2, . . . e^n; thus, p) as a second-level argument for us, so that ordinarily it will be epistemically rational for us to believe p if it is epistemically rational for us to believe that all the premises of this argument are true. In turn, this second-level argument along with other such second-level arguments might provide us with the material for yet additional law-like connections (or highly reliable correlations)—in effect, additional second-level arguments. And so on. Unless we could use second-level arguments in this way—a way that allows us to piggy-back one argument on top of another, with arguments at one level supporting arguments at a higher level—much of what we believe could not be epistemically rational for us. Second-level arguments, like testimony, give us tools with which we are able to generate arguments for a huge variety of propositions for which we otherwise would lack good arguments. They do so, in effect, by increasing our body of available evidence, so that not just properly basic propositions can be used to argue for other propositions.[38]

2.6   Is Subjective Foundationalism Incoherent?

According to an Aristotelian conception of rationality, if an individual S has a goal X and if upon careful reflection he would believe Y to be an effective means to X, then it is rational, all else being equal, for S to bring about Y. This is the conception of rationality that provides the underpinning for subjective foundationalism. Subjective foundationalism can be understood as an attempt to idealize this general conception—not just careful reflection is required but ideally careful reflection—with respect to a distinctly epistemic goal—the goal of now believing truths and now not believing falsehoods. According to the subjective foundationalist, it is epistemically rational for a person to believe the conclusions of arguments that are uncontroversial for him (that is, arguments whose premises are properly basic for him and whose premises in addition tend to make their conclusions epistemically rational for him), since were he to engage in reflection of an appropriate ideal sort he would think that believing these conclusions is an effective way of satisfying his epistemic goal. More precisely, were he to engage in reflection of an appropriate ideal sort, he would think that the arguments in question are sufficiently likely to be truth preserving and he would uncover no good reason to be suspicious of their premises.

But why this emphasis upon arguments? Might not a person think that argumentation is an ineffective means to his epistemic goal? And if so, would not the general conception of rationality that underpins subjective foundationalism be at odds with subjective foundationalism? That is, would not the general conception suggest that it is epistemically *irrational* for him to believe the conclusions of arguments that are uncontroversial to him? Or at the very least, might not a person believe that there are other means to his epistemic goal that are as effective as believing the conclusions of such arguments, and if so does not the general conception suggest that an account of epistemic rationality in terms of argument is inevitably incomplete?

Consider the first question. Might not a person S believe of the arguments that are uncontroversial for him (in the subjective foundationalist's sense) that their conclusions often are false, and as a result might not he also think that his believing such conclusions is not an effective means to his epistemic goal? Suppose, for example, S believes that there is an evil demon who does not like S to be reflective. This demon, S believes, is prepared to deceive S about what arguments are truth preserving if S reflects about what arguments are truth preserving. Does not the possibility of S believing this reveal an incoherence between the general conception of rationality and subjective foundationalism? After all, according to the subjective foundationalist, arguments that seem to be truth preserving to S on reflection tend to make their conclusions epistemically rational for him, and yet in this case S thinks that believing the conclusions of such arguments is not an effective means to his epistemic goal (even if their premises are true).

The key issue, however, is not whether S thinks, perhaps without much reflection, that the conclusions of such arguments often are false. The general schema of rationality is that it is rational, all else being equal, for S to bring about Y if he has a goal X and upon reflection he would believe that Y is an effective means to X. So the key issue is whether or not believing the conclusions of such arguments represents what S on reflection would regard as an effective means to his epistemic goal of now believing truths and now not believing falsehoods.

However, suppose that even given ideal reflection S would not believe this. In other words, suppose that on ideal reflection S would think that believing the conclusions of those arguments that seem best to him on reflection is *not* an effective way for him to believe truths and not to believe falsehoods (even when their premises are true).

Even so, such a case does not exhibit any kind of incoherence between subjective foundationalism and the general conception of rationality that underpins it. In particular, it is not a case in which S on reflection would think of the arguments that are uncontroversial for him that they are not likely to be an effective means to his epistemic goal. For insofar as *S* on reflection thinks that believing the conclusions of the arguments that seem best to him on reflection is not an effective means to his epistemic goal (even if their premises are true), not even these arguments are uncontroversial for him. Indeed, with respect to these arguments, *S* is a skeptic.[39]

What about the second question? Might not *S* on reflection believe that there are other means to his epistemic goal that are as effective as believing the conclusions of good arguments? The means would have to be "direct," since the epistemic goal is now to have true beliefs and now not to have false beliefs. So no causal means will do. A person *S* might think that something he could do now would be a causally effective means to his having true beliefs and not having false beliefs in a few seconds or in a few hours or in a few days, but not that it would be an effective way to satisfy his goal of now having true beliefs and now not having false beliefs.[40]

But might not it be the case that *S* on reflection would believe that there is some effective, direct means of satisfying his goal, a means other than that of believing the conclusions of good arguments? For example, might not *S,* on reflection, think that believing what his perceptual equipment inclines him to believe is such a means? Or might he not, on reflection, think that believing what his friend Jones tells him is such a means? Or might he not even on reflection think that something relatively bizarre—such as believing the first thing that pops into his head—is an effective way to satisfy his epistemic goal? If so, will not the general conception of rationality that under-pins subjective foundationalism imply that it is epistemically rational for him to believe what his perceptual equipment inclines him to believe, or what Jones tells him, or what first pops into his head? But then, is there not a kind of incoherence between this general concep-tion and subjective foundationalism, since the latter implies that it is epistemically rational for *S* to believe *p* only if he either has a good argument for *p* or *p* is properly basic for him?

No, since (subject to a qualification that I will bring up shortly) for any means that *S,* on reflection, would take to be an effective means to his epistemic goal, there is a corresponding argument that *S* on reflection would regard as likely to be truth preserving. Thus, if *S,* on reflection, would think that believing what his perceptual equip-ment inclines him to believe is an effective way to satisfy his epistemic goal, then the argument (*S* is perceptually inclined to believe *p;* thus, *p*) is one that *S,* on reflection, would regard as likely to be truth preserving. Accordingly, on any occasion when it is uncontroversial for S to assume that he is perceptually inclined to believe p and all else is equal, p is epistemically rational for him. In a like manner, if S on reflection would think that believing what Jones tells him is an effective way to satisfy his epistemic goal, then the argument (Jones says that p; thus, p) is one that he, on reflection, would regard as likely to be truth preserving. So on any occasion where it is uncontroversial for S to assume that Jones has said p and where all else is equal, it is epistemically rational for S to believe p. Finally, if S is unlike most of the rest of us and on reflection would think that believing the first thing that pops into his head is an effective means to his epistemic goal, then the argument (p is the first thing that pops into S's head; thus, p) is an argument he, on reflection, would regard as likely to be truth preserving. Accordingly, p is epistemically rational for him if it is uncontroversial for him to assume that p is in fact the first thing that pops into his head and if in addition all else is equal.

However, in each of these cases there is a potential complication. To illustrate this, consider the case involving Jones's testimony. Suppose, as is not unlikely, that although S thinks that Jones's testimony is in fact reliable, he, on reflection, would *not* think that the argument (Jones says that p; thus, p) is sufficiently likely to be truth preserving, since he, on reflection, would think that there are many relevant possible situations in which Jones's testimony is not reliable. If so, then contrary to what I assumed above, the proposition that Jones says that p does not by itself tend to make p epistemically rational for S. Nevertheless, it in conjunction with the proposition that Jones is highly reliable presumably does. In other words, presumably the argument (Jones says that p, Jones is highly reliable; thus, p) is one that S, on reflection, would think is truth preserving in a sufficiently large percentage of possible situations even if the simpler argument (Jones says that p; thus, p) is not. But then, the point at issue here can be made with respect to this more complex argument. If the premises of this argument are properly basic for S and all else is equal, then p is epistemically rational for S. And even if these premises are not properly basic for S, the argument might nonetheless be a second-level argument that helps make p epistemically rational for S.

So while it is true that S, on reflection, might be disposed to think that there are effective nonargumentative means to his epistemic goal, subjective foundationalism has a way of capturing (in terms of argument) how these nonargumentative means influence what is epistemically rational for S. Subjective foundationalism has a way of incorporating these nonargumentative means into arguments.

Once it is appreciated how nonargumentative means to the epistemic goal can be incorporated into arguments, it is hard to see how the Aristotelian conception of rationality that originally motivated subjective foundationalism can be used to generate results that are at odds with the account. But in addition, there is a deeper and more interesting way of eliminating the possibility of any kind of incoherence between the two. This can be done by using the account of epistemic rationality to make more precise the very conception of rationality that underpins it. What I have in mind is this: The Aristotelian conception of rationality implies that if S has a goal X and if upon careful reflection he would believe that Y is an effective means to X, then it is rational, all else being equal, for S to bring about Y. However, the phrase "upon careful reflection he would believe" is vague here. How long must a person reflect in order for his reflection to be careful? And in what kind of reflection must he engage? Some of this vagueness can be eliminated by stipulating that the reflection in question be reflection from an epistemic point of view (where what is of concern is to have true beliefs and to avoid false beliefs about what is an effective means to the goal X) and by stipulating also that the reflection be ideal reflection (where a person is ideally reflective if further reflection would not change his mind). So suppose we make these stipulations, and suppose we give expression to them by substituting the phrase "given ideal reflection from an epistemic point of view he would believe" for the phrase "upon careful reflection he would believe" in the original Aristotelian conception. This revised, idealized conception can then be thought of as the conception that underpins the subjective foundationalist account of epistemic rationality. Subjective foundationalism tries to capture what an individual S, given ideal reflection from an epistemic point of view, would believe to be an effective means to his epistemic goal. However, once the subjective foundationalist account of epistemic rationality is in place, we can return to the revised, idealized Aristotelian conception that underpins it and makes this conception even more precise. We can use the subjective foundationalist account to make more precise the very conception that motivates it. This can be done by substituting the phrase "it is epistemically rational for S to believe" for the phrase "given ideal reflection from an epistemic point of view he would believe." With these changes, the general conception of rationality will then imply that it is rational, all else being equal, for S to bring about Y if he has a goal X and if it is epistemically rational for him to believe that Y is an effective means to X.

The idea here is that we begin with an Aristotelian conception of rationality, which implies that, all else being equal, it is rational for S to bring about Y if he has a goal X and if on reflection he would believe that Y is an effective means to X. We then revise this conception, stipulating that the relevant kind of reflection be ideal reflection from an epistemic point of view. This revised conception motivates the subjective foundationalist account of epistemic rationality. Since this account tries to specify in a relatively precise way what an individual S would believe were he ideally reflective from an epistemic point of view, it can be used to further revise the original, Aristotelian conception, so that now this conception can be expressed by saying that, all else being equal, it is rational in sense K for S to bring about Y if he has a goal X of kind K and it is epistemically rational for him to believe Y is an effective means to X. In this way, epistemic rationality becomes a constituent of other kinds of rationality. For example, what is rational for S to bring about from a prudential point of view is partially a function of what it is epistemically rational for him to believe. If S has a prudential goal X and it is epistemically rational for him to believe that Y is an effective means to X, then all else being equal it is rational in a prudential sense for S to bring about Y.

This same point applies, albeit more trivially, to epistemic rationality itself. Given that the epistemic goal is now to believe truths and now not to believe falsehoods, the revised general conception of rationality implies that all else being equal it is rational from an epistemic point of view for S to believe a proposition *p* if it is epistemically rational for him to believe that believing *p* is an effective means to his now believing truths and now not believing falsehoods. But it trivially is the case that it is epistemically rational for S to believe that his believing *p* is an effective means to the epistemic goal only if *p* is epistemically rational for S. In this way, then, any fear that the conception that motivates subjective foundationalism might be at odds with subjective foundationalism disappears altogether.

2.7   *The Purely Epistemic Point of View*

I suggested in section 2.2 that there may be conceptual reasons for why we have at least some of the epistemic standards that we do. But even if this is not so, given the general similarities in our psychological makeups and in our environments it is unlikely that the deepest epistemic standards of one person will differ radically from the deepest epistemic standards of most other people. Consequently, it also is unlikely that the kinds of propositions it is epistemically rational for one person to believe will differ radically from the kinds of propositions it is epistemically rational for most other people to believe. If, for example, propositions about physical objects or propositions about other people's psychological states are epistemically rational for some of us, it is unlikely there are many other people for whom such propositions are never epistemically rational. However, this is not to say that more moderate differences will not be common. On the contrary, they will be. Often a proposition *p* will be epistemically rational for a person *S* while its negation not*p* will be epistemically rational for another person *R*. If in such a situation *S* believes *p* and *R* believes not*p*, it can be tempting for *S* and *R* each to charge that the other is being irrational, despite the fact that each such charge is incorrect. Indeed, whenever there is a difference of opinion, it can be tempting for the parties involved to try to explain away the disagreement by each claiming that the other is being irrational. And this is so even when the disagreement is the result of differences in the evidence available to the parties. One may have talked to people to whom the other has not, seen things that the other has not, and so on.[41]

On the other hand, not all differences in what it is epistemically rational for two people to believe need be the result of differences in the kind of evidence available to them. It is at least possible for such differences to exist even though the evidence available to an individual *S* and an individual *R* is roughly the same—even though, for example, they have talked to the same people, seen the same things, and so on. It is what they do or what they would do on reflection with this evidence that differs. Given this evidence, *S* may have what he, on reflection, would regard as a good argument for *p*, while *R* may have what he, on reflection, would regard as a good argument for not*p*. If so, *p* is epistemically rational for *S* and not*p* epistemically rational for *R*, despite the fact that they have been exposed to roughly the same evidence. In such cases, it can be especially tempting for each person to charge the other with believing a proposition that is not epistemically rational. It is especially tempting because from each person's perspective the other is believing a proposition that is false, and perhaps even obviously false, and is doing so despite having access to the relevant evidence.

Moreover, even though in such cases the charges of *epistemic irrationality* are incorrect, it need not be inappropriate for the individuals involved to engage in *epistemic criticism* of one another. It need not, for example, be inappropriate for *S* to charge that *R* is not believing that which it is best for a person with his (*R*'s) evidence to

believe insofar as he wants to believe truths and not to believe falsehoods. In particular, it is not inappropriate for S to charge that a
person with R's evidence is likely to do a better job of satisfying his
epistemic goal were he to believe *p* instead of not*p*. Of course, S here
will be disposed to make this charge just because given his (S's) perspective—specifically, given his epistemic standards—the evidence that
R has constitutes a good argument for *p*. From this, it in no way
follows that R does not have an equally good argument from his
perspective—given his own epistemic standards—for not*p*. Indeed, it
is worth remembering that by hypothesis R's *deepest* epistemic standards—that is, the arguments that R would find sufficiently truth
preserving were he ideally reflective—imply that not*p* is likely given
his evidence. So by hypothesis no further consideration that would
occur to R on reflection would convince him that S is right in thinking
that such evidence makes *p* likely. But despite this, S's criticism of R
nonetheless is a legitimate kind of epistemic criticism. It is a criticism
of R in terms of R's own epistemic goals, albeit not from R's own
epistemic perspective. It is a criticism that implies that R has not
effectively pursued his epistemic goals, given his evidence.

In a similar way, it is possible to evaluate a person's beliefs, and
to evaluate them epistemically, not from that person's own perspective
but rather from the perspective of most people who share his culture,
or from the perspective of the best scientists, or from the perspective
of his intellectual peers, or from the perspective of yet some other
group. In order for such evaluations to be epistemic, it must be that
the person's beliefs are measured against the standard of how good
a job they do of realizing his goal of now believing truths and now
not believing falsehoods. But in making such evaluations, instead of
adopting an internal perspective, where we describe what means the
person S himself, on reflection, would regard as effective to reach his
goal, we instead adopt an external perspective, where we describe
what means we or what means the best scientists or what means the
people in some other group would regard as effective to reach this
goal were they in something like S's position. In particular, we make
use not of the arguments S would regard as sufficiently truth preserving but rather of the arguments the members of this external group
regard as sufficiently truth preserving. We then go on to describe what
conclusions such people could argue for were they to have seen roughly
what S has seen and were they to have talked to the people he has
talked to, and so on. We describe, in other words, what propositions
they would have had good arguments for, given their epistemic standards, had they roughly the same evidence that S has.

Moreover, it can be perfectly appropriate for the rest of us to evaluate S's beliefs in this way even if S is a radical skeptic who on reflection would regard relatively few arguments as sufficiently likely to be truth preserving. In so evaluating his beliefs, we in effect would be judging that with respect to the goal of his believing truths and not believing falsehoods it is best for him not to take a skeptical attitude. We would be judging that a person in his position, one who has had the sensory experiences that he has had, would better satisfy his epistemic goal by believing various propositions about the external world, the past, and the future than by not believing them.

It is helpful to think about these points in terms of a notion of the purely epistemic. To describe what it is rational for S to believe from a purely epistemic point of view is to describe what S himself from his own perspective on reflection would believe to be an effective means to his epistemic goal of now believing truths and now not believing falsehoods. It is easy enough as well as altogether appropriate to depart from this purely epistemic point of view in order to evaluate S's beliefs from other points of view. Indeed, theoretically there is no limit to the number of viewpoints other than the purely epistemic one from which S's beliefs can be evaluated. Nevertheless, these viewpoints can be categorized. Since the purely epistemic point of view is made up of two components—first, the epistemic goal of S's now believing truths and now not believing falsehoods and, second, what S from his perspective on reflection would take to be an effective means to this goal—departures from the purely epistemic point of view can be categorized in terms of whether they alter the first of these components or the second or both.

If only the first of these components is altered, S's beliefs are evaluated from his own perspective on reflection but with respect to goals other than the epistemic one. His beliefs, for instance, might be evaluated with respect to his prudential goals or perhaps with respect to his total constellation of goals. Since these evaluations are made from S's own perspective on reflection, they are evaluations of the rationality of S's beliefs, albeit not the epistemic rationality of these beliefs. (See sections 1.1, 2.6, and chapter 5.) So, if given S's own perspective on reflection, his beliefs seem to be effective means to his prudential goals, then these beliefs, all else being equal, are rational for him in a prudential sense, even if they are not epistemically rational for him. Similarly, if given this perspective, his beliefs seem to promote effectively his total constellation of goals, then these beliefs, all else being equal, are rational for him in an overall sense.

By way of contrast, if the second of the above components is altered and S's beliefs are evaluated with respect to S's epistemic goal but from a perspective other than S's own, then these evaluations, given what I have said so far, are not to be construed as evaluations of the rationality of S's beliefs.[42] Nevertheless, it is perfectly appropriate to make such evaluations. It is perfectly appropriate, that is, to evaluate S's beliefs using the epistemic standards of most scientists or his peers or the members of some other group. In making such evaluations, we take the propositions that S believes and then criticize them by comparing them to the propositions that the members of one of these groups would have good arguments for had they been in something like S's position. Likewise, it can be appropriate to alter both of the above components, such that S's beliefs are evaluated with respect to some nonepistemic goal and from some perspective other than S's own.

There is nothing wrong about evaluating S's beliefs from points of view other than the purely epistemic one—from perspectives other than his own or with respect to goals other than the epistemic one. At least there is nothing wrong with this as long as we do not forget what we are doing. In particular, it is important not to forget that with respect to a practical goal or from an external perspective it can seem appropriate for S to believe a proposition p that from his own perspective seems obviously false (either because not$p$ is properly basic for him or because not$p$ is the conclusion of an argument that is uncontroversial for him). Thus from a purely epistemic point of view it is inappropriate for him to believe p even if there are various other points of view from which believing p is altogether appropriate.

There are points of view other than the few already mentioned from which S's beliefs also can be evaluated. Indeed, there theoretically is no limit to the number of such viewpoints. There is no limit to the number of perspectives from which his beliefs can be evaluated and no limit to the kinds of goals with respect to which his beliefs can be evaluated. We can make distinctions among perspectives and among kinds of goals as fine-grained as we find convenient. However, two goals with respect to which the beliefs of an individual can be evaluated deserve special mention. First, an individual S's belief can be evaluated with respect to a goal that is relatively similar to the epistemic goal of now believing truths and now not believing falsehoods, only it is more demanding. It is the goal of believing all propositions with the appropriate degree of confidence. The goal is concerned not just with believing what the evidence warrants and not believing what the evidence does not warrant (believing that and only that for which there is a good argument), but in addition, with believing everything with the exact degree of confidence that the evidence warrants.[43]

Again, there is nothing inappropriate about evaluating the confidence with which S believes various propositions, although perhaps a bit of pessimism is warranted both about the chances of success in developing an account of the exact degree of confidence with which people should believe various propositions and about its interest as a standard by which to evaluate the everyday attitudes people have toward propositions. The important point is that evaluations of a person's degrees of belief differ from purely epistemic evaluations. Indeed, nothing precludes the possibility that each and every one of S's beliefs is correct with respect to the purely epistemic standard (that is, every proposition he believes is either properly basic for him or is made epistemically rational for him by propositions properly basic for him), while each and every one of S's beliefs is incorrect with respect to this more demanding standard (that is, every proposition he believes is believed with at least a slightly inappropriate degree of confidence).

What this illustrates, in turn, is that the two standards reflect different goals. The goal implicit in the more demanding standard is concerned with an individual believing propositions with appropriate degrees of confidence. However, with respect to any given proposition there presumably are infinitely many degrees of confidence with which an individual can believe the proposition. Accordingly, with respect to any given proposition, an individual satisfies the goal in question only if he believes that proposition with the exact degree of confidence, out of the presumably infinitely many possible degrees of confidence, that is the most appropriate one, given his evidence. The epistemic goal is considerably simpler. It is to believe a proposition if it is true and not to believe it if it is false. So, the range of options is pared down to three. With respect to any given proposition, there are three fundamental options—one can believe it, disbelieve it, or withhold on it. Accordingly, with respect to any given proposition, one satisfies the epistemic goal just in case one's attitude toward the proposition is the one attitude out of the three relevant attitudes that is the most appropriate one, given his evidence. (Cf. chap. 1, note 33.)

The second kind of goal that deserves special mention is what might be called a "diachronic" goal. The epistemic point of view is concerned with the goal of S now having true beliefs and now not having false beliefs. This goal is a synchronic goal, one that concerns only the present time-slice. But all of us have diachronic goals as well. We want not just to do well at the present moment; we also want to do well over time. This applies to our intellectual goals as well as to our practical goals. In particular, most of us want or need to have true beliefs and not to have false beliefs not just now; we also want or need this at future times as well, if only because we think this will help us obtain our future nonepistemic goals. However, insofar as *S* does want or need this and insofar as he, on reflection, would believe that the regular use of some belief-acquisition method M will maximize his chances of satisfying this goal, then it is rational, all else being equal, for him to use this method to acquire beliefs. Accordingly, it also will be rational, all else being equal, for him now to believe *p* if this is what M recommends in the current situation. This will be rational relative to his long-term goal of believing truths and not believing falsehoods.[44]

This long-term goal might also be combined, or constrained, by other kinds of goals. For example, the long-term goal of believing truths and not believing falsehoods might be constrained by an interest in acquiring truths that will be useful. From this viewpoint the idea would be to use a method of belief acquisition that is likely to yield not just truths per se but in addition truths that are themselves usable or that have a good chance of guiding our investigations toward other truths that are. Indeed, the work done in many areas of science seems to presuppose an interest in a complex goal of roughly this sort. Accordingly, a promising suggestion concerning how to interpret talk of "scientific rationality" would be in terms of such a goal. Given this suggestion, the scientific point of view (or at least one scientific point of view) would differ from the epistemic point of view not only by being concerned with a diachronic goal (where what is of interest is to find a method that eventually will lead one to truths) but also by being concerned with a practical goal (where what is of interest is to find usable truths). This practical aspect of the scientific point of view may help explain why so many philosophers of science endorse the notion that it is rational, all else being equal, to accept the simpler of two theories—the simpler one is likely to be easier to use. Analogously, the diachronic aspect of the scientific point of view may help explain why so many philosophers of science endorse the notion that it is rational, all else being equal, to accept the more fertile of two theories—the theory that is more likely to generate promising research projects is more likely to lead us eventually to truths.[45]

Not surprisingly, it also is possible to evaluate *S*'s methods of belief acquisition and his resulting beliefs with respect to the long-term goal of believing truths (with or without the practical constraint that the truths be usable) and from an external perspective. We or the community of scientists or some other group can decide that given what we regard as reliable methods and given that S has a long-run goal of believing truths and not believing falsehoods, it is appropriate for him to use some belief-acquisition method M. Hence, we also can conclude in a particular situation that it is appropriate for him to believe proposition p, since this is what he would believe were he to use M.

Indeed, once we adopt this kind of diachronic goal, where the goal in terms of which we are evaluating S's beliefs is the long-term goal of his believing truths and not believing falsehoods, and once we also adopt an external point of view, we in effect have adopted the point of view taken by those who defend so-called reliabilist accounts of rational belief. What such reliabilist accounts suggest, in broadest terms, is that S rationally believes p only if his belief p is the result of his using a reliable method of belief acquisition,[46] or alternatively is the result of his having an intellectual virtue, which, roughly, is a stable disposition to acquire truths.[47] In the terminology I have been using, what such accounts are expressing is the idea that with respect to the goal of S in the long run having true beliefs and not having false beliefs and from an external perspective, it seems appropriate for S to use method M (or to have a stable disposition to use M), since M is a method that we or most scientists or (in the limiting case) omniscient observers regard as reliable. Accordingly, if in some particular situation S would believe p were he to use M, it is appropriate in this reliabilist sense of him to believe p.

Once again, there is nothing wrong about evaluating S's beliefs from such a reliabilist viewpoint, especially since if he is anything like most of the rest of us S will want to have intellectual virtues. He will want to build habits that result in his having stable dispositions to acquire truths. But in making such evaluations, it again is important not to forget what we are doing. We are evaluating S's beliefs from some perspective other than his own and with respect to a goal other than the epistemic one. In particular, it is important not to forget that although from the external perspective of most people or most scientists or an omniscient observer, M may seem to be an obviously effective means to S's long-term goal of believing truths and not believing falsehoods, it is possible that from S's perspective M may seem to be an obviously ineffective means to this long-term goal. A fortiori, although from such an external perspective it may seem appropriate for S to believe p, since this is what he would believe were he to use method M, p from S's perspective may seem obviously false. In particular, not$p$ may be properly basic for S or not$p$ may be the conclusion of an argument that is uncontroversial for S. But then, from S's perspective and with respect to the goal of his now believing truths and now not believing falsehoods, it is not appropriate for him to believe p. It is not, in other words, epistemically rational for him to believe p.[48]

2.8   Different General Conceptions of Rationality

The purely epistemic point of view, I have said, consists of two components, one having to do with the kinds of goal at issue and the other having to do with the perspective from which an individual's attempts to secure his goal are to be evaluated. The epistemic goal is that of now believing truths and now not believing falsehoods, and the epistemic perspective is that of the reflective individual himself. It is from this point of view, I have claimed, that judgments concerning the epistemic rationality of a person's beliefs are to be made. But why need this be so? Why are such judgments to be made from the person's own perspective on reflection? Why not make such judgments from some other perspective, say, a more objective one? For example, why not make the propositions that are epistemically rational for a person a function of what arguments are in fact truth preserving rather than a function of what arguments he on reflection would take to be truth preserving?

Such questions, I have suggested, are to be answered by appealing to a general conception of rationality, one that I have called an "Aristotelian conception." According to this conception, it is rational, all else being equal, for a person S to bring about Y if he has a goal X and he on reflection would believe Y to be an effective means to X. Given this general conception, judgments concerning the rationality of a person's beliefs or actions are to be made from the perspective of the person himself on reflection. An account of epistemic rationality is an idealization of this conception as applied to the epistemic goal, the goal of now believing truths and now not believing falsehoods.

Having said this, however, I now want, at least partially, to take it back. In particular, I want to take back the assumption—implicit in much of what I have said—that judgments about what it is rational for a person to do or to believe are to be made only from the perspective of the reflective individual himself. I have already pointed out that it can be altogether appropriate to make judgments concerning how effectively a person is pursuing his goals from other perspectives. The point now is that such judgments often are as entitled to be construed as judgments about the rationality of a person's beliefs or actions as are judgments that are made from the person's own perspective on reflection. Moreover, there is a straightforward explanation as to why this is so. Namely, an Aristotelian conception of rationality is not the only plausible general conception of rationality, and non-Aristotelian conceptions of rationality imply that a perspective other than that of the reflective individual himself is the appropriate one from which to make judgments about what it is rational for a person to do or to believe.

To illustrate this, it is helpful to identify three general conceptions of rationality, although theoretically there need be no limit to the number that might be identified. Conceptions 2 and 3 below are radical conceptions that perhaps might be more attractive were they less extreme. Even so, for the sake of having a sharp contrast among the conceptions as well for the sake of simplicity, it is preferable to leave them in a radical form.

1. The Aristotelian (or reflective subjective, or epistemic) conception: All else being equal, it is rational for S to bring about Y if he has a goal X and on reflection would believe that Y is an effective means to X.

2. The radically subjective conception: All else being equal, it is rational for S to bring about Y if he has a goal X and believes that Y is an effective means to X.

3. The radically objective conception: All else being equal, it is rational for S to bring about Y if he has a goal X and Y is an effective means to X.

None of these conceptions is clearly counterintuitive. On the contrary, each when thought about in a certain way can seem appealing.

Consider an example. Suppose S is betting on a horse race in which only three horses are entered, and suppose further he must bet on one of the horses to win and that the odds on each of the horses is the same. On which horse is it rational for him to bet, assuming that his goal is to win the bet?

The answer seems to depend on what elements in the betting situation one emphasizes. Suppose S has evidence indicating that horse A will win, evidence that he himself would acknowledge, were he to be reflective. Suppose, for example, that he has evidence to the effect that A's record is much better than the records of the other two horses, that his recent workout times are faster than those of the other two horses, and that the best jockey at the track is riding him. Then he would seem to have good reason, all else being equal, to bet on A.

Indeed, if he were to be reflective, he himself would be critical of any other bet; he would think it a mistake to bet on any other horse. And so, in accordance with conception 1, it would seem to be rational for him, all else being equal, to bet on A.

However, suppose S does not consider carefully enough the evidence he has for believing that A will win. As a result, he believes that horse B will win. In such a case, we can be critical of S for not attending to his evidence more carefully. Even so, given that he believes B will win, it seems that at least in one sense he would be acting irrationally if he were to bet on either of the other horses. For a decision to bet on one of the other horses would amount to a decision to bet on a horse that he believes will lose. And would this not be a paradigm of irrationality? If so, then in accordance with conception 2, it would seem to be rational, all else being equal, for him to bet on B.

But now, suppose that although S has good evidence for thinking A will win and although he believes B will win, in fact C will win. Then does he not have a good reason, all else being equal, to bet on C? After all, this is the only bet that actually will succeed in getting him what he wants—to win the bet. And so, in accordance with conception 3, it would seem to be rational, all else being equal, to bet on C.

Which of the three bets is the rational one for S to make? And which general conception of rationality is *the* correct one? I do not think there is an answer. Each of the conceptions is plausible. Each simply reflects a different perspective—the Aristotelian perspective, the radically subjective perspective, and the radically objective perspective—from which evaluations concerning how effectively an individual S is pursuing his goals can be made. And as the example illustrates, depending upon our purposes, interest, and so forth, any one of these perspectives (or any one of a number of other perspectives) can seem to be the appropriate one for such evaluations. If, for example, S bets on horse B, conception 2 allows us to see the reasonability of his decision, given his present (unreflective) perspective. However, by hypothesis S himself would be critical of this decision were he to have been reflective. So if we want to give expression to this sense in which S has violated his own standards, we will be drawn to conception 1. On the other hand, if we realize that neither S's actual decision nor a decision in accordance with his own standards is likely to accomplish what S wants such a decision to accomplish and if we want to give expression to this sense in which he has a reason not to make either decision, we will be drawn to conception 3.

So none of these perspectives and no other perspective is the only correct perspective from which to make judgments about what is rational for an individual to do or to believe. None constitutes a privileged perspective. Rather, judgments of rationality can be and are made from a variety of perspectives. In trying to provide a philosophical account of rational belief or rational action, it is especially important to keep this in mind, since the perspective one adopts (either implicitly or explicitly) is likely to shape one's judgments (or "intuitions") about what it is rational for an individual to do or to believe in various situations, and as a result it is also likely to shape one's account of what is involved in making such judgments. For example, when one tries to formulate an account of what it is rational for an individual to believe insofar as he has the goal of now believing truths and now not believing falsehoods, the kind of account toward which one will be inclined is likely to be shaped by which of these perspectives one emphasizes.

Thus, insofar as an epistemologist adopts something like the radically objective perspective represented in conception 3, his judgments, or intuitions, about what it is rational for people to believe in various situations is likely to incline him toward an account of rational belief that is more objective than subjective foundationalism. The most extreme move to be made in this direction is one that would collapse altogether the distinction between rational beliefs and true beliefs: Insofar as one has the goal of believing truths and not believing falsehoods, it is rational to believe all and only truths. This would represent a purely objective perspective—in effect, the perspective of an omniscient being. Short of this, one might be inclined toward an account that shrinks but does not altogether eliminate the gap between rational belief and true belief. For example, one might be inclined to emphasize, as do traditional foundationalists, the rationality of a person believing the conclusions of arguments that in fact are likely to be truth preserving. Or if one is interested in methods of belief acquisition (perhaps because one is interested not just in the epistemic goal but also in the diachronic goal of believing truths and not believing falsehoods over the long run), then from this objective perspective one might claim that a belief is rational just if it is the product of reliable belief-acquisition methods, or more generally the product of reliably functioning cognitive equipment.

Another kind of move away from the perspective adopted by the subjective foundationalist is one that emphasizes not what arguments in fact are truth preserving or what methods of belief acquisition in fact are reliable but rather the arguments that some social group takes to be truth preserving or methods of belief acquisition that some relevant social group takes to be reliable. It is best to think of any move in this direction as a move toward an intersubjective rather than an objective account of rational belief. For unless a number of dubious assumptions are made, there is no reason for thinking that most members of a social group cannot be mistaken in their judgments about what arguments are truth preserving and what methods of belief acquisition are reliable (just as the individual members of the group can be mistaken about these matters). In any event, introducing social considerations into one's account of rational beliefs is a move toward an externalist account even if it is not a move toward an objective account. Moreover, as is the case with other externalist considerations, there are a variety of ways in which social considerations might be brought into an account. For example, one might emphasize the rationality of an individual believing the conclusions of arguments that would be regarded favorably on reflection by most members of the individual's community.[49] Or instead of emphasizing the epistemic standards of the general community in a direct way, one might emphasize the rationality of an individual believing the conclusions of arguments that reflect the epistemic standards of those recognized by the general community as experts on the issue in question.[50]

Suppose, on the other hand, one is more inclined toward something like the radically subjective perspective represented in conception 2. Pushed to the extreme, this perspective might incline one to collapse altogether the distinction between belief and rational belief. Insofar as a person believes p (that is, believes that p is true) and is aware that he believes p, he presumably thinks that believing p is a more effective means to his epistemic goal than disbelieving p or withholding judgment on p. So, from the viewpoint of this goal and from a radically subjective perspective, it would be perverse for him to try to believe not$p$ or to try to withhold on p.[51] Less extreme moves in the direction of the subjective perspective have the effect of shrinking but not altogether eliminating the distinction between belief and rational belief. For example, one might adopt a position that implies each of a person's beliefs is prima facie rational, such that it is rational for a person to believe what he does as long as there is no positive reason to doubt what he believes. Some coherentist positions, for example, can be construed as endorsing this kind of idea, since some such positions seem to recommend changes in a person's beliefs only if an incoherence develops (that is, only if the rest of what a person believes gives him a positive reason to doubt something else he believes) and then only the minimum changes needed to restore coherence.[52] Likewise, some positions advocated by decision-theoretic epistemologists may be of this sort, since some such positions seem to recommend changes in the confidence with which a person believes a proposition only if it is possible to make a Dutch Book against the person (given that the person is willing to bet on the propositions he believes and is willing to give odds in proportion to the confidence he has in the truth of these propositions) and then only the minimum changes needed to avoid this possibility.[53]

Between perspectives that tend toward the radically subjective and ones that tend toward the radically objective is the Aristotelian perspective. One who is interested in this perspective and in the epistemic goal will be inclined to favor something like subjective foundationalism, or at least so I have been arguing. The way to think about this perspective is to regard it as the perspective from which it is appropriate to make judgments of rationality insofar as one is interested in exploring in an empathetic but nonetheless thoroughly critical way how well an individual is pursuing his goals. The idea is to adopt the person's own perspective but not to do so in such a wholehearted way that one ignores the possibility that were he to be reflective the person himself might be willing to admit that he has silly views about how to pursue his goals. With respect to the epistemic goal, this means we leave open the possibility that the person might have silly beliefs and that he might make silly inferences, but we nonetheless determine what constitutes a silly belief or a silly inference from his perspective rather than from our perspective or from some other external perspective. Given this approach, it is not appropriate in our evaluations of another person's beliefs to take an altogether uncritical attitude toward his current beliefs (in effect, assuming that he can do no better) or even a generally uncritical attitude (in effect, assuming that each belief is all right unless there is a positive reason for thinking otherwise). On the other hand, neither is it appropriate to evaulate his beliefs against some altogether objective standard. After all, what constitutes an effective means to his epistemic goal of now believing truths and now not believing falsehoods need not be something that an individual can read off from the world unproblematically. He need not be able to read off what is true and he need not be able to read off what methods of belief acquisition are likely to generate true beliefs. So, from an Aristotelian perspective, telling an individual to believe some claim only if his belief would be true or only if it would be the product of a reliable belief-acquisition process is altogether unhelpful. For, from an Aristotelian perspective, the interesting questions are the ones of determining from an individual's own perspective what should be regarded as true and what should be regarded as a reliable belief-acquisition method. It is equally unhelpful to tell an individual to believe some claim only if he can defend the claim in a way that would be acceptable to the best scientists, or to most members of his community. Again, the individual need not be able to read off what would be acceptable to the best scientists or to most members of his community. But even more important, from an Aristotelian perspective, the interesting question is not what the best scientists or the members of the individual's community would regard to be an effective strategy for securing his epistemic goal; it is not the question, in other words, of what they would believe were they in something like *S*'s position. From an Aristotelian perspective, the interesting questions about the best scientists and the members of *S*'s community are ones concerning whether their standards are standards that *S* should adopt and whether their opinions are ones to which *S* should defer. But these questions are ones that are to be settled from *S*'s perspective on reflection. After all, even scientists make mistakes. So, from an Aristotelian perspective, the interesting questions are ones of what the person himself from his own perspective is to make of the world, what he is to make of others' testimony, including the testimony of experts, what he is to make of current science, and so on. This is not to say, it bears repeating, that he cannot have silly views about these matters. He can have silly views about what is an effective means to his epistemic goal just as he can have silly views about other matters. It is only to say that the standards that determine which of his views are silly are his own *deep* standards; they are standards that are a function of what he would take to be an effective means to his epistemic goal, were he to be reflective. In the idealized version of this perspective, a person's deepest standards are identified, standards that are a function of what he would take to be an effective means to the epistemic goal, were he ideally reflective.

I have no argument that indicates that this perspective—the subjective reflective one—is intrinsically any more important or any more appropriate for making judgments of rationality than other perspectives. Indeed, I do not think that it is intrinsically more appropriate. It is one perspective from which such judgments can be made, but neither it nor any other perspective is the only perspective from which such judgments can be made; there is no privileged perspective for making judgments of rationality.[54] Likewise, I have no argument to show that the label "epistemic" is appropriate only for evaluations of a person's beliefs from what I have called "the purely epistemic point of view," the point of view that consists of the epistemic goal and the subjective reflective (or Aristotelian) perspective. My calling this point of view "purely epistemic" is a matter of stipulation. Although I think that this point of view is closely related to the points of view adopted (at least implicitly) by a good number of the great figures of epistemology,[55] I do not want to attach too much importance to the label. If others insist on reserving the label for evaluation from other points of view—say, an objective point of view or an intersubjective point of view—they are welcome to it. The label is of little importance. What does matter is that this point of view and the perspective associated with it be distinguished from other points of view and their associated perspectives. It is important to make these distinctions because these other points of view may well imply that it is appropriate for S to believe p even though from S's current perspective on reflection, p seems obviously false; they also may well imply that it is inappropriate for S to believe p even though from S's current perspective, on reflection, p seems obviously true. And so, if the concern is to evaluate S's beliefs with respect to the goal of his now believing truths and now not believing falsehoods (rather than with respect to the goal of his having true beliefs and not having false beliefs in a few moments or in a few days or in a few years and rather than with respect to the goal of his having beliefs that are useful) and if the concern also is to evaluate S's beliefs against the standard of what he himself, given ideal reflection, would take to be an effective means to this goal (rather than against some standard—say, an objective or an intersubjective one—that S even on ideal reflection might regard as mistaken, or that he on ideal reflection might not even be capable of grasping), then none of these other points of view is the appropriate one to adopt; the only point of view that it is appropriate to adopt is the one that I have called "the purely epistemic point of view."

Moreover, it is important to distinguish these points of view because insofar as seemingly rival accounts of rationality—for example, seemingly rival accounts of epistemic rationality—are attempting to give expression to different points of view, they are not in the strict sense rivals at all, despite a tendency to view them as such. Rather, they are accounts with different subject matters. The suspicion that this might be so, in turn, makes explicit an important thesis about rationality, a thesis implicit in much of what I have already said. The thesis is that judgments about what it is rational for an individual to do or to believe tend to be elliptical. Judgments of rationality are judgments about how effectively an individual is pursuing some goal. This is what all judgments of rationality have in common. However, such judgments are commonly elliptical. For one, they commonly fail to make explicit what goals are in question. Is the judgment a judgment about how well the person's actions or beliefs satisfy a certain kind of goal—say, a practical goal or an intellectual goal—or is it a judgment about how well these actions or beliefs satisfy his total constellation of goals? For another, judgments of rationality commonly fail to make explicit the perspective in question. Is the judgment about how effectively the person's actions or beliefs satisfy the goal (or goals) in question one that is made from an external perspective or is it one that is made from the individual's own perspective?

One consequence of this thesis is that it is necessary for any account of rationality to demarcate its subject matter—that is, to identify the kind of rationality that is the concern of the account. The way to do this is by identifying the kind of goal that is being sought and by identifying also the perspective from which the evaluation of how effectively the person is pursuing this goal is to be made. The idea is that whenever someone claims it is rational to believe some proposition (or to perform some action) and a fortiori whenever someone tries to give an account of what is involved in such claims, we are entitled to ask two questions: Rational for what, with respect to what goal? And rational from what perspective?

In doing epistemology it is especially important to take these two questions seriously, because by taking them seriously we may very well be driven to the conclusion that although subjective foundationalism, traditional foundationalism, coherentism, realiabilism, decision-theoretic accounts, various accounts of scientific rationality, and so on, at first glance seem to be rivals, perhaps in a strict sense many of them are not rivals at all. In particular, it is not altogether implausible to suggest that of these accounts perhaps only subjective foundationalism adopts what I have called "the purely epistemic point of view." As I have already suggested, reliabilist accounts, decision-theoretic accounts, and various accounts of scientific rationality perhaps are all best construed as being concerned with a goal other than the epistemic one. The suggestion is that this is the way to make the strongest case for such accounts; this is the way to see what is right about them. Construe them, for example, as being concerned with the goal of believing propositions with the appropriate degree of confidence, or with having true beliefs and not having false beliefs over the long run, or with having true beliefs that are easily used, or with some other goal distinct from that of simply now having true beliefs and now not having false beliefs. And likewise, perhaps each of the accounts (except subjective foundationalism) is best construed as attempting to describe what it is rational for a person to believe from some perspective other than an Aristotelian one. Perhaps they are best construed as adopting either a more subjective or a more objective perspective—for example, the perspective of what the person himself believes (perhaps without much thought) to be effective means to his goal or the perspective of what an omniscient being would believe to be a generally effective means.

This constitutes at least the beginnings of a meta-account of rationality; it constitutes the beginnings of an account of how best to evaluate proposed accounts of rational belief (and mutatis mutandis the beginnings of an account of how best to evaluate proposed accounts of rational action). Out of this meta-account come two recommendations, one negative in spirit and one positive. The negative recommendation is that in evaluating a proposed account of rational belief, one should not rely too heavily upon simple intuitions about what it is rational for an individual to believe in various situations. For one's intuitions about what it is rational for an individual to believe will be shaped by the point of view one implicitly adopts, and this point of view need not be the one that it is most charitable to adopt in evaluating the proposed account. The positive recommendation is that in evaluating a proposed account of rational belief, one should try to find a point of view that makes the account a plausible one. When does a point of view make an account of rational belief plausible? Think of the matter in this way. A judgment to the effect that an individual S's belief p is rational, like all judgments of rationality, is a judgment that is made from some point of view, where a point of view is defined by a goal (or goals) and a perspective. Specifically, a judgment that S's belief p is rational is a judgment made from some particular perspective that S's believing p is an effective means to some particular goal (or goals). So, if an account of rational belief implies that S's belief p is rational just in case S's belief has characteristics _____, this account will be plausible just to the extent that there is some important perspective P and some major goal G such that from perspective P S's believing p seems to be an effective (and nontrivial) means to goal G just in case S's belief p has characteristics _____. (See section 1.1.) The restriction that the goal G be a major goal is needed here to ensure that goal G is of sufficient breadth, coherence, and centrality that it is of interest to us. For example, even if S wants to have true beliefs and wants also to own a leopard, we are unlikely to be interested in an account of rational belief whose concern is judgments about whether S's beliefs effectively promote the disjunctive goal of his having true beliefs or his owning a leopard.

Similarly, the restriction that the perspective be an important one is needed because although in principle there is no limit to the number of perspectives from which judgments of how effectively an individual is pursuing his goals can be made, only a limited number of these will be of much interest to us. For instance, we are not likely to find it interesting that from the perspective of the shortest man living in Chile something Y seems to be an effective means to goal G. Indeed, if we did not in some such way restrict the number of perspectives that interest us and the kinds of goals that interest us, it presumably would be possible to find for any proposed account of rational belief some point of view that makes it plausible. For, regardless of what conditions are laid down by a proposed account of rational belief, there is likely to be some possible point of view (some combination of a weird goal and a weird perspective) such that from this weird perspective a belief p would seem to be an effective means to this weird goal just in case the conditions laid down by the account are met. The point I am making, then, is simply this: The greater the lengths that we have to go to in order to find a point of view in terms in which a proposed account of rational belief can be represented, the less plausible the account—and what is perhaps as damning, the less interesting the account.

The main thesis here is that claims of rationality—claims about the rationality of a person's actions or beliefs—tend to be elliptical, and the corresponding thesis is that such claims tend to be elliptical because they fail to make explicit the point of view from which they are made. A point of view, in turn, can be identified by identifying a goal and by identifying a perspective from which the evaluation concerning how effectively the person is satisfying the goal is made. Accordingly, one can remove the ellipsis from a claim of rationality by making explicit the point of view it presupposes.

The corollary of these theses is that any proposed account of rational belief or rational action, if it is to be plausible, must be capable of being plausibly represented as an account of judgments made from some nonweird perspective P about how effectively the beliefs or actions of an individual promote some nonweird goal G. Expressed more simply, the corollary is that any proposed account of rational belief or rational action must be capable of being plausibly represented as an account of judgments of rationality from some important point of view. This corollary in turn gives us a tool with which we can determine what, if anything, is right about various proposed accounts of rational belief or rational action. Consider, for example, proposed accounts of rational belief whose requirements differ significantly from those laid down by subjective foundationalism. If such an account of rational belief can be represented in terms of some important point of view, it will be a plausible account of rational belief, albeit not a plausible account of epistemically rational belief, which is to be represented in terms of an idealized Aristotelian perspective and the goal of now believing those propositions that are true and now not believing those propositions that are false. On the other hand, if a proposed account of rational belief cannot be plausibly represented in terms of some important point of view, it will not be a plausible account of epistemically rational belief or of any other kind of rational belief.

These remarks about the elliptical nature of claims of rationality can be illustrated by organizing the various particular notions of rationality in terms of the perspective adopted, as represented by the three general conceptions of rationality, and in terms of the kind of goals being sought (remember that depending upon our interests finer divisions might be made, both in respect to the perspective adopted and the goal being sought):

1. Aristotelian (or reflective sub-   a. Practical goal
   jective) conception   b. Epistemic goal
                                    c. Long-term intellectual goals
                                       etc.
                                       etc.

2. Radically subjective conception a. Practical goal
                                    b. Epistemic goal
                                    c. Long-term intellectual goals
                                       etc.
                                       etc.

3. Radically objective conception   a. Practical goal
                                    b. Epistemic goal
                                    c. Long-term intellectual goals
                                       etc.
                                       etc.

To return to the example of S at the race track, it is rational in sense 1a for S to bet on horse A (since given the appropriate kind of reflection he would conclude that A will win); it is rational in sense 2a for S to bet on horse B (since he believes that B will win); and it is rational in sense 3a for S to bet on horse C (since C will in fact win). On the other hand, rationality in sense 1b, or at least an idealized form of it, is described by subjective foundationalism, whereas perhaps the kind of rationality described by many traditional foundationalists is closer to sense 3b.[56] Correspondingly, perhaps the kind of rationality described by some coherentists is closer to sense 2b. The kind of rationality described by reliabilists and some philosophers of science, by contrast, perhaps is closer to sense 3c. Other kinds of rationality might be classified in analogous ways.

It is important to note also that within each of the general conceptions of rationality, the various senses of rationality identified above can be combined. For instance, since what a person believes can affect the likelihood of his achieving not only his epistemic goals but also his practical goals, one can ask what it is rational for an individual to believe when both his epistemic goals and his practical goals are taken into account. (Indeed, as I suggested earlier, it may be an interest in a combination of epistemic and practical goals that motivates much work on scientific rationality, the rough idea being that the scientific point of view presupposes an interest in the goal of acquiring beliefs that are both true and useful.)[57] Or one might ask what it is rational for him to believe, all things considered, that is, when all his goals are taken into account.

How are these combinatory senses of rational belief to be understood? Consider the Aristotelian conception of rationality, or at least the idealized version of it. How within this conception are we to understand what it is rational for a person S to believe, all things considered?

What it is rational for S to believe, all things considered, is a function of his goals, the relative value of these goals, and what S on ideal reflection would believe (what it is epistemically rational for S to believe) about how his believing or withholding on a proposition will affect the likelihood of his achieving these various goals. Suppose that what is at issue is whether it is rational, all things considered, to believe, disbelieve, or withhold judgment on a proposition p. Then, at least in the simplest cases, which of these options is rational for S, all things considered, is a function of the relative values of the affected goals and of what is epistemically rational for S to believe about the chances of obtaining these goals on each of his options (believing, disbelieving, and withholding). At least in the simplest cases then, what is rational, all things considered, is the option with the highest estimated value, where the estimated value is determined by multiplying the weighted value of the goals by the probability it is epistemically rational for S to assign to the option bringing about these goals.

What it is rational, all things considered, for S to believe on the radically subjective conception and on the radically objective conception can be determined in analogous ways. On the subjective conception, what is rational for S is a function of the weighting of S's various goals and what S believes about the chances of obtaining these goals on each of the options. On the objective conception, it is a function of the weighting of the goals and what in fact are the chances of his obtaining these goals on each of the options.

Of course, this is but a sketch—much more would have to be said. Among other things, much more would have to be said about what makes something a goal for somebody as well as about how the various goals of an individual are to be weighted. Suppose, for example, a goal is understood to be something that the person wants or needs. Then perhaps the weighting will be a function of the strength of the want or of the seriousness of the need. But if goals are understood in some other way, we would need some other weighting procedure. The important point here, however, is that whatever is the proper way to understand the goals of a person—whatever one's "theory" of goals—that notion of goal can be plugged into the above schema along with the appropriate weightings to generate a notion of what is rational for a person, all things considered.

These brief remarks concerning goals suggest a natural way in which the threefold classification of general conceptions of rationality could be made more fine-grained. (I already have noted that in principle there is no limit to the number of general conceptions that might be identified.) The three conceptions I have mentioned are generated by assuming that the person S has a goal X and then by distinguishing situations in which something Y in fact is an effective means to X from situations in which S merely believes this and distinguishing both of these from situations in which S would believe this on reflection (that is, in which it is epistemically rational for S to believe this). Other general conceptions can be generated by making analogous distinctions with respect to the goal itself. Suppose, for example, that S believes that he has a goal X and believes that Y is an effective means to X. Then, even if X is in fact not one of his goals, all else being equal, it would seem to be rational for S in one sense—a "doubly subjective" sense—to bring about Y. Similarly, if it is epistemically rational for S to believe that he has a goal X and that Y is an effective means to X, then in a "doubly epistemic" sense it would seem rational, all else being equal, for S to bring about Y. There can be mixed conceptions as well. Suppose, for example, it is epistemically rational for S to believe he has a goal X and suppose that in fact Y is an effective means to X. Then even if X is not one of S's goals and even if S neither believes nor has reason to believe that Y is an effective means to X, in one sense—in an "epistemic-objective" sense—it is rational, all else being equal, for S to bring about Y.

With a little imagination it is not difficult to see how these conceptions might be multiplied, and hence how the classification scheme might be made more complex. However, the important issue here is not a classificatory one; it is a therapeutic one. For unless one is sensitive about the point of view from which one is making judgments of rationality, one is likely to find it all too easy to argue that any proposed account of rational belief or rational action has consequences that at least appear to be counterintuitive. One can do so simply by adopting a point of view that is at odds with the point of view of the account. To be sure, the burden upon one proposing an account of rational belief or rational action is to forestall such easy objections by making explicit the point of view presupposed by the account. But correspondingly, the burden upon one evaluating an account of rational belief or rational action is to try to find a point of view that makes the account seem at least prima facie plausible. Accordingly, it is likely to be of little interest to object to, say, reliabilist accounts of rational belief on the grounds that they are committed to claiming that if an individual's belief p is the product of reliably functioning cognitive equipment, his belief p might be rational even if he does not have what he, on reflection, would take to be good reasons for thinking that p is true. Reliabilist accounts of rational belief are not accounts that are most charitably interpreted as accounts that try to assess from the person's own perspective on reflection how effectively he is satisfying the epistemic goal.

Correspondingly, criticisms of subjective foundationalism that implicitly adopt an external point of view are not likely to be very persuasive either, since the subjective foundationalist adopts the perspective of the reflective subject himself. For example, one might point out that, given subjective foundationalism, what propositions are epistemically rational for an individual is a function of what the individual himself on ideal reflection would think about the truth-preservingness of various arguments. One might then ask (rhetorically) whether an individual might not be so constituted that he would reflect wrongly. In particular, one might ask whether it might not be the case that even if an individual S were to reflect without limit on an argument A, he would irrationally persist in thinking that A is likely to be truth preserving, even though it is obvious (to the rest of us) that the argument is a terrible one. The answer to such a question is "yes, a person S might be constituted so that even if he were to be ideally reflective, he would irrationally continue to think that A is likely to be truth preserving." But given that claims of rationality and irrationality are elliptical, the subjective foundationalist need not deny that the answer to this question can be yes. He need only insist that when we judge it to be irrational for S to think that A is likely to be truth preserving, we are making this judgment not from S's own perspective but rather from our perspective or from some other perspective external to S. He need only insist, in other words, that the kind of irrationality that can be ascribed to S here is not epistemic irrationality. Again, it is important to remember that none of those considerations that convince us that A is not likely to be truth preserving are considerations that S on reflection would find persuasive; it may seem obvious to us that A is not likely to be truth preserving, but it would seem equally obvious to S on reflection that A is likely to be truth preserving.

2.9   Is Subjective Foundationalism Self-refuting?

Although the notion of epistemic rationality that I have been defending is not a radically subjective notion, it does involve important subjective elements. It adopts the perspective of a reflective subject, in the sense that what propositions are epistemically rational for a person is a function of what he believes, the confidence with which he believes what he does, and the arguments that on reflection he would think are sufficiently likely to be truth preserving. Since the account is intended as a general one, such that any proposition whatsoever that is epistemically rational for any person whatsoever, and only these propositions, meet the requirements laid down by the account, it is natural to wonder whether the subjective elements in the account create any special difficulties for defending it.

There are at least two sources of difficulty that an account of epistemic rationality might face in its own defense. The first potential problem is that any account of epistemic rationality, whether subjective or not, must allow for the possibility of it being epistemically rational for people to believe that it is an acceptable account. Thus, for example, a defender of a traditional foundationalist account must show how it is possible in a way consistent with his foundationalism to defend the adequacy of his foundationalism, and a defender of a coherentist account must show how it is possible in a way consistent with his coherentism to defend the adequacy of his coherentism.[58]

It may be tempting to dismiss as question-begging any attempt to use either traditional foundationalist doctrines in a defense of foundationalism or coherent doctrines in a defense of coherentism. But in fact, this is the least we should expect from traditional foundationalists and coherentists.[59] The difficulties arise not from providing such defenses but rather from being unable to provide them. In particular, if the belief that an epistemic theory is an acceptable theory cannot satisfy the conditions of rational belief imposed by the theory, then the defenders of the theory face a dilemma: Either it can be after all epistemically rational for people to believe the theory, in which case the theory itself must be false (since the requirements of the theory are not satisfied by this belief), or it cannot be epistemically rational for people to accept it, in which case there cannot be good epistemic reasons to think that it is an acceptable theory.[60]

The question, then, is whether subjective foundationalism faces such a dilemma. The answer should be obvious. Nothing in the account implies that it cannot be epistemically rational for someone to think that subjective foundationalism is an adequate account. If the claims that make up the account are conclusions of arguments that are uncontroversial for a person, then it is epistemically rational for that person to believe that the account is adequate. Indeed, I think that I am such a person.

So there is no reason to think that subjective foundationalism is vulnerable to the above dilemma. However, perhaps it is vulnerable to a second kind of problem, one that is just the opposite of the first. Given the subjective nature of the account, it can be epistemically rational for a person to believe that the account is inadequate. So the account can apparently be used against itself. In particular, it is possible for people to have good arguments (according to the account itself) for thinking that the account is inadequate. And thus, it might be argued, subjective foundationalism tends in this way to be self-refuting.

By why does the possibility of an account of epistemic rationality being used against itself in this way show that the account tends to be self-refuting? Nothing in subjective foundationalism implies that it cannot be epistemically rational for someone to believe that the account is inadequate, but this is as it should be. It would be presumptuous to claim otherwise. Most true claims on most accounts of epistemic rationality are such that it is at least possible for their negations to be epistemically rational for someone. Why then should the claim that subjective foundationalism is an acceptable account of epistemic rationality be any different?

The answer is that it should not. A theory of epistemic rationality must allow the possibility that it can be epistemically rational for someone to believe the theory, but it need not and should not preclude the possibility of it being epistemically rational for someone to reject the theory.

Even so, it might be thought that there still is a problem lurking here. Suppose it is epistemically rational, given subjective foundationalism, for a person S to accept, say, a coherentist account of epistemic rationality. Suppose, in other words, that it is epistemically rational, given subjective foundationalism, for S to think that some version of coherentism identifies all and only those propositions that are epistemically rational. Suppose, moreover, that it is epistemically rational for S to believe that a proposition p coheres with the rest of his beliefs in the way that this version of coherentism requires. Then will it not be epistemically rational for him to believe p? And yet, might not there be no argument for p that is uncontroversial for him? That is, might not there be no argument whose premises are properly basic for him and whose premises in addition can be used to argue for p in a way that he, on reflection, would regard as sufficiently truth preserving? And if there is no such argument, will not subjective foundationalism once again be subject to the charge that it can be self-refuting? After all, if, given subjective foundationalism, it can be epistemically rational for S to be a coherentist, then it seems as if it could be epistemically rational, according to subjective foundationalism, for S to believe what coherentism recommends rather than what subjective foundationalism recommends.

However, this worry is unfounded. The way to see that it is unfounded is to remind ourselves that in situations where it is epistemically rational for S to accept coherentism and to accept also that proposition p coheres with the rest of what he believes, S either has a good (subjective foundationalist) argument for p or he does not. Suppose he does. Then there is no worry about subjective foundationalism being self-refuting, since the recommendations of the coherentist and the subjective foundationalist with respect to p are identical—both recommend that S believe p. On the other hand, suppose that S does not have a good (subjective foundationalist) argument for p. Then again there is no worry about subjective foundationalism being self-refuting, since under these conditions p is not epistemically rational for him, even if it is epistemically rational for S to believe both that a coherentist criterion of epistemic rationality is adequate and that coherentism recommends p—even if it is epistemically rational for S to believe that p is epistemically rational for him. How is this possible? It is possible because a falsehood can be epistemically rational for S. In particular, it can be epistemically rational for S to believe that p is epistemically rational for him without p in fact being epistemically rational for him. In this case, for example, it is epistemically rational for S to believe this falsehood because it is epistemically rational for him to believe both that coherentism successfully identifies just those propositions that are epistemically rational and that coherentism implies that p is epistemically rational for him. But at least one of these claims is false.

There is, however, a complication. Suppose we assume that because it is epistemically rational for S to believe that coherentism is an adequate account of epistemic rationality, it also is epistemically rational for him to believe that propositions that cohere in an appropriate way with the rest of what he believes are likely to be true. Will it not then be epistemically rational for S to believe p, given that it is epistemically rational for him to believe that p coheres in the appropriate way with the rest of what he believes? Ordinarily, p will be epistemically rational for S in such a situation. But even so, there again is no real difficulty. Compare the situation with one in which it is epistemically rational for S to believe both that a certain kind of second-level argument is likely to have a true conclusion and that he has such a second-level argument for p. In such situations, p ordinarily will be epistemically rational for him, and this second-level argument will help make it so. (But there are exceptions—see note 37.) Ordinarily, in such situations, S will have a good first-level argument for p by virtue of having a good first-level argument for the claim that this second-level argument for p is likely to have a true conclusion. Analogously, if it is epistemically rational for S to believe that coherentism recommends p and that what coherentism recommends is likely to be true, then ordinarily p will be epistemically rational for S,[61] and coherentism will help make it so. For it is by virtue of having a good first-level argument—that is, a good subjective foundationalist argument—for the claim that what coherentism recommends is likely to be true that S has a good first-level argument for p.

Thus, there is no real difficulty. There is no difficulty, that is, with it being epistemically rational, given subjective foundationalism, for a person S to believe both that some other account of epistemic rationality is adequate and that as such the propositions it picks out as rational are highly likely to be true. For insofar as it is epistemically rational for S to believe this, the other account can play a secondary, albeit important, role in making propositions epistemically rational for S (just as second-level arguments can play such a secondary, albeit important, role). Indeed, any account of epistemic rationality, at least any account that allows there to be rational but false beliefs, encounters the same phenomenon. For instance, it in principle ought to be possible on coherentist accounts for a person S to rationally believe that a traditional foundationalist account is adequate. And insofar as this is possible, it ought also to be possible on a coherentist account for foundationalist principles to play a secondary role in making propositions rational for S—in much the way that coherentist principles, traditional foundationalist principles, and the like can play such a role in a subjective foundationalist account.

2.10 Subjective Foundationalism and Relativism

According to the subjective foundationalist, it is epistemically rational for an individual to believe p just if there is an argument for p that is uncontroversial for him. But as the writings of Thomas Kuhn, Paul Feyerabend and many others suggest, what arguments a person finds uncontroversial are likely to be a function of the culture in which he lives (where culture is understood in a suitably broad sense).[62] If this is so, then, given subjective foundationalism, what is epistemically rational for a person is also likely to be relative to his culture. Accordingly, it seems as if subjective foundationalism commits one to a form of epistemic relativism.

Whether or not this is so depends upon what is meant by "relativism." If by "relativism" one merely means that various cultural factors influence what propositions are epistemically rational for a person, then subjective foundationalism does commit one to epistemic relativism. But then it is hard to see how any plausible account of epistemic rationality could fail to be relativistic, if for no other reason than that a person's culture can affect what he hears, sees, and so forth. On the other hand, if by "relativism" one means something considerably stronger—if, say, one means that the criteria that determine what it is epistemically rational for people in one culture to believe need not be the same as the criteria that determine what it is epistemically rational for people in another culture to believe—then subjective foundationalism is not relativistic. To the contrary, it implies that the same criteria of epistemic rationality are to be used for evaluating the beliefs of every person in our culture as well as the beliefs of every person in every other culture that ever has been, now is, or will be. If a proposition that a person believes is to be epistemically rational for him, it must either be properly basic for him or it must be made epistemically rational for him by what is properly basic for him. Thus, the account in this sense is as nonrelativistic, or as categorical, as an account of epistemic rationality can be.

On the other hand, the account is subjective. It implies that what it is epistemically rational for a person S to believe is a function of what he believes, the confidence with which he believes what he does, and the arguments that on reflection he would regard as sufficiently likely to be truth preserving. And of course, insofar as these subjective factors are influenced by cultural factors, cultural factors influence what it is epistemically rational for S to believe. However, the interesting question is not the classificatory one of whether the presence of these culturally influenced, subjective factors makes the account a relativistic one. The interesting question is whether one has a reason to be suspicious of arguments that otherwise would be uncontroversial for him, given that his opinion of these arguments (and what he would think of them were he to be reflective) has been culturally influenced and given that he realizes this. The interesting question, in other words, is whether the relativism here, if that is what it is, is a destructive, internal kind of relativism—a relativism that encourages skepticism.

However, it is difficult to see why the mere belief that our culture inclines us to favor certain kinds of arguments should in itself give us a reason to be suspicious of these arguments, a reason that would prevent their conclusions from being epistemically rational for us. Analogously, it is hard to see why the mere belief (if we have such a belief) that our genetic makeup inclines us to favor certain kinds of arguments in itself should give us a reason to be suspicious of these arguments. Indeed, many of us may have good epistemic reasons (that is, good subjective foundationalist reasons) to believe that our culture and our genes are epistemically benevolent. We may have good epistemic reasons, in other words, to believe that our genes and our culture influence our beliefs and our epistemic standards in such a way that truths rather than falsehoods are likely to be epistemically rational for us. For example, perhaps many of us may have good epistemic reasons to believe that the processes of natural selection have influenced our beliefs and our epistemic standards, that these influences tend to be survival-enhancing, and that they would not be survival-enhancing if they did not incline us to believe truths. But if so, we have good epistemic reasons to believe that our genes are epistemically benevolent.

Moreover, there is a more general reason for thinking that our culture and our genes are epistemically benevolent. Or at least this is so if we suppose that most of the propositions that are epistemically rational for us are propositions that we realize are epistemically rational for us, and if we suppose in addition that it is epistemically rational for us to believe that cultural and genetic factors are at least partially responsible for our having the beliefs, dispositions, and so on that make these propositions epistemically rational for us. For then it also is epistemically rational for us to believe that these factors are epistemically benevolent, since the propositions that these factors cause to be epistemically rational for us are propositions that it is epistemically rational for us to regard as true. But if so, we need not be worried that our epistemic standards are culturally and genetically influenced; their being so influenced need give us no reason to be suspicious of them. On the contrary, we have reasons for thinking that these influences are epistemically benevolent.

But do not arguments such as these beg the question? Do they not presuppose that we have reasons to think that the conclusions of arguments that we are inclined to favor (on reflection) are true? But should we not be looking for an independent reason for trusting such arguments?

No. At least we should not if we are to be subjective foundationalists. For insofar as subjective foundationalism is an acceptable account of epistemic rationality, every epistemic reason to believe a proposition must be a "subjective foundationalist reason," a reason that is generated by virtue of the person having an argument that is uncontroversial for him. Analogously, we might ask of a coherentist, what reasons are there for thinking that propositions that cohere are likely to be true? Insofar as the reason that is being requested here is supposed to be an epistemic reason, the coherentist had better supply a coherentist reason if he supplies a reason at all. Otherwise, his answer will presuppose the inadequacy of coherentism.

None of this is to say, however, that it is impossible for facts about cultural relativity or our genetic makeup to give us a good reason to be suspicious of arguments that otherwise would be uncontroversial for us. If, for example, we had good reasons to think that the people in another culture do not make many of the inferences that we are inclined to think unproblematic and if in addition we had good reasons to think that they are in as good a position as we to decide whether such inferences are likely to be truth preserving, then we might very well have a reason to be suspicious of these inferences and of the arguments that recommend such inferences. An argument based on considerations of this sort, if plausible, might very well provide us with a reason (albeit perhaps not a decisive reason) to be suspicious of arguments that we otherwise would be inclined to find unproblematic. Indeed, this kind of argument from cultural relativity might even provide us with a reason to be suspicious of the argument itself, for it too might be a kind of argument that people in this other culture might find problematic. Thus this kind of argument from cultural relativity might tend to undercut itself; it might tend to generate suspicions even about itself. This is not to say, however, that the skeptical implications of the argument can be dismissed for this reason. An argument does not itself have to be uncontroversial to keep other arguments from being uncontroversial, and this is exactly what an argument from cultural relativity *might* do. It might ensure that there is relatively little that we can argue for in an uncontroversial way.

This is not an objection against subjective foundationalism, however. It only illustrates that, given subjective foundationalism, it is possible for there to be situations in which relatively little is epistemically rational for us. But this is as it should be. It is implausible for an account of epistemic rationality to imply that regardless of the circumstances it is epistemically rational for our beliefs to be comprehensive—for example, to be about as comprehensive as they are now. And one kind of circumstance in which it might not be epistemically rational for us to have as comprehensive a belief system as we now have is a circumstance that involves radical cultural relativity with respect to epistemic standards.

Fortunately, this is not our situation. Among the cultures with which we are familiar, there is general agreement about what constitutes acceptable kinds of inferences and what does not. So, for example, among the cultures with which we are familiar, there is broad agreement about the general reliability of memory, about our sense-experiences generally being a good guide to what physical objects there are in our immediate environment, about the past behavior of physical objects being a good guide to their future behavior, and so on. To be sure, there may be some areas of disagreement. However, it is important not to exaggerate these differences.[63] For any culture that we know anything about, these areas of disagreement are outnumbered by the areas of agreement. Indeed, were there not this huge background of agreement concerning what are acceptable arguments (or inferences), it is difficult to see how we (or beings similar to us) could come to understand what differences there are between another culture's "conceptual scheme" and ours.[64] Accordingly, nothing that we now know about the variety of cultures here on earth gives us any general reason to be suspicious of the arguments that we in our culture are inclined to favor. Nothing that we know, in other words, encourages a destructive, internal kind of relativism.[65]

What then is the worry here? Is it the worry that there *could be* —that it is possible for there to be—a culture (or a genetic makeup) that influences beings like us to have epistemic standards radically different from those we have? But even if we grant that this is possible, what does this show?[66] Does it show that we have a reason to be suspicious of our standards, of the arguments that our culture and our genetic inheritance (we are assuming) have inclined us to favor? No. It does show that it is possible for cultural and genetic factors to influence beings similar to us in such a way that most of the arguments they are inclined to favor are not likely to be truth pre-serving. But from this it does not follow that we have a reason to be suspicious of the arguments we are inclined to favor. The mere pos-sibility that we might be wrong in regarding these arguments as truth preserving is not enough to give us a reason to be suspicious of them.

There is no denying that genetic and cultural factors influence what we believe, what we believe with confidence, and what arguments we on reflection would find acceptable. There also is no denying that the propositions we believe with confidence might be false and that the arguments we on reflection regard as truth preserving might not be truth preserving. However, it is equally important to remember that although our having beliefs that are for the most part true is the goal we are seeking insofar as we are trying to be epistemically rational, our having beliefs that are for the most part true is not a prerequisite of our being epistemically rational. Our beliefs can be epistemically rational even if many, perhaps even most, of them are false. This is one of the lessons to be learned from the demon hypothesis and the brain-in-the-vat hypothesis. Even if an evil demon manipulates us so that most of our beliefs are false, such manipulation does not in itself guarantee that any, much less most, of those beliefs are epistemically irrational.

Similarly, it is possible that our history, our culture, or our genetic inheritance have influenced us in such a way that the propositions that we regard as obviously true are not true and the arguments that we regard as obviously truth preserving are not truth preserving. But this in no way implies that it is not epistemically rational for us to believe the conclusions of arguments that are uncontroversial for us. What arguments are uncontroversial for us are historically, culturally, and genetically conditioned. Had we a different history or a different culture or a different genetic inheritance, we might not have thought that such arguments were effective means to the epistemic goal of believing truths and not believing falsehoods. But such means are nonetheless *our* means. We cannot be certain that using such means will generate beliefs that are mostly true. This is just part of the human predicament, and any adequate account of epistemic rationality must recognize it. It must recognize, in other words, that what it is epistemically rational for a person to believe is a function of his historically conditioned and culturally conditioned and genetically conditioned and admittedly imperfect perspective.

3

EPISTEMIC RATIONALITY
AND TRUTH

3.1 Reliabilism and Epistemic Rationality

Epistemic rationality is distinguished from other kinds of rationality by its truth-directed goal. The goal is for one now to believe those propositions that are true and now not to believe those propositions that are false.

However, to say that the goal that helps distinguish epistemic rationality from other kinds of rationality is a truth-directed goal is not to say that truth is a prerequisite of epistemic rationality. In particular, it is not to say that it is impossible for what is epistemically rational to be false, and likewise it is not even to say that it is impossible for most of what is epistemically rational to be false. Nevertheless, epistemologists have had a tendency to presuppose that there must be some sort of intimate link between rational belief and truth. For example, Descartes can be interpreted as having assumed that it cannot be rational for us to believe what is clear and distinct unless propositions that are clear and distinct for us are true; this assumption prompted him to try to prove that God would not allow us to be deceived about what is clear and distinct. Similarly, Hume can be interpreted as having assumed that it cannot be rational for us to believe the conclusions of inductive arguments unless most such conclusions are true; this assumption prompted him to try to prove the uniformity of nature.

Contemporary philosophers also have displayed a tendency to presuppose that rational belief is intimately linked with truth. For example, Alvin Goldman defends a view that he calls "historical reliabilism," which implies that a belief is rational only if it is the result of a belief-forming process that is reliable. And since not every proposition that is rational for a person is believed by the person, Goldman proposes an analogous view concerning the propositions it is rational for a person to believe. He says that a proposition is rational for a person to believe only if there is available to him a reliable belief-forming process that if used would result in his believing the proposition.[1] Similarly, Marshall Swain claims that a person S rationally believes p only if S has cognitive characteristics such that, given those characteristics, his believing p on the basis of reasons r is a reliable indicator that p is true.[2] Ernest Sosa claims that the most promising way of understanding rational beliefs is as beliefs that are the products of intellectual virtues, where an intellectual virtue is understood in terms of the person having a stable disposition to acquire truths.[3] And William Alston claims that a belief is rational only if it is acquired or held in such a way that beliefs of that sort are reliable.[4]

Suppose we assume that these philosophers are offering accounts of epistemically rational beliefs. This may well be not the most charitable way to interpret them. (See section 2.8.) Nevertheless, for the sake of discussing the relationship between epistemic rationality and truth, let us assume (at least temporarily) that each of the above suggestions is a suggestion about epistemically rational belief. Then each of these suggestions implies that there is some sort of logical, or conceptual, tie between what is epistemically rational and what is true. The exact nature of this tie depends upon what it takes for a belief-forming process to be reliable, or what it takes to have a stable disposition to acquire truths. For example, is a belief-forming process reliable just if it has produced mostly true beliefs, or just if it will in the long run produce mostly true beliefs, or just if it would produce mostly true beliefs in situations relevantly similar to our actual situation, or what? I will have more to say about this problem of explication shortly, but for now let us consider positions that imply the thesis that if one gathered into a set each proposition it is epistemically rational for a person now to believe, it would be impossible for the set to contain more falsehoods than truths. Or at least let us consider positions that imply the thesis that this is so provided that the set of propositions that are epistemically rational for the person is relatively large. This proviso allows the possibility of there being situations in which relatively little is epistemically rational for an individual but in which the few propositions that are epistemically rational for him are mostly false. What the thesis precludes is this being the case when the set of epistemically rational propositions is relatively large—when, say, it is approximately as large as the set of propositions that we take to be rational for us. And along with this thesis, let us consider an analogous thesis concerning what a person now rationally believes, as opposed to what now is rational for him to believe—the thesis that it is impossible for more of what a person now rationally believes to be false than true, provided again that the set of his rational beliefs is relatively large.[5]

Since these theses imply that what we now rationally believe, or what it is now rational for us to believe, must be a reliable indicator of what is true, any account of epistemic rationality that implies such theses can be regarded as a version of reliabilism. Moreover, for the moment I also will assume that any account of rational belief that does not imply such theses should not be regarded as a reliabilist account. After all, if an account does not imply such theses, it allows the possibility that most of what an individual rationally believes might be false, and on the face of it this does not seem like a possibility that a reliabilist account should allow. Even so, I later will discuss variations of these reliabilist theses—counterfactual variations and the like—that do not imply these basic reliabilist theses.

In (temporarily) restricting reliabilist accounts of rational belief to ones that imply one of the above theses, my use of the term "reliabilism" is narrower than the usual. But in other respects it is broader. The term often is reserved for positions that focus upon the process that causes a person to believe a proposition (or the process that causally sustains his belief). However, here I want to distinguish the reliability component of such accounts from the causal component. The advantage of doing so is that this makes obvious that an account of rational belief might require most epistemically rational beliefs to be true without also requiring epistemically rational beliefs to have some appropriate kind of causal history. So, for example, consider an account that implies that a belief is epistemically rational just if it is supported by adequate evidence, where adequate evidence in turn is understood in such a way that necessarily most beliefs supported by such evidence are true. An account of this sort can plausibly be regarded as a reliabilist account, since it implies that most rational beliefs are true; it implies, in other words, that the set of rational beliefs reliably indicates what is true. But it is not a causal account, because it does not require a belief to have had an appropriate causal history in order to be epistemically rational. (See chapter 4.)

My use of the term "reliabilism" is weak in another way. It does not require that the connection between truth and epistemic rationality be terribly intimate. In particular, it does not require that a large percentage of rational beliefs be true; it only requires that more propositions that are epistemically rational for us, or more propositions that we rationally believe, be true than false.

Nevertheless, insisting upon even this very weak connection between epistemic rationality and truth is incompatible with the version of subjective foundationalism that I have been defending. Given subjective foundationalism, what propositions are epistemically rational for a person is a function of what propositions are properly basic for him and what propositions these properly basic propositions tend to make rational. There is no requirement that properly basic propositions be true or even mostly true. Likewise, there is no requirement that the propositions made rational by properly basic propositions are mostly true or even that they would be mostly true were the properly basic propositions true. Accordingly, what reliabilism takes to be impossible, subjective foundationalism allows. It allows the possibility that more propositions that are epistemically rational for us are false than are true. Likewise, it allows the possibility that more propositions that both are believed by us and are epistemically rational for us are false than are true.[6] Moreover, it is right to allow for these possibilities.

Consider one way of illustrating the reason for this. Consider a world in which we believe, seem to remember, experience, and so forth, just what we in fact believe, seem to remember, experience, and so forth, but in which our beliefs are often false. Suppose further that in this other world the confidence with which we believe and the clarity with which we seem to remember and the intensity with which we experience is identical with the actual world. Suppose even that what we would believe on reflection (about, say, what arguments are likely to be truth preserving) is identical with what we would believe on reflection in this world. So if we somehow were to be switched instantaneously from our situation to the corresponding situation in this other world, we would not distinguish any difference regardless of how hard we tried. To use the familiar example, suppose a demon ensures that this is the case. Call such a demon world w and then consider this question: Could some of the propositions that we believe in w be epistemically rational for us? The answer is yes. If we are willing to grant that in our world some of the propositions we believe are epistemically rational, then these same propositions would be epistemically rational for us in w as well. After all, world w by hypothesis is one that from our viewpoint is indistinguishable from our own.

Of course, in one sense this is not a particularly surprising result. But in another sense, it can seem somewhat surprising. Notice that the possibility of there being such a world w follows from the fact that our being in the epistemic situation in which we are is compatible with our world being w. This fact in no way shows that it is not epistemically rational for us to believe what we do. But, and this is what might seem somewhat surprising, if the mere possibility of our world being a demon world is not sufficient to defeat the epistemical rationality of our believing what we do, then neither should the actuality. Even if, contrary to what we believe, our world is world *w*, it still can be epistemically rational for us to believe many of the propositions we do, since the epistemic situation in world *w* is indistinguishable from the epistemic situation in a world that has the characteristics we take our world to have.

The point here is a simple one. In effect, I am asking you: Are not some of the propositions we believe epistemically rational for us to believe? And would not whatever it is that makes these propositions epistemically rational for us also be present in a world where these propositions are regularly false but where a demon hid this from us by making the world from our viewpoint indistinguishable from this world (so that what we believed, and what we would believe on reflection, and what we seemed to remember, and what we experienced were identical to this world)? The intuitive answer is yes. The intuitive answer, in other words, is that although the demon's deceits may deprive us of truths, they need not also deprive us of a chance of being epistemically rational; they need not make it impossible for us to have epistemically rational beliefs.

Moreover, this answer illustrates something concerning the way we think about epistemic rationality. Namely, we think that what it is epistemically rational for a person to believe is a function of what it is appropriate for him to believe given his perspective. More exactly, what it is epistemically rational for an individual to believe is a function of what it is appropriate for him to believe given his perspective and given that one of his goals is to believe truths and not to believe falsehoods. Reliabilist theses of epistemic rationality are unacceptable precisely because they do not sufficiently emphasize this element of perspective. They imply that it is impossible for our beliefs to be epistemically rational if they are not reliable. And they imply that this is so regardless of what our perspective might be—even if, for example, it is indistinguishable from our current perspective.

So demon worlds and the like can be used to generate an antireliabilist lesson. The possibility of there being such worlds illustrates that subjective foundationalism is right in allowing the possibility that more of what we rationally believe might be false than true and is right also in allowing the possibility that more of what it is rational for us to believe (regardless of what we do in fact believe) might be false than true. Correspondingly, it illustrates that reliabilist theses are wrong insofar as they imply that these are not genuine possibilities.

Moreover, this antireliabilist lesson can be drawn even if it is not assumed, as I have above, that many of the propositions that we believe are epistemically rational for us to believe. For convenience, I have made this assumption, but the lesson here can be illustrated without it. Strictly, all that is needed is the assumption that what we take to be our epistemic situation is such that it would make some of what we believe epistemically rational for us if it did obtain. We no doubt think that we have good arguments for many of the propositions we believe, and no doubt we often do. And if we do, these propositions are epistemically rational for us. But our judgments about whether we have a good argument for a proposition, and hence our judgments about whether it is epistemically rational for us to believe a proposition, are not infallible. And so, given what is properly basic for us and given what arguments are uncontroversial for us, it is at least possible that only a few of the propositions we believe can be defended. Even so, reliabilist theses about epistemic rationality are still implausible, since if we were to have good arguments for these propositions, they would be epistemically rational for us. Moreover, they would be epistemically rational even if a demon ensured that most of them were false. And this is enough to illustrate the implausibility of this kind of reliabilism.

This same lesson, moreover, applies to variations on what I have been calling "reliabilism," variations that need not imply that more of what we rationally believe, or more of what is rational for us to believe, must be true than false. Consider, for example, a position implying the thesis that over the long run more beliefs that are epistemically rational must be true than false. This variation does not rule out the possibility that the set of our current rational beliefs might contain more falsehoods than truths, but it does rule out the possibility that the total set of propositions that we now rationally believe or have rationally believed or will rationally believe might contain more falsehoods than truths.

But again, this is not really impossible, and a demon situation once again can be used to illustrate this. It is possible for there to be a world in which we are under the control of a demon who ensures that much of what we believe or have believed or will believe is false, and it also is possible for this demon to ensure that such a world from our viewpoint is, has been, and will be indistinguishable from the actual world. So if we now have good arguments for some of the propositions we believe, we would also have good arguments for these propositions in the demon world. And if we will have good arguments for what we will believe, or did have good arguments for what we did believe, this also would be the case in the demon world. Any proposition that we either did rationally believe or are now rationally believing or will rationally believe is a proposition we would rationally believe in the demon world as well. But by hypothesis, in the demon world more of these propositions are false than true.

So, reliability over the long run is not a prerequisite of epistemic rationality. Similarly, reliability in close counterfactual situations is not a prerequisite of epistemic rationality. For example, consider the thesis that the set comprised of the propositions we now rationally believe plus the propositions we would rationally believe in close counterfactual situations must contain more truths than falsehoods. According to such a thesis, it again is possible for the set of propositions that we now rationally believe to contain more falsehoods than truths. What is impossible is for the set of propositions that we either do rationally believe or would rationally believe in close counterfactual situations to contain more false beliefs than true beliefs.

But once more, this is not really impossible; the set comprised of both our rational beliefs and the rational beliefs we would have in close counterfactual situations might very well contain more falsehoods than truths. Moreover, this might be so even if most of our actual rational beliefs are true. Imagine a world in which there is a demon who in fact does not interfere with us but who is (and was) prepared to do so had this demon world been even a little different from what it is. In particular, imagine that the percentage of rational beliefs that are true in such a world is no different from the percentage of rational beliefs that are true in this the actual world, since the demon does not interfere with us in this demon world. Moreover, suppose that what we in this demon world experience, seem to re-member, believe, would believe on reflection, is the same as in the actual world. Nonetheless, in this demon world the set comprised of the propositions we rationally believe plus the propositions we would rationally believe in close counterfactual situations might very well contain more false beliefs than true beliefs, since by hypothesis the demon was (and is) prepared to interfere had this world been even a little different.

Neither of these variations on what I have regarded as the basic version of reliabilism is any more plausible than the basic version itself. The set of our current beliefs need not contain mostly truths. And the same holds for the set of our rational beliefs over the long run and the set of rational beliefs we would have in close counterfactual situations. None of these reliabilist theses about epistemically rational belief is acceptable.

This is not to say, however, that there are no nonepistemic senses of rational belief for which reliability is a prerequisite. Indeed, in sections 2.7 and 2.8, I already have admitted that there are. For instance, if one adopts a diachronic goal, such that one is interested in true beliefs over the long run and if in addition one adopts an externalist perspective, it might be appropriate to say that with respect to this goal and from this perspective, S rationally believes p only if his belief is the product of a belief-forming process that is reliable over the long run. However, it is possible for S in this sense to rationally believe a proposition for whose negation he now has a good argument. And thus, from his perspective and with respect to the goal of his now believing truths and now not believing falsehoods—that is, from a purely epistemic point of view—it need not be appropriate for him to believe this proposition. In other words, it need not be epistemically rational for him to believe this proposition. So, the "only" point I am insisting upon here is that although one can define senses of rational belief for which reliability is a prerequisite, these senses of rational belief must be distinguished from the purely epistemic sense of rational belief, for which reliability is not a prerequisite. The point is that any account of rational belief that makes reliability a prerequisite of rational belief is an account that is not most charitably interpreted as an account of epistemically rational belief. (See section 2.8.)

3.2   Evil Demons and Brains in a Vat

Is there anything suspicious about using evil-demon examples or brains-in-a-vat examples or other such bizarre examples to illustrate how truth and epistemic rationality can come apart? Descartes would have thought so, for he thought that God would not allow us to be deceived about what is epistemically rational for us. For Descartes, this meant that God would not allow us to be deceived about what is clear and distinct for us. A fortiori, God would not allow most of what is clear and distinct for us to be false. If we grant that God necessarily exists, it then follows that it is impossible for there to be a situation in which most of what is clear and distinct for us is false. It is impossible, for example, for there to be an evil demon who regularly deceives us about what is clear and distinct, and likewise it is impossible for us to be brains in a vat who are regularly prompted to have false beliefs even about that which is clear and distinct. Accordingly, evil-demon examples and brains-in-the-vat examples cannot be used to illustrate that it is possible for most of what is epistemically rational for us to be false.

Even if we grant that it is clear and distinct that God exists, there is much that can be questioned about this line of reasoning, not the least of which is that it does not seem altogether clear and distinct that God would not permit us to be regularly deceived about what is clear and distinct. But suppose we waive this difficulty and just grant that Descartes was right in arguing that God would not allow us to be regularly deceived about what is epistemically rational (even if he was wrong in claiming that only what is clear and distinct can be epistemically rational). What does this show about subjective foundationalism? The answer is that it shows very little. Given this Cartesian assumption, a reliabilist thesis about epistemically rational belief is acceptable. However, this does not in any way imply that subjective foundationalism is unacceptable, for on this assumption reliabilism is not incompatible with subjective foundationalism. Originally it seemed important to illustrate the implausibility of reliabilist theses about epistemically rational belief, since nothing about subjective foundationalism seemed to rule out the possibility that much of what we rationally believe might be false. But if Descartes' assumption is accepted—if it is assumed that God would not allow us to be regularly mistaken about what we rationally believe—there is after all something about subjective foundationalism that rules out this possibility. Subjective foundationalism is an account of epistemically rational belief; insofar as it succeeds in picking out epistemically rational beliefs, it also succeeds, given the Cartesian assumption, in picking out beliefs that are mostly true.

Seen in this light, it is easy to appreciate that the Cartesian assumption makes a reliabilist thesis about rational beliefs true but uninteresting as a test by which to judge the adequacy of an account of epistemically rational belief. It is true because, given this assumption, it is impossible for more of what we rationally believe to be false than is true; it is uninteresting because, given this assumption, a proponent of almost any kind of account of epistemically rational beliefs can endorse reliabilism, even proponents of accounts that initially would seem at odds with reliabilism, such as subjective foundationalism.

The same kind of lesson applies to positions defended by some contemporary philosophers. What I have in mind are the positions defended by those who claim that it is impossible for there to be situations in which more of our beliefs or at least more of our simplest, most psychologically basic beliefs—for example, simple perceptual beliefs, simple memory beliefs, simple introspective beliefs, and so on—are false than are true.[7] This is not to suggest that it is impossible for there to be situations, or worlds, in which there are, say, no tables, no chairs, no trees, and in which an evil demon prompts people to have the beliefs that they do. Likewise, it is not to say that it is impossible for there to be worlds in which there are only brains in a vat hooked up to a computer. What is not possible, such philosophers claim, is for us with the beliefs we now have about tables, chairs, and trees, to be in the clutches of such a demon, or for us with the beliefs we now have to be brains in a vat hooked up to a computer. For, they say, in such situations it would be impossible for us to have beliefs about tables, chairs, and trees.

The reason this is supposed to be impossible has nothing to do with the nature of God, as Descartes would have claimed. Rather, it has to do with the nature of belief. The claim is that what we believe is not so much a function of our entertaining certain thoughts and having the appropriate attitudes of assent toward these thoughts. It is more a function of that with which we interact in our environment.[8] Thus, suppose an evil demon ensures that people do not causally interact with tables, chairs, and trees. He ensures that these things never cause people to have the experiences they do. So, he ensures that they never see these things, never touch them. Whenever they have a visual experience or a tactile experience, it is the demon who causes the experience and never a real table or a real chair. Under these conditions, it is claimed, people cannot have beliefs about real tables, chairs, or trees. Similarly, if instead of people with bodies who interact with tables, chairs, trees, there are only brains in a vat hooked up to a computer, then these brains in the vat cannot have beliefs about such common objects. On the other hand, they may very well have beliefs about the electronic impulses produced by the computer or about the computer's program, since they do interact with these things. These are the things that cause the brains in the vat to have the experiences they do, and these are things to which the brains in the vat react.

The claim is that although at first glance it may seem as if it is possible for there to be evil-demon situations and brains-in-the-vat situations in which we believe the same propositions that we do now but in which more of these propositions are false than are true, this is in fact impossible. Our thinking that it is possible rests on a mistaken internalist view about beliefs and an associated mistaken internalist view about reference. In particular, it rests on the mistaken assumption that "qualitative similarity (amounting, if you like, to qualitative identity) between the thoughts of the brain in the vat and the thoughts of someone in the actual world . . . implies sameness of reference."[9] What goes on in our brains and what goes on in the brains in the vat may be exactly the same, but what we believe and what the brains in the vat believe nonetheless may be radically different.

This is but a very rough sketch of a way of thinking about the nature of belief and reference, but even this rough sketch is enough to indicate how controversial such a view is. However, rather than pursuing the question of the plausibility of this view, I propose simply to assume, as I did with the Cartesian view, that such a view is plausible, or at least could be made plausible. In other words, I will assume that it really is impossible for more of our beliefs, or at least more of our simplest, most psychologically basic beliefs, to be false than true. I do this because even if this view is correct, it does not affect the plausibility of subjective foundationalism.

There are two reasons why this is so. First, even if it is impossible for more of our beliefs, or more of our simplest beliefs, to be false than true, it does not follow that it is impossible for more of our rational beliefs, or more of our rational simple beliefs, to be false than true. For not everything we believe is something we rationally believe. Normally, the set of propositions we rationally believe is a proper subset of the set of propositions we believe. So, even if the latter must contain more truths than falsehoods, this is no guarantee that the former must as well.

Suppose, however, that this point is waived, and we just assume that a reliabilist thesis must be true if it is impossible for more of our beliefs to be false than true. Let us just assume, in other words, that the percentage of our beliefs that are rational is sufficiently large that the set of our rational beliefs, like the total set of our beliefs, must contain more true beliefs than false beliefs.[10] Does this then create difficulties for subjective foundationalism? No; it creates no more difficulty than does the Cartesian assumption, for this assumption, like the Cartesian, makes subjective foundationalism compatible with reliabilism. According to subjective foundationalism, what it is epistemically rational for people to believe is a function of what they believe, the confidence with which they believe what they do, and the arguments they on reflection would regard as sufficiently truth preserving. At first glance, there seemed to be nothing in this view to imply that most propositions that we rationally believe have to be true. So the view seemed to be incompatible with reliabilism. This is what made it important to show that reliabilism is false. But if the above assumption is accepted—if it really is impossible for most of what we believe to be false and hence also impossible for most of what we rationally believe to be false—there need be no incompatibility between subjective foundationalism and reliabilism. Insofar as subjective foundationalism succeeds in picking out beliefs that are rational, it also succeeds, given this assumption, in picking out beliefs that are mostly true. Once this assumption is granted, there is no reason why a proponent of subjective foundationalism cannot also be a proponent of reliabilism. Indeed, given this assumption, there is no reason why a proponent of almost any account of epistemically rational belief cannot be a proponent of reliabilism. Accordingly, this assumption, like the Cartesian, makes reliabilist theses about rational belief true but uninteresting as a test by which to judge the adequacy of accounts of epistemically rational beliefs; almost anyone properly can claim to be a reliabilist.[11]

All this, of course, hinges on the assumption that it really is impossible for more of our beliefs (or more of our simple beliefs) to be false than are true and hence also impossible for more of our epistemically rational beliefs to be false than are true. I am skeptical about this assumption. And if this skepticism is warranted, then what I claimed earlier still stands: Reliabilism is implausible, and demon examples and the like illustrate its implausibility. But if this skepticism is not warranted, reliabilism is uninteresting. Either way there is not much to recommend reliabilist theses about epistemically rational belief.

Even so, this is not to say that considerations of reliability are altogether unimportant epistemically. On the contrary, insofar as a person believes what is epistemically rational for him, he believes what he on reflection would think it is appropriate for him to believe insofar as his goal is to have true beliefs and not to have false beliefs. Reliability in effect is his goal. The point I have been making is that although this is the goal of one who tries to be epistemically rational, it is not a prerequisite of his being epistemically rational. One can believe just what a person who is seeking to have true beliefs and not to have false beliefs should believe, given his perspective, and yet still be often mistaken, whether through the intervention of a demon or for some more prosaic reason.

3.3   Why Should We Be Interested in Being Epistemically Rational?

Reliability, then, is not a prerequisite of epistemic rationality. But if it is not, can the theory of epistemic rationality be of much help in developing an adequate account of knowledge? After all, at first glance it would not seem implausible to think that reliability is in some appropriate sense a prerequisite of knowledge. And if it is, this might raise the suspicion that epistemic rationality is not a prerequisite of knowledge.

But suppose it is not. Suppose that it is possible for S to know p without his belief p being epistemically rational. What of interest follows from this?

Very little follows that is of interest for the theory of epistemic rationality. It may follow that the notion of knowledge is somewhat less interesting than is sometimes thought, since given this assumption a person can know p without having what he on reflection would take to be a good argument for p. On the other hand, what does not follow is that subjective foundationalism is in any way inadequate as an account of epistemic rationality. Such an account may be only marginally useful in developing an account of knowledge, but if this is so, so be it. The emphasis here is not to provide an adequate theory of knowledge, but rather an adequate theory of epistemic rationality. By its very nature, an adequate theory of epistemic rationality must be an internalist theory, one that seeks to describe from the person's own perspective what it is appropriate for him to believe insofar as he is interested in believing truths and not believing falsehoods. The theory of knowledge, in contrast, is at least partially an externalist theory; it seeks to describe all the conditions, both internal and external (such as that the belief be true and presumably other external conditions as well) that have to be met in order for a person to know something.

Almost everyone agrees, of course, that the conditions of epistemic rationality, whatever they might be, can be met without all the conditions of knowledge being met—for example, S's belief p can be epistemically rational without p being true. However, the suggestion under examination now is that the reverse also holds, that S can know p without his belief p being epistemically rational. But if this is so, and I think that perhaps it is, it does not indicate that there is anything implausible about subjective foundationalism. It indicates only something about the nature of knowledge—that it is not as closely linked with epistemic rationality as is sometimes thought.

Consider a case in which it perhaps is plausible to think that a person knows *p* without his belief *p* being epistemically rational. Consider, in particular, an extreme case—the case of chicken-sexers who, it is claimed, are able to determine reliably the sex of very young chicks but who are not aware of any distinguishing marks on the basis of which they are able to do this. Although they are able to distinguish male chicks from female chicks, they cannot describe to themselves or to others how they do this. Nor can they teach others to do it, for they do not have a conscious technique to teach. They simply pick up each chick, and after a moment or two, by some process that they themselves do not understand, they become convinced either that the chick is male or that the chick is female. And they are almost always right.

It can be questioned whether there really are chicken-sexers who meet this description, although some people testify that there are. It may be, for instance, that these chicken-sexers in fact are aware of some mark that can be used to distinguish the sex of the chicks but that they claim otherwise, perhaps for reasons of job security. And of course, if they are aware of such a mark, then their beliefs about the sex of the chicks that they handle may very well be epistemically rational for them. But for the sake of discussion, let us suppose that this is not so, or at least let us suppose that this need not be so. Suppose that there is, or at least that there might be, one chicken-sexer who is able to determine reliably the sex of very young chicks, despite being unaware of any such distinguishing marks. Suppose further that this chicken-sexer has no inductive evidence that his past beliefs about the sex of the chicks usually have been correct, and suppose he has no other reason to think his beliefs have been correct. He has never been told, for instance, whether he has been right in his judgments about the sex of the chicks; he simply picks up a chick, he waits for the belief that it is male or the belief that it is female to arise in him, he puts the chick down, and he never finds out whether he is right or not. But in fact, he almost always is right. Moreover, since he has correctly identified the sex of chicks a huge number of times, his being right almost certainly is not merely an accident. Even so, the chicken-sexer has no good argument indicating, for example, that the chick now in his hand is male. Yet he does believe this, and the process by which he has come to believe this, whatever this process may be, is a process that consistently produces true beliefs.

It is not implausible to claim that such a chicken-sexer somehow, in a way that neither he and perhaps no one else understands, knows that the chick in his hand is male. However, the proposition that the chick in his hand is male need not be epistemically rational for him. It need not be properly basic for him; it need not be the case, for example, that on reflection he would think that in most relevant possible situations in which he believes such propositions, his beliefs are true. Likewise, the proposition here need not be made epistemically rational for him by propositions that are properly basic for him. And so, if we grant that the chicken-sexer here knows that the chick in his hand is male, we are granting that it is possible for a person to know a proposition that it is not epistemically rational for him to believe.

But is it really plausible to claim that the chicken-sexer here *knows* that the chick in his hand is male? One way of trying to show that this is not plausible is to raise the possibility that the knowledge of the chicken-sexer is not propositional knowledge. It might be argued, for example, that although the chicken-sexer knows how to pick out male chicks from female chicks, it does not follow from this that, say, he knows that the chick now in his hand is male.[12]

The problem with this response, however, is that it is far from clear in cases such as the chicken-sexer that knowing-that does not follow from knowing-how. To be sure, there is a distinction between knowing-that and knowing-how. Witness the person who knows how to tie a Windsor knot in his necktie without knowing that one does so by first making sure that the thick end is longer and then grasping the thick end, placing it over the narrow end, and so on. However, one not implausible way to think about chicken-sexer cases and the like is in terms of there being a certain range of cases, of which the chicken-sexer case is but an extreme one, in which knowing-how does imply knowing-that. Very roughly, we might say that if an individual knows how (perhaps in a way that neither he nor others understand) to generate correct beliefs as answers to a certain kind of question and if in some particular case he in fact does generate a correct belief in answer to such a question—say, the belief that p is true—then he knows *that p*. Moreover, this is so whether the kind of question to which the individual knows how to generate correct answers and the mechanism that he uses to generate these answers are familiar ones (say, questions about what one did this morning, where one's memory is used to generate correct answers) or whether the questions and mechanisms are less familiar, as in the chicken-sexer case. Likewise, this is so whether the answers that the individual knows how to generate are epistemically rational for the individual (as many of the pronouncements of memory presumably are)[13] or whether, as I have stipulated in the chicken-sexer case, they are not. But if all this is so, then it is possible for an individual to know a proposition that it is not epistemically rational for him to believe.

This possibility is not in itself particularly troublesome for the theory of epistemic rationality, but it is interesting for what it suggests about the nature of knowledge. And what it suggests is that knowledge cannot be understood, as it has had a tendency to be understood since Gettier's 1963 article in *Analysis,* in terms of rational true belief plus some other condition. Although these conditions may very well be sufficient for knowledge, they are not necessary.

However, drawing such a conclusion from this example or other similar examples may be somewhat hasty, for strictly speaking what such examples illustrate is that knowledge cannot be understood in terms of rational true belief plus some other condition if the kind of rational belief being referred to is epistemically rational belief. There are other senses of rational belief, and perhaps a belief being rational in one of these other senses is a necessary condition of knowledge, even if its being epistemically rational is not. Moreover, if it really is the case that reliability is in some sense a prerequisite of knowledge, it is not unnatural to wonder whether some reliabilist sense of rational belief might not be a necessary condition of knowledge. Consider, for example, a reliabilist sense of rational belief that implies that S rationally believes p just if his belief p is caused by a reliable belief-forming process. Let us for the moment ignore the problem of what makes a belief-forming process reliable, and let us just assume that the chicken-sexer's belief is reliably produced. We then could say of the chicken-sexer that he not only knows the chick in his hand is a male but also rationally believes this. Accordingly, the chicken-sexer case could not be used to show that knowledge need not involve rational true belief. It could only be used to show that knowledge need not involve belief that is epistemically rational.

No doubt there is a hint of verbal hocus-pocus about this maneuver. Even so, there is nothing inherently wrong with appealing to such a reliabilist sense of rational belief in an attempt to preserve the traditional analysis of knowledge.[14] At least there is nothing wrong with this as long as we remember what we are doing. Specifically, it is important to remember that in this sense of rational belief, a person—

such as the chicken-sexer—can rationally believe a proposition *p* even though *p* is not properly basic for him and even though nothing that is properly basic for him indicates that *p* is true. In this sense of rational belief, a person can rationally believe *p* even though from his perspective there are no epistemic reasons to think that *p* is true. Thus, even if knowledge does require this kind of rational belief, it is not the kind of rational belief that implies that the person from his perspective now has an argument indicating that what he believes is true. It is not an epistemic sense of rational belief. Rather, this sense of rational belief merely indicates that somehow the person is capable of forming true beliefs about, say, the sex of young chickens. It does not imply that he is aware that he has this ability, or that there are reasons for him to think that he has it. All it implies is that he has it.

All this is somewhat beside the point, however, since any attempt of this sort to preserve the traditional analysis of knowledge as rational true belief, where rational belief now means beliefs that are the products of a reliable belief-forming process, will be inadequate. Being the product of a reliable belief-forming process may be an important ingredient in a set of conditions sufficient for knowledge; chicken-sexer cases and the like may illustrate this. But even if this is so, nothing like this is a necessary condition for knowledge.

When I say "nothing like this" is a necessary condition of knowledge, I mean that the problem here is not one of formulation. It does not matter whether we understand a reliable belief-forming process to be one that is statistically reliable for most people, or one that is statistically reliable for the believer himself, or one that is counter-factually reliable. It does not even matter if we alter somewhat the reliabilist's central idea, replacing it with the idea of cognitive equipment that is functioning in the way it was designed to function.[15] All these notions have in common the idea that a belief is an instance of knowledge only if it is a true belief that has an appropriate causal history—only if, that is, it is a true belief that is the product of an appropriate cognitive process. They differ only in what they understand the appropriate cognitive process to be. However, all these views are implausible insofar as they purport to be offering not only sufficient but also necessary conditions of knowledge. A person's belief *p* can be an instance of knowledge even if it lacks an "appropriate history," whether this appropriate history be understood in terms of reliable cognitive processes or in some other way.

I propose to postpone until section 4.3 the defense of this claim, since what is of primary interest here is not the analysis of knowledge but rather the relation between truth and epistemic rationality. And if what I have been saying about this relationship is plausible, one might wonder why we should be interested in being epistemically rational. After all, I have said that reliability is not a prerequisite of epistemic rationality. It is possible for more of the propositions that are epistemically rational for us to be false than are true. Thus, there is no guarantee that by being epistemically rational we will do any better with respect to believing truths and not believing falsehoods than we would by believing what the ouija board tells us or by deciding what to believe by the flip of a coin. There is even no guarantee that we are likely (in an objective sense) to do better. And to make matters worse, I have said that we need not be epistemically rational in order to have knowledge. So why be interested in epistemic rationality?

A full answer to this question would involve reference to nonepistemic considerations, since there are good nonepistemic reasons to be epistemically rational. (See section 5.3.) But in addition, there is at least a partial answer that does not depend on nonepistemic reasons. It is this: We as humans have certain goals, and yet by the very nature of our situation there normally is no guarantee that the means we choose to achieve these goals will be effective. And this is so no matter how much time we might spend deliberating about these means. The lack of such a guarantee, however, does not imply that we should abandon systematic efforts to achieve our goals and that we should proceed instead in a random fashion—say, deciding how to proceed by a flip of the coin. And it does not imply that we should give up pursuing these goals altogether. It only implies there is no guarantee that our attempts to pursue our goals by what on reflection we would regard as the most promising means in fact will turn out any better than if we had flipped a coin.

Suppose, for example, that we go to the race track and there gather information that indicates to us that our best bet is on Fool's Gold; his workout times consistently have been better than any of the other horses in the race, the most successful jockey at the track is riding him, the only other horse of his quality has an injured hoof, and moreover the odds on him are better than on any other horse. We reflect upon these considerations and decide that insofar as we have the goal of winning money, it is best to bet on Fool's Gold. Is this decision rational? The answer is clear: In one straightforward sense, this is rational;[16] if we are going to bet at all, it is rational to bet on Fool's Gold. But is there any guarantee that Fool's Gold will win? Again the answer is clear: No. Is there any guarantee that by betting in accordance with information that on reflection we think that we can trust we as a rule will do better than we would do by drawing lots to decide how to act? Yet again, the answer is clear: There is no such guarantee. Why then should we rely on the information we have and bet on Fool's Gold? One perfectly good answer is: Because it is rational to do so.

The situation is essentially no different with epistemic rationality. If someone asks why we should be interested in being epistemically rational, one perfectly good answer is that insofar as we have the goal of now believing truths and now not believing falsehoods, it is rational for us to be epistemically rational. Indeed, this is trivially so. Of course, there is no guarantee that by believing what is epistemically rational for us we will effectively satisfy our epistemic goal. Moreover, there is no guarantee that believing what is epistemically rational for us is a more effective way of satisfying our epistemic goal than is deciding what to believe by a flip of a coin. But this just is part of the human predicament. Typically, there is no guarantee that what we on reflection would think to be an effective means to our goals will yield better results than a flip of the coin or some other random method. But what are the alternatives? If we do not altogether give up pursuing our goals, we have the choice of pursuing them in a way that on reflection we would judge to be effective or pursuing them in a way that on reflection we would judge not to be effective. Insofar as we are rational we opt for the former.

4

EPISTEMIC LUCK

4.1 Epistemic Rationality and the History of a Belief

According to the subjective foundationalist account of epistemic rationality I have been defending, a proposition p is epistemically rational for a person S just if either p is properly basic for S or propositions that are properly basic for S constitute the premises of what S on reflection would regard as a good argument for p. If under these conditions S believes p, then he is believing what it is appropriate for him to believe from an epistemic point of view. In this sense then, his belief that p, as well as the proposition p, is epistemically rational for him.

This notion of epistemically rational belief is thoroughly ahistorical. In order for a belief to be epistemically rational, it need not have been caused in an appropriate way or in any other sense had an appropriate history. Of course, its history might be important in a secondary way, since it might not have had all those characteristics that make it epistemically rational had its history been different. However, having had a specific sort of history is not a prerequisite of the belief being epistemically rational. If S now has an adequate argument for a proposition that he believes, then regardless of what led him to have that argument or that belief, S's belief is epistemically rational.

Thus, just as subjective foundationalism implies that there is no necessary link between a belief being epistemically rational and its being true, so too it implies that there is no necessary link between a belief being epistemically rational and its having an appropriate causal history. Indeed, the same kinds of situations that were used to illustrate the separation of truth and epistemic rationality also can be used to illustrate the separation of epistemic rationality and historical considerations. Consider a pair of situations. In one, suppose that S

has a good argument for p and that he believes p. So his belief p is epistemically rational. In the second situation, suppose that S believes, thinks, experiences, seems to remember, exactly what he does in the first situation, and moreover suppose that what he would believe on reflection is the same. This second situation, then, is such that S would not be able to distinguish any difference between it and the first situation were he somehow to be switched instantaneously from one to the other.

Situations of this sort are epistemic twins. If S's belief p is epistemically rational in one situation, then it is epistemically rational in the other as well. Similarly, if in one situation his belief is not epistemically rational, it is not epistemically rational in the other either. After all, what S believes, the confidence with which he believes it, and what he would believe on reflection is the same in the two situations. So, if S has a good argument for p in the first situation, he also has a good argument for p in the second situation; and if he lacks a good argument for p in one situation, he lacks it in the other as well.

Such pairs of situations illustrate that having had an appropriate history is not a necessary condition of a belief being epistemically rational. For regardless of what historical consideration is proposed as a necessary condition of epistemically rational belief, it will be possible to imagine a pair of situations that from S's viewpoint are indistinguishable but in only one of which does his belief p meet the proposed historical requirement.[1] But if the situations are indistinguishable from S's viewpoint, then on the assumption that S has a good argument for p in one of the situations, he will have a good argument for it in the other as well. Accordingly, if his belief p is epistemically rational in one situation, it will be epistemically rational in the other as well. Thus, the proposed historical consideration, whatever it is, is not a prerequisite of S's belief p being epistemically rational.

4.2 Propositionally Rational Beliefs and Doxastically Rational Beliefs

Suppose S believes p and p is epistemically rational for him. Then, either p is properly basic for S or there is some good argument for p with premises that are properly basic for him. However, to say that S has such an argument for a proposition p is not to say that he now realizes he has this argument. Suppose this to be the case. Suppose that S as he is now, without having reflected much, does not recognize the good argument he has for p. Suppose, in particular, that although he does think he has a good argument for *p*, this argument is not in fact the one that is good. Moreover, suppose that it is this argument, and not the good argument, that prompts *S* to believe *p*.

Under these conditions, the proposition *p* is epistemically rational for *S* to believe, since he has a good argument for it. So, in believing *p* he is believing just what it is appropriate for him to believe from an epistemic point of view. Even so, *S*'s belief *p* here does leave something to be desired from an epistemic point of view. There is a sense in which *S*'s belief here is less rational epistemically than it might have been. The question is: Exactly what is this sense?

Consider some other cases in which this same question can be raised. Roderick Firth, for example, describes a case in which both Holmes and Watson have surveyed the scene of a murder. Holmes has pointed out to Watson all the crucial evidence—the footprints, the ripped piece of cloth, the position of the body. Holmes recognizes how all this evidence points to the guilt of the coachman. On the other hand, although Watson has all the evidence that Holmes has, he does not see how it indicates that it is the coachman who is the murderer. He nonetheless believes the coachman to be the murderer, perhaps because he believes that coachmen generally have criminal tendencies.[2] Similarly, John Pollock describes a man who has strong evidence that his wife has been unfaithful but who discounts this evidence and instead regards the testimony of his mother as convincing evidence of his wife's infidelity, even though his mother in the past has been noticeably untrustworthy about these sorts of matters.[3] Marshall Swain talks of a bank teller who has good evidence that she will be promoted for her competence but who nonetheless believes she will be promoted only because she believes her employers will favor her for her good looks.[4] Hilary Kornblith talks of a man who rationally believes *p* and rationally believes if *p* then *q* but who distrusts modus ponens and who is caused to believe *q* only because the sound of the sentence expressing *q* is attractive to him.[5]

Each of these philosophers claims that the person they describe lacks an important kind of rational belief. Of course, as these cases are described, it is not altogether clear that the proposition the person believes is one that is epistemically rational for him. And if it is not, it is easy to account for the irrationality in these cases—the people involved believe a proposition that is not epistemically rational for them. In Firth's case, for example, it is not clear that it is epistemically rational for Watson to believe that the coachman is guilty. Even though he has been exposed to the same evidence to which Holmes has been exposed, it is not clear that on reflection he would take this evidence as constituting a good argument for the claim that the coachman is guilty. But if he would not, the proposition that the coachman is guilty need not be epistemically rational for him.

However, in order to preclude too easy an answer to the problems that these cases raise, let us assume that the proposition at issue in each of these cases is epistemically rational for the person. Let us assume, for example, that it is epistemically rational for Watson to believe that the coachman is guilty (not on Holmes's authority— perhaps Holmes has not said whom he believes to be the murderer— but rather on the basis of the evidence to which Holmes has drawn Watson's attention). Given this assumption, the question is, what exactly is it about these cases that suggests something is epistemically wrong with the person's belief, even though by hypothesis the proposition that is believed is epistemically rational for the person? All the philosophers I have mentioned make a similar suggestion about how to answer this question. They all suggest that the people they describe lack an important kind of rational belief because their beliefs are not caused in an appropriate way by their evidence. Each of them claims that the person they describe lacks an important kind of rational belief because the belief in question lacks an appropriate causal history, where causal history is understood broadly to include not only what causally originates but also what causally sustains the belief.

Firth makes his suggestion in terms of a distinction between the propositional rationality and doxastic rationality of a belief. Firth says that in the propositional sense of rational belief, both Holmes's belief and Watson's belief that the coachman is guilty are rational, since both have evidence that support their believing this proposition. However, in the doxastic sense only Holmes's belief is rational, since only for Holmes is there an appropriate causal relation between the "evidential states" indicating that the coachman is guilty and the belief that the coachman is guilty. The exact nature of this causal relationship Firth leaves open, saying only that Holmes's belief is caused "in a way that corresponds in the appropriate way to the evidential relationships in virtue of which the belief is propositionally warranted for him" (Firth, p. 220).

For Firth then, although in the propositional sense of rational belief historical considerations are not important, in the doxastic sense they are. In the doxastic sense, a belief's having had an appropriate history is a prerequisite of its being rational.

Any such attempt to introduce a historical sense of epistemically rational belief faces a number of problems. Consider two such problems, both of which concern the nature of the causal relationship that must obtain between a person's belief and his evidence in order for the belief to have an appropriate history. The first problem arises because the person's evidence for p might cause him to believe p in a wayward manner. Ordinarily, when a person becomes aware that he has good evidence for a proposition p, this in a straightforward way causes him to believe p. But his becoming aware that he has this evidence might also cause him to believe p in an indirect way. Suppose, for example, that S's becoming aware that he has good evidence for p somehow causes him to become excited, and this in turn causes him to trip and to hit his head, which then somehow causes him to believe p. This is a case where Firth and like-minded epistemologists would want to deny that the person's belief has the appropriate kind of causal history in order to be doxastically rational. But if so, they need to provide an explication of "appropriate causal history" that rules out such wayward causation, and this will be none too easy to do.[6]

However, suppose we waive this difficulty, assuming that it can be solved somehow. Then a second problem remains. This second problem concerns how much of S's evidence for p must play an appropriate causal role in his believing p in order for his belief to be doxastically rational. Since normally the evidence required to make a proposition epistemically rational is relatively complex, it will be much too stringent to require that S reflect upon *all* the evidence needed to make a proposition p rational for him (including, for example, all the "background assumptions") and then to have these reflections cause him to believe p. It presumably also is too stringent to require that all this evidence causally contribute to his belief in some other way—for example, in an unconscious way. But if the entire body of evidence needed to make his belief p propositionally rational for S need not causally contribute to his believing p, how much of it must causally contribute to his believing p in order for his belief to be doxastically rational? It will have to be admitted, I think, that there can be no very precise answer to this question. Accordingly, it also will have to be admitted, I think, that the notion of doxastic rationality may very well be irremediably vague.

However, this is not to say that the notion is unintelligible or useless. On the contrary, the general idea Firth is trying to express is clear enough—in order for S's belief p to be doxastically rational, his belief must be propositionally rational (he must have adequate evidence for p), he must be aware at least in some rough way that he has this evidence for p, and this awareness must causally contribute (in some nonwayward manner) to his believing p. Moreover, his notion is not useless either, at least if Firth is right. For according to Firth, it is in terms of this notion that we can explain why Holmes's belief is epistemically rational in a way that Watson's is not.

Suppose, then, that all this is at least roughly on the right track. That is, suppose that the cases above illustrate the need for a richer sense of epistemically rational belief than I have so far allowed (what Firth calls "the doxastic sense"), and suppose also that these cases illustrate that in this doxastic sense having had an appropriate history is a necessary condition of a belief being epistemically rational. If all this is right, then there is no reason why this doxastic sense cannot be tacked on to a subjective foundationalist account of epistemic rationality. Subjective foundationalism implies that a proposition p is epistemically rational for S just if p either is properly basic for S or is the conclusion of a good argument that S has. S's belief p, in turn, is epistemically rational in a propositional sense just if he believes the proposition p and this proposition is epistemically rational for him. And then, following Firth's suggestion, we can say that S's belief p is epistemically rational in a doxastic sense just if the evidence that makes his belief p propositionally rational causes him (non-waywardly) to believe p. What this means, details aside, is that S believes p because he believes the premises of an argument that makes p epistemically rational for him.[7]

Thus, there is nothing in what Firth or in what others have suggested about cases such as the Holmes-Watson case that is fundamentally at odds with subjective foundationalism. Subjective foundationalism is first and foremost an account of what propositions are epistemically rational for an individual to believe—of what propositions he can argue for in an uncontroversial way. It is not first and foremost an account of epistemically rational belief. But this is not to say that various notions of epistemically rational beliefs, including a causal-historical sense (for example, Firth's doxastic sense), cannot be tacked on to the account.

Nevertheless, I do not think that it really is necessary to introduce a causal-historical sense of epistemically rational belief. For even if it is granted that Watson lacks an important kind of epistemically rational belief, it need not be granted that the explanation for this has to do with the history of Watson's belief. The same holds for the other cases. Although the people described in those cases may lack an important kind of epistemically rational belief, it need not be granted that this is due to their beliefs lacking some kind of appropriate history. For in each of those cases, the irrationality that intuitively seems to attach to the person's belief can be accounted for without citing the history of the belief in question and without citing any other causal or historical consideration.

My suggestion is that in each of the cases, there is something about the person's present beliefs that taints the epistemic rationality of his beliefs. Watson, for example, does not understand how his evidence indicates that it is the coachman who is guilty. In Pollock's case, the man does not believe that the good evidence he has for his wife's infidelity really is good evidence, and he instead takes his mother's testimony to be good evidence. Swain's teller in a similar way does not appreciate the force of the good evidence she has for thinking that she will be promoted. And in Kornblith's case, the man distrusts modus ponens. He does not think that modus ponens arguments are truth preserving, even though he would think this were he to be more reflective.

Once these failings are noticed, a suspicion arises: If the present belief systems of the people involved in these cases were not inadequate in the ways mentioned, we might not be inclined to think that the beliefs in question are in some sense epistemically irrational, and this might be so regardless of their causal histories. Notice especially that in each of the cases, the person by hypothesis has adequate evidence for the proposition he believes—he has a good argument for the proposition—but he either is unaware even in a rough sense of what this argument is or if he is aware of it he dismisses it as inadequate. In each of the cases, then, there is something wrong with the person's current belief system, and this current failing can be used to account for the sense in which each of these people lacks an important kind of epistemically rational belief.

More specifically, the failing in the current belief systems of these people can be used as the basis for introducing a richer notion of epistemically rational belief than I have so far allowed, a notion analogous to Firth's doxastic sense of rational belief but one that does not impose any causal-historical requirements. Following Firth, let us say that S's belief p is epistemically rational in a propositional sense just if he believes the proposition p and this proposition is epistemically rational for him. Then the richer but noncausal sense of epistemically rational belief—let us again follow Firth and call it "the doxastic sense"—can be introduced in terms of this propositional sense. In particular, we can say that S's belief p is epistemically rational in the doxastic sense just if (1) S's belief p is epistemically rational in the propositional sense, (2) there is an argument A that S believes is a good argument for p, (3) this belief also is epistemically rational for S in the propositional sense, and (4) argument A roughly resembles an argument that is in fact a good argument for p.

These four conditions require a number of comments. First, consider the belief mentioned in conditions (2) and (3), S's belief that he has a good argument for p. Might not this belief itself be doxastically irrational? Yes, but this need not contaminate S's belief p, preventing it from being doxastically rational. Let p^1 be the claim that S has a good argument A for p. Suppose that p^1 is true (that is, that A *is* a good argument for p) and that S believes p^1 and that p^1 is epistemically rational for S. However, suppose that S is not even roughly aware of an argument A^1 that makes p^1 epistemically rational for him. Perhaps he thinks he has a good argument B for p^1, but if so, this argument does not even roughly resemble A^1 or any other good argument for p^1. Then, S's belief p^1 is not doxastically rational. But his belief p is. In other words, there is something wrong with S's belief system here, but what is wrong concerns his belief p^1 and not his belief p. After all, by hypothesis his belief p is epistemically rational, he is at least roughly aware of an argument A that makes it so, and it is epistemically rational for him to believe that A makes it so.

Notice also that each of the above conditions (2), (3) and (4) makes use of the notion of a good argument. What for present purposes constitutes a good argument for p? It would be too stringent to require that S always be aware of an argument for p that has as its premises propositions that are properly basic for him. So let us say that the argument A that S here believes to be a good argument for p need not be a first-level argument. It might be a second-level argument. In particular, it might be an argument whose premises are not properly basic for S.[8] What *is* required is that it be epistemically rational for S to believe that the argument is highly likely to have a true conclusion. However, it cannot be p itself that makes this epistemically rational for S. Expressed in terms of a notion that I will explicate later, it being epistemically rational for S to believe that argument A is likely to have a true conclusion cannot be grounded on p itself. (See section 4.3.)

Although S does need to be aware of propositions that can be used to defend p if his belief p is to be doxastically rational, these propositions need not be properly basic for him. It is enough if the propositions roughly resemble the premises of some good argument for p, where the good argument here might be a good second-level argument for p.

But what if the proposition p that S believes is itself properly basic? Then S need not have a good argument for p in order for his belief

p to be propositionally rational. However, according to the conditions above, in order for this belief to be doxastically rational, he does need to be aware of some good argument for p. What might this argument be? It might be the argument (S believes p; thus, p). Since p is properly basic for S, it must be the case that S on reflection would think that this argument is sufficiently likely to be truth preserving; it must be that he on reflection would think that when he believes p, p is sufficiently likely to be true. And for a proposition q that is properly basic a priori for him, it must also be the case that he on reflection would think that his understanding q is itself enough to provide him with an understanding of why q cannot be false; it must be the case, in other words, that he on reflection would think that q is in this sense self-evident.

Of course, from the fact that S, on reflection, would think that p is likely to be true when he believes p, it does not follow that he now thinks this. And likewise, with respect to a proposition q that is properly basic a priori for S, from the fact that he on reflection would think that understanding q is enough to provide him with an understanding of why q cannot be false, it does not follow that he now thinks this. But, suppose that he does; suppose that he does believe (perhaps nonoccurrently) these things about p and q respectively. In addition, suppose that he believes (again perhaps nonoccurrently) that he believes p and that he believes q. Suppose finally that it is epistemically rational for S to believe all these things.[9] Then his belief p and his belief q are doxastically rational for him.

In order for S's belief p and S's belief q to be propositionally rational for him, he need not be aware of any good way to defend p and q respectively. But if these beliefs are to be doxastically rational, he does need to be aware of some good way to defend them. One way for him to be able to defend p is for him to be aware that he believes p and to be aware that p is likely to be true when he believes p, while one way for him to be able to defend q is for him to be aware that he believes q and to be aware that his understanding q is enough to provide him with an understanding of why q cannot be false.

These are not the only ways, however. S might also have some other argument for p or for q. In fact, this will often be the case. For example, suppose p is the proposition that S sees a cat on the mat, and suppose p here is properly basic for S. Even so, S might believe (at least nonoccurrently) that there are other propositions that can be used to argue for p. For example, perhaps he believes (again, at least nonoccurrently) that he is having a cat-on-the-mat kind of visual gestalt and believes also that his visual equipment is reliable. Moreover, perhaps it is epistemically rational for him to believe these propositions. Then, if in no other way, his belief p is likely to be doxastically rational by virtue of his believing these propositions, since these propositions are likely to constitute a good argument for p.

The intuitive idea here, then, is this. When a proposition p is properly basic for S, either properly basic a posteriori or properly basic a priori, S's belief p can be made doxastically rational by virtue of his having at least a rough awareness of the conditions that make p properly basic for him. But even when this is not so, his belief p nonetheless can be doxastically rational for him. For to say that p is properly basic for S is to say that S need not have an argument for p; it is not to say that he cannot have arguments, even many arguments, for p. But then, S might be aware of some such argument for p, and moreover his awareness of this argument (perhaps a second-level argument) might make his belief p doxastically rational.

The effect of this is to make it somewhat easier for beliefs about properly basic propositions to be doxastically rational. And in turn this may make it easier for an individual to have evidential knowledge of propositions that are properly basic for him. For if S is to have evidential knowledge of a proposition p, his belief p must be doxastically rational.[10]

If we set these qualifications concerning properly basic propositions aside and instead focus on propositions that are not properly basic, then what the above characterization of a doxastically rational belief suggests is that if S's belief p fails to meet any one of the four conditions comprising the characterization, then S is subject to epistemic criticism. If (1) is not met, he is subject to the criticism that in believing p he believes a proposition for which he does not have an adequate argument. If (2) is not met, he is subject to the criticism that in believing p he believes a proposition for which he does not believe he has a good argument. If (3) is not met, he is subject to the criticism that in believing p he believes a proposition for which it is not epistemically rational for him to believe he has a good argument. And if (4) is not met, he is subject to the criticism that in believing p he believes a proposition for which no argument that he rationally takes to be a good argument even roughly resembles an argument that in fact is a good one. S's belief p can be epistemically rational in the propositional sense even if not all of these conditions are met. But in the richer doxastic sense, his belief will not be epistemically rational if any one of these conditions is not met. It will be subject to one of the above criticisms. Moreover, it is plausible to think that the beliefs of Watson, and the husband who believes his wife has been unfaithful, and the bank teller, and the man who distrusts modus ponens are subject to one of these criticisms. Accordingly, the irrationality in those cases can be explained by reference to this noncausal notion of doxastically rational belief.

Of course, this notion of doxastically rational belief is somewhat vague, just as Firth's historical notion upon which it is patterned is somewhat vague. Firth's notion left vague how much of S's evidence for *p* must causally contribute to his believing *p;* this notion leaves vague how closely the argument that S rationally takes to be a good argument for *p* has to resemble an argument that actually is a good argument for S. It is too stringent to require that what S takes to be a good argument for *p* be in every one of its details identical with what in fact is a good argument for *p*. Good arguments are likely to be relatively complex. But on the other hand, it is not too stringent (even if it is somewhat vague) to insist that what he takes to be a good argument for *p* roughly resemble an argument that in fact is a good argument for *p*.

I do not want to apologize too much for this vagueness, however. My purpose here is simply to show that the kind of case that is cited by Firth, Pollock, Swain, and others does not illustrate the need to introduce historical considerations into the discussion of epistemic rationality. What these cases *do* illustrate is the need to introduce a sense of epistemically rational belief that is richer than one that requires only that the person have adequate evidence for what he believes. For in each of the above cases, the person does have adequate evidence for what he believes, but his belief is nonetheless subject to a significant kind of epistemic criticism. So, there is an important sense of epistemically rational belief such that the person in each of these cases lacks a rational belief in this sense. However, there is no reason to think this has to be a causal-historical sense of rational belief. Rather, the irrationality of the person's belief in these cases can be accounted for straightforwardly in terms of a nonhistorical sense of rational belief—a sense of rational belief that requires a person not only to have adequate evidence for his belief but also to appreciate at least roughly how this evidence can be used to argue for the proposition he believes.

But is it not possible to redescribe any of the cases in such a way that the person's belief is doxastically rational in my sense even though his belief is not caused by his recognizing that he has adequate evidence for what he believes? And if so, will not the same motivation for introducing a causal-historical sense of rational belief pop up once again? For example, is it not possible to imagine Holmes in a situation where he believes that the coachman is guilty and where he is well aware of the good evidence he has for believing this but where his awareness of this evidence plays no causal role in producing his belief? Situations of this sort, no doubt, are rare (since ordinarily one's awareness of what one takes to be good evidence for p prompts one to believe p), but at least at first glance they would not seem to be impossible. Nevertheless, situations of this sort do not illustrate the need for introducing a causal-historical sense of epistemically rational belief any more than do the original situations described by Firth, Pollock, and the others. For in these unusual situations, it is not at all clear that there is any straightforward, intuitive sense in which Holmes's belief is not epistemically rational. In other words, insofar as Holmes's belief that the coachman is guilty is propositionally rational and insofar as Holmes's belief that he has good evidence for this claim also is propositionally rational and insofar finally as what Holmes takes to be good evidence for this claim resembles what in fact is good evidence for the claim, it is no longer clear that his belief properly is subject to any kind of epistemic criticism, even if it was caused in some peculiar way. Similarly, if a person who rationally believes both p and if p then q and who rationally believes that modus ponens is truth preserving is nonetheless caused to believe q in some unusual way (perhaps due to some recent neurological malfunction about which he knows nothing), then it is no longer clear that his belief is irrational in any epistemic sense.

As an illustration of this, consider a pair of situations of a sort which by now should be familiar. In the first situation, imagine that Holmes has very strong evidence for believing that the coachman is guilty and that he appreciates how this evidence indicates that the coachman is guilty. Specifically, suppose that his belief that the coachman is guilty is epistemically rational for him in both the propositional and the doxastic sense (my doxastic sense). Also, suppose that his having such evidence causes him in a normal way to believe that the coachman is guilty. Now imagine Holmes in a second situation that from his viewpoint is indistinguishable from the first but in which his belief has not been caused by his evidence. He thinks, believes, experiences, seems to remember, exactly what he does in the first situation. What he would believe on reflection is the same. He discerns just as well how his evidence indicates that the coachman is guilty. We even can suppose that in both situations Holmes believes, and with as much evidence, that his belief about the coachman is caused by his evidence. But in the second situation, he is wrong. His belief has a wholly nonevidential cause, although he neither believes nor could be expected to believe anything about this cause. There is nothing in this second situation, which from his point of view is indistinguishable from the first, to indicate that his evidence has not caused him to believe that the coachman is guilty.

Given these assumptions, my suggestion is that we draw the same conclusion that was drawn earlier with respect to analogous cases—we should conclude that these situations are epistemic twins. The situations *are* twins with respect to the propositions that are epistemically rational for him and with respect to the kinds of epistemically rational beliefs I have defined: Since the two situations are indistinguishable from Holmes's point of view, any proposition p that is epistemically rational for Holmes to believe in one situation also is epistemically rational for him to believe in the other; any belief that is propositionally rational for Holmes in one situation is propositionally rational for him in the second as well; and any belief that is doxastically rational for him in one is doxastically rational for him in the other. However, the point I now am making is broader than the claim that the two situations are twins with respect to these kinds of epistemically rational beliefs. The point is that any account of rational belief that implies that such situations are not twins is not an account that adopts a purely epistemic point of view. Rather, the account is interested in evaluating the individual's beliefs from some perspective other than the individual's own perspective on reflection (and perhaps also with respect to some goal other than the individual's epistemic goal).

However, to conclude this is just to conclude that any account of rational belief that requires an individual's belief to be caused in an appropriate way by his evidence is not an account of epistemically rational belief.[11] Indeed, since for any nontrivial, causal-historical requirement[12] it is possible to imagine pairs of situations of the above sort, such that in only one is the purported requirement met even though what the person thinks, what he believes, what he would believe on reflection, what he experiences, and so on, is the same in both, a more general conclusion follows. Any account of rational belief that requires an individual's belief to have an appropriate history is not an account of epistemically rational belief.[13]

4.3   Two Senses of Knowledge

Why do so many philosophers resist this conclusion? Why, that is, are so many philosophers tempted to insist that there must be some sense of epistemically rational belief that makes the causal history of a belief important?

Part of the temptation may arise from the view that a belief cannot be an instance of knowledge unless it has an appropriate history. If one then also thought that a belief cannot be an instance of knowledge unless it is epistemically rational, one might be tempted to claim that a belief is epistemically rational in one important sense only if it has an appropriate history. Then any belief that is epistemically rational in this sense would satisfy the causal-historical prerequisites of knowledge; any such belief, in other words, would be a candidate for knowledge.

Insofar as the temptation does arise for these two claims, it is a temptation to be resisted. For one, chicken-sexer cases and the like suggest that a belief need not be epistemically rational to be an instance of knowledge. Second, a belief need not have an appropriate history in order to be an instance of knowledge. And this is so regardless of how the notion of "appropriate history" is understood, whether for example it be understood in terms of the belief being the product of a reliable cognitive process or in terms of the belief being the product of properly functioning cognitive equipment or in terms of the belief being caused in an appropriate way by the evidence that makes it propositionally rational.

Consider an extreme case to illustrate why this is so. Suppose for convenience we take "appropriate history" to mean that the belief must be the product of a reliable cognitive process, where a cognitive process is reliable just if it would produce mostly true beliefs in close counterfactual situations. If we understand "appropriate history" in this way, nothing would seem to preclude the possibility that all of a person's beliefs lack an appropriate history even though all are true. Indeed, nothing would seem to preclude the possibility that although all of a person's beliefs lack an appropriate history, he nonetheless believes everything that is true and nothing that is false, or at least that he comes as close to this as is humanly possible. Suppose, for example, that an individual S is struck by a lightning bolt and that this lightning bolt somehow alters S's cognitive equipment so that he comes to have something like an ideally veridical belief system. He has true and comprehensive beliefs about the past, the present, and the future. Moreover, suppose that the lightning bolt causes him to be epistemically perfect as well. Suppose, in other words, that all of these beliefs about the past, present, and future are epistemically rational for him, both in the propositional and in the doxastic sense. Thus, each claim that he believes is a claim that he knows how to defend; he is aware of a good argument, either a good first-level or a good second-level argument, for each such claim. Indeed, suppose he has not just a good argument for each such claim but something like a perfect argument for each claim, an argument that provides something like a perfect explanation for why each such claim is true. Suppose, for example, that he has true beliefs about what the basic laws of the universe are, and in terms of these basic laws he has true beliefs about how to explain everything that has happened or will happen (or at least everything that can be explained by these basic laws).

What are we to say of such a person? Are we to say that he has knowledge? The answer seems clear. He does have knowledge. He knows things that you and I do not. Indeed, he is as close to being omniscient as is humanly possible. For almost any question that we can imagine asking him, he has true beliefs about the answer to the question. Moreover, he would be able to explain in something like perfect detail why his answers are correct. At the very least, it would be extremely odd to claim of such a person that we know more than he does. It would be odd, for example, to say that we know but that he does not know that the surface of the sun is hotter than the surface of the earth, that one of the by-products of photosynthesis is oxygen, and that in a perfect vacuum light objects would fall at the same rate as heavy objects. After all, by hypothesis he has something approaching a perfect explanation as to why each of these claims is true.

But notice, this is exactly what a reliabilist about knowledge might be committed to saying. He might be committed to saying that we know such things but that our ideally veridical and epistemically perfect believer does not. Presumably some of us have beliefs about these matters that have an appropriate history—they are the products of reliable cognitive processes. And presumably some of us have beliefs about these matters that meet whatever other conditions are necessary for knowledge. But nothing in our story about the perfectly veridical believer implies that his beliefs are the products of reliable processes; there is nothing inconsistent about supposing that his beliefs are not caused by reliable processes. Suppose we stipulate that they are not. Suppose we stipulate that although the lightning bolt has caused S to have ideally true and evidentially perfect beliefs, the processes that caused these beliefs are not reliable. Suppose we stipulate, for example, that had the situation been even a little different, the lightning bolt would have caused S to have many false beliefs, and suppose we stipulate as well that the lightning bolt has altered S's faculties so that were he (as he is now) to be placed in close counterfactual situations, these faculties would not generate true beliefs.

But then, it might be objected, his present doxastic state—a state in which his beliefs are close to being ideally veridical—will not be stable. Yes, but so what? Why does knowledge have to be stable? Can one not have fleeting insights—in effect, fleeting knowledge? Many mystics have thought so, and on this issue, at least, they are right. It is at least possible for us to have isolated and fleeting moments of brilliant illumination, moments where we understand how things fit together, moments where we have something like perfect understanding. It is at least possible for an individual (if only for a moment) to be lifted to something of a higher epistemic plateau, where he has close to a perfect explanation of almost everything that has been and will be. It is at least possible for there to be such moments—and as far as I can see, such moments would be moments of something like perfect knowledge.

But if so, a belief need not be the product of a reliable cognitive process—a process that would produce mostly true beliefs in close counterfactual situations—in order to be an instance of knowledge. Likewise, a belief need not have any other kind of appropriate causal-history in order to be an instance of knowledge. For regardless of how we understand the notion of an appropriate history, it would seem possible for a person's beliefs to be ideally veridical and epistemically perfect even though they lack the appropriate kind of histories.

Or at least this is so for nontrivial, causal-historical requirements. It is easy to trivialize the thesis that a belief must have an appropriate history if it is to be an instance of knowledge. For example, one might say that a belief has a history appropriate for knowledge only if it is the product of a reliable cognitive process and then allow the notion of a reliable cognitive process to be understood in such a situation-specific way that any true belief is the product of a reliable cognitive process. Suppose, for instance, that the process that leads to a true belief is specified in such minute detail that these details in conjunction with the laws of nature imply that the belief is true. Such a process presumably will be reliable no matter how we understand reliability (whether in a statistical or in a counterfactual sense). Moreover, presumably any true belief will be the product of such a reliable process.[14] A fortiori, the beliefs of our ideally veridical and epistemically perfect believer will be the products of such processes, even though by hypothesis lightning bolts of very similar strength in a very similar condition hardly ever would generate mostly true beliefs, much less ideally veridical beliefs, in individuals very similar to *S*. And so, if having a history of this sort constitutes having an appropriate history, even the beliefs of our ideally veridical believer will have appropriate histories.

But this kind of causal-historical thesis is altogether trivial. It is trivial because *any* plausible account of knowledge will be compatible with this thesis. And this is so, in turn, because any plausible account will imply that a belief is a serious candidate for knowledge only if it is true.

So causal-historical theses, which imply that a belief is a serious candidate for knowledge only if it has an appropriate history, face a dilemma. On the one hand, if "appropriate history" is understood in such a way that just any true belief has an appropriate history (just because it is true), then the thesis is trivial; any plausible account of knowledge will be compatible with the thesis. On the other hand, if the notion of an appropriate history is understood in such a way that not just any true belief has an appropriate history and if the notion is not trivialized in some other fashion, it is hard to see without further explanation why it would be utterly impossible for a person's beliefs to be both epistemically perfect (in the doxastic as well as the propositional sense) and ideally veridical, so that he has something like a perfect explanation of the world, and yet not have appropriate histories. But then it is equally hard to see why a belief must have had an appropriate history if it is to be an instance of knowledge.[15]

Suppose then that this is so; suppose that having had an appropriate history is not a necessary condition of a belief being an instance of knowledge. Suppose, in other words, that just as it is possible (we have assumed) for a belief to be an instance of knowledge without it being epistemically rational—chicken-sexer cases and the like illustrate this—so too it is possible for a belief to be an instance of knowledge without it being the product of reliable or properly functioning cognitive equipment and without it having an appropriate history in some other nontrivial sense—cases of ideally veridical believers can be used to illustrate this. What does this suggest about the notion of knowledge?

It suggests that perhaps there are distinct senses in which an individual can know something. Chicken-sexer cases and the like suggest that there is a causal-historical sense of knowledge. What is crucial if a belief is to be a serious candidate for knowledge in this sense is that the belief be the product of reliable or properly functioning faculties (or processes).[16] It is not crucial that the person have adequate evidence for what he believes. It is not crucial that he be able to defend what he believes.

On the other hand, the possibility of a person having beliefs that constitute something like a perfect explanation of the universe even though his beliefs lack appropriate histories suggests that there also is a noncausal sense of knowledge. This sense seemingly is close to the traditional conception of knowledge, which understands knowledge as (roughly) true belief that is supported by adequate and true evidence. Call this "the evidential sense of knowledge" to distinguish it from "the causal-historical or nonevidential sense of knowledge." The idea, then, is that an ideally veridical and epistemically perfect believer can be said to know, say, that one of the by-products of photosynthesis is oxygen even if his belief in this proposition does not have an appropriate causal-history. He can be said to know this in the evidential sense. And he can be said to know this in the evidential sense because (loosely) his belief is true and because he has something approaching perfect evidence for it.

Of course, assuming that there is this distinct evidential sense of knowledge, it presumably is not necessary for an individual to have perfect evidence for a claim in order to know it in this evidential sense. But if so, the question arises as to how far from perfect a person's evidence can be and yet be good enough for evidential knowledge. It no doubt will be difficult to answer this question with any kind of precision.[17] Nonetheless, there is a traditional way of at least trying to answer this question, a way that in broad outline is endorsed by epistemologists as diverse as Roderick Chisholm, Gilbert Harman, and Keith Lehrer. Their answer, expressed roughly, is that the evidence must be strong enough to make the person's belief epistemically rational and also accurate enough so that there is no falsehood that is "essentially involved" in making his belief rational.[18] Ignore for the moment what "essential" means here. Instead, consider the general idea lying behind this suggestion. The general idea can be illustrated by Gettier-type examples, in which a person S rationally believes a falsehood p and from this deduces a truth (p or q). Even though S may rationally believe this disjunction and even though it may be true, S need not know that it is true. The reason he need not know it, according to the suggestion above, is that it being epistemically rational for him to believe the falsehood p may be essential for his rationally believing the disjunction.

Chisholm, Lehrer, and Harman all suggest that something like these conditions—the conditions that the belief be true, that it be epistemically rational, and that there be no falsehood essentially involved in making the belief rational—are both necessary and sufficient for knowledge. This is not my suggestion. My suggestion is that something like these conditions is sufficient but not necessary for knowledge. They represent, at least roughly, one way in which a person can come to know a proposition.

Is there a way of making this idea more precise? I think so. Let us begin by saying that an individual S knows p in this evidential sense only if his belief p is doxastically rational as well as propositionally rational. So S not only has adequate evidence for p, he is aware (at least roughly) of what this evidence is. For the subjective foundationalist, this means that S is aware (at least roughly) of some good arguments that he has for p. Of course, he may very well have many good arguments for p. If so, he need not be aware of them all, but he does have to be aware of at least one. Moreover, let us insist that this argument is one whose conclusion is in fact probable given the truth of its premises. In this way, we preclude the possibility that S might know p in virtue of having an argument for p that he on reflection would think is likely to be truth preserving but that in fact is not likely to be truth preserving.[19] Finally, let us add that there is no falsehood q such that it being rational for him to believe q is "essential" to the arguments that allow his belief p to be doxastically rational.

How are we to understand "essential" here? For the moment, let us not worry about the question of what makes the rationality of q essential to the arguments that allow S's belief p to be doxastically rational. Instead, consider the question of what makes q's being rational essential to the proposition p being rational for S. The answer to this question will help us answer the former question. As at least an initial attempt to answer this latter question, let us say that it being rational for S to believe q is essential for it being rational for him to believe p just if p is grounded on q for S. What is it for p to be grounded on q for S? Let us say that p is grounded on q for S just if p is epistemically rational for S and every set of propositions that makes p epistemically rational for S also makes q epistemically rational for him. In other words, every good argument that S has for p is an argument that employs as its premises all the premises needed for S to have a good argument for q, where for present purposes a good argument is a first-level argument; it is an undefeated argument whose premises are properly basic for S and whose premises tend to make its conclusion epistemically rational for S.

Given this initial characterization, it follows that if a proposition q itself is a premise in every good argument that S has for p, then p

is grounded on q for S. This follows because the premises of a good argument must be properly basic for S and propositions that are properly basic constitute good arguments for themselves. So one way a proposition can be grounded on another proposition for S is for the second to be a premise in every good argument S has for the first.

But this is not the only way in which p can be grounded on q for S. The former can be grounded on the latter even if q is not properly basic for him. In particular, p can be grounded on q for S if every argument that S has for p contains premises that make q epistemically rational for S. Thus, suppose proposition e^1 makes p rational for S and that proposition e^2 also makes p rational for S. Suppose in addition that any other set of propositions that makes p rational for S is a set whose conjunction entails either e^1 or e^2. Then, p is grounded on q for S. Suppose, however, that although e^1 makes q rational for S, e^2 does not. Then p is not grounded on q for S. On the other hand, suppose e^2 does make rational q^2 for S. Then, p might very well be grounded on the disjunction (q^1 or q^2), since presumably every set of propositions that makes p rational for S also makes this disjunction rational for him. Or consider again Gettier-like cases. If every good argument that S has for a disjunction (a or b) is an argument whose premises make a epistemically rational for him, then the disjunction (a or b) is grounded on a for S.

We are now in a position to say what is involved in there being no falsehood q such that it being epistemically rational for S to believe q is essential to the arguments that allow S's belief p to be doxastically rational. Recall that in order for S's belief p to be doxastically rational, there must be at least one argument A such that S believes A to be a good argument for p, it must be epistemically rational for S to believe this, and A must closely resemble an argument that in fact helps make p epistemically rational for S. The argument A here can be a first-level argument for p or a second-level argument for p. If A is a first-level argument, let us say it is one of the arguments that allows S's belief p to be doxastically rational. If A is a second-level argument, then there must be a first-level argument that backs it—a first-level argument that makes it rational for S to believe that A is a kind of argument that is likely to have a true conclusion. In order for S's belief p to be doxastically rational, S need not be aware of this argument that backs A; it is enough that he believes A to be a good argument for p and that this belief is propositionally rational for him. Nonetheless, let us say that, strictly, it is not argument A alone that allows S's belief p here to be doxastically rational. Rather, let us add to the premises of A the premises of the first-level argument that backs it and then say that it is an argument with these premises, strictly speaking, that allows S's belief p to be doxastically rational. And if there is more than one first-level argument that backs A, let us say that for each such argument, there is a corresponding argument, formed by conjoining its premises with the premises of A, that allows S's belief p to be doxastically rational.

Suppose we gather all these arguments that allow S's belief p to be doxastically rational into a set. Then, we can say (roughly) that it being epistemically rational for S to believe q is essential to the arguments that allow S's belief p to be doxastically rational just in case p would be grounded on q were these the only arguments that made p epistemically rational for S. We can make this more precise (avoiding the counterfactual) by saying that each of these arguments has premises that not only make p epistemically rational for S but also make q epistemically rational for S.

The important point here, however, is not so much whether this approach to understanding the grounding relation (and the related notion of what is essential to the arguments that allow S's belief p to be doxastically rational) is exactly right. Perhaps it is not exactly right. But even if it is not, the important point is likely to be unaffected, since this point presumably could be made using almost any plausible explication of the grounding relation. The important point is that something at least roughly resembling the following conditions is sufficient for knowledge: S believes p, p is true, his belief p is doxastically rational (and hence also propositionally rational), at least some of the arguments that allow his belief to be doxastically rational are in fact good arguments (arguments whose premises, if true, make p probable), and there is no falsehood q such that it being epistemically rational for S to believe q is essential to the good arguments that allow S's belief p to be doxastically rational (there is no falsehood q such that p would be grounded on q for S were these good arguments the only arguments that made p epistemically rational for S).[20]

The point, remember, is only that something like these conditions is sufficient for knowledge. The conditions may have to be tampered with a bit. And it is not just the explication of the grounding relation that may have to be tampered with a bit. Other tampering may also be needed. Perhaps, for example, the case of our ideally veridical believer suggests that the evidence that an individual has must be not only sufficient to make his belief rational but also "sufficiently comprehensive."[21] But even if this is so, it would not affect the claim that although something like these conditions seems sufficient for knowledge, nothing in them seems to imply that it is impossible for a belief that satisfies them not to have an appropriate history. Nothing in them seems to imply, for instance, that a belief that satisfies them need be the product of reliable or properly functioning cognitive equipment, and nothing in them seems to imply that a belief that satisfies them needs to have an appropriate history in some other nontrivial sense. But if this is so and if it also is possible (as the chicken-sexer case seems to indicate) for *S* to know *p* without having adequate evidence for *p*, there must be distinct senses of knowledge—a nonevidential sense and an evidential sense.

Moreover, intuitively this seems plausible. Some of the things we intuitively think we know seem to be such that we know them only because we have good evidence for them and are aware at least roughly of what this evidence is. We know them, in other words, only because we have, or at least are capable of generating, good arguments for their truth. Much scientific knowledge, mathematical knowledge, and other highly theoretical knowledge may be of this sort. But other things that we intuitively think we know cannot be so easily construed as evidential knowledge. Sometimes we take an individual to have knowledge even though the individual would be hard-pressed to defend such beliefs, to know how to argue for them. I have used the example of chicken-sexers as an extreme example to illustrate the possibility of this kind of knowledge, but there are perhaps many more mundane examples of nonevidential knowledge as well. Some of our knowledge of propositions that are properly basic a posteriori perhaps is like this. An individual's knowledge that he sees a chair in front of him and his knowledge that he remembers being at the zoo last Saturday and his knowledge that he now has a headache are at least sometimes not easily construed as instances of evidential knowledge. For at least sometimes ordinary people may not even be roughly aware of how to defend such claims. But if so, such knowledge is most naturally construed as nonevidential, as knowledge that an individual has not because he is aware of the good evidence he has for the claim but rather because his belief in the claim has been appropriately generated (whether "appropriate generation" be understood in terms of one's cognitive faculties being reliable or in terms of one's cognitive faculties functioning properly or in some other way). It is no accident that proponents of nonevidential accounts of knowledge, in which the favored nonevidential conditions are forwarded as being both necessary and sufficient for knowledge, focus upon instances of perceptual knowledge, memory knowledge, and the like. For these are the kinds of knowledge for which a nonevidential conception of knowledge normally seems most appropriate. It is likewise no accident that proponents of these nonevidential accounts have not focused upon instances of highly theoretical knowledge. For this is the kind of knowledge for which a nonevidential conception of knowledge normally seems least appropriate.

Of course, it presumably is the case that much of our knowledge can be construed either evidentially or nonevidentially. Much of our knowledge presumably consists of true beliefs that are caused by reliable processes (in some significant but no doubt vague sense of reliable process). Correspondingly, many if not most of these very same true beliefs are beliefs that we could defend (at least in a rough and ready way) were we forced to do so. It is often the case and perhaps even usually the case that when an individual knows something, his belief is both one that he can defend and one that is caused by a reliable process. However, there are exceptions, as the case of the ideally veridical believer and the case of the chicken-sexer illustrate. To be sure, these are extreme examples, far removed from the knowledge that most of us have. But not infrequently we need extreme examples to put our concepts into sharp relief. The hope is that these extreme examples will provide us with a tool by which we can strip away complications, allowing us to see more clearly the core of the concept in question. However, with the concept of knowledge, the extreme examples seem to reveal two distinct cores—two fundamentally distinct senses in which an individual's beliefs might constitute knowledge. Accordingly, we seem to be pressured into admitting that knowledge is not univocal, that there is an evidential as well as a nonevidential sense of knowledge.

No doubt some will be disposed to respond to this pressure by simply denying either that the chicken-sexer has knowledge or that the ideally veridical and evidentially perfect believer has knowledge. But any such denial would have all the appearances of a solution too easily won; it would appear to be the philosophical analogue of an ostrich sticking its head in the sand as a way of dealing with a danger with which it otherwise cannot cope. Short of such a "solution," there perhaps is some plausible and straightforward way of maintaining an univocal account of knowledge. Perhaps, for instance, someone eventually will find a way of stretching a nonevidential conception of knowledge so that it can plausibly account for all instances of knowledge, even the knowledge of our ideally veridical believer. Or perhaps someone eventually will find a way of stretching an evidential conception of knowledge so that it can plausibly account for all instances of knowledge, even the knowledge of the chicken-sexer. However, it is not easy to see how. So, for the time being, it seems best just to admit that there are these two different ways in which an individual can come to have knowledge.

4.4 Epistemic Luck

Is there any other consideration that might tempt one to think that there must be some sense of epistemically rational belief that makes the causal history of a belief important? I think there is, but it perhaps is best to approach this consideration indirectly. Consider an extreme voluntarist conception of a belief, a conception that implies that we regularly choose not only what to believe but also the reasons that motivate us to believe what we do. Thus, suppose a person has what he takes to be a good argument for a proposition p, but in addition suppose he has what he takes to be good practical reasons for believing p. Such a person, according to this extreme voluntarist conception of belief acquisition, is free to decide whether or not to believe p. He also is free to decide whether to believe p for epistemic reasons or for practical reasons or both. So, he might decide to "allow" what he takes to be the good argument for p to motivate him to believe p. Or he might decide to allow the practical advantages that he thinks will accrue to him if he believes p to motivate him to believe p. Or he might decide to allow neither of these to motivate him to believe p and to allow nothing else to so motivate him either. If so, he would not come to believe p.

I am not suggesting that this is even a remotely plausible conception of belief acquisition, but the conception is useful for purposes of illustration. For the moment, simply assume that something like this view of belief acquisition is adequate, and then consider this case. Suppose Holmes has strong evidence indicating that the coachman is guilty, he rationally believes in the propositional sense that he has good evidence indicating that this is so, and the evidence he takes to be good evidence closely resembles the actual good evidence he has for thinking that the coachman is guilty. So, Holmes's belief that the coachman is guilty is epistemically rational both in the propositional sense and in the doxastic sense.

Nevertheless, given the voluntarist conception of belief acquisition, what motivated Holmes to acquire his belief may have had nothing to do with his having good evidence for the proposition that the coachman is guilty. Despite the fact that he has this good evidence and despite the fact that he is aware that he has it, this may not be what motivated him to believe that the coachman is guilty (and it may not be what motivates him to sustain the belief). Perhaps he chose to acquire his belief for reasons of self-interest. Perhaps, for example, Holmes stands to gain financially if the coachman is found guilty and Holmes knows he will be able to convince others of the coachman's guilt only if he himself believes that the coachman is guilty.

But notice, if Holmes did choose to acquire his belief for reasons of self-interest, it can be tempting to conclude that although Holmes's belief is epistemically rational in both the propositional sense and the doxastic sense, in some other sense his belief is far from epistemically rational. After all, Holmes here has not been as good an epistemic agent as he could have been. He did not choose to acquire his belief because he has good evidence for it. His having a belief for which he has adequate evidence is just a fortuitous consequence of his choice. He chose to acquire the belief for reasons of self-interest. It just happened to be the case that what he had self-interested reasons to believe was a proposition for which he also has adequate epistemic reasons. In this sense then, he has been epistemically lucky. And given that it is just a matter of luck that Holmes here believes what it is epistemically rational for him to believe, it can be tempting to conclude that there must be a sense in which Holmes's belief about the coachman is epistemically irrational, despite the fact that it is both propositionally and doxastically rational. His belief must be epistemically irrational in some sense, it can be tempting to think, just because the manner in which Holmes chose the belief is properly subject to criticism.

Of course, relatively few philosophers are prepared to endorse the view of belief acquisition that is being presupposed here. Nevertheless, this voluntarist conception of belief acquisition is instructive, since it makes tempting the claim that having an appropriate history is a prerequisite of a belief being epistemically rational. Moreover, the way in which it makes this tempting has an analogue for less voluntaristic conceptions of belief acquisition.

Consider, for instance, the conception of belief acquisition implicit in the views of Roderick Firth, who claims that in one important sense S's belief p is rational only if it is caused by his evidence for p. Both Firth and one who is interested in defending an extreme voluntarist account of belief acquisition could agree that the reason S's belief p might not be epistemically rational in some significant sense despite the fact that it is both propositionally and doxastically rational (in my sense of doxastically rational) is that it lacks an appropriate history. In addition, they could agree that a belief has an appropriate history, and thus is epistemically rational in the sense in question only if the person's evidence for *p* plays a role in getting the person to believe *p*. What they would disagree about is doxastic voluntarism; Firth gives no indication that he is willing to endorse a radical voluntaristic conception of belief acquisition. Even so, if Firth or like-minded epistemologists were pressed to explain why beliefs that are not prompted by the person's evidence must be epistemically irrational in some important sense, their explanation presumably would be analogous to that given by the voluntarist. According to the voluntarist, if *S* is not motivated to believe *p* for acceptable epistemic reasons, then his choice and the resulting belief are properly subject to criticism. His choice reflects unpraiseworthy intellectual characteristics. So even if *S*'s belief *p* is doxastically rational in my sense, he is not being as good an epistemic agent as could be expected. His believing a proposition for which he has adequate evidence is just a matter of luck. For Firth and like-minded epistemologists, the explanation presumably would be similar, only it would be stripped of an emphasis upon agency. The explanation, for example, might be in terms of the person's cognitive equipment not working properly. *S*'s belief *p,* if not caused by the evidence that *S* has for *p,* is not epistemically rational in some important sense, because in such a case *S*'s cognitive equipment is not working in a proper manner. In particular, in order for *S*'s belief *p* to be rational in this sense, *S*'s cognitive equipment must be working in such a way that there is an appropriate causal connection between *S*'s having evidence for *p* and *S*'s believing *p*. Otherwise, it simply would be a matter of luck—a happy coincidence—that *S*'s belief conforms to his evidence.

To return to the question posed earlier, why are so many philosophers tempted to think that there must be some sense of epistemically rational belief that implies that the history of a belief is important? Part of the temptation may arise from the view that epistemic luck is impossible. It may arise, in other words, from the view that there is some sense of epistemically rational belief such that a necessary condition of *S*'s rationally believing *p* is that his having adequate evidence for this proposition *p* that he believes is not just a matter of luck.

4.5 *Is Epistemic Luck Impossible?*

Is epistemic luck really impossible? I think not. Any case where there is a temptation to use the impossibility of epistemic luck to claim that in some important sense *S*'s belief *p* is not epistemically rational even though it is both propositionally and doxastically rational is a case where this temptation can be explained away. It can be explained away by distinguishing the evaluation of a belief from the evaluation of whatever produced the belief. And it does not matter whether what produced the belief is a voluntary act of the believer, which reflects upon his intellectual character, or some involuntary process, which reflects upon how well his cognitive equipment is operating. Epistemically desirable intellectual characteristics and epistemically desirable cognitive equipment—characteristics or equipment that ordinarily produce beliefs for which the believer has adequate evidence—at times can produce beliefs that are epistemically unfavorable. However, the fact that such beliefs are produced in a way that usually does not produce howlers does not mean that the beliefs are any less howlers. The reverse is also true; epistemically unfavorable ways of producing beliefs at times can bring about epistemically favorable beliefs; one is not forced to say that these beliefs are epistemic howlers just because the process that produces them usually produces howlers.

Although for certain purposes it may be appropriate to collapse the distinction between the evaluation of a belief and the evaluation of the kind of process or the kind of intellectual character that produced the belief, there *is* such a distinction to be made. And for purposes of epistemic evaluation, it should be made. For epistemic evaluations of beliefs are evaluations of how effectively a person is satisfying the goal of now believing truths and now not believing falsehoods. Were we interested in evaluating how effectively the person is pursuing the goal of having true beliefs and not having false beliefs over the long run, we might have to be concerned with more than his present belief system. We might have to be concerned with how he came to believe what he does. For if unaltered, the processes, character, habits, or whatever produced or sustain his beliefs will affect his long-term prospects for believing truths. And so, with respect to this long-term goal it is not unnatural to collapse (or at least to collapse partially) the distinction between an evaluation of a belief and an evaluation of what produced the belief. It is not unnatural to make the evaluation of the belief at least partially a function of the history of the belief, so that the belief is to be favorably evaluated only if it has been produced in a proper way. But from an epistemic point of view, where what is of interest is now to have true beliefs and now not to have false beliefs, this is not appropriate.[22] From an epistemic point of view, what matters in the evaluation of a belief is whether the proposition believed is epistemically rational for the individual in question (the propositional sense of epistemically rational belief) and whether the individual is appropriately aware of the evidence that makes this proposition epistemically rational for him (the doxastic sense of epistemically rational belief).

These points may be obvious when stated abstractly, but when particular cases arise, especially cases involving a history of faulty reasoning, it is easy to become confused. Suppose, for example, that Watson yesterday on the basis of some obviously faulty reasoning came to believe irrationally that the coachman is the murderer. Moreover, suppose that as a result of believing this, Watson comes today to acquire additional evidence in favor of his belief. The maid, knowing that Watson believes the coachman is the murderer and wanting to please Watson, lies to him; she tells him that she saw the coachman commit the crime. So, Watson, let us assume, now has overwhelming evidence indicating that the coachman is guilty, and moreover he understands how this current evidence supports his belief. Unfortunately, his irrational belief of yesterday has caused him to be sloppy in his investigations of other suspects. In particular, he has failed to search the butler's room, where he would have found the murder weapon and other incriminating evidence—evidence, let us finally assume, that would make it epistemically rational for him to believe that the coachman is not guilty, despite the maid's testimony to the contrary.

In cases of this sort, it is especially tempting to smuggle an evaluation of the reasoning processes that originally led Watson to his belief about the coachman into the epistemic evaluation of the belief itself. It is tempting, that is, to note that there is much about the way Watson acquired his belief that rightly can be criticized and to conclude from this that the belief itself is not epistemically rational. But this temptation is one to be resisted. From an epistemic point of view, there is nothing wrong with Watson's belief now. Yesterday his belief was irrational, but today he has a good argument for what he believes, he recognizes that he has this argument, and so on. The mistakes in reasoning he made yesterday resulted in his having an irrational belief at that time about the murderer, and it also resulted in his now lacking evidence that would defeat the evidence for his present belief. But neither of these facts indicates that his present belief is epistemically irrational in some important sense. A person may lack evidence about *p*, even available defeating evidence, and still rationally believe *p*. Indeed, this happens all the time.[23] The fact that Watson would find defeating evidence in the butler's room does not indicate that Watson's belief about the coachman is not epistemically rational, especially since his present evidence overwhelmingly indicates that he would not find such evidence in the butler's room. Likewise, a person now may lack defeating evidence about *p* just because he earlier made a faulty inference that led him at this earlier time to irrationally believe *p*, and yet at the present moment he may still rationally believe *p*. This too may not be unusual. Our investigations, scientific and otherwise, ordinarily are shaped by what we believe. It is possible for a faulty inference and a resulting irrational belief in a proposition *p* to shape our investigations in such a way that we find additional support for *p* and fail to find available defeating evidence. And once in possession of this additional supporting evidence, we may very well come to believe *p* rationally. Thus, it is possible for us now to believe *p* rationally only because we earlier believed *p* irrationally. In such cases, the way in which we come to acquire our belief may be rightly criticized even though the present belief is epistemically rational.

Of course, ordinarily if a person reasons badly in coming to believe something, unwelcome consequences show up in the person's present belief system. The fact that this usually happens is another factor that can make it tempting to smuggle considerations that concern the origin or sustenance of a belief into the epistemic evaluation of the belief. But once again, the temptation is one to be resisted. If Watson has come to believe that the coachman is guilty as a result of a faulty reasoning process that prompts him to irrationally believe that in murder cases it almost always is the coachman who is guilty and if he still has this irrational general belief about coachmen, then presumably his present belief that the coachman is guilty is epistemically irrational. But his belief is epistemically irrational not in virtue of being one of the products of this faulty reasoning process. The problem lies in the present and not in the past. Watson's belief about the coachman is epistemically irrational either because he does not have a good argument indicating that the coachman is guilty or, if he does have such an argument, because he does not recognize that he has this argument. That is, his belief is epistemically irrational either because it is not rational in the propositional sense or because it is not rational in the doxastic sense. Had Watson's faulty process of reasoning somehow caused him to have an adequate argument for what he believes and to recognize that he has this argument, then regardless of how many mistakes led to such a state, his belief that the coachman is guilty would be both propositionally and doxastically rational.[24]

Moreover, this point can be generalized: *Any* case in which causal-historical considerations make it at all tempting to conclude that a belief is irrational in some epistemic sense despite the fact that the belief is both propositionally and doxastically rational is a case where what really is bothering us is some flaw in the believer's intellectual character or in his cognitive equipment. Thus, what troubles the voluntarist in cases where a person chooses to acquire a belief for reasons of self-interest is that this choice may reflect a tendency on the part of the person to believe claims even if he has no good reasons to think them true. It may reflect, in other words, a faulty intellectual character, which over the long run is likely to prompt the person to have many beliefs for which he lacks adequate evidence. Analogously, what troubles Firth in cases where a person's belief has not been caused by his having evidence for the truth of what he believes is that this may reflect a tendency of the person's cognitive equipment to generate beliefs for which he lacks adequate evidence. It may reflect, that is, faulty cognitive equipment, which again over the long run is likely to result in the person having many beliefs for which he lacks adequate evidence.

The fact that there is a flaw of one of these kinds in the believer's intellectual character or in his cognitive equipment perhaps *does* indicate something about his chances of having true beliefs over the long run or about his chances of having epistemically rational beliefs over the long run, but it does not indicate that there is something epistemically substandard about every belief that is the product of that character or equipment. We can criticize the person's intellectual character or his cognitive equipment without criticizing everything that is the product of that character or equipment. A belief can be epistemically rational even though what prompts the believer to choose his belief or what cognitive equipment causes him to have the belief regularly produces epistemic howlers. In such cases, we should admit just what those who want to insist that having an appropriate history is a necessary condition of a belief being epistemically rational are so reluctant to admit; we should admit that the believer has been epistemically lucky.

Moreover, this same lesson applies to evidential knowledge. A person can evidentially know p even though the intellectual characteristic or cognitive process that prompted him to believe p regularly produces beliefs that are not propositionally rational. A person can evidentially know p, in other words, even though he is lucky to have adequate evidence for p. Analogously, he can evidentially know p even though the intellectual characteristic or cognitive process that causes him to believe p is unreliable. He can evidentially know p, in other words, even if he is lucky that his belief p is true. The example of our ideally veridical and evidentially perfect believer, who has something approaching a perfect explanation of the world, illustrates that both of these kinds of epistemic luck are possible.

4.6   *The Purely Epistemic*

A proposition p is epistemically rational for S to believe just if p either is properly basic for S or is made epistemically rational for S by propositions that are properly basic. Using this notion, I have proposed two senses in which S's belief p might be epistemically rational. In the propositional sense, S's belief p is epistemically rational just if S believes the proposition p and this proposition is epistemically rational for S. In the doxastic sense, S's belief p is epistemically rational just if it is propositionally rational, S believes he has a good argument for p, this belief also is propositionally rational for S, and the argument that S takes to be a good one for p roughly resembles an argument that in fact is a good argument for him. In neither of these senses and, I have claimed, in no other sense is having an appropriate history a prerequisite of a belief being epistemically rational. To help illustrate this claim, I have considered pairs of situations that are indistinguishable from the perspective of the person involved. The person believes exactly the same things in both situations and with the same amount of confidence, he has the same sort of experiences in both situations and with the same degree of vividness and clarity, and what he would believe on reflection is the same. Situations of this sort are epistemic twins. If some proposition p is epistemically rational (or irrational) for the person to believe in one situation, it is equally rational for him to believe in the other. Similarly, if one of the person's beliefs is epistemically rational in either of the above senses in one situation, the corresponding belief is epistemically rational in that sense in the other situation as well. And this is so regardless of any differences there might be in the histories of the beliefs in the two situations.

Of course, if S's beliefs are evaluated from some perspective other than his own or with respect to some goal other than his epistemic goal, situations of this sort need not be twins. For example, suppose S's beliefs are evaluated with respect to the epistemic goal but from an external perspective (say, the perspective of a "normal" person in S's community or even the perspective of an omniscient observer). From such a point of view, it can be appropriate for S to believe p in one of the above situations but not in the other. For even if the two situations are indistinguishable from S's perspective, from an external perspective they need not be indistinguishable. In particular, from an external perspective it may be obvious that S's believing p will promote his epistemic goal in one situation but not in the other.

When we depart from a purely epistemic point of view and evaluate S's beliefs with respect to some other goal (whether this be a social goal, a prudential goal, a long-term intellectual goal, or whatever) or from some other perspective (whether this be the perspective of some other person, the perspective of most people in S's community, the perspective of most scientists, the perspective of an omniscient observer, or whatever), we depart from the perspective from which judgments of epistemic rationality are made. All these other goals and all these other perspectives are beside the point when we are making purely epistemic evaluations. They are irrelevant, and their irrelevance can be illustrated in the same way. With respect to each of these other goals and each of these other perspectives, it will be possible to imagine a situation in which it is appropriate for S to believe p even though from S's own perspective on reflection p seems obviously false. But then, it is not epistemically rational for S to believe the proposition p. Rather, it is epistemically rational for him to believe its negation.

Of course, if it is epistemically rational for S to believe that his believing p would produce future benefits (whether these be practical benefits or intellectual benefits) and if in addition it is epistemically rational for him to believe that his believing p would not produce such benefits were not p true, then it normally will be epistemically rational for S to believe p. In a similar manner, if it is epistemically rational for S to believe that his belief was produced by a reliable process or if it is epistemically rational for S to believe that the total evidence possessed by his community indicates p is true, then it normally will be epistemically rational for S to believe p. But even in such cases, the future considerations themselves or the causal-historical considerations themselves or the social considerations themselves are not in any way prerequisites of S's belief p being rational in an epistemic sense. Rather, his belief is epistemically rational for him because it is epistemically rational for him to believe that only true beliefs will produce the benefits in question (or because it is epistemically rational for him to believe that the process that caused his belief is reliable, or because it is epistemically rational for him to believe that the total evidence possessed by his community would support p). And as is the case with most propositions that are epistemically rational, it is possible for such propositions to be mistaken, so that, for example, the process in question did not really cause S to believe *p* even though it is epistemically rational for *S* to believe that it did, or so that the process in question is not really reliable even though it is epistemically rational for him to believe that it is.

Thus, although it being epistemically rational for *S* to believe that his belief *p* has an appropriate past or will help bring about an appropriate future or conforms appropriately with the community's evidence sometimes can be important in making his belief epistemically rational, whether the belief actually has these characteristics is never important. In order for a belief to be epistemically rational, it need not have been caused in an appropriate way, it need not bring about appropriate effects, and it need not conform in an appropriate way to the community's evidence. In this sense, past conditions and future conditions and social conditions are never epistemically important.

Such a conclusion is Cartesian in spirit if not in letter. Indeed, it is not hard to see how the venerable Cartesian-inspired argument, the argument from illusion, can be recast in my terms. The fundamentally sound idea contained in the argument from illusion is that even in ordinary perceptual situations the fact that there is an object that the person is perceiving is epistemically insignificant in determining the epistemic rationality of the person's perceptual belief. After all, we can imagine a second situation that from the perspective of the person is indistinguishable from the actual situation but in which there is no object corresponding to his perceptual belief, and in this second situation his perceptual belief would be as rational from a purely epistemic point of view as it is in the first situation. But then, if we want to account for the epistemic rationality of the person's belief in the first situation, we need not cite the fact that there is an object corresponding to this belief in that situation. Rather, we can account for the belief's being epistemically rational by citing only characteristics that the belief shares with the belief in the second situation.

One way of summarizing this approach to epistemology is to say that it emphasizes the epistemic priority of both the present and the first person. This does not mean that in adopting this approach I am embracing any kind of solipsism nor does it mean that I am in some sense denying the reality of the past and the future. All I am claiming is that if anything makes it epistemically rational for me now to believe propositions about the past, the future, and the external world and if anything makes my actual beliefs about these kinds of propositions epistemically rational, then that something is within me and within the present moment. It is in this sense that I associate myself with a

Cartesian approach to epistemology. I am claiming that the conditions that make it epistemically rational for me to have beliefs about the past, the future, and the external world do not obtain within you or within most members of my community or within the scientific community or in the past or in the future. They obtain within me now.

Indeed, this maxim is not even very controversial once one accepts the notion that the purely epistemic point of view is defined by the goal of now believing truths and now not believing falsehoods and by the perspective of the individual himself on reflection. After all, from my own perspective it need not be obvious what you think or what the scientific community generally thinks. And even if it is obvious what you think or what they think, it need not be obvious from my perspective that what you or they think is acceptable. Analogously, what cognitive processes are reliable, or what causes me to believe what I do, is not something that I unproblematically can read off from the situations in which I find myself. And so, a proposition *p* might be appropriate for me to believe, given my own perspective and given that I have the goal of now believing truths and now not believing falsehoods, even though it runs counter to what you think or to what the scientific community thinks and even though what causes me to believe it is unreliable or is in some other way unusual.

Of course, it may be tempting for some to try to trivialize the simple maxim that the conditions that make my beliefs epistemically rational are conditions that obtain within me now. For example, one might claim that even a reliabilist can agree with this maxim, since we might interpret the reliabilist to be claiming that my present belief *p* is epistemically rational just if I presently am in the state of having a belief *p* that was produced by the reliable workings of my own internal cognitive equipment. However, this is only a ploy. A reliabilist position of this sort does not really imply that what makes my present belief rational are conditions that obtain within me now, since what makes my cognitive equipment a reliable indicator of the external world depends not just on my internal states but also upon the external world. After all, the external world could have been such that my cognitive equipment would not be a reliable indicator of it. Moreover, my *now* having a belief *p* that was reliably produced is not strictly a condition that obtains within me now, since it involves my belief having had an appropriate past. It is not, in other words, a purely present state of mine.[25]

This then is the general approach I have been taking toward epistemology: The conditions that make it epistemically rational for *S* at a time *t* to believe a proposition *p* as well as the conditions that make his belief *p* epistemically rational are conditions that obtain within *S* at that time *t*. The specific account of epistemic rationality, consistent with this approach, that I favor is the subjective foundationalist one outlined in chapter 1—an account that makes epistemic rationality a function of what a person believes, the confidence with which he believes it, and what he as he is now would believe on reflection.

NONEPISTEMIC REASONS FOR BELIEVING

5.1 Rational and Epistemically Rational Beliefs

There are, I have said, different general conceptions of rationality (see section 2.8). These different conceptions reflect different perspectives from which evaluations of how effectively an individual is pursuing his goals can be made. One of these conceptions, the one that I have called "an idealized Aristotelian conception," is represented by the following schema: All else being equal, it is rational for a person S to bring about Y if he has a goal X and he would believe were he to be ideally reflective that Y is an effective means to X. I have used this schema to motivate a subjective foundationalist account of epistemic rationality. But once the account is in place, I pointed out, it can be turned around and used to make more precise the very schema that was used to motivate it (see section 2.6). In particular, the fundamental schema can be revised to read: All else being equal, it is rational for S to bring about Y if he has a goal X and it is epistemically rational for S to believe that Y is an effective means to X. In this way, epistemic rationality becomes a constituent in other kinds of rationality. If S has a goal of kind K, then it is rational in sense K for S to bring about Y, all else being equal, if it is epistemically rational for S to believe that Y is an effective means to this goal.

Consider, for example, practical rationality. Suppose that S has a practical goal X and that it is epistemically rational for him to believe that Y is an effective means to X. Then, all else being equal, it is rational—rational in a practical sense—for S to bring about Y. And this is so even if Y in fact is not an effective means to X. What it is rational in a practical sense for S to bring about is not a function of success. Just as it can be epistemically rational for S to believe p even though p is false, so in an analogous manner it can be rational in a practical sense for S to bring about Y even though Y is not an effective means to his practical goals.[1]

Of course, as is the case with respect to S's epistemic goals, it is possible to evaluate from a perspective other than S's own ideally reflective perspective what means would be effective to his practical goals. But for present purposes, let us continue to adopt this idealized Aristotelian perspective, which implies that it is rational in a practical sense for S to bring about Y, all else being equal, if it is epistemically rational for him to believe that Y is an effective means to his practical goal X. This is not to say, of course, that when all practical considerations are taken into account it is rational in a practical sense for S to bring about Y. Whether in the final analysis it is rational in a practical sense for S to bring about Y is a function of how valuable his goal X is in relation to other practical goals (where this in turn might be a function, for instance, of how much he cares about or how much he needs X), what it is epistemically rational for S to believe about the likelihood of Y bringing about X, what it is epistemically rational for S to believe about the likelihood of Y bringing about something that will make it more difficult to achieve his other practical goals, and so on. But for the discussion here, all these details can be left open, for the idea is not to develop an adequate account of practical rationality, but rather to look at how practical rationality and other kinds of rationality interact with epistemic rationality. And for this purpose, the brief remarks above should suffice.

In particular, they should suffice to indicate how it is that considerations of practical rationality can be relevant to the question of what it is rational for S to believe. For insofar as it is epistemically rational for S to believe that his believing p would increase the likelihood of his achieving his practical goals, it is rational in a practical sense, all else being equal, for S to believe p.

This in turn creates a difficulty for anyone who is interested in the question of what it is rational for individuals to believe, since it is possible for an individual's practical reasons for believing to conflict with his epistemic reasons for believing. For example, suppose that it is epistemically rational for S to believe that his believing he will recover from his illness will aid his recovery (by improving his attitude). Then, all else being equal, it is rational in a practical sense for him to believe that he will recover. Or suppose it is epistemically rational for S to believe that his believing that he is more talented than his peers will help him succeed at his job (by adding to his self-confidence). Then, all else being equal, it is rational in a practical sense for him to believe that he is more talented than his peers. Like-wise, suppose that it is epistemically rational for S to believe that an eccentric philanthropist will give him a million dollars if he comes to believe that the earth is flat (the philanthropist has a way of distin-guishing S's actually believing this from his merely acting as if he believes it). Then, all else being equal, it is rational in a practical sense for S to believe that the earth is flat.[2] Yet it is easy to imagine that what it is rational in a practical sense for S to believe in each of these cases is not epistemically rational for him to believe. It can be rational in a practical sense for S to believe that he will recover from his ill-ness, or that he is more talented than his peers, or that the earth is flat, even though it is not epistemically rational for him to believe any of these claims. Thus, there can be conflicts between practical rationality and epistemic rationality. And as is the case with other conflicts, the question naturally arises: How should such conflicts be resolved? Is there some rational procedure by which they can be resolved?

In trying to answer this question, the first thing to notice is that the question is one that a theory of epistemic rationality cannot pos-sibly answer. It is not within the province of a theory of epistemic rationality to answer it. Rather, the question is within the province of the theory of rational belief, of which the theory of epistemically rational belief is but a part. The theory of epistemically rational belief seeks to describe what it is rational for a person to believe insofar as he has the goal of now believing truths and now not believing false-hoods. The theory of rational belief, in contrast, seeks to describe what is rational for S to believe all things being considered. That is, it seeks to describe what it is rational for S to believe when all of his goals—his epistemic goal, his practical goals, his long-term intellec-tual goals—are taken into account. Following the general schema of rationality, we can say as a rough approximation that it is rational all things being considered for S to believe p if it is epistemically rational for S to believe that the estimated benefits of his believing p are greater than either the estimated benefits of his withholding judgment on p or the estimated benefits of his believing not$p$, where the estimated benefits of these options are determined by the relative importance of S's various goals, epistemic and other-wise, and the relative likelihood that S's believing p (or disbelieving p or withholding judgment on p) will secure (or help secure) these goals for him.

So insofar as we are interested in how conflicts among epistemic goals, practical goals, and other goals are to be resolved rationally, it is the theory of rational belief rather than the theory of epistemically rational belief to which we must turn.

5.2   Evidentialism

What, then, does the theory of rational belief tell us about what it is rational for a person to believe when there is a conflict between his epistemic goal and one of his nonepistemic goals? It tells us, very roughly, that what it is rational for him to believe is determined by which of the goals is more important. If the epistemic goal is more important and if all else is equal (if, say, it is epistemically rational for him to believe that the chances of securing it are as good as the chances of securing the nonepistemic goal), it is rational for him to believe what he has epistemic reasons to believe. On the other hand, if the nonepistemic goal is more important, it is rational for him to believe what he has nonepistemic reasons to believe.

But of course this only pushes the question back one step. Now the question becomes, what goals are likely to be more important, epistemic ones or nonepistemic ones? How one answers this question is likely to be a function of one's theory of goals. If, for example, an individual's goals are just those things that he wants or needs, then the relative value of his goals presumably will be a function of how much he wants or needs these things. On the other hand, if an individual can have as one of his goals something that he neither wants nor needs, then the relative value of his goals will have to be determined in some other way. In any event, I do not intend to propose here a theory of goals, for the question at hand is a limited one, one concerning the relative importance of an individual's epistemic goal. And at least a provisional answer to this question might be forthcoming even without a complete theory of goals. For example, one simple answer to this question is that whatever one's theory of goals, that theory, if it is to be adequate, must imply that an individual's epistemic goal is always more important than his other goals. In other words, one's theory of goals ought to imply that epistemic reasons to believe something always take precedence over nonepistemic reasons to believe something.[3] Hence, if there is a nonepistemic reason for S to believe a proposition p but p is not epistemically rational for S to believe p, then all things being considered it is not rational for S to believe p.

This is the position that sometimes is known as evidentialism. Evidentialism implies that in the final analysis it is rational for an individual to believe just that for which he has adequate evidence. Indeed, since the evidentialist says that epistemic considerations always override nonepistemic considerations and since overridingness is often taken to be a key characteristic of moral considerations, it is natural to interpret the evidentialist as saying that morality requires that the epistemic goal take precedence over other goals, so that a person has a moral duty to believe, or at least to try to believe, what it is epistemically rational for him to believe. It is immoral to knowingly allow any nonepistemic consideration to prompt one to believe a proposition that it is not epistemically rational for one to believe.[4]

Evidentialism, then, embodies a kind of epistemic chauvinism: Epistemic reasons for believing something by their very nature are thought superior to nonepistemic reasons for believing. Indeed, they are thought to be so superior that it always is rational, all things considered, to believe only that for which one has good epistemic reasons.

This is an extreme position, far too extreme. To show how extreme, consider an extreme example. Suppose that the survival of the earth somehow is dependent upon a person S believing a proposition p that he has good epistemic reason to believe is false. Suppose, for example, a mad scientist will blow up the earth if S does not come to believe p. Surely any plausible theory of goals will imply that in such a case it might be rational, all things being considered, for S to believe p. That is, it surely might be the case that when all of S's goals and their relative values are taken into account, S has stronger reasons to believe p than not to believe p. But, this is just what the evidentialist is committed to denying.

There presumably are also less extreme cases in which it is rational all things being considered for a person to believe what is not epistemically rational for him. William James, for one, thought there are less extreme cases of this sort. In particular, James sought to describe a set of conditions that are sufficient to make believing p morally appropriate and hence (in James's view) rational for a person even though the person lacks adequate evidence for believing p. Roughly, James claimed that if (1) believing a proposition p is a "live" option for S, in that the question of whether p is true "cannot by its very nature be decided on intellectual grounds," and if (2) the question of whether or not to believe p is for S a "momentous" issue, in that his believing p will help bring about some morally desirable result (perhaps the truth of p itself), and if (3) his believing p is a "forced" issue, in that only if he gets himself to believe p will this morally desirable result occur (so withholding judgment on p will have the same effect as disbelieving p), then S ought to believe p—it is rational all things considered for him to believe *p*—despite the fact that he lacks adequate evidence for it. Moreover, these conditions are met, James thought, in a variety of actual situations by a variety of propositions. For many people in many situations, the proposition that the person they have just met likes them is such a proposition, James thought. Believing this proposition is an option that is likely to be live (since we normally will not have decisive evidence for it or against it), momentous (since believing it is likely to promote friendship), and forced (since withholding on it will not help promote friendship). More notoriously, the proposition that God exists also can be a proposition of this sort, James thought.[5]

Whether or not James is right in thinking that these three conditions are sufficient for it being rational to believe what is not epistemically rational[6] and whether or not he is right in thinking that the proposition that God exists satisfies these conditions, the general point he is making is the same general point that I have made with my more extreme case. Epistemic chauvinism, as embodied in evidentialism, is indefensible. All things being considered, it can be rational for an individual to believe what it is not epistemically rational for him to believe.[7]

It is important not to misunderstand what this rejection of evidentialism involves. In particular, to reject evidentialism is not to be committed to the claim that it can be rational for an individual to believe what he has no reasons to believe. To the contrary, it is trivially true that it is rational for someone to believe *p* only if he has adequate reasons to believe *p*. Rejecting evidentialism merely commits one to the claim that there can be adequate, nonepistemic reasons for believing *p*. It commits one to the claim that there can be adequate reasons to believe that for which there is not adequate evidence.

Why does this seem so odd? Why does it seem so odd for practical reasons, or for other nonepistemic reasons, to override epistemic reasons for believing, making it rational all things considered to believe what is not epistemically rational? That it does seem odd, I think, cannot be denied. Indeed, when people reflect upon what reasons they have to believe something, as opposed to what reasons they have to say something or what reasons they have to act as if they believed something, they rarely even consider the practical advantages that might accrue to them by believing it. But insofar as they wish to believe what all things being considered it is rational for them to believe, it seems as if they should. Likewise, when someone tries to convince another person that he has reasons to believe something (again, as opposed to convincing him that he has reasons for saying something or reasons for acting as if he believed something), they rarely even mention the practical benefits that might result from believing it. And yet, insofar as one is trying to convince the other person that it is rational all things being considered for him to believe the proposition in question, it seems as if one should mention these practical benefits.

Why is there this almost total disregard for anything other than epistemic reasons for believing? Perhaps because it is impossible for someone to believe a proposition p as long as he is convinced that his evidence indicates that p is likely to be false. Just as it may be impossible for a person S to believe p and also to believe its contradictory not$p$, so too it may be impossible for him to have "near contradictory" beliefs, such that he believes p while also believing that his evidence indicates that p is likely to be false. (See section 7.5.) Perhaps it is even impossible for him to believe p while also believing that he has no evidence indicating that p is likely to be true.[8] The nature of believing may prevent this, since belief by its very nature "aims at the truth."[9] If p here, for example, is the proposition that the earth is flat and S is convinced that his evidence indicates that p is likely to be false or even if he is merely convinced that he lacks evidence for thinking p is true, he may not be able to believe p no matter how much money is at stake. Similarly, if p is the proposition that he will recover from his illness or the proposition that he is more talented than his peers and S is convinced that he either lacks evidence for p or has evidence against it, S may not be able to believe p even if his health or his future job prospects depend upon it.

If it really is impossible for a person to believe a proposition when he is convinced that he either lacks evidence for it or has evidence against it, or even if this is merely difficult instead of impossible, this may help explain why people only rarely consider what nonepistemic reasons they have to believe a proposition. It may also help explain why they only rarely mention to other people what nonepistemic reasons these other people have to believe a proposition. Namely, it normally is pointless to do so. It normally is pointless for a person S to try to convince himself of the truth of p by convincing himself that he has good nonepistemic reasons to believe p. Likewise, it normally is pointless for others to try to convince S of the truth of p in this way. For even if S becomes convinced that he does have good nonepistemic reasons for believing p, unless he also becomes convinced that there are good epistemic reasons for p (or at least unless he ceases to be convinced that there are *not* good epistemic reasons for p), he may find it difficult or even impossible to believe p. On the other hand, if he becomes convinced that he has good epistemic reasons for p (that is, good evidence for p), this normally is enough to convince him of p. It normally is enough to make him believe p; most of us are such that when we become convinced there is good evidence for a proposition p, we "automatically" come to believe it. So, being convinced that one lacks evidence for p normally will prevent one from believing p (whatever practical reasons there might be for believing it), and on the other hand being convinced that one has good evidence for p normally is enough to ensure that one believes p (whatever practical reasons there might be against believing it). This then may be the explanation for why it seems so odd for a person even to consider the nonepistemic reasons he has for believing something and what makes it so odd for others in their efforts to persuade him to so much as mention these kinds of reasons for believing.

Even if all this is right, however, it does not imply that it is impossible for practical or other nonepistemic considerations to give a person a good reason to believe something. Likewise, it does not imply that such considerations cannot effectively motivate a person to get himself to believe a proposition that is not now epistemically rational for him. It implies only that insofar as these nonepistemic considerations do play a role in getting the person to believe the proposition, they must do so indirectly, since it is impossible, or at least unlikely, that he will believe the proposition as long as he believes that there is no evidence indicating it is true. On the other hand, if somehow he were to come to believe that there is good evidence for the proposition, all this would change. It might then be possible for him to believe the proposition.

How are we to understand this talk of evidence? For a subjective foundationalist, it is natural to say that an individual's evidence consists of those propositions that are properly basic for the individual (and perhaps in addition those propositions that are the premises of the good second-level arguments he has). But for present purposes (where we are concerned with the individual coming to believe that he has good evidence for a proposition), it will be better to understand evidence in a more objective manner. Let us say that a proposition e is evidence for p for an individual S just in case (roughly) e is true and e along with other true propositions that S believes helps make p probable.[10] And then we can say that in order for e to be part of what S takes to be his evidence for p, S must believe both that e is true and that e in conjunction with true propositions $e^1, e^2, \ldots e^n$ make p probable.

Given this notion of evidence, assume that S somehow arranges things so that he comes to believe propositions that he takes to constitute good evidence for *p*. Then the obstacles that (we are assuming) previously prevented him from believing *p* have been removed. He might then come to believe what previously was rational but not epistemically rational for him. This becomes possible because he has manipulated himself and his situation so that at this later time he has what he takes to be good evidence for believing *p*.

Accordingly, even if it is impossible for a person to believe a proposition *p* that he takes to be rational all things being considered but not epistemically rational for him, his nonepistemic reasons for believing *p* nonetheless might motivate him to undertake a project of manipulating his situation so that at some future time he comes to have what he takes to be good evidence for *p*. As a result, he might then "automatically" come to believe *p*.

However, in order for any such project to be successful, it must hide its own tracks. In other words, it must involve a measure of self-deception, so that *S* at the future time will no longer be aware that he undertook such a project.[11] For if *S* remains aware that he has deliberately manipulated his situation for the express purpose of garnering evidence for a proposition *p* against which he previously thought he lacked good evidence, he presumably will not think that in the final analysis he has evidence indicating that *p* is likely to be true. His manipulations may succeed in giving him what he takes to be prima facie evidence for *p,* but he presumably will think that this prima facie support is defeated by other evidence relevant to *p*, evidence indicating that his newly acquired evidence for *p* is nonrandom. He will still be aware that he has deliberately skewed his evidence in favor of *p*.

On the other hand, if *S* somehow can get himself to forget that he has deliberately skewed his evidence in favor of *p*, his project stands a chance of succeeding. Perhaps, for example, *S* could have himself hypnotized and given posthypnotic suggestions that will result in his placing himself in situations in which what he sees, hears, and so on will cause him to believe propositions that he thinks make *p* likely and will not cause him to believe propositions that he thinks make *p* unlikely. In addition, perhaps these posthypnotic suggestions also will result in his forgetting that he has been hypnotized or that he has in any other way skewed his situation in order to get evidence for *p* and to exclude evidence against it. Or perhaps there is some other, less extreme way that he can get himself to forget he has skewed his evidence.

So even if it is impossible for *S* to get himself to believe *p* as long as he believes he has no good evidence for *p*, he nonetheless may be able indirectly to get himself to believe *p*. He can do this by altering his epistemic situation so that he comes to believe that he has good evidence for *p*. Unfortunately, it frequently will be the case that altering his epistemic situation in this way will not be a narrowly contained project. Given the holistic nature of beliefs, such a project frequently will involve *S* not just in changing his attitudes toward *p* but also in changing his attitudes toward an enormous number of other propositions. For ordinarily, beliefs cannot be altered in a piecemeal fashion. Significant chunks of beliefs have to be altered in order for any one belief to be altered.

But then, if one undertakes a project of getting himself to believe a proposition for which he now lacks evidence, it frequently will be the case that he will be involved in a project that will result in his believing not just one isolated proposition for which he now lacks good evidence. Rather, he will be involved in a project that will result in his believing a whole host of propositions for which he now thinks he lacks good evidence. And so, deliberately altering one's beliefs for nonepistemic reasons frequently will involve a person in what that person now has good epistemic reason to regard as massive error. For example, if in order to win a million dollars, *S* must come to believe that the earth is flat, he also is going to have to come to believe a whole range of other propositions that are now epistemically irrational for him. Indeed, he presumably will have to come to believe that there is an enormous worldwide conspiracy to make it appear as if the earth is round when in fact it is flat. Similarly, if it is now epistemically rational for *S* to believe that he generally is less talented than his peers but he undertakes to get himself to believe that he is more talented so as to increase his self-confidence, he must get himself to "reinterpret" an enormous amount of data about his life history. In addition, he must take steps to ensure that he has suitable stories or scenarios for explaining away any new data that might indicate that he is less talented than his peers.

This is not to say, however, that a project of getting oneself to believe what is now epistemically irrational for him to believe need always be so far-reaching. There presumably are some relatively noncentral and unimportant propositions that are now epistemically irrational for an individual *S* but that also are such that a project to get himself to believe them would not involve *S* in what he now has good epistemic reasons to regard as massive error. Suppose, for example, that *S* now believes and now has good epistemic reasons to believe that some swans are nonwhite. (He believes this because he remembers seeing a black swan.) Then, in order to get himself to believe that all swans are white, S presumably must somehow get himself to forget that he has seen a black swan. He presumably must also find some way of ensuring that he will not find himself in situations in which he is likely to see another nonwhite swan or in which he is likely to hear someone he trusts talk about the color of swans. Even so, none of this, it seems, need result in his believing a huge number of propositions that he now (with good reason) regards as false.

Here there is a range of relevant cases. In certain situations, undertaking to get himself to believe a proposition that is now epistemically irrational for him is likely to involve S in what he now has epistemic reasons to regard as massive error. In other cases, such a project is likely to involve him in what he now has reason to regard as moderate error. And in still other cases, such a project is likely to involve relatively insignificant error.

In any event, the project of undertaking to get oneself to believe what is now epistemically irrational is not a project to be undertaken lightly. Not infrequently, the effects will ripple throughout a large part of one's belief system. The possibility of there being such a ripple effect no doubt at least partially accounts for why it can be so tempting to think that there is something inevitably and deeply irrational about allowing practical considerations to override epistemic considerations in shaping what one believes.

It is important to notice, however, that even if there is something inevitably and deeply irrational about this, the irrationality does not arise simply because one has tampered with one's evidential situation with the intention of influencing what one believes. On the contrary, we properly engage in such tampering all the time. For example, it is characteristic of the scientific enterprise that it encourages such tampering. A key component of scientific investigation is to manipulate one's environment (as one does when one conducts an experiment) in such a way that one's evidence about various propositions is likely to be altered and as a result one's beliefs also are likely to be altered. There need be nothing that even hints of irrationality in manipulations of this sort. Moreover, this is so even if a scientist is motivated to tamper with his evidential situation for reasons that are only indirectly related to discovering the truth. If, for example, a scientist for reasons of self-aggrandizement wants to get himself as well as others to believe a hypothesis that he has proposed, it is perfectly appropriate for him to set up the kind of experiment that he deems most likely to generate convincing evidence for its truth. What distinguishes this kind of case, in which a person deliberately seeks to expose himself to evidence that supports a proposition he wants to believe but which is not now epistemically rational for him to believe, from the kind of case where such manipulations are suspicious, is that in the suspicious cases the person deliberately worsens his epistemic situation. He deliberately tries to get himself in a situation where his evidence is likely to support falsehoods. By contrast, our scientist tries to get himself to believe what he wants to believe by improving his epistemic situation—by getting himself in a situation where (he hopes) the truth of his hypothesis will become compelling. Moreover, it presumably is epistemically rational for the scientist to believe that his manipulations will have this result. It is, in other words, epistemically rational for him to believe that the kind of control he is exercising over his situation, and hence the kind of control he is exercising over the evidence to which he will be exposed, is likely to result in his being in a better position to evaluate the truth of his hypothesis. On the other hand, in the suspicious cases this is not so. When a person S in order to win a million dollars tampers with his evidence in a way that (he hopes) will result in his believing that the earth is flat, it presumably is epistemically rational for him to believe that such tampering will leave him in a worse position to determine whether or not it is true that the earth is flat. Likewise, it presumably is epistemically rational for him to believe that it also will leave him in a worse position to determine the truth of a variety of other propositions. Indeed, this is the point of his manipulations. The point is to get himself in an evidential position that he takes to be worse than his current one, so that he can come to have the belief that the earth is flat.

So, if there is something deeply irrational about S trying to get himself to believe that the earth is flat in order to win a million dollars, the irrationality does not arise simply because he has manipulated his evidence. It does not even arise because he has manipulated his evidence with the intention of getting himself to believe a specific proposition that he now has good epistemic reasons to think false. Rather, if there is something deeply irrational about S trying to get himself to believe that the earth is flat, the irrationality is likely to arise because he has manipulated his evidence with the intention of making it more likely that his evidence will support what is false.

Even so, the irrationality here, if it be such, occurs when the tampering is initiated. There need be no irrationality at the end of the project. At the end of the tampering, S may very well believe precisely what it *then* is epistemically rational for him to believe (and what it is *now* epistemically rational for him to believe false). The point of the tampering is for S to get himself to believe the proposition in question, whether this be the proposition that the earth is flat or some other proposition *p,* by getting himself to believe he has good evidence for it. But ordinarily, the best way for S to get himself to believe that he has good evidence for a proposition *p* is in fact to acquire what he takes to be good evidence for *p.* If S can manipulate his situation so that he sees, hears, and remembers the appropriate things and if he also can manipulate his situation so that he forgets (or is unaware of) this manipulation, he can generate what he takes to be genuinely good evidence for *p.* But then, assuming that sufficient reflection would not alter his opinion about this evidence, *p* is likely to be epistemically rational for him. So, the inevitable irrationality involved in such tampering, if it be such, must be the irrationality involved in undertaking such a project. There is no inevitable epistemic irrationality at the end of the project.

The fact that there need be no epistemic irrationality at the end of the project reflects one of the characteristic marks of rationality, both in the epistemic sense and in the practical sense: The sins of the past are not, as it were, passed down from generation to generation. Past mistakes may make it more difficult to achieve one's goals, whether these be epistemic or practical, but success in achieving one's goal is not a prerequisite of being rational in either the practical or the epistemic sense. Thus, past mistakes may affect and affect for the worse the situation in which a person now finds himself, but this does not imply that it is impossible for him to be rational in his current situation. Whether or not he is now being rational depends on whether or not he is dealing in an appropriate way with his current situation, regardless of what that situation is and regardless of whether he himself is responsible for making it as bad as it is. So, for example, suppose a person does something that results in his being in a position where he cannot help but do something immensely harmful to his self-interest, but suppose that once he is in this position he does what he recognizes to be the least harmful thing he can do. This latter action, then, is rational in a prudential sense even if the earlier action was not.

The interesting question is not whether a person who deliberately worsens his epistemic situation with the hope that he will come to believe what is now epistemically irrational for him inevitably ends up with epistemically irrational beliefs. The answer to this question is no.[12] Rather, the interesting question is whether there is something inevitably irrational about a person undertaking such a project. Is there, in other words, something inevitably irrational, all things considered, about a person deliberately trying to worsen his epistemic situation?

But so far at least, it is not obvious that there is. What has been established so far is that if such a project is successful, it frequently will involve the person in what he now has epistemic reasons to regard as massive error. But not all such projects are like this, and for those projects that are not, it is hard to see why undertaking them would have to be irrational, all things considered. And even when such a project would involve the person in what he now has epistemic reasons to regard as massive error, it still is hard to see why undertaking it would have to be irrational, all things considered. After all, if the person has goals other than ones related to his believing truths and if these other goals are sufficiently more important than the epistemic ones, what is there to prevent these goals from making it rational, all things considered, for him to deliberately worsen his epistemic situation?

The answer is that in principle there is nothing to prevent this. Even in those cases where it is epistemically rational for the person to believe that such a project will lead to massive error, it can be rational, all things considered, for a person to undertake the project. It can be rational, that is, for him to try to worsen his epistemic situation in order to get himself to believe what he now with good epistemic reasons regards as false. Some of the cases already mentioned illustrate how this can be rational. If, to return to the most extreme case, it is epistemically rational for S to believe that the earth will be destroyed unless he somehow gets himself to believe p, which he now with good epistemic reasons believes to be false, it will be rational on any plausible theory of goals for S to undertake a project of getting himself to believe p. And this is so even if the only way to do this is to get himself to believe a whole host of other propositions that he now has good epistemic reasons to regard as false.

5.3   Reasons for Not Worsening One's Epistemic Situation

Although it can be rational, all things considered, for an individual deliberately to worsen his epistemic situation in an attempt to get himself to believe what he now has no good epistemic reasons to regard as true, this is not likely to be common. On the contrary, a project of this sort is likely to be rational, all things considered, only infrequently. But this is not, as the evidentialist suggests, because the goal of believing truths and not believing falsehoods is intrinsically so much more important than other goals. Far from it; believing truths and not believing falsehoods for most of us is probably intrinsically less important than many other goals.

So, what does make it almost always irrational, all things considered, for a person to allow practical considerations to override epistemic considerations? The answer is that practical considerations themselves normally make this irrational. There normally are good practical reasons against allowing practical considerations to motivate one to try to worsen one's epistemic situation. For although by deliberately worsening one's epistemic situation one may get oneself to believe what one has a practical reason to believe, worsening one's epistemic situation ordinarily will affect adversely one's chances of achieving one's other practical goals. Or at the very least, it normally will be epistemically rational for an individual S to believe that this is so. It normally will be epistemically rational for S to believe both that worsening his epistemic situation is likely to result in his having more false beliefs than would otherwise be the case and that the more false beliefs he has the less likely it is that he will be able to pursue his practical goals effectively. Thus, under normal conditions it is likely to be epistemically rational for an individual to believe that in trying to worsen his epistemic situation he also will worsen his practical situation. This is particularly likely to be the case when worsening one's epistemic situation has a significant ripple effect on what else one believes.

Although by deliberately worsening one's epistemic situation a person may get himself to believe what he has a good practical reason to believe and in this way achieve one of his practical goals, he ordinarily also will worsen his chances of achieving a host of his other practical goals. But if so, when all of his goals are taken into consideration, it is unlikely to be rational for him to undertake this project of worsening his epistemic situation.

Of course, the extent to which a project of worsening one's epistemic situation will worsen one's practical situation as well will be a function of how much error such a project is likely to generate. If it is epistemically rational for an individual to believe that such a project is likely to produce massive error, then (at least normally) it also will be epistemically rational for him to believe that the project will worsen significantly his chances of achieving his various practical goals, since he is likely to end up with false beliefs about how to obtain his goals. On the other hand, if it is not epistemically rational for him to believe that the project is likely to produce significant error, he is unlikely to have significant practical reasons to undertake the project. Suppose, for example, that the project is one of getting himself to believe a proposition p. Then, he is likely to have significant non-epistemic reasons to believe such a proposition p only in "funny" situations—situations, say, in which someone has offered him a million dollars to come to believe p. In relatively normal situations, the only propositions that a person is likely to have significant nonepistemic reasons to believe (despite the fact that they are epistemically irrational) are propositions that are relatively central to how he lives his life—for example, propositions about his own abilities, talents, and so on—but these propositions are just the ones that are least likely to be relatively isolated from other propositions. Accordingly, a project to get oneself to believe these propositions is just the kind of project that is likely to involve the person in what he now has epistemic reasons to regard as massive error. And hence, there normally will be strong practical reasons not to undertake such a project.

This is not to say that there cannot be exceptions. There can be cases in which deliberately worsening one's epistemic situation in order to get oneself to believe a proposition p is rational, all things considered. The point here is simply that there are considerations that make it highly improbable that this will happen frequently. Such a project either will be a project that is likely to generate what the person now has epistemic reasons to regard as significant errors or it will not be such a project. If the former, then the person is likely to have strong practical reasons not to undertake the project (since it is likely to affect adversely his chances of achieving a whole range of his practical goals). On the other hand, if the latter, then the person is unlikely to have strong practical reasons to undertake the project (since the proposition is unlikely to be one that is important to how he lives his life).

Moreover, this point can be generalized. It is not just that it normally will be epistemically rational for a person to believe that worsening his epistemic situation will result in a worsening of his practical situation, such that he may well be involved in massive practical error as well as massive epistemic error. It is also that an analogous point can be made for any of his other goals, whether these be long-term intellectual goals, moral goals, aesthetic goals, or whatever. Insofar as it now is epistemically rational for an individual to believe that a deliberate worsening of his epistemic situation is likely to result in his choosing less effective means to these goals than he would otherwise, he has reasons not to worsen his epistemic situation.

So it is not just from the standpoint of having true beliefs and not having false beliefs that an individual normally has reasons not to worsen his epistemic situation. And it is not just that he normally has practical reasons not to do so. Rather, he normally has as many kinds of reasons not to worsen his epistemic situation as he has kinds of goals.

Thus, although it may not be unusual for practical and other nonepistemic considerations to give an individual a reason to believe what is epistemically irrational for him, the total set of practical and nonepistemic considerations normally prevents a nonepistemic reason for believing from making it rational, all things considered, for the individual to worsen his epistemic situation in an effort to acquire the belief in question. In most cases, there are good practical reasons and other good nonepistemic reasons not to deliberately worsen one's epistemic situation in order to get oneself to believe what one now does not have good epistemic reasons to believe. Practical rationality and other kinds of nonepistemic rationality in this way encourage epistemic rationality.

Moreover, in encouraging epistemic rationality, nonepistemic considerations also help supply an answer to the question, "Why should one believe what is epistemically rational for him?" In addition to the trivial answer, because it is epistemically rational for one to do so, we now can add the nontrivial answer, because normally it is rational, all things considered, for one to do so.

5.4   Reasons for Not Improving One's Epistemic Situation

Practical considerations and other nonepistemic considerations only rarely give a person a good reason to worsen his epistemic situation, but on the other hand they also only rarely give a person a good reason to try as hard as he can to try to improve his epistemic situation—to try as hard as he can to get himself in a better position to believe truths and not to believe falsehoods. Rather, nonepistemic considerations normally encourage one to set limits upon the amount of time and effort one devotes to trying to believe truths and not to believe falsehoods. A fair amount of such effort (in the form, for example, of gathering evidence, studying that evidence, and so on) is reasonable, since it is plausible to think that such effort will increase the likelihood that what one will believe to be effective means to one's various goals really are effective. But beyond a certain point, additional epistemic effort is not likely to be reasonable. For one, it may be that epistemic effort is subject to a rule of diminishing epistemic return, in the sense that additional epistemic effort is likely to bring little or no improvement in one's epistemic situation. And if it is epistemically rational for a person to believe that this is so, it very likely also will be epistemically rational for him to believe that additional epistemic effort will not improve his overall situation either; it will not make it more likely that what he takes to be effective means to his various goals really are effective means. Second, and perhaps more important, the time and effort one spends in trying to improve one's epistemic situation reduces the time and effort one has to devote to the pursuit of one's nonepistemic goals, and at some point additional increments of epistemic effort will begin to worsen significantly the chances one has of achieving these nonepistemic goals. Accordingly, at some point it becomes epistemically rational for one to believe that additional epistemic efforts—studying one's evidence, generating new evidence, and the like—is likely to worsen instead of improve one's overall situation. At this point, it becomes rational, all things considered, not to spend additional time or effort in improving one's epistemic situation.

Of course, the exact point at which this happens will differ for different people, especially in a society where division of labor is customary and where the labor expected of some people requires them to spend much of their time improving their epistemic situation. But even for these people, for health reasons if for nothing else, there will be a point at which it becomes rational, all things considered, not to spend additional time and effort studying their evidence, gathering additional evidence, or doing something else to improve their chances of believing truths and not believing falsehoods.

Although there normally are good practical reasons for not worsening one's epistemic situation, there normally also are good practical reasons for not spending a huge amount of time and effort on improving one's epistemic situation. Practical considerations as well as other nonepistemic considerations act in this way as a kind of moderating influence upon epistemic pursuits; they tend to make it rational, all things considered, for a person to be neither slovenly nor fanatical in his search to believe truths and not to believe falsehoods.

5.5   The Deductive Consequence Thesis and Epistemic Blame

When evaluating an account of epistemic rationality, it is important to keep in mind how nonepistemic considerations tend to make it rational for an individual to be moderate in his attempts to believe truths and not to believe falsehoods. Unless this is kept in mind, it is easy to be misled into thinking that an otherwise adequate account of epistemic rationality is overly demanding. For example, consider all those propositions that are deductively implied by a proposition *p* that is epistemically rational for a person *S*. Given subjective foundationalism, it is likely that many if not most of these implied propositions will themselves be epistemically rational for *S*. Many if not most will be such that were *S* to be sufficiently reflective, he would realize that they are implied by *p*. So if *S* has what he on reflection would regard as a good argument for *p*, he is also likely to have what he on reflection would regard as good arguments for many if not most of the propositions that are implied by *p*. But then, a huge number of propositions are likely to be epistemically rational for *S*. For example, any disjunction whatsoever that has *p* as one of its disjuncts is implied by *p*. So if *p* is epistemically rational for *S*, all these disjunctions (or at least all that are not too complex for him to understand) are also likely to be epistemically rational for him. Moreover, *p* is likely to imply many other propositions in more subtle ways, ways which *S* does not recognize but which he would recognize were he to be sufficiently reflective. And of course, the same is likely to be true of any other proposition that is epistemically rational for *S*.

Let us call this thesis—the thesis that most of the relatively uncomplex deductive consequences of a proposition that is epistemically rational for a person are also epistemically rational for that person—"the deductive consequence thesis."[13] It can be tempting to regard this thesis as constituting a reductio against any view of epistemic rationality that implies it, since it would seem to be impossible for any person to believe anywhere near all the propositions that the thesis implies are epistemically rational for him. For one, an individual presumably will not believe every proposition that is epistemically rational for him. But if he fails to believe even one such proposition *p*, he presumably also will fail to believe a huge number of the deductive consequences of *p*. And even if *p* here is a proposition that he believes, there presumably still will be many deductive consequences of *p* that he does not believe.

Thus, if anything like the deductive consequence thesis is acceptable, it is likely that every person fails to believe a huge number of propositions that are epistemically rational for him. Moreover, this presumably would be the case even if a person were to devote all of his time to epistemic pursuits. If an individual were to do this, no doubt he would come to see additional implications of the propositions that are now epistemically rational for him. As a result, no doubt he would come to believe additional propositions that are epistemically rational for him. But even so, there presumably would be many implications of the propositions that are epistemically rational for him that he still would not believe.

So if anything like the deductive consequence thesis is true, a person can try as hard as he possibly can to believe all that and only that which is epistemically rational for him and still fail to believe an enormous number of propositions that are epistemically rational for him. This might make it all the more tempting to think that the deductive consequence thesis and any account of epistemic rationality that implies it is overly demanding.

Is the deductive consequence thesis really overly demanding? Notice that the thesis does not imply that it is rational, all things considered, for a person to believe as many of the deductive consequences of propositions that are epistemically rational for him as he possibly can. It does not even imply that it is rational, all things considered, for an individual to *try* to believe all these propositions (say, by devoting all his time to working out the implications of those propositions for which he thinks he has good evidence). If it did imply this, the thesis would be clearly unacceptable, since it would be recommending that people try to do what it is obviously absurd for them to do. But in fact, the deductive consequence thesis makes no such recommendation, and neither does any theory of epistemic rationality that implies it. Indeed, a theory of epistemic rationality makes no recommendation whatsoever about what it is rational for people to believe, all things considered. Likewise, it makes no recommendations about how much time and effort it is rational, all things considered, for people to devote to deliberating about what to believe. By its very nature, a theory of epistemic rationality only makes recommendations concerning what it is rational for a person to believe insofar as he has the goal of now believing truths and now not believing falsehoods.

Of course, if one assumes that the only goal, or at least by far the most important goal, that people have is this epistemic goal, then absurd consequences would follow given the deductive consequence thesis. One then would be committed to the view that people should devote most of their lives to trying to figure all the implications of the propositions for which they think they have good evidence, in the hope that this will result in their believing all the deductive consequences of propositions that are epistemically rational for them. But even here, the absurdity attaches not to the deductive consequence thesis, or to a theory of epistemic rationality that implies it, but rather to the assumption that the epistemic goal is far more important than any of our other goals.[14]

Still, there may be a lingering suspicion that any account of epistemic rationality that implies anything like the deductive consequence thesis is overly demanding. As a way of making explicit this suspicion, consider two assumptions: (1) A person who tries as hard as he can to believe truths and not to believe falsehoods cannot be faulted for believing what he does;[15] (2) if a person cannot be faulted for believing what he does, he believes just what it is epistemically rational for him to believe.[16]

When these two assumptions are joined with the deductive consequence thesis, absurd consequences once again follow. For if we assume there is a person S who tries as hard as he possibly can to believe truths and not to believe falsehoods (by gathering evidence, studying his evidence, and so on), then there almost certainly will be propositions that are both epistemically rational and not epistemically rational for him to believe. For try as he may, he almost certainly will not be able to believe all the propositions that the deductive consequence thesis implies are epistemically rational for him. Let p be one of these propositions that is epistemically rational for him but that he fails to believe. But by hypothesis, S has tried as hard as he possibly can to believe truths and not to believe falsehoods, and yet he does not believe p. Since he has tried as hard as he can, he cannot be faulted for failing to believe p. This follows from (1). But then, by (2) it cannot be epistemically rational for him to believe p. Thus, given the deductive consequence thesis and given assumptions (1) and (2), p is both epistemically rational for S and not epistemically rational for S.

There may be a suspicion, then, that what leads to this contradiction is an account of epistemic rationality that is overly demanding, an account that implies the deductive consequence thesis. But again, the real problem lies not with the deductive consequence thesis, nor with a theory of epistemic rationality that implies it; rather, it lies with assumption (2) above, the assumption that doxastic faultlessness implies epistemic rationality. It may be true that if a person tries as hard as he possibly can to believe truths and not to believe falsehoods, then he cannot be faulted for not having done a good enough job of satisfying his epistemic goals.[17] But from the fact that he cannot be so faulted, it does not follow that everything he believes and nothing that he fails to believe is epistemically rational for him. It does not follow that he has perfectly satisfied his own epistemic standards. Consider a proposition p that he fails to believe even though it is the deductive consequence of another proposition that he does believe and that is epistemically rational for him to believe. Suppose further that the deductive relation between this other proposition and p is such that were he to have been more reflective, S himself would have realized that the proposition implies p. However, by hypothesis S has tried as hard as he possibly can to satisfy his epistemic goal. So, were he to have been more reflective about p and about the proposition that implies it, he would have spent less time thinking about other propositions. As a result, he might well have made a mistake somewhere else. In particular, he might well have failed to believe some other proposition that is epistemically rational for him. But this is irrelevant. Even if we suppose that S here could not have done a better overall epistemic job than he has done, it nonetheless is true that he has good epistemic reasons to believe p, and had he reflected more on the consequences of the proposition that implies p, he himself would have admitted that this is so. In other words, even if S could not have done any better epistemically than he has done, it nonetheless is true that in failing to believe p he has failed to believe a proposition it is epistemically rational for him to believe. He has failed to believe a proposition that, given his own deepest epistemic standards, he has good reasons to believe.

The lesson, then, is that although it perhaps is possible for people to believe only propositions that are epistemically rational for them to believe, it may very well not be possible for people to believe all propositions that are epistemically rational for them. Or at least, this may very well not be possible for any person who is at all like most of the rest of us. One way to express this lesson is by saying that epistemic sins of omission may be inevitable even if epistemic sins of commission are not. However, expressing the lesson in this way may be misleading. It may be misleading because it may suggest that people ought to be concerned about such omissions, whereas in fact they should not be; it almost always is rational, all things considered, for people not even to try to believe everything that is epistemically rational for them to believe. In addition, talk of "epistemic sins" of omission may be misleading because it may suggest that if people do not believe *all* those propositions that are epistemically rational for them to believe, they must have been sloppy or careless or in some other way "sinful." But in fact this is not so; a person can be as careful and as thorough as he possibly can be in gathering evidence, studying his evidence, and so on, and yet still fail to believe propositions that are epistemically rational for him.

Talk of "epistemic sins" of commission can be misleading in an analogous way. It may suggest that if people do not believe only propositions that are epistemically rational for them, they must have been sloppy or careless in some way. But again, this need not be so. It is possible for a person to be as careful in his deliberations as he possibly can be and yet for these deliberations to generate beliefs that are not epistemically rational for him. Consider an extreme case. Suppose S is under the control of a demon who ensures that no matter how carefully S deliberates, he will believe all sorts of propositions that he himself on reflection would admit are obviously false. Suppose, for instance, that S deliberates upon a certain sector of his belief system and comes to see that he has no good reasons for many of these beliefs. As a result, suppose he ceases to have these beliefs. But suppose also that while S is correcting these beliefs, the demon somehow causes him to believe all sorts of other crazy propositions, propositions that S himself on reflection would admit are highly unlikely to be true. If S then finds time to reflect upon and to correct these beliefs, the demon will contaminate yet some other sector of S's belief system. In this way, the demon stays one step ahead of S, ensuring that despite S's best efforts he believes all sorts of propositions that are not epistemically rational for him.

What this illustrates is that epistemic irrationality does not necessarily go hand-in-hand with doxastic blameworthiness. But why would anyone be tempted to think otherwise? Why would anyone be tempted to think that they do go hand-in-hand? Why, in particular, would anyone be tempted to think that if a person believes what is not epistemically rational for him, he must not be altogether doxastically blameless? No doubt there are many reasons why someone might think this, but one that is of particular interest involves a position that might be called "extreme internalism." Let internalism be the position that implies, roughly, that what is now epistemically rational for a person S is a function of conditions that obtain within him now. (See section 2.7, esp. note 48; and section 4.6.) Extreme internalism, by contrast, is the more radical position that a person must have reflective access both to the conditions that make propositions epistemically rational for him and to the fact that these conditions do so. By this I mean that if a condition c makes a proposition p epistemically rational for S, then S must be able (at least on careful reflection) to determine that c obtains and to determine as well that c makes p epistemically rational for him. Accordingly, if S reflects carefully, he can always determine whether or not a proposition p is epistemically rational.[18]

On the face of it, there does not seem to be much to recommend extreme internalism. On most other issues we can be mistaken in our judgments even if we reflect carefully, and there do not seem to be strong reasons to think that the situation is any different with epistemic issues. Even so, what is of interest here is that if extreme internalism were a plausible position, there would be a rationale for claiming that whenever a person *S* believes a proposition *p* that is not epistemically rational for him, then he has not carefully reflected about *p*. Accordingly, there also would be a rationale for claiming that *S* is not altogether doxastically faultless with respect to his believing *p*. For had he reflected carefully about *p,* he would have realized that he does not have good epistemic reasons for *p*. And this in turn, we can suppose, would have kept him from believing *p*.

If extreme internalism were plausible, it would make possible an intimate connection between questions of doxastic blameworthiness and questions of epistemic rationality. The connection would not be altogether tight, however, since all things considered (when all of his goals are taken into account) an individual *S* might have no reason to reflect carefully about a proposition *p*. But then, even if *p* is not epistemically rational for him, he could not be faulted, all things considered, for failing to reflect carefully about *p* and likewise could not be faulted for believing *p*.

Nevertheless, extreme internalism does manage to bring questions of doxastic blameworthiness and questions of epistemic rationality closer to one another. It guarantees that the criteria of epistemic rationality are accessible to a reflective individual and in this way guarantees that the very conditions that make a proposition *p* epistemically rational for the individual can be used by him in his deliberations about *p*. It in effect guarantees that the rationality-making criteria also can be the decision-making criteria.[19]

However, as long as the issue is the criteria of epistemic rationality, none of this is very plausible. A person can be as careful as can be reasonably expected and still believe many propositions that are not epistemically rational for him. It is no more plausible to think that a carefully reflective person cannot be mistaken about whether he has good epistemic reasons to believe a proposition *p* than it is to think that he cannot be mistaken about other difficult issues.[20]

Moreover, there is a simple explanation of why questions of epistemic rationality are not as closely linked with questions of doxastic blameworthiness as extreme internalism suggests. The notion of epistemic rationality is an idealized notion. It seeks to describe what it is rational for an individual to believe (given the epistemic goal) from an idealized Aristotelian perspective. The subjective foundationalist tries to provide this description by identifying the arguments that an individual *S* would regard as sufficiently truth preserving were he ideally reflec ive. These arguments reflect *S*'s deepest epistemic standards. In terms of these standards and in terms of what *S* believes, the propositions that are uncontroversial for *S* to use as premises are identified. A proposition *p* is epistemically rational for *S*, then, just in case *p* is the conclusion of an undefeated argument that reflects *S*'s deepest epistemic standards and that has premises that are uncontroversial for him.

On any such account of epistemic rationality, questions of doxastic blame cannot be intimately linked with questions of epistemic rationality. Questions about the epistemic rationality of a proposition *p* are intimately linked with questions about what arguments the person would regard as sufficiently truth preserving were he ideally reflective. But a person cannot be reasonably faulted for failing to be ideally reflective.

Having said this, however, there is nothing in principle to prevent one from constructing an account of rational belief that seeks to describe how effectively an individual *S* is satisfying his epistemic goal not from the perspective of what *S* would think were he ideally reflective but rather from the perspective of what *S* would think were he to be, say, reasonably reflective. Such an account would be linked more intimately with issues of doxastic blame than an account of epistemic rationality is. Moreover, although such an account would be a different kind than an account of epistemic rationality (since its evaluations are made from a different perspective), the latter might well give us clues about how to approach the task of constructing the former.

In particular, following the clues provided by subjective foundationalism, let us say that it is rational for *S* to believe *p*, given a nonidealized Aristotelian perspective, just in case *S* has an uncontroversial argument for *p*, but let us understand "uncontroversial" in a nonidealized way. Let us say as at least a rough approximation that in this nonidealized sense *S* has an uncontroversial argument for *p* just if (1) there is an argument for *p* that *S* would believe to be sufficiently likely to be truth preserving were he to be reasonably reflective about this argument,[21] (2) the premises of this argument are uncontroversial for him, and (3) there is no defeater of this argument that is uncontroversial for him. Moreover, let us say (again very roughly) that a proposition *q* is uncontroversial for *S* just in case (a) were he to be reasonably reflective he would think that the argument (*S* believes *q*; thus, *q*) is sufficiently likely to be truth preserving, and (b) nothing else that he believes with comparable confidence can be used to argue against q in a way that he would regard as sufficiently likely to be truth preserving were he to be reasonably reflective.[22] Finally, let us say that S has been reasonably reflective about an argument just in case S has reflected about the argument as carefully as it would be rational, all things considered, for him to reflect were he to have the epistemic goal as his most important goal.

All of this, of course, is extremely vague, but since I am interested in describing only in a very rough way how a nonidealized Aristotelian perspective might be developed, it will do for now. The key idea is that we determine what it is rational for an individual S to believe (in this nonidealized Aristotelian sense) by imagining what he would think were he to be reflective. However, instead of imagining him to be ideally reflective, we imagine only that he is reasonably reflective. How long must an individual reflect in order to be reasonably reflective? He must reflect for as long as it is rational, all things considered (when all of his goals are taken into account) for him to reflect.[23] But in order to keep the emphasis on epistemic concerns rather than on practical concerns, we also imagine that his most important goal is the epistemic goal. In this way, the length of time that it would be rational, all things considered, for him to spend reflecting upon an argument will be dominated by his desire to have true beliefs and not to have false beliefs, rather than by his (perhaps more pressing) practical concerns. Even so, given the scarcity of time and given the need for him to sleep and eat and given that he is concerned not just with proposition p and the arguments he has for it but also with many other propositions, he cannot spend an unlimited time reflecting about his argument for p. He must balance all these considerations. Suppose there is an argument for p that S would regard as truth preserving were he to reflect for a moment or two on it, and suppose its premises are uncontroversial for him in the sense sketched above. Then, from this nonidealized Aristotelian perspective, it might very well be rational for S to believe p. Moreover, p might very well be rational for S even if it is the case that had he reflected only a moment more he would have seen that his argument for p is not truth preserving after all. In other words, p might be rational for him in this nonidealized sense even if he himself would have admitted had he reflected a bit more that it is an obvious mistake for him to believe p. It might be rational for him to believe p here, because it might be the case that he cannot have been reasonably expected to have engaged in this additional reflection.

This nonidealized notion of what it is rational for an individual to believe is perhaps close to what at least some philosophers have in mind when they speak of what an individual is justified in believing.[24] But whether or not this is so, the important point is that such a notion of rationality links questions of rationality with questions of doxastic blame much more intimately than does the notion of epistemic rationality. For given this nonidealized notion, what is rational is a function not of ideal reflection but rather of the kind of reflection that could reasonably be expected of a person were the epistemic goal his most important goal.

However, even on this nonidealized notion of rational belief, there is a gap between questions of rational belief and questions of doxastic blame. Suppose, for example, that an individual S does not reflect on the question of whether he has any good arguments for a proposition p that he believes, and suppose also that if he had engaged in the reflection that reasonably could be expected of him were the epistemic goal his most important goal he would have seen that he has no good argument for p. And suppose that as a result he would have ceased to believe p. Nevertheless, S here might still be blameless, since he may have had more pressing nonepistemic concerns. In such a case, he would have been doxastically blameworthy if the epistemic goal were his most important goal. But if we suppose that it is not, he need not be doxastically blameworthy.

Nevertheless, this nonidealized notion of rationality does link blame with rationality much more closely than does the notion of epistemic rationality. It does so precisely because it is a nonidealized notion— precisely because it seeks to describe what it is appropriate for an individual to believe from a nonidealized point of view. The point of view it adopts is one of evaluating the individual's beliefs with respect to how well they are satisfying his epistemic goal, where the evaluations are made from the perspective of what the individual himself would believe were he reasonably reflective.

It can be every bit as appropriate to make such judgments about how effectively a person is satisfying his epistemic goal from this perspective as it is to make such judgments from a purely epistemic perspective (that is, from an idealized Aristotelian perspective) or from some external perspective. Indeed, for many of our everyday purposes and needs, judgments from this nonidealized Aristotelian perspective may very well be of more interest than judgments from a purely epistemic perspective. Be this as it may, what is important for our (theoretical) purposes here is that these judgments be distinguished from judgments from a purely epistemic perspective. It is important, in other words, not to confuse such judgments with judgments of epistemic rationality.

CONSISTENCY AND COHERENCE

6.1 Inconsistent and Nearly Inconsistent Propositions

Every proposition that is epistemically rational for a person is either a proposition that is properly basic for him or a proposition that is made epistemically rational for him by propositions that are properly basic for him. Call the latter "nonbasic propositions." I have claimed that a set of propositions of either kind can be inconsistent. (See sections 2.3 and 2.4.) It may be rare for a set of propositions that are properly basic for a person to be inconsistent, but it is not impossible. And with nonbasic propositions, this need not be even rare. On the other hand, for sets of propositions that are *obviously* inconsistent, the situation is somewhat different. For purposes of the discussion, let us say that a set of propositions is obviously inconsistent for an individual S only if he realizes that it is impossible for all of the members of the set to be true and only if further reflection would not alter his opinion. Nonbasic propositions, I have claimed, can be obviously inconsistent in this way; lottery cases illustrate this. On the other hand, propositions that are properly basic for S cannot be obviously inconsistent. If a set of propositions is obviously inconsistent, at least one proposition in the set is such that propositions believed by S as confidently as the proposition in question tend to make epistemically rational for S the negation of that proposition.[1] But then, that proposition is not uncontroversial for S to assume; it is not properly basic for him.

The same holds for nearly inconsistent sets of propositions. A nearly inconsistent set of propositions is such that the negation of any member in the set is made highly probable by the remaining members of the set. Propositions that are properly basic for S, as well as propositions that are nonbasic for him, can be nearly inconsistent, but again only the latter can be nearly inconsistent in an obvious way. For if a set of propositions is nearly inconsistent in an obvious way and if all else is equal (if there are no appropriate defeater propositions), at least one proposition in the set is such that there is an undefeated argument against it with premises that are as confidently believed by S as is the proposition. But then this proposition cannot be properly basic for him.

Of course, to say that it is possible for a set of propositions to be epistemically rational for S and yet to be inconsistent (or nearly inconsistent) in an obvious way is not to say that this has to be the case for every person at every time. Even in lotterylike situations, it need not be epistemically rational for an individual to believe the obviously inconsistent propositions involved in such cases—the propositions that ticket one will not win, that ticket two will not win, and so on, and that some ticket will win. What propositions are epistemically rational for a person is a function of what arguments he on reflection would regard as sufficiently likely to be truth preserving. It is possible, although presumably unusual, for the situation of a person when confronted with a lottery to be such that on reflection he would not regard the probabilistic arguments that have as their conclusions that ticket one will not win, that ticket two will not win, and so on, as being sufficiently likely to be truth preserving.

So strictly speaking, subjective foundationalism is neutral with respect to what it is epistemically rational for a person to believe in lottery cases and other similar cases. What subjective foundationalism does do is to remove the obstacles that might be thought to rule out the possibility of it being epistemically rational for a person to believe that some ticket in the lottery will win and yet also epistemically rational for him to believe of each individual ticket that it will not win.

But even this might be thought to be overly permissive. It might be thought that neutrality on this issue is unacceptable. So it is worth reconsidering the relation between consistency and epistemic rationality, to see if consistency might after all be a prerequisite of epistemic rationality, and if, as I claimed earlier, it is not, to see exactly why it is not.

6.2 Can Contradictory Propositions Be Epistemically Rational?

Before considering the more general category of inconsistent sets of propositions, consider a particular kind of inconsistent set of propositions—explicitly contradictory propositions. It is impossible, as I will suggest in section 7.5, to believe explicitly contradictory propositions; it is impossible, that is, for an individual to believe a proposition p and also to believe its negation, not$p$. Even so, it might occur to some that perhaps one of the defects of subjective foundationalism is that with its emphasis upon what arguments an individual on reflection would take to be truth preserving it might allow explicitly contradictory propositions to be epistemically rational for an individual.

Let us ask whether, given subjective foundationalism, this is possible. Consider all the possibilities. Begin by considering whether there could be a pair of contradictory propositions such that each is properly basic for someone. Assume for purposes of a reductio that this is possible. Specifically, assume that p as well as not$p$ is properly basic for S. However, this immediately implies that S believes p as well as not$p$, which is impossible. So, contrary to the original assumption, p and not$p$ cannot both be properly basic for S. Moreover, even if we waive this point, assuming for the moment that it is possible to have explicitly contradictory beliefs, it still will not be possible for p and not$p$ to be properly basic for S. For if S believes p as well as not$p$, he either believes p with as much confidence as he believes not$p$ or he does not. Suppose that he does. Then not$p$ cannot be properly basic for him, since there is an argument against not$p$ (that is, an argument for p) that S, on reflection, would regard as truth preserving and that has premises he believes as confidently as not$p$—the argument (p; thus, p). Every proposition (or at least every proposition a person understands) constitutes an argument for itself. Indeed, this is trivial. To say that p constitutes an argument for itself is only to say that a person S, on reflection, would believe that if p is true, p is sufficiently likely to be true. And presumably everyone, or at least everyone who is at all like the rest of us, would, on reflection, believe this to be the case.

So, if p is believed by S as confidently as not$p$, then not$p$ cannot be properly basic for S. On the other hand, if p is not believed by S as confidently as not$p$, then p cannot be properly basic for him. For then there will be a good argument against p with premises he believes as confidently as p—the argument (not$p$; thus, not$p$). Accordingly, even if it is possible for S to believe p as well as not$p$, it is impossible for both p and not$p$ to be properly basic for S. It is impossible, in other words, for contradictory propositions to be epistemically rational for S by virtue of each being properly basic for him.

What about the possibility of p being properly basic for S and his having a good argument for its negation, not$p$? Is this possible? Again the answer is no. To see why, notice that any argument for not$p$ either is one that S, on reflection, would regard as deductive or it is one that he would not regard as deductive. Suppose the former. Suppose, in other words, that, on reflection, he would believe that the premises of the argument for not$p$—let these premises be $e^1, e^2, \ldots e^n$—imply not$p$. Then either p is not properly basic for him or not all these premises are properly basic for him. In particular, if all of these premises are believed by S as confidently as p, then p cannot be properly basic for him. For there is a good argument against p with premises that S believes as confidently as p. On the other hand, if one of these premises—say, premise e^1—is believed less confidently than p, then e^1 cannot be properly basic for him. For there is a good argument against e^1 with premises he believes as confidently as e^1—the argument $(p, e^2, \ldots e^n;$ thus, not$e^1)$. The premises of this argument tend to make rational its conclusion for S, since by hypothesis he on reflection would believe it is impossible for $e^1, e^2, \ldots e^n$ all to be true and yet for p to be true. So, he on reflection would believe that if p is true and if $e^2, \ldots e^n$ likewise are true, e^1 must be false. Suppose, on the other hand, that S on reflection does not think that the premises $(e^1, e^2, \ldots e^n)$ imply not$p$. Then even if p is properly basic for S, it is at least possible that $(e^1, e^2, \ldots e^n)$ also are all properly basic for him. But if they are, p will be a defeater of the argument $(e^1, e^2, \ldots e^n;$ thus, not$p)$, since S on reflection would not think that not$p$ is likely to be true, given that $e^1, e^2 \ldots e^n$ and p are all true. At the very least, he would not think this if he is anything at all like the rest of us. For if he is anything like the rest of us, he, on reflection, would realize that if $e^1, e^2, \ldots e^n$ and p are all true, not$p$ cannot be true.

Consider, then, the final possibility. Might there be an argument for p as well as an argument for not$p$ with premises that are properly basic for S and with premises that S, on reflection, would think tend to make probable its conclusion? The answer seems to be yes. Nothing altogether precludes there being a situation of this sort. On the other hand, such a situation will not be one in which both p and not$p$ are rational for S, because at least one of the arguments will be defeated. To see why, suppose for purposes of a reductio that neither is defeated. This means that the premises of S's argument for not$p$—let these premises be $d^1, d^2, \ldots d^n$—do not defeat his argument for p and that likewise the premises of his argument for p—let these premises be $e^1, e^2, \ldots e^n$—do not defeat his argument for not$p$. But again, if S is at all like most of the rest of us, this cannot be the case. If, on reflection, *S* would think that propositions e^1, e^2, . . . e^n make likely *p* and if, on reflection, he would think that propositions d^1, d^2, . . . d^n make likely not*p*, then at least one set of these propositions is a defeater of the other. For, if he is at all like the rest of us, he, on reflection, would realize that relative to the truth of e^1, e^2, . . . e^n *and* d^1, d^2, . . . d^n, it cannot be the case both that *p* is likely and that not*p* is likely. He, on reflection, would realize, in other words, that if the set made up of the conjunction of these sets—the set $(e^1, e^2, . . . e^n, d^1, d^2, . . . d^n)$— contains only truths, then it is not the case that both *p* and not*p* are sufficiently likely to be true. But then, *S*'s argument for *p* or his argument for not*p* or both arguments will be defeated.[2]

Accordingly, subjective foundationalism implies that for any remotely normal person there is no way in which both a proposition *p* and its negation not*p* can be epistemically rational for him. It is impossible for both to be properly basic for him. Likewise, it is impossible for one to be properly basic for him and for the other to be the conclusion of a good (that is, undefeated) argument. And it is impossible for both to be conclusions of good arguments.

Does this then imply that, given subjective foundationalism, it is possible for contradictory propositions to be epistemically rational for someone who is *not* remotely normal? No, for it may very well not be possible for anyone, no matter how abnormal, to have those characteristics he would need to have in order for contradictory propositions to be epistemically rational for him. The nature of belief or our nature as believers may make this impossible. It may make it impossible, for example, for an individual on reflection to believe that a set of propositions—say, the set of propositions $(e^1, e^2, . . . e^n, d^1, d^2, . . . d^n)$—makes likely *p* as well as not*p*. But even if this is not so, it is easy enough simply to stipulate that the subjective foundationalist criterion of epistemic rationality applies only to individuals who are relatively normal, enough so that contradictory propositions cannot be epistemically rational for them. Or instead of simply stipulating this, perhaps there is a plausible way of arguing for this. Other individuals, if there are any, might plausibly be regarded as lacking the prerequisites of rationality. It might be argued that, strictly speaking, their beliefs are neither rational nor irrational, the idea being that an individual has to be at least minimally like us in order for charges of irrationality even to make sense. Indeed, the work of some philosophers suggests a stronger conclusion; it suggests that only individuals whose basic epistemic standards are at least somewhat like ours can be said to have beliefs at all.[3]

6.3   Can Inconsistent Propositions Be
Epistemically Rational?

A set of propositions is inconsistent just if it is impossible for all of the propositions in the set to be true. So, if a set of propositions contains explicitly contradictory propositions, the set is inconsistent. But since not every set of propositions that is inconsistent contains explicitly contradictory propositions, nothing that has been said so far implies that it is impossible for each member of an inconsistent set of propositions to be epistemically rational. On the contrary, subjective foundationalism allows that this is possible.

Are there any reasons for thinking that an adequate account of epistemic rationality should not allow each member of an inconsistent set of propositions to be epistemically rational for a person? It is difficult to think of any. One reason is that it is difficult to see why it should be impossible for a person to have very good evidence for p and very good evidence for q while having no evidence at all indicating that p implies not$q$. After all, the way in which p implies not$q$ may be very complicated. Indeed, it may be so complicated that even given ideal reflection most people would not see that the one implies the other. And if so, there would seem to be nothing to prevent a person from having what, given ideal reflection, he would regard as a good argument for p as well as a good argument for q even though the first implies the negation of the second.

Moreover, if a proposition that is necessarily false can be epistemically rational for an individual S, then it follows trivially that each member of an inconsistent of propositions can be epistemically rational for S. Any set of propositions that contains a necessarily false proposition is inconsistent; it is impossible for all members of such a set to be true. For example, imagine that it is epistemically rational for S to believe a false mathematical proposition. Suppose his normally reliable computer has convinced him that the expansion of pi carried out to one thousand decimal places does not contain three consecutive ones. And suppose a friend has used his normally reliable computer to verify this result. Then this proposition might be epistemically rational for S. But it is necessarily false. Accordingly, it in conjunction with any other propositions that are epistemically rational for S creates a set of inconsistent propositions each of which is epistemically rational for him.

What is more controversial is whether sets of propositions that are blatantly inconsistent can be epistemically rational, as is also allowed by subjective foundationalism. For example, suppose S believes p, believes p^1, believes p^2, . . . believes p^n and suppose that the conjunction (p^1 and p^2 . . . and p^n) implies not$p$. Further suppose that S recognizes that this conjunction implies not$p$. He recognizes that what he believes is inconsistent. However, suppose that he does not have explicitly contradictory beliefs; he does not, for example, both believe p and believe not$p$. Moreover, suppose that no particular proposition that he believes implies not$p$. He believes p^1 but it alone does not imply not$p$; likewise he believes p^2, believes p^3, and so on, but none of these propositions alone implies not$p$ either. Even so, the fact that S believes (and, we can suppose, would continue to believe on reflection) that these propositions together imply not$p$—the fact that he recognizes that their conjunction implies not$p$—might be thought to preclude the possibility that each of them is epistemically rational for S. After all, if S himself, on reflection, would admit that an argument with p^1, p^2, . . . p^n as premises and not$p$ as its conclusion is truth preserving and if in addition p^1, p^2, and so on, are epistemically rational for S, then it might seem that so too is proposition not$p$. But if not$p$ is epistemically rational for S, its contradictory—proposition p—cannot be. Accordingly, it might be argued that in such a situation, despite my suggestion to the contrary, each member in the set (p, p^1, p^2, . . . p^n) cannot be epistemically rational for S.

However, none of this follows. For even if p^1, p^2, and so on, are epistemically rational for S and even if S himself, on reflection, would recognize as deductively valid an argument for not$p$ that has as its premises p^1, p^2, and so on, it does not follow that not$p$ is epistemically rational for S. This *would* follow if p^1, p^2, and so on, were all properly basic. But from the fact that p^1, p^2, and so on, are all epistemically rational for S, it does not follow that they are all properly basic. Hence, it does not follow that their truth can be assumed in order to argue for not$p$; it does not follow that they can be used as evidence for not$p$.

So the argument fails to show that if the propositions p, p^1, p^2, and so on, are all epistemically rational for S and if in addition S on reflection correctly believes that (p^1 and p^2, . . . and p^n) implies not$p$, it must also be epistemically rational for S to believe not$p$. Hence, it fails to show that there is anything wrong with supposing that it is possible for all of these propositions to be epistemically rational for S; it fails to show that it is impossible for each member of an obviously inconsistent set of propositions to be epistemically rational for S.

Suppose, however, that a conjunctive rule applied to epistemic rationality, such that necessarily if it is epistemically rational for S to believe p and epistemically rational for S to believe q, it also is epistemically rational for S to believe the conjunction (p and q). There then would be a reason to deny that each member of an obviously inconsistent set of propositions can be epistemically rational for S. For, to return to the above example, suppose that the propositions $p, p^1, p^2, \ldots p^n$ are all epistemically rational for S and that they are obviously inconsistent. Then given a conjunctive rule, it also is epistemically rational for S to believe the conjunction (p^1 and $p^2 \ldots$ and p^n). But by hypothesis, S on reflection would realize that his conjunction implies not$p$. Thus, not$p$ also will be rational for S. For if S has a good argument for the conjunction and if, given ideal reflection, he would realize that this conjunction implies not$p$, then he also has a good argument for not$p$—an argument with properly basic propositions as premises and an argument that S on ideal reflection would regard as sufficiently likely to be truth preserving.

So, if a conjunctive rule did apply to epistemic rationality, then we would be forced to conclude either that it is impossible for an obviously inconsistent set of propositions to be epistemically rational or that it is possible for explicitly contradictory propositions to be epistemically rational even for relatively normal people. However, in fact we are not forced to conclude either of these things, because a conjunctive rule does not apply to epistemic rationality. It is possible for a proposition p to be epistemically rational for S and a proposition q also to be epistemically rational for S without their conjunction (p and q) being epistemically rational for him.

On the simplest, most intuitive level, this is possible because an individual might recognize that the risk of error involved in believing a conjunction can be greater than the risk of error involved in believing either conjunct. Of course, if the individual thinks that the conjuncts complement one another, in the sense that the truth of one makes it more likely that the other is also true, then he may well believe that the risk of error involved in believing the conjunction is no greater than the risk of error involved in believing the weaker (i.e., the more risky) conjunct. But if he does not think that the conjuncts complement one another, he may think that the risk is significantly greater. It is hard to see why he might not think that the risk of error has increased to the point where believing the conjunction is unacceptable. In particular, it is hard to see why a person S, on reflection, might not regard the arguments for the individual conjuncts as sufficiently likely to be truth preserving and yet, on reflection, not think this of the more complicated argument that is needed for their conjunction. It is especially hard to see why repeated applications of the conjunctive rule might not lead to this result. In fact, by repeated applications the conjunctive rule implies that it is epistemically rational for every person to believe the conjunction that is comprised of *every* proposition that is epistemically rational for him. So, if $(p, p^1, p^2, \ldots p^n)$ are propositions that are epistemically rational for S, given a conjunctive rule it is epistemically rational for S to believe the conjunction $(p$ and p^1 and $p^2 \ldots$ and $p^n)$. And this is so no matter how many propositions are epistemically rational for S; it always is epistemically rational for S to believe that this set contains not even one falsehood. In other words, it is always epistemically rational for a person to be an infallibilist with respect to the propositions that are epistemically rational for him. But of course, this is preposterous. It normally is not epistemically rational for a person to believe the conjunction of all the propositions that are epistemically rational for him.

Indeed, if a conjunctive rule were applicable to epistemic rationality, it could be used to argue in favor of a skepticism that implies that very few propositions beyond those that are properly basic and those that can be deduced from such propositions are likely to be epistemically rational for an individual. Consider any set of propositions that S on reflection would not regard as being deducible from propositions properly basic for him (and that therefore have at least a small chance of being false, even given that the propositions that are properly basic for S are all true). If this set is relatively large, it ordinarily will be epistemically rational for S to believe that the set is likely to contain at least one falsehood. But if a conjunctive rule were acceptable, not all of these propositions could be epistemically rational for S (since it is not epistemically rational for him to believe their conjunction).

Moreover, this kind of problem is not limited to sets of propositions that are large—it can occur even when the set is of only moderate size. This is especially so if some of the propositions in the set are negatively relevant to some of the others, in the sense that the truth of one somewhat diminishes the chances of the other being true. It again is difficult to see why S on reflection might not regard the risk of error involved in believing the conjunction of such propositions to be unacceptably great and why as a result it might not be epistemically irrational for him to believe their conjunction. But then, given a conjunctive rule, not all of these propositions can be epistemically rational for S.

Of course, one could try taking a heroic course here and simply deny that a situation of this sort is possible. One might claim, for example, that it is impossible for a set of propositions to be epistemically rational for S if even one member of the set is negatively relevant to any other member of the set.⁴ But this is strongly counterintuitive. Take, for example, the claim that *S* now sees a table and the claim that people sometimes hallucinate without being aware that they are hallucinating. It seems as if *S* might have very good arguments for each of these claims. That is, it seems as if both of these claims might be epistemically rational for *S*. Yet the second is negatively relevant to the first, and moreover *S,* on reflection, might recognize that this is so. But then, one claim can be negatively relevant to another even though both are epistemically rational for a person.

The lottery case is but an extreme illustration of this general point. In the lottery case, it is not just that some proposition in a set is negatively relevant to some other proposition in the set even though all of them are epistemically rational for *S*; it is that each of the propositions involved in the case is such that each of the remaining members is negatively relevant to it. But despite this, *S* might have a very good argument for each member in this set of propositions; each member, in other words, might be epistemically rational for *S*.

Of course, just as one can be tempted to take a heroic course and deny that two propositions can be epistemically rational for *S* if they are negatively relevant to one another, so too one can be tempted to take an analogous heroic course and deny that all the propositions in the lottery case could be epistemically rational for *S*. But the result of this heroism is not much different than in the earlier case, since one is thereby forced to claim that propositions for which a person has incredibly strong arguments—indeed, arguments as strong as he has for almost any proposition—are not epistemically rational for him. Suppose, for example, that a lottery is extremely large. Suppose, in fact, that it has a billion tickets. Then most of us, on reflection, would be likely to regard the evidence we have for the claim that ticket one will not win to be as strong as the evidence we have for most of the claims that we believe. For instance, we would be likely to regard the evidence for it as being at least as strong as the evidence we have for the claim that the room we just left still has furniture in it, and at least as strong as the evidence we have for the claim that the person who has promised to meet us for dinner will be there, and at least as strong as the evidence we have for the claim that it will not snow in Chicago next August. And so, if these claims are epistemically rational for us to believe, as they surely are for many of us, then so too, it seems, is the claim that ticket one will not win.

Moreover, if *S* on reflection would think that the probabilistic argument indicating that ticket one will not win is sufficiently likely to be truth preserving, then presumably he also, on reflection, would think this of the probabilistic arguments that indicate of each of the various other tickets, from ticket two to ticket one billion, that it will not win either. For each of these arguments is essentially the same as the argument that indicates that ticket one will not win. Accordingly, if the proposition that ticket one will not win is epistemically rational for *S,* then presumably so too is the proposition that ticket two will not win, the proposition that ticket three will not win, and so on. But then, if it also is epistemically rational for *S* to believe that some ticket will win, there is a set of propositions that are all epistemically rational for *S* and that are obviously inconsistent.

I am not suggesting that *necessarily* if an individual is confronted with a billion-ticket fair lottery, it is epistemically rational for him to believe that ticket one will not win, ticket two will not win, and so on. It is at least possible for such propositions not to be epistemically rational for an individual. All I am claiming is that, contrary to what is sometimes suggested, it also is possible for these propositions to be epistemically rational for someone. I am, furthermore, suggesting that this is likely to be the rule rather than the exception. I am suggesting that most people, on reflection, would regard the argument they have for the claim that ticket one will not win to be as good as the arguments they have for most of the claims they believe. And so, insofar as they, on reflection, would believe that some of these latter arguments are good ones, they presumably also, on reflection, would believe that the argument in favor of the proposition that ticket one will not win is a good one. I am also suggesting that they, on reflection, would regard with favor the analogous arguments for the proposition that ticket two will not win, and for the proposition that ticket three will not win, and so on. That is, I am suggesting that for most people, if they were confronted with a billion-ticket lottery, all these propositions would be epistemically rational for them. And I am claiming, not merely suggesting, that it in no way follows from this that it must be epistemically rational for them to believe contradictory propositions.

On the other hand, I am not claiming that in typical lottery situations, an individual *S* can evidentially know that, say, ticket one will not win. Indeed, the explication of evidential knowledge given in chapter 4 suggests that *S* does not evidentially know that ticket one will not win, even if it turns out to be true that ticket one does not win.[5] For in typical lottery situations, it being epistemically rational for *S* to believe that ticket one will not win is grounded on falsehood. This is so because the only argument that makes this claim epistemically rational for *S* is an argument whose premises also make epistemically rational for him, with respect to each of the other tickets in the lottery, the claim that it will not win either. But on the assumption that the lottery is a fair, normal lottery, one of these claims is false. And thus, it being epistemically rational for S to believe that ticket one will not win is grounded on a falsehood.

By way of contrast, situations involving a fallibilist belief are typically not like this. Thus, suppose that S believes propositions p, $p^1, \ldots p^n$ as well as the proposition that at least one of these propositions is false. Moreover, suppose that each of these propositions, including the fallibilist proposition, is epistemically rational for S. The fact that these propositions, like the propositions in the lottery case, are obviously inconsistent does not prevent S from evidentially knowing most of them. (He cannot know them all, since at least one is false.) For, unlike the propositions in the lottery case, S typically will have distinct arguments for these propositions. His argument for p, for example, typically will not have premises that make p^2, p^3, and so on epistemically rational for him. So even if we assume that at least one proposition in the set $(p, p^1, \ldots p^n)$ is false, it being epistemically rational for S to believe p need not be grounded on a falsehood. Accordingly, he may very well have evidential knowledge of p.

6.4 Lotteries Reconsidered

Subjective foundationalism implies that it is possible for all of the propositions involved in lottery cases to be epistemically rational for an individual. It is possible, for instance, for each member in the following obviously inconsistent set of propositions to be epistemically rational for an individual: Some ticket will win, ticket one will not win, ticket two will not win, . . . ticket one billion will not win. On the other hand, subjective foundationalism also allows the possibility that these propositions are *not* epistemically rational for an individual. However, this presumably is the exception; there presumably are not many people who, on reflection, would so emphasize the importance of not believing falsehoods over the importance of believing truths that they would think this. After all, the chances of ticket one not winning are very, very high.

This then is how the subjective foundationalist deals with lottery cases and the like. But might there be other, preferable ways of dealing with such cases? Consider some alternatives. Consider, for example, the claim that a person who is confronted with a lottery does not have as good an argument for the proposition that ticket one billion will not win as he does for the proposition that ticket one will not win. Suppose, in particular, that the order in which a person considers propositions is thought to be important in determining whether a proposition is epistemically rational or not. Thus, if in a lottery situation S first considers the proposition that ticket one will not win, this proposition may very well be epistemically rational for him. Suppose S accepts this proposition and then considers the proposition that ticket two will not win. On the assumption that he was right about ticket one not winning, it is a little less likely that ticket two will not win. Nevertheless, it too is highly likely to be true. Suppose he accepts it as well and then considers next the proposition that ticket three will not win. On the assumption that he was right about the first two tickets, it is again a little less likely that this ticket will not win. And of course, as he continues this process, on the assumption that he was right about all the previous tickets not winning, it becomes increasingly likely that the next ticket will be the winner. So, if he had sufficient time to get around to considering the proposition that ticket number 999,999,999 will not win, then on the assumption that all the previous propositions he has considered are true, this proposition would have only about a 50–50 chance of being true. Accordingly, it would not be epistemically rational for S to believe it. On the other hand, if S had started by considering the proposition that ticket one billion will not win and had worked his way down to the proposition that ticket two will not win, then the latter would have been epistemically rational for S.

This is not a plausible way of dealing with lotterylike cases. The most obvious mistake it makes (although not the only one) is that of supposing that if it is epistemically rational for S to believe a proposition, it is always appropriate for S to assume the truth of that proposition for purposes of evaluating other propositions. Most simply put, it makes the mistake of presupposing that those propositions for which there is good evidence can themselves be unproblematically used as evidence. However, this need not be so; the fact that it is epistemically rational for S to believe that ticket one will not win does not imply that the truth of this proposition can be assumed in order to evaluate whether ticket two will not win, whether ticket three will not win, and so on. Moreover, it is not just lotterylike cases that illustrate this, although they do provide particularly striking illustrations. Any proposition that is the conclusion of a good nondeductive argument is a candidate for illustrating the point also. For even if the premises of such an argument are absolutely certain, there is at least some chance of its conclusion being false, given that the argument is nondeductive. So if one then tries to use the conclusion of this first nondeductive argument as a premise in a second nondeductive argument, the chances of this second conclusion being in error may very well be even more significant. Indeed, it may be significant enough so that S himself on reflection might think that he lacks a good argument for this second conclusion. (See section 1.6.)

Are there, then, any other ways of dealing with lottery cases? Suppose one made an appeal to different degrees of epistemic rationality. Suppose, for example, one claimed that there is a degree of epistemic rationality such that if a proposition p is rational to this degree for S, it is rational for him either to believe p or to withhold judgment on p. We might say of such a proposition that it is epistemically permissible (or acceptable) but not epistemically required for S, the idea being that his failing to believe p does not imply that with respect to p he is being epistemically irrational.

One might try to use this distinction between propositions that are epistemically required and those that are only epistemically permissible to resuscitate a conjunctive rule. Specifically, one might argue that with respect to the weaker degree of epistemic rationality, a conjunctive rule does not apply. From the fact that one is epistemically permitted to believe p and to believe q, it does not follow that one is permitted to believe their conjunction. On the other hand, with respect to the stronger degree of epistemic rationality, one might insist that a conjunctive rule does apply. If one is epistemically required both to believe p and to believe q (so that failure to believe either would be epistemically irrational), then one also is epistemically required to believe the conjunction (p and q). Accordingly, a set of propositions that one is only epistemically permitted to believe might very well be obviously inconsistent, but a set of propositions that one is epistemically required to believe cannot be obviously inconsistent, for then one would be epistemically required to believe contradictory propositions. In the lottery case, for example, one might be permitted to believe each of the following propositions: Ticket one will not win, ticket two will not win, . . . ticket one billion will not win. However, not all of these propositions could be epistemically required, for given that a conjunctive rule is in force for required propositions, the conjunction of these propositions would also be required. But on the assumption that the denial of this conjunction is also required for him (since the proposition that some ticket will win is required), this is impossible.[6]

In one sense, this suggestion mirrors the one I have endorsed. I have claimed that there are two different ways in which a proposition can be made epistemically rational for a person—by being properly basic and by being made epistemically rational by propositions that are properly basic—and I have claimed that a conjunctive rule applies to propositions of the first kind but not to propositions of the second kind. It applies to properly basic propositions because all or at least almost all people, on reflection, would regard as truth preserving arguments that have as their conclusions the conjunction of their premises. And so, if the premises of such arguments are properly basic for a person *S,* the conjunction of these premises is epistemically rational for him to believe. (See section 2.4 and chapter 7.) On the other hand, for propositions that are epistemically rational for a person *S* but that are not properly basic for him, it cannot be assumed that it will be epistemically rational for *S* to believe their conjunction, even if *S* on reflection does approve of conjunctive arguments. For it cannot be assumed that there are properly basic propositions that can be used to argue for the conjunction.

So at least on the surface, there is a similarity between the suggestion for dealing with lottery cases and my view: Both grant that a conjunctive rule is applicable to some but not all of the propositions that are epistemically rational for a person. But in claiming that a conjunctive rule applies to all propositions that are epistemically required, the suggestion goes far beyond anything I have claimed. Indeed, claiming this has the effect of making a certain kind of epistemic irrationality—the irrationality involved in not believing what one is epistemically required to believe—far too rare a thing. For most propositions cannot be conjoined with impunity. As a result, on the view above, most propositions that are epistemically rational for a person *S* will be propositions that he is epistemically permitted but not epistemically required to believe. Failing to believe them, accordingly, need not be irrational.

There are two ways of seeing that this is so. Recall the lottery. In the lottery case, a person *S* is likely to have very strong evidence for believing that ticket one will not win and equally strong evidence for believing of each of the other tickets that it will not win either. In fact, if the lottery is large enough—if it is, as I have assumed previously, a billion-ticket lottery—then the evidence *S* has for believing such propositions is likely to be at least as strong as the evidence he has for most of what he believes. After all, how much of what he believes is likely to have less than a .000000001 chance of being false? And yet, given the suggestion above, not all the propositions involved in the lottery can be epistemically required, since they cannot be properly conjoined. At least one of them must be such that it is not irrational for S not to believe it. At least one, in other words, must be at best only epistemically permitted rather than epistemically required. But if at least one of these propositions is permitted but not required for S and if the evidence he has for this proposition is as strong as that which he has for the vast majority of propositions for which he has good evidence, it is hard to see how there could be very many propositions that S is epistemically required to believe, on pain of irrationality. Thus, if the suggestion above were accepted, only rarely would a person be epistemically irrational by virtue of failing to believe a proposition that is epistemically rational for him. But of course, this is not particularly rare at all.

The second way of seeing that, given the suggestion above, relatively few propositions would be epistemically required is to remember that lotterylike situations, in which an individual has obviously inconsistent beliefs, are not unusual. So, if the propositions involved in the lottery case cannot be epistemically required, then neither can the propositions in these more common cases. Take, for example, almost any large set of propositions that are epistemically rational for S to believe by virtue of his having good nondeductive arguments for them. Suppose that the set contains a thousand, or ten thousand, or even a million members, and suppose that the arguments for the various members of the set are (at least roughly) equally strong. Let $(p^1, p^2, p^3, \ldots p^n)$ be the set of such propositions. Consider then this question: Is it epistemically rational for S to believe that the set $(p^1, p^2, p^3, \ldots p^n)$ contains only truths? Ordinarily, the answer will be no. Given that the arguments for these propositions are nondeductive, there is some risk of error involved in believing them even if the premises of these arguments are true. Moreover, since the set of such propositions is likely to be very large, the risk of there being a false proposition somewhere in the set presumably might become significant enough to prevent the conjunction $(p^1$ and p^2 and $p^3 \ldots$ and $p^n)$ from being epistemically rational for S. But then, on the suggestion above, although it might be epistemically permissible for S to believe each of these propositions, it could not be epistemically required of him to believe each. In other words, at least one member of the set must be such that it is not epistemically irrational for S not to believe it. But since each member in the set (as in the lottery case) is supported by an equally good argument, if this is true of one member, it is difficult to see why it would not be true of the other members as well. Moreover, since almost any proposition that is neither properly basic for S nor deducible from propositions properly basic for S is a member of some such set, almost any proposition will be such that at best S is epistemically permitted to believe it. Putting the point the other way around, almost no proposition will be such that S is epistemically required to believe it. But this is not so. Many propositions can be such that it is epistemically irrational for a person not to believe them.

So an appeal to degrees of epistemic rationality is not likely to be of much use in dealing with lottery cases and others involving obviously inconsistent propositions. Related sorts of considerations, moreover, can be used to illustrate the implausibility of suggesting that in the lottery case what is epistemically rational for S are not propositions such as that ticket one will not win but rather propositions such as that it is very likely (or highly probable) that ticket one will not win. Such a suggestion at first glance might be thought to be helpful in dealing with lottery cases, since the set of such probability claims in the lottery case need not be inconsistent. For example, the set of propositions (some ticket will win, it is probable that ticket one will not win, it is probable that ticket two will not win, . . . it is probable that ticket one billion will not win) is not inconsistent. Accordingly, no unwelcome consequence need follow from the claim that it might be rational to believe their conjunction.

Unfortunately, the suggestion also has a significant disadvantage. The suggestion implies that the proper conclusion of a nondeductive argument is almost never the proposition we ordinarily take to be the conclusion. Rather, the proper conclusion is the proposition that this proposition probably is true. So, for example, an argument that we ordinarily would take to be a good argument for the proposition that Venus is closer to the sun than the earth is, on this view, not a good argument for this proposition at all. Instead, it is a good argument for the proposition that it is probable that Venus is closer to the sun than the earth is. For suppose that the proper conclusion of this argument were thought simply to be that Venus is closer to the sun than the earth is (and not the probability claim). Then this proposition presumably will be a member of an incredibly large set of propositions that are equally well supported but that nonetheless are such that it is not epistemically rational for S to believe of this set that it contains not even one falsehood. In other words, this proposition will belong to a set composed of other like propositions whose conjunction is not epistemically rational for S. But given a conjunctive rule, it would then follow that not every proposition in this set could be epistemically rational for S. But if one proposition in the set is not epistemically rational for S, it is hard to see how any of the others could be either, since by hypothesis each proposition in the set is equally well supported. It is hard to see, for example, how it could be epistemically rational for *S* to believe that Venus is closer to the sun than the earth is. At best, it will be epistemically rational for him to believe that this proposition is probable.

Worse yet, it is far from clear, given the suggestion above, that even such probabilistic propositions can be epistemically rational. It is far from clear that the same kinds of considerations that (according to the suggestion above) prevent most ordinary claims from being epistemically rational will not also prevent their probabilistic counterparts from being epistemically rational. In particular, just as the claim that Venus is closer to the sun than the earth is might belong to a set of equally well supported propositions such that it is epistemically rational for an individual *S* to believe that at least one of these propositions is false (since none of these propositions are certain for *S*), so too the probabilistic counterpart of this claim, the claim that it is highly probable, given the available evidence, that Venus is closer to the sun than the earth is, might belong to a set of equally well-supported probabilistic claims such that it is epistemically rational for *S* to believe that at least one of these probabilistic claims is false. After all, the probabilistic counterparts of ordinary propositions are not likely to be certain for *S* either. Accordingly, it looks as if lotterylike situations could arise with respect to them as well as for ordinary nonprobabilistic propositions. But if so, then the same kinds of consideration that forces us, given the suggestion above, to say that only the probabilistic counterpart of an ordinary proposition *p* is epistemically rational for *S* is likely to force us to say something similar about the probabilistic counterpart itself. We may be forced to say that the proposition that *p* is probable is not epistemically rational for *S*; only the proposition that *p* is probably probable is epistemically rational for *S*. But then it seems as if the same kind of considerations could arise yet again, with respect to this "doubly probabilized" claim. And if so, the suggestion above for dealing with lotterylike cases may well ultimately reduce us, recalling C. I. Lewis's phrase, to a perpetual stutter.

However, suppose we waive this difficulty, assuming that it can be resolved somehow. Even so, we are still left with the difficulty mentioned previously—the suggestion above seems to commit us to a skepticism about ordinary claims. The ordinary claims that all of us believe are almost never epistemically rational for us; at best, only their probabilistic counterparts are. But what, it might be asked, is wrong with this kind of skepticism? After all, few if any people believe with absolute certainty that the earth revolves around the sun and few if any people, if they were confronted with a billion-ticket lottery, would believe with absolute certainty that ticket one will not win. It might be claimed that in effect all the suggestion above does is to approve of this lack of certainty.

The problem with this response, however, is that it conflates the issue of *what* a person believes with the issue of *how* he believes it. Normally, people do feel, and should feel, at least a little tentative in accepting claims of the sort mentioned above, but this in no way shows that they neither do nor should believe such claims. *What* a person believes must be distinguished from *how* he believes it. (See chapter 1, note 33.) The fact that a person both is and should be somewhat uncertain about the truth of a proposition does not preclude the possibility that it is epistemically rational for him to believe that proposition. It only indicates something about the degree of confidence with which the person believes or should believe the proposition.

However, might it not be possible to save a version of the conjunctive principle by appealing to degrees of belief, where the degree of belief with which a person believes a proposition is a measure of the confidence with which he believes it? It does not seem so, for even if the concern here were the development of an adequate account of rational degrees of belief (rather than an adequate account of epistemically rational belief), the problems discussed above would remain essentially the same. In particular, we could still ask whether if it is rational for S to believe p with degree of confidence X and rational for S to believe q with degree of confidence X, then it also is rational for S to believe the conjunction (p and q) with degree of confidence X. We could ask, in other words, whether a conjunctive rule is applicable to rational degrees of belief. And if someone were to claim that it is, all the same problems involving lotteries and other obviously inconsistent sets of propositions would occur once again.

It is important also to notice that although those who propose accounts of rational degrees of belief often talk of a requirement of coherence or consistency, typically what they have in mind is not the kind of coherence and consistency with which I have been concerned here. Rather, the kind they normally have in mind is one that requires a person's degrees of belief not to violate the axioms of the probability calculus, a kind of consistency that prevents others from making a Dutch Book against a person. The degrees of confidence with which one person believes what he does, allow a second person to make a Dutch Book against the first if the first is willing to make a series of bets on the truth of the propositions he believes, giving odds that correspond to the degree of confidence he has in their truth, and if these odds are such that the second person is able to place a series of bets that make it impossible for him to lose but not impossible for the first person to lose. So, for example, in a fair lottery with ten tickets, suppose that *S* believes that ticket one will not win with enough confidence that he is willing to give 9:1 odds on its denial. And suppose he believes with the same degree of confidence of each of the other tickets that it will not win either. Thus, he is willing to give 9:1 odds on their denials also. From this it does not follow that a Dutch Book can be made against *S*. On the other hand, if *S* also believes with this same degree of confidence the conjunction (ticket one will not win and ticket two will not win . . . and ticket five will not win), then a Dutch Book can be made against *S*. One way of doing so, for example, is to bet $1 on the denial of this conjunction, $1 on each of the tickets one through five to win, and $2 on each of tickets six through ten to win, taking the 9:1 odds that *S* is willing to give on each bet.

For reasons of this sort, accounts of rational degrees of belief usually insist that in order for a person's degrees of belief to be rational, they must not violate the axioms of the probability calculus.[7] But in addition, such accounts typically allow a person to rationally believe with great confidence propositions that are obviously inconsistent. Likewise, they allow that the degree of confidence with which a conjunction can be rationally believed might be less than the degree of confidence with which the conjuncts can be rationally believed. And of course, the subjective foundationalist can and presumably should agree with all this. In particular, although his interest is not to develop an account of rational degrees of belief, he presumably should agree that even in a very large lottery an individual should not believe with absolute confidence that ticket one will not win. At the very least, the subjective foundationalist should agree that it is best for an individual to avoid betting on each of the propositions involved in the lottery case as if they were absolutely certain.

The conclusion to be drawn from all these discussions, then, is that it is very difficult to defend a conjunctive rule with respect to epistemic rationality. Accordingly, it also is very difficult to avoid the conclusion that it can be epistemically rational for a person to believe obviously relatively few propositions beyond those that are properly basic and those that can be deduced from propositions that are properly basic.

6.5 *Coherentist Accounts of Epistemic Rationality*

Despite difficulties discussed in section 6.4, one kind of account of epistemic rationality—perhaps even the dominant one—implies that obviously inconsistent propositions cannot be epistemically rational. This is the coherence account.[8]

The identifying mark of a coherence theory is its claim that each member of a set of propositions is epistemically rational for a person just if the propositions are mutually supportive. What "mutual support" means is a matter of some controversy among coherentists. For some early coherentists, mutual support seemed to require mutual implication. Each proposition in a coherent set must be implied by the remaining members.[9] More recent coherentists agree that such a notion of mutual support is overly stringent, but beyond this there is little agreement. Some, the so-called explanatory coherentists, suggest that mutual support be understood in terms of some sort of explanatory relation. Of course, it is no trivial matter understanding what it is for one proposition (or set of propositions) to explain another, and to do so without making use of some other epistemic notion that is equally hard to understand. But at least the rough idea is that propositions are mutually supportive, and hence coherent, only if each proposition in the set either is explained by or helps explain the rest.[10] Other coherentists understand the support relation more subjectively; they insist that each proposition in a mutually supportive set of propositions must be such that the person believes (or at least would believe were he to be reflective) that it is likely to be true if the other members of the set are true.[11] Although it is more difficult to find proponents of such a view, it also is possible to understand mutual support "negatively." The idea would be that in order for a set of propositions to be mutually supportive in the way required for coherence, there need not be relations of "positive support" among the propositions. It is enough for there not to be a relation of "negative support," where this means that no proposition in the set can be such that its negation is positively supported by the remaining members. There then would be the usual range of options available for understanding what constitutes "positive support." It might be understood stringently, in terms of implication. If so, then a set of propositions would be coherent as long as the negation of no proposition in the set is implied by the remaining members—it would be coherent as long as it is consistent. Alternatively, positive support might be understood in terms of some kind of explanatory relation or it might be understood more subjectively.[12]

Despite the significant differences among these notions of mutual support, none allows obviously inconsistent propositions to be mutually supportive. If a set of propositions is obviously inconsistent, no proposition in the set is supported (in any of the above senses) by the remaining members. On the contrary, each proposition in the set is such that its negation is implied in an obvious way by the remaining members. So, according to coherentists, whatever the details of their accounts, not all the propositions in such a set could be epistemically rational.

What reasons are there for coherentists to make this claim, despite its apparent difficulties? Keith Lehrer is one coherentist who has tried hard to defend such claims.[13] Consider, for example, his defense of the claim that obviously inconsistent propositions cannot all be epistemically rational. According to Lehrer, it is best to try to understand epistemic rationality in terms of what "the veracious man" should believe. The veracious man, says Lehrer, seeks "optimum success," where optimum success is defined as believing all and only truths. Lehrer argues that if an account of epistemic rationality is one that describes what a veracious man should believe in his search for optimum success, then such an account ought to preclude the possibility of it being rational for such a man to believe obviously inconsistent propositions. For an individual who believes obviously inconsistent propositions "automatically foregoes the chance of optimum success in the search for truth."[14] He cannot help but believe something false.

Lehrer concludes from this that in lottery cases it cannot be epistemically rational for a person to believe that ticket one will not win and that it likewise cannot be epistemically rational for him to believe of any of the other tickets in the lottery that it will not win. To believe all of these propositions as well as the proposition that some ticket will win is to believe obviously inconsistent propositions and hence to give up the chance of optimum success. On the other hand, to believe of some of the tickets that they will not win but not to believe this of other tickets is arbitrary, since *S*'s epistemic position with respect to the proposition that ticket one will not win is no different from his position with respect to the proposition that ticket two will not win, and likewise no different from his position with respect to the proposition that ticket three will not win, and so on. So, according to Lehrer, it is epistemically rational for *S* to believe none of these propositions.

Unfortunately, Lehrer's suggestion here does no better with regard to keeping open the possibility of optimum success than does the suggestion that it is epistemically rational to believe each of these propositions. It is true that if *S* believes none of these propositions, he will avoid believing propositions that are obviously inconsistent, and hence he will avoid making it impossible for himself to have only true beliefs. This is not to say, of course, that he cannot have many false beliefs; it is only to say that he has kept open the possibility that all of what he believes is true. But in keeping open this possibility, he has closed off another. In failing to believe of any of the tickets that it will not win, it is guaranteed that he will lack true beliefs. For if his belief that the lottery is a normal fair lottery (in which one ticket will win and the others will lose) is true, then the propositions that ticket one will not win, that ticket two will not win, and so on, cannot all be false. On the contrary, all but one must be true. But the veracious man, says Lehrer, is supposed to try not just to believe *only* that which is true but also *all* that which is true. So, by failing to believe any of these propositions, a person "automatically foregoes the chance of optimum success in the search for truth" just as much as he does by believing all of them. More exactly, by believing that the lottery is a normal, fair lottery in which exactly one ticket will win and by failing to believe of any of the particular tickets that it will not win, it is guaranteed that either there is a false proposition he believes (the proposition about the lottery having exactly one winner) or there are true propositions he fails to believe (propositions about individual tickets not being winners).

So Lehrer's suggestion does no better with respect to keeping open the possibility of optimum success than does the suggestion that it is epistemically rational for S to believe of each of the individual tickets in the lottery that it will not win. Indeed, it might even be argued that the latter suggestion comes closer to optimum success than does the former. After all, on the assumption that S's belief about the lottery being fair and normal is true, believing of each ticket that it will not win guarantees that S will have one false belief but believing this of none of the tickets guarantees that in a billion-ticket lottery he will lack 999,999,999 true beliefs.

More important, if it is assumed that the lottery is fair, then the only general strategy a person can use to keep open the possibility of optimum success (that is, the only way he can keep open the possibility of his believing all and only truths) is for him to believe of some particular ticket—say, ticket #334,568,112—that it will win and to believe of every other ticket that it will lose. But of course, this would be patently irrational rather than rational. And if we broaden our focus beyond lotterylike situations, the only strategy an individual can use in general to keep open the possibility of optimum success is for him either to believe or to disbelieve each and every proposition, whatever it may be. But again, this is patently irrational. There are many propositions that a person should neither believe nor disbelieve; he should withhold judgment on them.

Thus, the claim that one should try to keep open the possibility of optimum success is not likely to be helpful in explaining why coherence accounts (and their accompanying claim that obviously inconsistent propositions cannot be epistemically rational) should not be dismissed as implausible. Indeed, this appeal to keep open the possibility of optimum success makes the mistake (once again) of failing to distinguish the goal that characterizes epistemic rationality from the prerequisites of epistemic rationality. Epistemic rationality is characterized by the goal of now believing those propositions that are true and now not believing those propositions that are false. Insofar as a person tries to be epistemically rational, he tries to find effective means to this goal. But this in no way implies that it is impossible for a false proposition to be epistemically rational for a person *S*, and it in no way implies that it is impossible for most of what is epistemically rational for *S* to be false, and it likewise in no way implies that it is impossible for *S* to be aware that one of the propositions that he believes must be false and yet for all of these propositions to be epistemically rational for him. For even if *S* is aware that one of the propositions that he believes is false, it nonetheless may be the case that he thinks, and would continue to think on reflection, that having such beliefs is an effective, albeit not a perfect strategy, to his epistemic goal. So just as what is epistemically rational for him can be false and just as what is epistemically rational for him can be unreliable, so too what is epistemically rational for him can be obviously inconsistent.

Indeed, it is difficult to avoid a wide-ranging skepticism—implying that little of what we believe is epistemically rational—if it is granted that obviously inconsistent propositions cannot be epistemically rational. Granting this creates a tension: If it is claimed that even in a fair billion-ticket lottery, it cannot be epistemically rational for a person to believe the proposition that ticket one will not win (for fear that it then will be epistemically rational to believe obviously inconsistent propositions), it is hard to avoid the position that relatively little of what we believe is epistemically rational. After all, it does not seem that very much of what we believe is more likely to be true than this proposition. Moreover, any set of propositions that we believe can be made obviously inconsistent by adding the proposition that one of these propositions is false. The problem facing the coherentist, or anyone else who wants to claim that obviously inconsistent propositions cannot be epistemically rational, is the problem of claiming this while at the same time avoiding a position that allows very little to be epistemically rational.

6.6   *Coherentist Principles of Epistemic Rationality*

I have insisted that what is acceptable as a conclusion of an argument need not be acceptable as a premise. A failure to keep this in mind makes tempting a number of closely related mistakes. It makes tempting the claim that it is impossible for obviously inconsistent propositions to be epistemically rational, the claim that a conjunctive rule is applicable to epistemic rationality, and the claim that only propositions that are mutually supportive (that is, coherent) can be epistemically rational.

Nevertheless, it is one thing to suggest that not all propositions that are epistemically rational can be used as premises to argue for the truth of other propositions. It is quite another to suggest, as I might seem to be doing, that only propositions that are properly basic can be used as premises to argue for other propositions. I have said that if a proposition p is not properly basic for a person S, then p is epistemically rational for S only if there is an argument with premises properly basic for him that tend to make p epistemically rational for him. This seems to suggest that if a proposition is not properly basic for S, then no matter how well it is supported, it cannot be used as evidence for another proposition; it cannot be used as a premise in an argument that makes another proposition epistemically rational for S. But then, it may look as if the conclusions of good arguments can never be added to one's evidence; they can never be added to the stock of premises available to argue for other propositions. And this, it might be claimed, is as implausible as the suggestion that the conclusions of good arguments always can be added to one's evidence and used to argue for other propositions.

Indeed, most epistemologists—even those who might be thought most prone to dispute it—have agreed that it is sometimes permissible to add the conclusions of good arguments to one's evidence. The epistemologists I have in mind are ones with sympathies for foundationalism—such as Roderick Chisholm, C. I. Lewis, H. H. Price, Roderick Firth, and Bertrand Russell. Each of these philosophers endorses the view that it is sometimes permissible to use the conclusions of good foundationalist arguments as evidence for other propositions. Thus, each in effect allows propositions that are not properly basic (given their accounts) to function as premises in arguments that help make other propositions rational, or that at least help give them a higher degree of epistemic warrant than they otherwise would have. In fact, each of these philosophers endorses what might be called "a coherence principle," a principle that implies that the epistemic status of each member of a set of propositions is raised if the propositions are mutually supportive.[15] So, for example, if the propositions $(p, p^1, p^2, \ldots p^n)$ are mutually supportive, then the propositions $(p^1, p^2, \ldots p^n)$ can be used to provide additional evidence for p. And they can be so used even if they are not properly basic.

Consider Chisholm's view on this matter. Chisholm distinguishes between propositions that are merely acceptable, or permissible, for a person (that are such that withholding on them is not more reasonable than believing them) and propositions that are beyond reasonable doubt, or required, for a person (that are such that believing them is more reasonable than withholding on them). He then claims that if each member of a set of propositions is acceptable for S and if in addition the members are mutually supportive (in the sense that each member is such that the remaining members tend to confirm it) and if finally all of the members are in an appropriate sense independent of one another (in the sense that what makes each acceptable for S is distinct from what makes the others acceptable),[16] then the epistemic status of each proposition in the set is raised from acceptable to beyond reasonable doubt.

This endorsement of a coherence *principle* does not make Chisholm a coherentist. It does not mean that he endorses a coherentist *account* of epistemic rationality. On the contrary, he insists that each of the members in what he regards as a coherent set of propositions be made acceptable by foundational evidence. All he claims is that if these propositions have been made acceptable for a person S by foundational evidence and if in addition the propositions are in the appropriate senses both mutually supportive and independent, then these propositions are capable of generating additional evidence for each other. In effect, Chisholm is claiming that this is one way in which propositions that are not properly basic for S can come to serve as evidence for other propositions; it is one way in which propositions that are not properly basic for S can be used as premises in arguments that augment the foundational arguments that S already has.

Chisholm provides this example to illustrate his coherence principle. The following four propositions, he suggests, might be mutually supportive for a person S: (1) There is a cat on the roof of my house today; (2) a cat was on the roof yesterday; (3) a cat was on the roof the day before that; (4) there has been a cat on the roof of my house at least four days this week. Moreover, each of these four propositions, says Chisholm, might be made acceptable for S by distinct evidence. Thus, they in the appropriate sense might be independent of one another. For example, Chisholm suggests that proposition (1) might be made acceptable for S by his seeming to see a cat on the roof; (2) might be made acceptable for him by his seeming to remember that there was a cat on the roof yesterday; (3) might be made acceptable by his seeming to remember that there was a cat there the day before yesterday; and (4) might be made acceptable for him by his being assured by a reliable observer that there has been a cat on the roof at least four days this week. If all this is so, says Chisholm, each of these propositions is not just acceptable for S; each is beyond reasonable doubt. Each is beyond reasonable doubt for S because of the relation of mutual support that obtains among these propositions.

So what Chisholm is claiming with respect to proposition (1), for example, is that under the conditions he describes, S has stronger evidence for (1) than is provided by his seeming to see a cat on the roof. In addition to this evidence for (1), which Chisholm regards as foundational evidence, he has the evidence provided by propositions (2), (3) and (4)—none of which, according to Chisholm, are properly basic.[17] Under these conditions, propositions (2), (3) and (4) in effect can be added to S's evidence and used as premises to provide additional support for (1).

What Chisholm seems to be suggesting is a picture of the structure of epistemic rationality that at least appears to be at odds with the one I have been suggesting. He seems to be suggesting that in some instances nonbasic propositions can serve as premises in arguments for other nonbasic propositions. I, on the other hand, might seem to be denying this.

However, there may be less of a conflict than seems to be the case at first glance. Notice that there is no reason why Chisholm's principle of coherence, or some similar principle, might not at least usually succeed and perhaps even always succeed (at least if S is relatively normal) in identifying propositions for which S has a very strong foundationalist argument, an argument using only premises that are properly basic for him. Indeed, it seems plausible to think that this is the case.

Reconsider Chisholm's example. Suppose S has a good argument for (1), an argument that S on reflection would regard as sufficiently truth preserving and that has premises that are properly basic for him. Suppose moreover, as Chisholm suggests, that the crucial (and perhaps the only) premise in this argument is the proposition that he seems to see a cat on the roof. Suppose also that S has good arguments for

(2), (3), and (4). Let us assume, to return to Chisholm's vocabulary, that all of these propositions are acceptable for S. According to Chisholm, the relation of mutual support among these propositions raises the epistemic status of (1) to beyond reasonable doubt. But surely whenever all of Chisholm's conditions are met, including his condition of mutual support and independence, it is at least likely that S also has a more complicated argument for (1)—an argument more complicated than the one that originally made (1) acceptable for him (the one whose crucial premise is that he seems to see a cat on the roof). In particular, it is likely that the premises that make acceptable for S propositions (2), (3), and (4) can be combined with the premise that he seems to see a cat on the roof, to construct a more complex and stronger argument for (1) than would otherwise be possible. To follow Chisholm's suggestions again, perhaps basic propositions such as that S seems to remember that there was a cat on the roof yesterday, that he seems to remember that there was a cat on the roof the day before that, and that he seems to remember being told by a reliable observer that there has been a cat on the roof at least four days this week, when combined with the basic proposition that he now seems to see a cat on the roof, provide him with a much stronger argument for (1) than does this last basic proposition alone.

So at least ordinarily it may be the case that when Chisholm's conditions of coherence are met, a proposition such as (1) has more evidence in its favor for S than the evidence that made it originally acceptable. But if this is the case, subjective foundationalism can help explain why. The explanation, for instance, in the example that Chisholm describes is that in addition to the original, relatively simple and relatively obvious argument that S has for (1), there is a stronger, more complicated, and perhaps somewhat less direct argument for (1) as well—an argument that S on reflection would regard as more likely to be truth preserving than the original argument and an argument that has as its premises propositions that are properly basic for S.

More generally, the lesson here is that from the fact that, given subjective foundationalism, it is epistemically rational for S to believe p just if p is properly basic for S or p is the conclusion of a good argument whose premises are properly basic for him, it does not follow that there cannot be secondary principles or rules or arguments that succeed (or ordinarily succeed) in identifying in some other way propositions that are epistemically rational for S to believe. Chisholm's principle of coherence, of some closely related principle, may very well be such a principle.[18]

Moreover, it is not just that secondary principles, rules, and arguments sometimes can succeed in identifying propositions that, given subjective foundationalism, are epistemically rational for an indivdual *S*. In addition, such secondary principles, rules, and arguments can play a crucial role in helping to make a variety of propositions epistemically rational for *S*. They can help to do so when it is epistemically rational for *S* to believe that the propositions "recommended" by such principles, rules, or arguments are likely to be true. For example, although the propositions that are epistemically rational for an individual *S* need not cohere, considerations of coherence nonetheless can be epistemically important. Thus, suppose (not implausibly) that it is epistemically rational for *S* to believe that when his beliefs (or certain kinds of his beliefs) cohere with one another in an appropriate way, each of these beliefs (all else being equal) is highly likely to be true. What he has seen, what he remembers, and so on, might well provide *S* with the premises of a good inductive argument for a claim of this sort, making it epistemically rational for him. But if so and if it is epistemically rational for him to think that a certain set of his beliefs do in fact cohere, then, all else being equal, the propositions that are the objects of these beliefs will be epistemically rational for him. In this way, a subjective foundationalist can say that considerations of coherence typically play precisely the epistemic role that Chisholm envisions. A subjective foundationalist can say, in other words, that propositions that are not properly basic for an individual *S* can provide support for one another, support that they need in order to be epistemically rational; he can say, in effect, that these propositions can be used as evidence even though they are not properly basic; they can be so used by virtue of their being the premises of good second-level arguments.[19]

VARIETIES OF EPISTEMIC CONSERVATISM

7.1 *Conjoining Propositions That Are Properly Basic*

There are two ways in which a proposition can be epistemically rational for a person: It can be epistemically rational for him by virtue of being properly basic for him or it can be epistemically rational for him by virtue of being the conclusion of a good argument—an argument that reflects his own deepest epistemic standards and that has premises that are properly basic for him. Subjective foundationalism implies that although it often is not epistemically rational for a person to believe the conjunction of propositions of the second kind, it normally is epistemically rational for him to believe the conjunction of propositions of the first kind.

Why is this so? Why, given subjective foundationalism, is it epistemically rational for any relatively normal person to believe the conjunction of propositions that are properly basic for him? After all, it is possible for a proposition to be properly basic without being true. But if such propositions need not be true, it seems as if the chances of at least one of them being false could be significant and that the person might realize that this is so. But then, why might not it be epistemically rational for him to believe *of* the set of properly basic propositions[1] that not all are true? Or short of this, why might not it be epistemically rational for him to withhold judgment on the conjunction of them?

The most straightforward answer to this question is the one mentioned in section 2.4, namely, that conjunctive arguments reflect the deepest epistemic standards of all, or at least almost all, people. A conjunctive argument is one whose conclusion is the conjunction of its premises. For example, the argument (*a; b;* thus, *a* and *b*) is a conjunctive argument. All, or almost all, people, on reflection, would regard this argument as truth preserving; they would think that in situations where the premises are true, the conclusion also has to be true. They would think the same of other conjunctive arguments, except those that are too complex for them to understand. But then, the conjunction of any set of propositions that are properly basic for a normal individual *S* must be epistemically rational for him, subject again to the proviso that the conjunction is not so complex that *S* would not be able to understand it even if he were ideally reflective. For any conjunction of properly basic propositions that is not too complex for him to understand will be the conclusion of an argument that reflects *S*'s deepest epistemic standards and that has premises that are properly basic for him.

To return to the original question: Why cannot it be rational, given subjective foundationalism, for a relatively normal person either to disbelieve or to withhold judgment on a conjunction made up of propositions that are properly basic for him? Because if it were rational for him either to disbelieve or to withhold judgment on the conjunction, then contrary to the original assumption not all of its conjuncts could be properly basic for him. A properly basic proposition is one whose truth can be uncontroversially assumed in order to argue for other propositions. And so, given that conjunctive arguments are acceptable to almost all people, to say of propositions that they cannot be properly conjoined is to say that they cannot be uncontroversially assumed; it is to say that they are not properly basic.[2]

This is the most straightforward answer to the question. But on the other hand, it may not be an altogether satisfying answer, since it encourages yet another question, the question of whether this consequence of subjective foundationalism is intuitively plausible. No doubt subjective foundationalism does imply that the conjunction of propositions that are properly basic for any relatively normal individual is epistemically rational for him, but the question remains of whether intuitively this seems right, given that the set of such propositions might be relatively large, and given that the individual's beliefs in at least many of these propositions are fallible. At first glance, it might seem as if there is likely to be some good way of arguing from an individual's perspective (given his doxastic system and his epistemic standards) for the proposition that there is a good chance of at least one of these propositions being false—a way of arguing that intuitively would seem to provide him with good epistemic reasons for believing this proposition, despite what is implied by subjective foundationalism. What might such an argument be? The most natural candidate is a probabilistic argument that begins by emphasizing the fallibility of the belief-acquisition processes and faculties that produced the individual's beliefs in these propositions and then goes on to point out that if each of these individual beliefs has even a small chance of being false, then given the large number of such beliefs there would seem to be a much larger chance of at least one of them being false. Indeed, it might be thought that most normal individuals are such that, on reflection, they would think that such fallibilistic considerations indicate that there is a good chance of there being at least one falsehood in *any* relatively large set of propositions that they believe.

But is this really so? Consider those propositions that I have identified as good candidates for being properly basic for a relatively normal individual S—propositions about his own current psychological states (for example, that he has a headache, or that he is having a tablelike visual experience), simple propositions about what he is perceiving in his immediate environment (for example, that he now sees a table in front of him, or that he now feels a pencil in his hand), simple propositions about what he remembers about the not-too-distant past (for example, that he remembers entering this room about ten minutes ago, or that he remembers working in his office at home this morning), simple propositions of mathematics and logic (for example, that $2 + 2 = 4$), and so on. Is it really the case that S, assuming that he is not much different from most of the rest of us, would be willing to admit on reflection that when considerations of the general fallibility of his beliefs are combined with general probabilistic considerations, these considerations together indicate that there is a good chance that at least some of these simplest and seemingly most obviously true of his perceptual beliefs, memory beliefs, psychological beliefs, and the like, are false? I think not. Notice, first, that although no doubt most of us would be willing to admit that there are possible situations in which our beliefs about such propositions are false, most of these situations will be ones that we regard as radically unrealistic, as being so improbable as not to be worth worrying about in our deliberations about what arguments are sufficiently likely to be truth preserving. So, even if we admit that *theoretically* there is a possibility of error with respect to each of these beliefs, we, on reflection, may very well think that in any situation remotely similar to what we take to be our own, this possibility can be ignored for many if not most of these beliefs. A normal individual S may very well think, for example, that although theoretically there is a possibility that his present belief that he sees clearly and distinctly a chair directly in front of him is mistaken, the kinds of situations in which it would be mistaken—say, situations in which someone has devised an elaborate illusion of a chair, situations in which he has been given a drug that prompts him to have chairlike visual experiences, evil demon situations, and so on—are so improbable as to be irrelevant for an assessment of the likely truth of this belief.[3] A fortiori he is likely to think this of his simple beliefs about his current psychological states— the belief that he has a headache, the belief that he is having a tablelike visual experience, and so on.

Accordingly, although our beliefs in propositions that are properly basic for us need not be absolutely certain, many and perhaps even most of these beliefs might very well have what can be called a "relevant certainty." That is, many if not most of them might be such that we, on reflection, would think that in any relevant situation in which we believe such propositions, these propositions are true.

Moreover, even if for most of these beliefs we, on reflection, would not be disposed to dismiss as irrelevant all those possible situations in which they are mistaken, at the very least we would be disposed to think that there are very few relevant situations in which they are mistaken. We are likely to think, in other words, that the chances of these simple beliefs being mistaken are minute—so minute that even taking these chances into account, it still is highly improbable that even one of these beliefs is false. On reflection, we perhaps would think that the chances of at least one being false are fairly high, were we to think that the truth of each of these propositions is independent of the truth of the others, for then the likelihood of their conjunction being true could be calculated by simply multiplying their individual likelihoods, the result presumably being that we would regard the likelihood of the conjunction being false as relatively high. But in fact, the propositions that are properly basic for any remotely normal individual will not be such that he, on reflection, would regard them as being independent of one another. Indeed, given the weblike nature of belief, it will be impossible for the proposition, say, that he sees a chair in front of him to be properly basic for an individual S without his believing a host of other propositions that he takes to be positively relevant to this perceptual proposition, many of which are themselves good candidates for being properly basic for him—such as the proposition that he is having a chairlike visual experience. So if the propositions that are properly basic for S are anything like the propositions that are properly basic for the rest of us, they will not be such that, on reflection, S would think that the likelihood of their conjunction being true is to be calculated simply by multiplying their individual likelihoods. On the contrary, he may even think that once the support relations among these various propositions are taken into account, the conjunction is almost as likely as the individual propositions themselves.

However, suppose that none of this is so. Suppose that the propositions that S believes about what he is now experiencing, what he is now perceiving, what he now remembers about the not-too-distant past, and so on, are not relevantly certain for him, and suppose in addition that they do not hang together in the way that they do for most of us. Then it is unlikely that these propositions are properly basic for S. There are elements within the structure of subjective foundationalism that ensure that it will be unlikely for all these propositions to be properly basic. At a minimum, the least confidently believed of these propositions—say, proposition p—is unlikely to be properly basic for S. For it is likely that there will be propositions in the set that can be used to construct an argument for the conclusion that at least one proposition in the set is false. And then, these fallibilistic considerations can be combined with the other propositions of the set to create an argument for not$p$ that has premises as confidently believed as p, thus preventing p from being properly basic for S. Or if the fallibilistic considerations indicate only that there is about a 50–50 chance of one of these propositions being false (suggesting that it may be best to neither believe nor disbelieve but rather to withhold on the conjunction of these propositions), then it is likely that these considerations when combined with the other (more confidently believed) propositions of the set will defeat the argument (S believes p; thus, p), once again preventing p from being properly basic for S. (See section 1.6, including note 47.)

Indeed, if these propositions about what S is experiencing, perceiving, remembering, and so on, do not hang together and if in addition his beliefs in them are not relevantly certain for him, it is likely, at least if S is similar to the rest of us, that he will believe, albeit perhaps nonoccurrently, with great confidence of the set of such propositions that at least one is false. It is doubtful whether many of the rest of us believe this of such propositions. Although we may think that it is theoretically possible for our beliefs about at least many of these propositions to be false, it is doubtful whether many of us believe that in fact any of our beliefs about such matters are false. And even if some of us do believe that some of our beliefs are false, we are unlikely to believe this with anything like the confidence with which we believe these propositions themselves. Think in your own case, for example, of what you take to be the most obviously true of the propositions you believe about what sense experiences you are now having, about what you are perceiving in your immediate environment, and about what you did today. The set of such propositions is likely to be relatively large, and if you are like the rest of us, you are likely to think that your beliefs about at least some of these matters are not absolutely guaranteed to be true. Even so, do you believe with as much confidence as you believe the individual propositions in this set that at least one proposition in the set is false? I think that you do not.

However, if these propositions did not hang together and if your beliefs in them were not relevantly certain for you, all this might change. You then might very well believe, at least nonoccurrently, that there is a good chance of one being false. So, consider our person S who, we are now assuming, does believe this. The propositions that he believes about what he is experiencing, perceiving, remembering, and so on, do not hang together, and his beliefs in these propositions are not relevantly certain for him either; as a result, he believes with great confidence that at least one is false. But then, not all of these propositions can be properly basic for him. Let $(p, p^1, \ldots p^n)$ be the set of such propositions. If S believes of this set that at least one is false and if he believes this with as much confidence as, say, p, then this proposition p is not properly basic for him. For there is an argument against p with premises that S believes as confidently as p— the argument that has as its premises $(p^1, p^2, \ldots p^n)$ as well as the proposition that set $(p, p^1, \ldots p^n)$ contains a falsehood.[4]

So whenever from S's perspective there are considerations that intuitively might seem to indicate of a set of believed propositions $(p, p^1, \ldots p^n)$ that there is a good chance that one is false, the structure of subjective foundationalism ensures that at best it is highly unlikely for all these propositions to be properly basic for S and that at worst it is altogether impossible for all of them to be properly basic (for example, if he believes with sufficient confidence of the set that one is false). In particular, it is unlikely or impossible for the least confidently believed proposition in the set to be properly basic. Nevertheless, most of the other propositions in this set might still be properly basic for him. For example, suppose that S believes of the set $(p, p^1, \ldots p^n)$ that at least one of its members is false and that he believes this with as much confidence as he does p. Then, p cannot be properly basic for S but most of the other propositions in the set might be. To see how, suppose we subtract p from the original set; we are then left with the set $(p^1, p^2, \ldots p^n)$. Might all the members of this new set be properly basic for S? Perhaps, but perhaps not. The relevant question now is whether S believes (occurrently or nonoccurrently) of this new set that at least one member is false, and whether he believes this with as much confidence as the least confidently believed member of this new set. Suppose that he does; suppose that he believes this with as much confidence as p^1. Then p^1 is not properly basic for him. We now can repeat the process, deleting p^1 from the set and then asking whether S believes (again, either occurrently or nonoccurrently) of this latest set $(p^2, p^3, \ldots p^n)$, that at least one member of the set is false and whether he believes this as confidently as the least confidently believed member of this set. As we continue this process, two things happen. First, the least confidently believed member in each succeeding set is more confidently believed than the least confidently believed proposition in the preceding set. Second, since we decrease the size of the sets in question by deleting the propositions of whose truth S feels the least sure, we reduce the motivation for S believing with confidence that at least one member of the next set is false. So with respect to each succeeding set, it is likely that S believes with ever less confidence that at least one member of the set is false. Presumably at some point one of these sets will be such that S does not believe (even nonoccurrently) with as much confidence as the least confidently believed member of the set that one member is false. But then, all the members of this pared-down set will be properly basic for S (assuming all else is well with them).

Accordingly, even if an individual S for some reason comes to believe of the simple propositions that he believes about what he is experiencing, perceiving, remembering, and so on, that at least one is false and even if he comes to believe this with as much confidence as he believes some of these propositions themselves, many and probably even most of these propositions are still likely to be properly basic for him.

7.2 Three Kinds of Epistemic Conservatism

Subjective foundationalism may strike some as being overly conservative, since it makes epistemic rationality a function of what is properly basic for a person, which in turn is a function of what a person believes and the confidence with which he believes it. So the account, it might be claimed, contains a built-in bias in favor of what a person already believes.

It will be instructive to see if this worry can be made more precise and to see if it is a serious worry. In particular, it will be instructive to consider some different ways in which an account of epistemic rationality might be conservative and to consider which, if any, of these kinds of conservatism is plausible and to consider finally to which, if any, of these kinds of conservatism subjective foundation-alism is committed.

Begin by considering a political analogy. Political conservatism might be understood as a political philosophy that recommends main-taining the social, political, and economic traditions of the past. Such a political philosophy tends to favor the status quo and tends to disfavor any radical shifts in social, political, or economic policy. It generally disapproves of any kind of broad overhaul of past policies. Political conservatism, so understood, is essentially a diachronic po-litical view. It concerns itself with the maintenance of traditions over time. Suppose we consider an analogous kind of doxastic conserva-tism. Suppose, in particular, we consider a kind of conservatism that recommends, all else being equal, that a person continue to believe as much of what he in the past has believed as is possible. In other words, it recommends the pursuit of doxastic stability, where steps are taken to ensure that what we believe does not change significantly from moment to moment, or from day to day, or perhaps even from year to year.

There may be much to recommend this kind of conservatism. There especially may be all sorts of long-term reasons in favor of it, since without some doxastic stability intellectual progress is likely to be difficult, and this in turn is likely in the long run to affect adversely our chances of securing our various nonintellectual goals. Be this as it may, subjective foundationalism is altogether neutral with respect to this kind of conservatism. It in no way approves of it and in no way disapproves of it. Indeed, it is the same with all accounts of epistemic rationality. They are neutral with respect to this kind of conservatism, for accounts of epistemic rationality are synchronic accounts. They seek to describe what it is rational for a person to believe at a time t insofar as he has the goal of having true beliefs and not having false beliefs at that time t. As such, they are not concerned with describing and evaluating what the effects might be of repeated, radical shifts in beliefs from one moment to the next, or from one day to the next, or from one year to the next. These effects might well be disastrous. But if they are, it is no business of an account of epistemic rationality to say so; its business simply is to describe what at any particular moment it is appropriate for a person to believe insofar as his goal is at that moment to believe propositions that are true and not to believe propositions that are false. Its business, in other words, is a synchronic account of rational belief.

Let us restrict ourselves, then, to synchronic views. For example, consider a view that implies that necessarily it is epistemically rational for a person to believe of the propositions that he believes, regardless of what these propositions are, that a high percentage of them are true. According to this view, if $(p, p^1, p^2, \ldots p^n)$ is the set of propositions that S believes, then it must be epistemically rational for him to believe that $(p, p^1, p^2, \ldots p^n)$ contains mostly truths. This is a strong claim, and it is strong precisely because it is put forth as being necessarily true. The claim that it often, or even that it almost always, is epistemically rational for people to believe of the propositions they believe that a high percentage are true is far less controversial. Or at least this is so given the assumption that individuals pretty well know what they believe and what they do not believe.[5] For example, it may be that it is epistemically rational for many people nowadays to believe of the propositions they believe that most are true because of what many of us know about natural selection. What we know about the process of natural selection may give many of us a good argument for the claim that most of what we believe is true and this in turn, given that we can identify what it is that we believe, may make it rational for us to believe of the set of propositions we believe that most are true. For instance, the argument might go this way: Natural selection favors characteristics that enhance chances of survival; true beliefs are more likely to enhance our chances of survival than false beliefs; so, what people believe—including what I believe—is likely to be true (or at least mostly true); thus, given that I believe propositions $(p, p^1, p^2, \ldots p^n)$, most of these propositions are likely to be true.[6]

There is much that could be said about this sort of argument, but for present purposes the only important points about it are, first, that it is but one kind of argument that might make it epistemically rational for a person to believe of the propositions he believes that most are true, and second, that even if it is a good argument it is of no help in defending the conservative view. For nothing in this argument suggests that analogous arguments must make it epistemically rational for all people at all times to believe of the propositions they believe that most are true. Nothing in the argument suggests, for example, that it was epistemically rational for people three hundred years ago to believe this of the propositions they believed, nor does it suggest that it is epistemically rational for all people now, even those who have never heard of natural selection, to believe this. At best, the argument can be used to illustrate that under present conditions it is epistemically rational for many people to believe this. And of course, presumably almost any account of epistemic rationality will allow that this might be the case.

The stronger view, the one implying that *necessarily* it is epistemically rational for a person to believe of the propositions he believes that a high percentage are true, is much more controversial. Indeed, the view has a number of radical consequences. Its most direct consequence is that it precludes the possibility of a person rationally but extensively criticizing the set of propositions that he believes. For if the view set forth here is adequate, it never can be epistemically rational for a person to believe that a sizeable proportion of these propositions are false. In this sense, the view here makes rational and extensive self-criticism of one's beliefs altogether impossible. Regardless of the circumstances in which a person finds himself and regardless of what evidence he has and regardless of what he believes, given this evidence, it cannot, given this view, be epistemically rational for a person to believe of the propositions that he believes that a sizeable proportion of them are mistaken.

Second, this view, if acceptable, has the consequence that every believed proposition, regardless of what it is, is such that merely by believing it the person, all else being equal, is provided with a strong reason for thinking it is true. For if it is epistemically rational for every person at every time to believe of the propositions he believes that most are true, all else being equal he has a strong reason to believe of any particular believed proposition that it is true.

This consequence, in turn, at least encourages the acceptance of yet another radical view. It encourages the idea that necessarily most of the propositions that a person believes are epistemically rational for him to believe. After all, if necessarily it is epistemically rational for an individual S to believe of the propositions he believes that a high percentage are true and if in addition he necessarily has a strong reason, all else being equal, to believe of every particular proposition that he believes that it is true, it is difficult to understand how it could fail to be the case that most of the propositions he believes are epistemically rational for him. For this not to be the case, he must have defeaters with respect to most of the propositions he believes—that is, defeaters of the strong reasons he has for each of these propositions. But it is hard to understand what kind of considerations could defeat most of these reasons without violating the assumption that it is epistemically rational for S to believe of the propositions he believes that most are true.

In any event, whether or not this is so, we have here three distinct claims: (1) necessarily, it is epistemically rational for a person S to believe of the propositions he believes that most are true; (2) necessarily, a person S has a strong reason, all else being equal, to believe of any proposition that he believes that it is true; and (3) necessarily, most of the propositions that a person *S* believes are epistemically rational for him to believe. Moreover, each of these claims can be regarded as a version of epistemic conservatism, since each implies that there is something epistemically favorable to be said of the propositions that an individual believes, whatever those propositions might be.

Unfortunately, none of these conservative views, at least at first glance, seems very plausible. Contrary to what is suggested by (3), for example, at first glance it does not seem to be absolutely impossible—rather than perhaps just rare or unusual—for a person to believe many propositions that are not epistemically rational for him. And if it is possible for a person to believe many propositions that are not epistemically rational for him, then it also should be possible, contrary to what is suggested by (1), for it not to be epistemically rational for a person to believe of the propositions he believes that most are true. If, for example, a person believes propositions p, p^1, p^2, ... p^n, despite the fact that many of these propositions are not epistemically rational for him, then presumably it might not be epistemically rational for him to believe of these propositions that most are true. For he lacks arguments for many of them. It also is hard to see why (2) is plausible. It is hard to see why merely by virtue of believing a proposition, whatever the proposition is, an individual inevitably acquires a strong reason for thinking it is true. At the very least, it is hard to see why this should be the case unless a claim such as (1) is true, which it seems it is not.[7]

However, although at first glance (1), (2), and (3) may not seem very plausible, it might be thought that there is a way of arguing for them, or at least a way of arguing for claims very similar to them. In particular, it might be thought that these conservative claims can be defended by appealing to a metaphysical thesis about the nature of belief—the thesis that necessarily most of what an individual believes is true.[8] Unfortunately, even if this thesis is true and it is impossible for most of what a person believes to be false, it still does not follow, at least in any straightforward way, that any of the above conservative views are at all plausible. For example, it does not follow that (1) is plausible. Notice that even if the arguments that are used to defend this metaphysical thesis are good arguments, nothing follows about it being epistemically rational for people to believe the thesis; nothing follows, that is, about it being epistemically rational for people to believe of the propositions that they believe that they are mostly true. (See section 3.2.) After all, not everyone is familiar with these philosophical arguments, which purportedly establish that necessarily most of what any individual believes is true. And more generally, there are many other necessary truths that it need not be epistemically rational for people to believe. So it is hard to think why it would have to be epistemically rational for every person to believe this one.

It is easy to get confused when thinking about these issues, however. It is easy, for instance, not to distinguish the claim that it is epistemically rational for any person S to believe of the *propositions he believes* that most are true, from the claim that it is epistemically rational for a person to believe of the *propositions that are epistemically rational for him to believe* that most are true. This latter claim does not imply a version of epistemic conservatism. It does not imply that believed propositions necessarily have a special epistemic status. It implies only that insofar as a person S has good arguments for propositions $(p, p^1, p^2, \ldots p^n)$—or insofar as these propositions are properly basic for him—he has a good argument for the proposition that most of them are true. The former claim, on the other hand, implies that if propositions $(p, p^1, p^2, \ldots p^n)$ are believed by S, then regardless of his situation—regardless, for example, of whether he has good arguments for many of these propositions—it is epistemically rational for him to believe that most are true.

So the latter claim is much more modest than the former claim. If people only believed what it is epistemically rational for them to believe, the differences between the two would not be important. But of course, people do not believe only what it is epistemically rational for them to believe. There is an important difference between the two claims, and the difference is such as to make the one claim plausible and the other implausible. It is plausible to claim that necessarily if $(p, p^1, p^2, \ldots p^n)$ is a set of propositions that are epistemically rational for S, then the proposition that $(p, p^1, p^2, \ldots p^n)$ contains mostly truths is also epistemically rational for him.[9] On the other hand, it does not seem particularly plausible to claim (even if we assume that S is aware of what he believes) that necessarily if $(p, p^1, p^2, \ldots p^n)$ is the set of propositions that are believed by S, then the proposition that $(p, p^1, p^2, \ldots p^n)$ contains mostly truths is epistemically rational for him. And likewise, it does not seem particularly plausible to accept either of the other conservative views described above, that is, claims (2) and (3).

The subjective foundationalist account of epistemic rationality I have been defending agrees with these conclusions. Although subjective foundationalism makes epistemic rationality a function of what a person believes, what he believes with confidence, and what he would believe on reflection, nothing in the account implies any of these conservative views. For example, nothing in the account precludes the possibility of a person believing many propositions that are not the conclusions of premises that are properly basic for him and that reflect his deepest epistemic standards. Accordingly, nothing in the account implies that most of what an individual believes must be epistemically rational for him. And likewise, nothing in the account implies that it must be epistemically rational for an individual to believe of the propositions he believes (even assuming that he is aware of what he believes) that most are true. And finally, nothing in the account implies that an individual merely by coming to believe a proposition (any proposition) inevitably acquires a strong reason to think that the propositions are true.

7.3   A Weaker Kind of Epistemic Conservatism

The second of the conservative claims—the claim that merely by believing a proposition an individual acquires a strong epistemic reason to believe that proposition—represents what is perhaps the purest form of epistemic conservatism. It implies that, regardless of a person's epistemic situation, there is a strong presumption in favor of a proposition being epistemically rational for him if he merely believes it. This kind of conservative claim, I have suggested, is not very plausible. But perhaps weaker versions of the claim would be more plausible— say, a claim that there is for an individual S some kind of presumption, even if only a very weak one, in favor of any proposition that is believed by him.

Roderick Chisholm, for one, thinks that a claim of this sort is plausible. In particular, Chisholm says that the following is true: "Anything we find ourselves believing may be said to have some presumption in its favor—provided it is not explicitly contradicted by the set of other things we believe."[10] This is not quite a purely conservative position, since not just any proposition that is believed acquires this presumption in its favor. Only those that are not *explicitly contradicted* by the rest of what one believes acquires it. However, Chisholm apparently intends explicit contradiction to be a strong notion, such that it is relatively unusual for a believed proposition to be explicitly contradicted by the set (that is, by the conjunction) of propositions that the person believes. Accordingly, he intends his conservative principle to apply to most believed propositions. (Indeed, this is apparently why he worries about his principle being overly permissive.) Specifically, Chisholm suggests that a proposition p explicitly contradicts another proposition q provided that two conditions are met. First, it must be necessary that if p is true not$q$ is true. Second, it must be necessary that whoever believes p also believes not$q$.[11]

However, it is not clear that this suggestion captures the strong notion that Chisholm apparently wants. The problem is one that has been mentioned several times—it may not be unusual for people to believe *of* a set of propositions that they believe that some are false. But if this is not unusual, it may not be unusual for people to believe propositions that are explicitly contradicted by the conjunction of the other propositions they believe. And if this is so, Chisholm's principle of conservatism, despite Chisholm's intentions to the contrary, may apply to relatively few believed propositions.

It is worth noting in passing here that this problem arises for Chisholm not because people frequently believe the proposition that some of the propositions they believe are false. No doubt it is common for people to believe such a proposition, but the threat of an explicit contradiction does not arise simply because of this.[12] Indeed, if this proposition is added to the other propositions a person S believes, the resulting set need not even be inconsistent. Suppose, for example, that S believes propositions $(p, p^1, p^2, \ldots p^n)$ and then also comes to believe the proposition that some proposition he believes is false. Suppose also that these are all the propositions he believes. This set of propositions need not be inconsistent, even though at first glance it might seem to be so. Imagine another world in which in addition to the propositions that he now believes in the actual world, S also believes the proposition p^{n+1}, and suppose that in this second world p^{n+1} is false but everything else he believes is true. Since this is possible, it is possible for every proposition that S in the actual world believes to be true. What this shows, in turn, is that the set of propositions that S in the actual world believes—the propositions $p, p^1, p^2, \ldots p^n$ as well as the proposition that something he believes is false—is not inconsistent. There is a possible world in which *all* of these propositions are true.

So this problem arises for Chisholm not because people frequently believe that some of what they believe is false. Rather, the problem arises because it perhaps is the case that people frequently believe of a set of propositions they believe that some are false. Suppose, for example, that $(p, p^1, p^2, \ldots p^n)$ is a set of propositions S believes. Then it may not be unusual, especially if the set is large, for S to believe—albeit perhaps nonoccurrently—that $(p, p^1, p^2, \ldots p^n)$ contains at least one falsehood. Indeed, it may be that most propositions that most people believe belong to such a set. But if so, it may very well be the case that most propositions that most people believe are explicitly contradicted (in Chisholm's sense) by the set of other propositions they believe. Consider, for example, the proposition p from the above set. Necessarily, if propositions $(p^1, p^2, \ldots p^n)$ are all true and if the proposition that the set $(p, p^1, p^2, \ldots p^n)$ contains at least one falsehood is also true, then not$p$ is true. Thus, Chisholm's first condition of explicit contradiction is met. Moreover, it perhaps is also necessary that whoever believes (and hence understands) the proposition that the set $(p, p^1, p^2, \ldots p^n)$ contains a falsehood but the set $(p^1, p^2, \ldots p^n)$ contains all truths, also believes the proposition not$p$. Thus, Chisholm's second condition of explicit contradiction perhaps is also met. But if both of these conditions are met, proposition p— and perhaps most other propositions that S believes—is explicitly contradicted (in Chisholm's sense) by the set of other propositions he believes. And accordingly, Chisholm's principle of conservatism will apply only to relatively few propositions.[13]

Be this as it may, I propose to ignore this potentially difficult problem in order to concentrate on the issue of epistemic conservatism. Let us simply assume that Chisholm's conservative principle applies, as he intends, to most believed propositions, or let us assume that it can be modified to do so. Then let us consider whether such a weakly conservative principle is at all plausible.

In considering whether Chisholm's principle of conservatism is plausible, it is important to keep in mind the distinction between fully epistemic defenses of his principle and defenses that are not fully epistemic. There are different ways of defending a policy of conservatism with respect to one's own beliefs. For example, there might be pragmatic reasons for being conservative with respect to one's beliefs; it might be that regardless of what one happens to believe one has at least a weak practical reason to continue holding that belief, given the practical advantages of doxastic stability. Similarly, one might argue that having relatively stable beliefs increases a person's chances of having true beliefs and not having false beliefs in the long run. Thus, from the viewpoint of this long-run intellectual goal, there is also at least a weak reason to believe, and to continue to believe, whatever one believes.

However, Chisholm's principle is meant to be an epistemic principle, one that is defended on epistemic grounds. It is meant to be of help in describing what it is rational for a person to believe insofar as he has the goal of now believing truths and now not believing falsehoods. Thus, appealing to practical benefits or to the goal of believing truths in the long run is irrelevant to an evaluation of it.

Moreover, Chisholm's principle is intended to represent what might be deemed a fundamentalist version of conservatism. By this I mean that Chisholm is not proposing that there is some argument—such as the argument from natural selection mentioned earlier—that makes it epistemically rational for many people, or even most people, to believe of the propositions they believe that most are true and that as a result also gives them at least a weak epistemic reason in favor of any particular proposition that they believe. Chisholm's principle of conservatism is intended to be stronger than this. It is meant to apply necessarily, so that whenever a person believes a proposition that is not explicitly contradicted by the rest of what he believes, then the believed proposition has some presumption in its favor for him, regardless of his situation and regardless of what else it is epistemically rational for him to believe in that situation.

Although Chisholm's principle is intended to be a fundamentalist version of conservatism, it also is intended to be a very weak fundamentalist position. Chisholm says that a believed proposition has some presumption in its favor, which for Chisholm is the very weakest form of epistemic praise. A proposition p has some presumption in its favor for a person S, according to Chisholm, just in case believing p is more reasonable for S than disbelieving p. Thus, for example, if we let p be the proposition that either 1 or 2 or 3 or 4 or 5 or 6 will come up on the first roll of a fair ten-sided die, then this proposition for most people will have some presumption in its favor. Believing it will be more reasonable than disbelieving it (that is, believing its negation), even though withholding judgment on it may be even more reasonable than either believing it or disbelieving it.

So Chisholm's principle is intended to be a very weak principle of epistemic conservatism.[14] Even so, it still is far too strong, as can be seen by considering a person whose beliefs are not marred by any explicit contradictions but who believes a proposition when, given his circumstances, it is more reasonable to believe its negation. Situations of this sort certainly are possible. It is possible, for example, for S to believe p when not$p$ is epistemically rational for him. Yet this is just what Chisholm's principle implies is impossible. According to his principle, if S believes p and p is not explicitly contradicted by any other proposition he believes, then proposition p, whatever it is and whatever S's circumstances, is a proposition that is more reasonable for S to believe than to disbelieve. But of course, this is strongly counterintuitive. Unfortunately, people do believe propositions whose negations are more reasonable for them to believe.

The problem with Chisholm's principle as stated is obvious enough. Propositions can have a favorable epistemic status for a person either in a prima facie sense or in a final, or overall, sense. So, for example, a proposition p can have some presumption in its favor for S in a prima facie sense, even though when everything is taken into account, believing p is not more reasonable for S than disbelieving it. Accordingly, an epistemic conservative in claiming that any proposition simply by being believed acquires a favorable epistemic status for the person can be claiming either that believed propositions prima facie have this status or that they finally or ultimately have this status. The difficulty with Chisholm's principle arises because it implies the latter, stronger claim. It implies that no matter what S's situation is, if he believes p, then believing p is for him more reasonable than disbelieving p. And of course, this is implausible. On the other hand, it might not be implausible to claim that prima facie any believed proposition is such that believing it is more reasonable than disbelieving it.

Let us revise Chisholm's principle, so that it makes only this weaker claim, and let us call the revised principle A. Principle A, then, implies that any believed proposition prima facie has some presumption in its favor.

Principle A is a very weak principle of epistemic conservatism. According to it, believing a proposition counts for something but not for much. It employs only a very weak term of epistemic praise, and it implies only that every believed proposition prima facie has this status. It says only that every believed proposition is such that, all else being equal, believing it is more reasonable than disbelieving it. So even if all else is equal, it does not follow that the proposition is epistemically rational; it still may be epistemically rational for the person to withhold judgment on the proposition rather than believe it. Indeed, the weakness of principle A constitutes part of its significance. It is one of the weakest principles of epistemic conservatism imaginable. If principle A is not plausible, it is unlikely that any other conservative principle will be plausible either.

Although principle A is a very weak principle of conservatism, it is not without significance. It implies that all propositions are such that merely by believing them an individual acquires at least a very weak epistemic reason to think that they are true. Accordingly, at a minimum, A commits one to the view that it is somewhat easier, even if only a little easier, for propositions that an individual S believes to be rational for him than it is for propositions that he does not believe to be rational for him. Believing a proposition, according to A, is not enough, all else being equal, to make a proposition rational, but believing a proposition does reduce the amount of other support the proposition has to have in order to be rational. So what this means, in effect, is that a believed proposition needs less evidence in its favor to make it epistemically rational than does a proposition that is not believed.[15]

But even given this relatively modest interpretation, principle A is still far too strong a doctrine. One way to illustrate this is to imagine pairs of situations of the following sort. In the first situation, imagine that S withholds judgment on p, and suppose that it is epistemically rational for him to do so. Suppose, in particular, that there is an argument for p that has premises that are properly basic for him but that on reflection he would think that this argument is just barely insufficiently likely to be truth preserving. So it is just barely rational for him to withhold on p. Now, suppose that we alter this situation slightly. Suppose that S comes to believe p but that nothing else changes. Other than p, what he believes, the confidence with which he believes it, and what he would believe on reflection (about, say, what arguments are likely to be truth preserving) does not change.[16] Then, given principle A, it is epistemically rational for S in this second situation to believe p. In other words, the kind of epistemic conservatism represented by principle A commits us to the view that S here, by coming to believe a proposition p that by hypothesis is epistemically irrational for him in the first situation, inevitably changes the situation into one in which p is epistemically rational for him. And this is so regardless of what the proposition p is. For principle A implies that any proposition simply by being believed has the amount of support needed to make it epistemically rational somewhat reduced. So if the proposition p in the first situation is just barely unacceptable for S and if the only change in this situation is that S comes to believe p, then principle A implies that in the second situation it must be as reasonable to believe p as to withhold on it. In other words, p must be epistemically rational. And principle A implies this despite the fact that intuitively we think that in the second situation it need be no more appropriate for S to believe p than in the first situation. After all, he still has exactly the same arguments for p and they are still as strong or as weak as they were before. All that has changed is that he has come to believe p, a proposition that by hypothesis was epistemically irrational for him to believe in the first situation.

Of course, there are all sorts of conceivable modifications of principle A, some of which might very well generate conservative principles that at least at first glance seem more plausible than A. But there is little point in getting bogged down in a discussion of such modifications, for implicit in the discussion above is a perfectly general lesson. Any principle of conservatism will be implausible insofar as it, like A, implies that simply by being believed a proposition (*any* proposition) acquires some kind of favorable epistemic status that in some way alters what is required to make that proposition epistemically rational for the person. Simply believing a proposition is never enough in and of itself to give a person an epistemic reason, even a weak epistemic reason, to think that the proposition is true. After all, people in all sorts of very odd ways can come to believe all sorts of very odd propositions—propositions that they themselves would regard as highly unlikely to be true were they at all reflective.

This is not to say, of course, that what an individual believes is in no way important to what is epistemically rational for him. On the contrary, no account of epistemic rationality, which by hypothesis is an account that emphasizes the individual's own perspective, can be at all plausible without giving a significant epistemic role to what an individual believes. The lesson is merely that this must not be done too blatantly—for example, by supposing that merely by believing a proposition, an individual inevitably acquires a reason to think that the proposition is true. It must not be done by supposing that mere belief is always epistemically significant.

A fortiori, the way to give belief a significant role in the theory of epistemic rationality is not to so strongly emphasize what an individual believes that it becomes the *only* significant factor in determining what it is epistemically rational for him to believe. An account of epistemic rationality is an account that emphasizes the individual's own perspective but it also by hypothesis is an account that emphasizes what the individual would believe were he sufficiently reflective, where this need not be something that he now believes, even non-occurrently. One consequence of this is that situations that are doxastically identical need not be epistemically identical. For example, imagine a pair of situations in which an individual S believes the same propositions and believes them with exactly the same degree of confidence. Even so, a proposition p might be epistemically rational for S in one situation but not in the other. For in the first situation but not in the second, there might be an argument for p (in terms of what else S believes) that S would take to be a good argument were he sufficiently reflective, where this argument is not one that he now (in either situation) believes to be a good argument.

Is this consequence plausible? Is it plausible to think that situations that are doxastic twins need not be epistemic twins? Yes, for the propositions that are epistemically rational for an individual S can be thought of (at least roughly) as those propositions that S would be able to defend using his current beliefs were he to be sufficiently reflective. But from the fact that S in two situations has identical beliefs, it in no way follows that in these two situations S is equally able on reflection to defend some proposition p.

So pairs of situations in which S has not only identical beliefs but also identical dispositions to generate new beliefs given sufficient reflection *are* epistemic twins; any proposition that is epistemically rational for him in one situation is epistemically rational in the other as well. However, pairs of situations in which S has identical beliefs but not identical dispositions to generate beliefs on reflection need not be epistemic twins.

7.4   *Epistemic Conservatism and Subjective Foundationalism*

As I have been using the expression, epistemic conservatism is a position that implies that necessarily a person acquires at least a weak epistemic reason in favor of a proposition (*any* proposition) merely by virtue of the fact that he believes it. Subjective foundationalism is not conservative in this sense. Nevertheless, it does imply that *some* propositions acquire a favorable epistemic status for an individual by virtue of being believed by him. Which propositions are these? They are the propositions that are candidates to be properly basic for him. They are, in other words, the propositions that S on reflection would think are sufficiently likely to be true when he believes them to be true. If p is such a proposition, then the proposition that he believes p tends to make p epistemically rational for him. His own deepest epistemic standards imply that his believing p is epistemically significant. When he believes such a proposition, his belief tends to be self-justifying.

However, not all propositions are like this. And for those that are not, the fact that the person believes them (even with great confidence) is ordinarily altogether irrelevant to these propositions being epistemically rational for him.[17]

On the other hand, the fact that an individual believes such a proposition need not be altogether irrelevant to the question of whether some other proposition is epistemically rational for him. Suppose that q is not a candidate to be properly basic for S, but suppose that it does tend to make the proposition not$p$ rational for him, where p is a proposition that is a candidate for being properly basic for him. Then if S comes to believe q with great confidence, p may be prevented from being properly basic. For *p* is properly basic for *S* only if nothing else he believes with as much confidence can be used to argue against it. Or suppose that although *q* here does not tend to make not*p* rational for *S*, it is a potential defeater of the argument (*S* believes *p*; thus, *p*). Then, once again the fact that *S* believes *q* can be epistemically relevant. If *S* believes *q* as confidently as *p*, then *p* cannot be properly basic for *S* (unless *q* itself is defeated).

So according to subjective foundationalism, there are at least these three ways in which the fact that a person *S* believes a proposition *p* can be epistemically significant. First, for any proposition *p* that is a candidate for being properly basic (that is, any proposition that is such that *S* on reflection would think that it is sufficiently likely to be true when he believes it), believing it, all else being equal, gives *S* a good epistemic reason to think that it is true. Second, for any proposition *q* that tends to make rational the negation of a proposition *p* that is a candidate to be properly basic (whether or not *q* itself is properly basic), believing *q* with enough confidence may prevent *p* from being properly basic. Finally, for any proposition *q* that tends to defeat the reason that *S*'s believing *p* tends to provide for *p*, *S*'s believing *q* with enough confidence may prevent *p* from being properly basic.

Thus, according to subjective foundationalism, the only propositions for which mere belief is positively relevant, giving an individual a reason to think that what he believes is true, are propositions that are candidates for being properly basic. On the other hand, propositions that are not candidates for being properly basic can be such that belief (or confident enough belief) in them makes them negatively relevant to other propositions, preventing these other propositions from being epistemically rational. But even here, there are sharp restrictions on the kind of propositions that can be affected. Once again, only propositions that are candidates for being properly basic can be directly affected. Of course, insofar as what a person happens to believe directly affects the rationality of propositions that are candidates for being properly basic, it indirectly affects the rationality of other propositions. For what other propositions are epistemically rational for the person is in part a function of what is properly basic for him.

Even so, subjective foundationalism does not imply any version of epistemic conservatism. Although properly basic propositions are identified in terms of what the individual believes, what he believes with confidence, and what he would believe on reflection about the truth-preservingness of arguments, there is nothing in subjective foundationalism that commits one to the thesis that an individual S necessarily acquires an epistemic reason in favor of a proposition p (*any* proposition p) merely by coming to believe it. And likewise, nothing in subjective foundationalism commits one to any other robust conservative thesis.

Nevertheless, given subjective foundationalism, might not it in fact be the case, even if it is not necessarily the case, that with respect to most propositions, mere belief *is* positively relevant for an individual S? In particular, might not an individual S in fact be such that, on reflection, he would believe with respect to most of the propositions that he believes that these propositions are sufficiently likely to be true when he believes them? But if so, might not most of his beliefs tend to be self-justifying, and correspondingly might not it be the case that most propositions that he believes tend to be properly basic for him?

Apparently, this is at least possible. The interesting question, however, is whether it is plausible to think that many of us are in fact like this. Is it plausible to think that relatively normal people, on reflection, would believe with respect to most of the propositions that they believe that these propositions are true in a sufficiently large percentage of relevant possible situations in which they believe them? I think not. It *is* likely, I have said, that a normal person S, on reflection, would believe this of simple propositions concerning his current psychological states, what he is now perceiving, what he is now remembering, and so on. But with other propositions, this is unlikely to be the case. Consider, for example, propositions such as that there are more inhabitants of India than of the United States, that women in the United States have a longer life expectancy than men, and that ouija boards are not a reliable way to foretell the future. These are propositions that S, like many of the rest of us, might believe with a fair amount of confidence. Even so, these propositions are not likely to be properly basic for S. On reflection, he is not likely to have much trouble imagining many situations that he takes to be very similar to the actual situation but in which he falsely believes such propositions. Acordingly, the proposition that S believes such a proposition is unlikely to constitute what he, on reflection, would regard as a good argument for the proposition.

Moreover, these propositions are unlikely to be properly basic even if S, on reflection, would believe, say, that the nature of belief implies that most of his beliefs must be true. If S were to believe this, he also may very well believe of all (or at least most) of the particular propositions that he believes that his believing them, all else being equal, makes them likely. But, from this it does not follow that, on reflection, he would think that his believing them makes them sufficiently likely, such that (all else being equal) they are epistemically rational for him even if nothing else that he believes gives him a reason to think they are true. It does not follow, in other words, that these propositions tend to be properly basic for him when he believes them.

And, even if these propositions do tend to be properly basic for him, they still are unlikely to be properly basic for him. For there are other constraints on proper basicality, and it is unlikely that all of these other constraints will be met. For one, there may well be a defeater of the reason that his believing such propositions (we are now assuming) provides for them. Indeed, this is all the more likely since, on reflection, he is unlikely to think that mere belief is as positively relevant to these propositions as it is to simple propositions about his current psychological states, simple propositions about what he is perceiving in his immediate environment, and the like. As a result, it will be relatively easier for there to be a defeater of the reasons that his beliefs provide for the former propositions. But second, and as important, even if these propositions tend to be properly basic for him, they are unlikely to be believed by him with as much confidence as he believes propositions about what he is experiencing, what he is perceiving in his immediate environment, what he is remembering about the not-too-distant past, and so on. But if so, they are likely to be the most weakly believed member of some set of propositions such that S believes with as much confidence as this member that at least one proposition in the set is likely to be false. Then this most weakly believed proposition cannot be properly basic for S, since there is an argument against it with premises that S believes just as confidently. Thus, consider some proposition p that S believes but that is not one of the kinds of propositions that I have said are likely to be good candidates for proper basicality. Suppose, for example, p is the proposition that women in the United States have a longer life expectancy than men. Then there is likely to be some set of propositions $(p, p^1, p^2, \ldots p^n)$ such that each of the other propositions in this set is believed by S with as much confidence as p and such that in addition S believes (perhaps nonoccurrently) with as much confidence as p that it is likely that at least one proposition in the set is false. But if so, p is not properly basic for S, since there is an argument for not p that has premises that S believes as confidently as p.

But isn't it plausible to think that this is also the case with respect to propositions that I have said *are* good candidates for being properly basic? No. Suppose we construct a set of propositions from those simple propositions that *S* believes about his current psychological states (for example, that he has a headache, that he is having a tablelike visual experience, and so on) and about what he is now perceiving (for example, that he now sees a table in front of him, that he now feels a pencil in his hand, and so on) and about what he is now remembering (for example, that he entered this room about ten minutes ago, that earlier this morning he worked in his office at home, and so on) as well as fundamental propositions about the nature of our world (that there are material objects, that there are other people, that our world has had a significant past). Even if this set is relatively large, *S* is unlikely to believe of this set that at least one member is false. He is not even likely to believe that this is probable. A fortiori, he is unlikely to believe this with as much confidence as he believes some member in this set.

The conclusion, then, is this: There are, according to subjective foundationalism, some propositions that are made epistemically rational for an individual *S* by virtue of the fact that he believes them. However, not all propositions need be like this. Indeed, the only propositions that *can* be like this for an individual *S* are those that are such that *S*'s believing them tends to make them epistemically rational for him, and it is not plausible to think that all or even most of the propositions that *S* believes are like this for *S*, at least if he is relatively normal. But even if most propositions are like this—that is, even if most propositions do tend to be properly basic for *S*—it still is unlikely that most propositions that *S* believes are properly basic for *S*. For it is unlikely that the other constraints on proper basicality are met.

7.5 Epistemic Rationality and the Nature of Belief

Nothing in subjective foundationalism implies that it is altogether impossible for an individual *S* to believe many propositions that are not epistemically rational for him. Likewise, nothing in subjective foundationalism implies that it must be epistemically rational for *S* to believe of the propositions that he believes that most are true. Moreover, this is so even if we assume that an individual is always aware of what he believes, and it is so even if a surprising metaphysical thesis about the nature of belief turns out to be true—the thesis that necessarily most of an individual's beliefs are true. For even if this thesis is true, it presumably need not be epistemically rational for an individual to believe that it is true.

Nevertheless, it *is* plausible to think that the nature of belief does impose limits upon the extent to which an individual's beliefs can be epistemically irrational. It is plausible to think in other words, that given the nature of belief, anything that constitutes a belief system must of necessity satisfy minimal standards of epistemic rationality.

To see why, consider a few simple principles about what it is possible and what it is not possible for an individual to believe, principles that might be construed as constituting the barest beginnings of a logic of believing. (Let "Bsp" stand for "S believes that p is true," let "B*sp" stand for "p is true and S believes that p is true," let the box stand for "it is necessary that," let the diamond stand for "it is possible that," and let the tilde stand for "it is not the case that.")

$(i) \sim \Diamond$ (Bsp & B$snotp$)

$(ii) \sim \Diamond$ (B$s(p$ & not$p$))

$(iii) \quad \Box$ (if B$s(p$ & q), then Bsp & Bsq)

$(iv) \quad \Diamond$ ((Bsp & Bsq) & $\sim$B$s(p$ & q))

$(v) \quad \Diamond$ ((Bsp^1 & Bsp^2 ... & Bsp^n) & $\Box \sim (p^1$ & p^2 ... & p^n))

$(vi) \quad \Diamond$ ((Bsp^1 & Bsp^2 ... & Bsp^n) & B*$s \Box \sim$ (B*sp^1 & B*sp^2 ... & B*sp^n))

Principle (i) says that it is impossible to have explicitly contradictory beliefs, such that an individual believes a proposition p as well as the negation of that same proposition p. Principle (ii) says that it is impossible to believe an explicitly contradictory proposition—say, the proposition $(p$ & not$p)$. Principle (iii) says that it is impossible to believe a conjunction without believing each of its conjuncts, while (iv) says that it is possible to believe two propositions without believing their conjunctions. Principle (v) says that it is possible to believe propositions that are inconsistent, and (vi) says that this is possible even if one realizes that the propositions that one believes are inconsistent.

Let us assume that each of these principles is plausible. Or at least let us assume that each could be made plausible, by explaining away any apparent counterexamples. With respect to principle (i), for example, let us assume that *any* situation in which an individual at first glance might be thought to have explicitly contradictory beliefs plausibly can be understood as a case where either (1) the person has inconsistent but not explicitly contradictory beliefs, or (2) the person believes p although his behavior may make it seem as if he believes not$p$, or (3) the person now believes p, although at an earlier time, perhaps only a slightly earlier time, he believed not*p*, or (4) the person believes *p* although in some other sense of belief, perhaps an unconscious, repressed sense, he believes not*p*, or (5) the person has contradictory de re beliefs such that he believes of an object O^1 that it has property X and believes of an object O^2 that it does not have X, where in fact O^1 and O^2 are identical but where S does not realize this (and where as a result he does not have contradictory de dicto beliefs), or (6) the person believes two sentences to be true, where these sentences express contradictory propositions but where in addition the person does not understand precisely what proposition at least one of the sentences expresses.[18] Likewise, let us assume that there are analogous strategies for explaining away any apparent counterexamples to the other principles.

Given the principles above, it is plausible to think that the nature of belief imposes constraints upon epistemic irrationality. For the principles together with plausible assumptions about the nature of epistemic rationality, assumptions implicit in subjective foundationalism, imply that necessarily the beliefs of any individual satisfy at least minimal standards of rationality. This is so because each of the principles concerning what it is possible or impossible for an individual to believe have epistemic counterparts. For example, the epistemic counterpart of (i) is that it cannot be rational to believe contradictory propositions; the epistemic counterpart of (ii) is that it cannot be rational to believe a contradiction; the counterpart of (iii) is that if it is rational to believe a conjunction it also is rational to believe each of its conjuncts.

Principles (iv), (v) and (vi) also have epistemic counterparts but of a different sort. The counterpart of (iv), for example, is that it *can* be rational to believe two propositions even if it is not rational to believe their conjunction. Accordingly, instead of precluding a certain kind of epistemic irrationality—as do principles (i), (ii), and (iii)— principle (iv) implies that it is possible for an individual to be epistemically rational in a certain kind of situation. More exactly, (iv) implies that there is nothing about the nature of belief that implies that a person S must have irrational beliefs in situations where each of two propositions is rational for S but their conjunction is not. For nothing about the nature of belief precludes one from believing each of these two propositions without believing their conjunction.

Analogously, the epistemic counterpart of (v) is that it can be rational for an individual S to believe inconsistent propositions, and the epistemic counterpart of (vi) is that it can be rational for S to believe obviously inconsistent propositions. So (v) implies that nothing in the nature of belief ensures that when inconsistent propositions are epistemically rational for an individual *S*, *S* will fail to believe one of these propositions. Similarly, principle (vi) implies that nothing in the nature of belief ensures that when obviously inconsistent propositions are epistemically rational for *S*, he will fail to believe one of them.

The fact that there are epistemic counterparts to these doxastic principles, principles describing what it is possible (or impossible) to believe, indicates that there are significant links between the nature of belief and the nature of epistemic rationality. Principles (i), (ii), and (iii) and their epistemic counterparts especially indicate this, since they imply that necessarily an individual's beliefs must satisfy certain minimal standards of epistemic rationality.

In saying that the above doxastic principles in conjunction with their epistemic counterparts imply that necessarily an individual's beliefs must satisfy at least minimal standards of epistemic rationality, the "minimal" needs to be emphasized. There is nothing here that commits one to any robust kind of epistemic conservatism. For example, there is nothing here to suggest that merely by believing a proposition an individual acquires an epistemic reason to think that the proposition is true. Likewise, there is nothing here to suggest that it is altogether impossible for an individual's beliefs to be largely irrational, such that much, perhaps even most, of what he believes is not rational for him. On the contrary, I already have expressed skepticism about such theses, suggesting that belief and rationality need not be linked this intimately. Nevertheless, like those who insist upon such theses, I am claiming that there is a significant link between belief and rationality. In one sense, belief just is minimally rational belief. The principles above in conjunction with their epistemic counterparts begin (but only begin) to illustrate what this sense is. An adequate logic of believing, no doubt, would provide the materials for a more complete illustration.

NOTES
INDEX

NOTES

1. Epistemic Rationality

1. For the most part, in what follows I ignore questions concerning the nature of propositions. However, I do assume that propositions, whatever exactly they are, can be believed. I also assume that a proposition can be true at one time, false at a later time, and true once again at a still later time. Against this latter assumption, some philosophers prefer to say that a proposition, if true at all, is eternally true—that is, true at all times. Anyone wishing to honor this preference can substitute "state of affairs" for "proposition" in the discussion that follows, where a proposition can be thought of as a special kind of state of affairs—a state of affairs that is necessarily such that it either obtains at all times or obtains at no time. Given this distinction, many ordinary states of affairs, say, the state of affairs of Aristotle sitting, can be turned into propositions by stipulating the times at which they purportedly obtain, for example, the state of affairs of Aristotle sitting at time t. Compare Roderick Chisholm, *Person and Object* (LaSalle, Ill.: Open Court, 1976), chap. 4.

2. One thesis that I will develop later is that there are other plausible, general conceptions of rationality. Accordingly, it would be more accurate to say that what I am calling "an Aristotelian conception of rationality" is best for present purposes—that is, best for use in trying to develop an adequate account of epistemic rationality. I discuss various conceptions of rationality and their relation to the theory of epistemic rationality in section 2.8.

3. For the sake of simplicity, I will sometimes characterize the epistemic goal as the goal of now having true beliefs and now not having false beliefs. This is not to suggest, however, that the goal could be satisfied, for example, by believing only tautologies. The goal is to believe all truths (or at least those that one can understand) and to believe no falsehoods. Of course, this goal, like many other goals, is one that we do not have any realistic hope of satisfying perfectly; it is an ideal—a goal that we can do better or worse jobs of approaching.

4. Nonetheless, there *are* ways of epistemically evaluating even such a radical skeptic, ways that imply that some propositions are rational for him and others are not. Likewise, an individual who, on reflection, takes himself to be both omniscient and infallible can be evaluated epistemically in a way that does not imply that he should believe precisely what he now believes. However, these

evaluations are not *purely epistemic* evaluations. See section 2.7 for the distinction between epistemic evaluations and purely epistemic evaluations and for a discussion of its relevance to epistemic evaluations of a skeptic's beliefs.

5. What remains to be shown, and what will be argued for later (see section 2.6), is that every means that a person, on careful reflection, would believe to be an effective means to his epistemic goal can be represented in terms of such arguments.

6. So, in the sense of goal that is relevant here, to say that something is a goal is not equivalent to saying that it is intrinsically wanted or intrinsically needed. (Many people have the goal of making lots of money, but from this it does not follow that they *intrinsically* want or need money.)

7. Analogously, it can be perfectly appropriate to evaluate *S*, his actions, and his beliefs from a pragmatic point of view or from an aesthetic point of view or from the point of view of some other goal even if *S* lacks the goal in question (even if, for example, he cares not at all for his own welfare, or for the beauty of things, or for whatever other goal is in question).

8. However, see section 5.5, where I introduce a notion of irrational belief that is more closely linked with blameworthiness.

9. Thus, the notion of it being epistemically rational for *S* to believe *p* and the associated notion of *S* having a good epistemic reason to believe *p* are idealized notions. *S* can have a good epistemic reason to believe even a proposition *p* that he cannot believe, since on reflection he would think that from the standpoint of believing a proposition if it is true and not believing it if it is false it ideally would be better for him to believe *p* than not to believe *p*. (*S* might have a good practical reason to run one hundred yards in ten seconds even though he cannot in fact do this—imagine that this is the only way he can avoid an oncoming train.) However, it is worth repeating here that to say that it can be epistemically rational for *S* to believe *p*, where *S* cannot believe *p*, is *not* to say that it is rational all things considered—when *all* of *S*'s goals are taken into account—for *S* to believe *p*. Likewise, it is not to say that it is rational, all things considered, for him even to try to believe *p*.

10. This is so because ordinarily when a person becomes convinced he has a good evidence for a proposition *p*, he will come to believe *p*.

11. I do think that this use of "make probable" is closely related to at least one commonly employed notion of probability. However, I make no assumption here about whether this in fact is so, and likewise I make no assumption about how best to understand the probability claims made in science, games of chance, or in our everyday lives.

12. Why not say all else is equal just if there is no defeating proposition that is true (regardless of whether it is uncontroversial)? From the standpoint of formulating an adequate account of epistemic rationality, this is both too weak and too strong. It is too strong because there can be a true defeater even though from *S*'s viewpoint it may seem obvious that there is not. Indeed, he may have no reason whatsoever to think there is such a defeater and every reason to think there is not. But then, if the premises of an argument are uncontroversial for him, it might very well be appropriate from an epistemic point of view for him to believe its conclusion even if there is a true defeater. It is too weak because it can seem obvious from *S*'s viewpoint that there is a true defeater *d* even though

d in fact is false. If so, it might very well not be epistemically rational for *S* to believe the conclusion of the argument even if there is no true defeater of it.

13. Even so, propositions e^1, e^2, . . . e^n might still play an important role in making *p* epistemically rational for *S*. For instance, there might be another proposition d^1 such that d^1 is uncontroversial for *S* and such that in addition *S* on reflection would regard the argument $(e^1, e^2, \ldots e^n, d^1;$ thus, $p)$ as sufficiently likely to be truth preserving. Moreover, *d* might *not* be a defeater of this argument.

14. The restriction that the premises in an obvious way conflict with some of *S*'s general beliefs is meant to ensure that *S* on reflection would realize that it is impossible for both the premises of the arguments and these general beliefs to be true.

15. Analogously, not every argument whose premises and conclusion are regarded by an individual *S* as necessarily true is uncontroversial for him. See the discussion later in this section of arguments whose conclusions *S*, on reflection, would regard as necessarily true. The epistemic issues I am concerned with here and in the later discussion bear obvious parallels to the concerns of some logicians with the so-called paradoxes of material implication and strict implication respectively. In particular, just as a concern with the paradoxes of material implication was part of the motivation for introducing modal logics, so too my requirement that *S*, on reflection, think that most relevant *possible* situations in which the premises of an argument are true be situations in which its conclusion is true is introduced at least in part in order to ensure that not just any argument with what *S* regards as true premises and a true conclusion is an uncontroversial argument for him. And just as a concern with the paradoxes of strict implication was part of the motivation for introducing relevance logics, so too my requirement (discussed below) that *S*, on reflection, regard the premises of an argument as *relevant* to the conclusion is introduced at least in part in order to ensure that not just any argument with a conclusion that *S* regards as necessarily true is an uncontroversial argument for him.

16. It is no accident that a crucial presupposition of most skeptical positions is that in assessing whether knowledge of the premises of an argument gives one a good reason to believe the argument's conclusion, all possible situations in which the argument's premises are true are treated as relevant.

17. This is not to cast any aspersions on reductio ad absurdum arguments. In reductio arguments, a proposition is conditionally assumed in order to show that given the premises of the argument—premises whose conjunction is not necessarily false—this proposition must be false.

18. Notice that *S* on reflection might think that the premises of an argument if jointly understood could be used to provide him with an understanding of why it is impossible for the conclusion of the argument to be false even if the argument is sufficiently complex that he does not grasp (all at once) the connection between the premises and the conclusion. So, even very complex arguments can satisfy the above requirement.

19. Compare the work on so-called relevance logics, especially A. R. Anderson and N. D. Belnap Jr., *Entailment,* 1 (Princeton: Princeton University Press, 1975), who insist that *q* is deducible *from p* only if the derivation of *q* genuinely *uses p,* rather than simply *takes a detour* via *p.* However, it needs to be noted here that in my discussion the point is not that the lack of a relevant connection

298 Notes to Pages 30–33

between the premises and the conclusion of an argument is a logical defect; the point is rather that it is an epistemic defect.

20. I assume that the argument here for Goldbach's conjecture, an argument that has contingent premises, plausibly can be construed as an inductive argument, albeit of a special type, even though (assuming that the conjecture is true) its premises imply its conclusion. One reason to regard it as a (special) kind of inductive argument is that it can be defeated. See note 21.

21. Notice that arguments of this sort can be defeated. In particular, they can be defeated by a proposition that when added to the premises turns the argument into a kind of argument that S, on reflection, would not think is sufficiently likely to have a true conclusion. Thus, for example, S's argument here for Goldbach's conjecture might be defeated by a proposition that implies that his evidence for the conjecture (that is, the instances of even numbers greater than two that he and others have examined in order to test the conjecture) is not genuinely random, that it is biased in some significant way.

22. Thus, in order for an argument to be uncontroversial for an individual S, at a minimum he needs to have the ordinary notions of truth, falsity, and possibility. What are we to say of someone who claims not to be able to grasp (even roughly) one of these notions—say, a person who claims not to be able to understand the notion of something being possible? Are we forced to say that for such a person no argument is uncontroversial and hence that no proposition is epistemically rational? Not necessarily. For one, we do not have to believe him when he says that he does not understand this notion. After all, people are not infallible judges of what they understand and what they do not understand, and thus insofar as most of the rest of us understand the notion of something being possible, so too, it may be plausible to infer, does the person in question here. Second, even if the person does not understand this notion, perhaps he would understand it were he to be sufficiently reflective. If so, then although he may not believe that any argument is sufficiently likely to be truth preserving, it may nonetheless be true that he would believe this of many arguments were he to be sufficiently reflective. Third, even if some people do not understand (and on reflection would not understand) the notions of truth, falsity, and possibility that the rest of us commonly employ, it would be surprising if they did not understand (and employ) notions that closely approximate our notions—in effect, counterpart notions. Moreover, these counterpart notions might be such that they could be substituted for the ordinary notions in determining what arguments are uncontroversial for such people. For some related remarks, see also note 50 in this chapter.

23. For the sake of convenience, I have been representing the decision that an individual S would make about whether an argument is sufficiently likely to be truth preserving as a two-step decision, first, a decision about what possible situations in which the argument's premises are true are relevant situations, and second, a decision about whether the conclusion is true in enough of these relevant possible situations. However, we need not imagine that S actually would proceed in this way were he to be ideally reflective. He might simply reflect enough to become convinced (where further reflection would not change his mind) that whatever exactly is to count as a relevant situation it is going to turn out that in a sufficiently great percentage of these relevant situations the conclusion would

be true. However, notice that even if we do represent his decision as a two-step decision, we need not represent the two decisions as being unrelated. Indeed, as a general rule we can say that if we represent a relatively normal individual as making a demanding decision with respect to one of these two steps, we can represent him as making a less demanding decision with respect to the other. For example, if we represent S as making a demanding decision with respect to what possible situations are relevant (counting as relevant even those situations that he regards as highly improbable), we can ordinarily represent him as being somewhat less demanding with respect to how great a percentage of relevant possible situations must be those in which the conclusion of the argument is true.

24. Here and in what follows, I continue to ignore (for the sake of simplicity) the complications posed by arguments whose conclusions S, on reflection, would take to be necessarily true. For such arguments, S, on reflection, must also think that their premises are relevant to their conclusions.

25. Notice, to say that were he to be ideally reflective, S would believe that an argument is sufficiently likely to be truth preserving, is not to say that he now believes (albeit perhaps nonoccurrently) that this argument is sufficiently likely to be truth preserving. One might be tempted to think that this is so if one thinks that an individual S nonoccurrently believes p just in case he would occurrently believe p were he to consider (or to reflect upon) p. From this one might be tempted to conclude that if S would believe p were he ideally reflective, he must now in some sense believe p, albeit perhaps in a deeply nonoccurrent sense. However, any attempt to understand nonoccurrent beliefs in terms of what an individual would believe were he to reflect upon various propositions runs into a formidable problem. Namely, reflection might well alter one's beliefs (so that were one to be reflective, one might well come to believe something that previously he had not believed). In any event, whatever we decide about the best way to understand nonoccurrent beliefs, it is safe to assume that from the fact that a person S would believe p were he ideally reflective it does not follow that he now in any interesting sense believes p. Accordingly, with respect to what is at issue here, an argument can conform to an individual's deepest epistemic standards even if he does not now believe, even nonoccurrently, that the argument is likely to be truth preserving. What does have to be the case is that given the individual's present inclinations, dispositions, and so on, he would believe that the argument is likely to be truth preserving were he to be ideally reflective.

26. Does it matter how we imagine S beginning his reflection on an argument A? In most cases it probably does not matter, since in determining whether A is uncontroversial for S we are to imagine S reflecting upon any consideration at all that might occur to him until his view of A stabilizes. So whether he begins with a consideration m or with a consideration n, ordinarily the other consideration ultimately would occur to him. Moreover, presumably in most cases his final view about A would not be dependent upon which he considers first. However, suppose we imagine a case in which this is not so. Suppose that if S were to begin his reflections on A by thinking about consideration m he ultimately and stably would approve of A, whereas this would not be the case if he were to begin by thinking about consideration n. Suppose, in other words, that the consideration with which he begins would influence his later reflections in such a way that the two reflective processes (the one that begins with m and the one

that begins with *n*) would never "coalesce" even in the ideal long run. What are we to make of such a case? Suppose for convenience we adopt a "closest possible world" approach to counterfactuals. Then if an *m*-world (that is, a world in which *S* is sufficiently reflective about A and in which he begins his reflections by considering *m*) is closer to the actual world, argument A is uncontroversial for *S*. On the other hand, if an *n*-world is closer to the actual world, argument A is not uncontroversial. Is it possible for the closest *m*-world and the closest *n*-world to be equally close to the actual world? Perhaps, but if so, argument A is not uncontroversial for *S*. Indeed, under these conditions, the sentence "*S* would think A is sufficiently truth preserving were he to be sufficiently reflective" presumably is either false or lacks a truth value.

27. To be sure, there are still plenty of problem cases. Suppose, for example, the scientist yesterday set up a machine that today would alter *S*'s primary dispositions were *S* to be reflective. Suppose he attaches the machine to *S*'s body. Or suppose it is small enough to fit inside *S*'s brain. In setting up the machine yesterday, did the scientist at that time alter *S*'s secondary dispositions (and thus alter what opinions *S* today on reflection would *self*-generate) or did he merely set up an external mechanism that would alter *S*'s dispositions were he today to be reflective? Compare this case with the following. Suppose that *S*'s brain is such that were he to reflect carefully the strain would cause him to suffer a stroke that would reduce his intellectual capacities, resulting in his being unable to understand certain arguments. Nevertheless, such arguments presumably might be uncontroversial for him. But if so, there must be a sense in which *S* as he is now is disposed to approve of such arguments on reflection, even though by hypothesis were he to reflect on these arguments he would suffer a stroke that would render him incapable of understanding the arguments. However, in order to say what this sense is, we need to know what distinguishes a thing having a disposition (especially a higher-order one) from its acquiring or losing such a disposition, and this in turn may very well require an answer to the question of what kind of entity the thing in question is. In the case of persons, it may very well require a theory of persons, since without such a theory it is difficult to distinguish cases in which "external factors" (whether these be the tamperings of a scientist or a stroke or something else) cause the person to acquire or to lose a disposition to approve of an argument from cases in which the acquisition or loss of such a disposition is *self*-generated (by virtue, say, of his reflections triggering one of his higher-order dispositions). So, depending on one's theory of persons, there may (at least in principle) very well be different answers to the question of whether a person would approve of an argument were he to be sufficiently reflective.

A theory of persons might also be of help in settling other kinds of problematic cases—for example, cases in which a person is drunk and in which his drunkenness temporarily alters what arguments he would be disposed to accept were he to be sufficiently reflective. In such cases we are faced with the choice of claiming that alcohol alters, if only temporarily, the person's deepest epistemic standards or of claiming that the alcohol (like the evil scientist and the stroke) is an "external factor," and that hence what he is disposed to believe on reflection while drunk does not reflect his deepest epistemic standards. Suppose we prefer the latter option. Then, to determine his deepest epistemic standards, we need to determine (assuming a closest possible world approach to counterfactuals) *not* what he believes in the closest possible world in which he is sufficiently reflective. For this might be a world in which he is drunk. Rather, we need to determine what he believes in the closest possible world in which he is both sufficiently reflective *and* sober. At least in this respect, the state of drunkenness is like the state of sleep. While sleeping a person cannot engage in the kind of reflection that determines what his epistemic standards are, but he nonetheless has epistemic standards even while sleeping. To determine what these standards are, we need to imagine what he would be disposed to think on reflection, but to imagine this we need to imagine him awake (instead of as he is now). Cases involving mental illness raise analogous problems. Again we are faced with deciding whether the psychological problem alters a person's deepest epistemic standards or whether it is an "external" or "abnormal" factor and that hence what he is disposed to believe while suffering from this problem does not reflect his own deepest epistemic standards. The relevance of a theory of persons in this context is that such a theory may be of some help in distinguishing states of a person that (like sleep) are either "temporary" or "external" or "abnormal" (and thus do not alter his deepest epistemic standards) from states that are more "normal" and "essential" and "permanent" (and thus might alter his deepest standards).

28. So, I am using the notion of the strength of a belief (or the degree of belief) to develop an account of when it is epistemically rational to believe a proposition. I am not using it to develop an account of rational degrees of belief. A fortiori I am not endorsing the suggestion that the notion of believing a proposition be replaced altogether with the notion of degrees of belief. For more on the differences between an account of epistemically rational belief and an account of rational degrees of belief, see section 2.7. See also note 33, this chapter.

29. Why not say that S has a good reason to be suspicious of p if there is an undefeated argument for not$p$ that has premises whose conjunction S believes as confidently as p? After all, each premise in the argument for not$p$ might be believed by S as confidently as p, and yet S might believe that there is very little chance that all of them are true. Accordingly, he might not have (given his own beliefs) a convincing argument for not$p$. However, the point here is not to describe when S has a convincing argument for not$p$ but rather to describe when he has a good reason to be suspicious of p. An argument for not$p$ can give S a good reason to be suspicious of p even if it is not a particularly convincing argument for not$p$. One example of this (but not the only one) involves a set of propositions that S on reflection would recognize to be inconsistent. Suppose S believes with equal confidence each member of such a set of propositions. Nevertheless, it might very well be the case that no proposition p in this set can be argued against using propositions whose conjunction S believes as confidently as p. Although the remaining members of the set imply not$p$, S may very well think that it is highly unlikely that the conjunction of these remaining members is true. (Think of a lottery, for example.) If so, the remaining members of the set do not provide him with a convincing argument for not$p$. However, they might very well provide him with a reason to be suspicious of p, preventing p from being uncontroversial for him.

30. Again, inductive arguments for a conclusion that S on reflection would regard as necessarily true (if true at all) need special treatment. See section 1.2—especially note 21.

31. Note that there is a disanalogy between what is required in order for S to have an argument that threatens to make p controversial for him and what is required in order for there to be a convincing defeater of such an argument. Namely, if propositions e^1, e^2, ... e^n together tend to make not$p$ epistemically rational for S and if each is believed by S as confidently as p, then these propositions threaten to make p controversial for S even if their conjunction is believed by S less confidently than p. (See note 29.) On the other hand, suppose that the conjunctive proposition (d^1 and d^2 ... and d^n) is a potential defeater of the support that e^1, e^2, ... e^n give not$p$ but that none of these propositions taken individually is a potential defeater. Then this conjunction is not a convincing defeater unless it is believed by S as confidently as p (even if each conjunct is believed by S as confidently as p). Why the disanalogy? Because it is more difficult to eradicate a reason that makes p suspicious for S than it is to create the reason for the suspicion in the first place.

32. For a defense of the view that apparently categorical probability claims (such as the claim that p is probable) always are best interpreted as relational claims (such as the claim that p is probable given some assumed body of evidence—say, the total relevant available evidence), see F. C. Benenson, *Probability, Objectivity and Evidence* (London: Routledge and Kegan Paul, 1984). For any view of this sort to be plausible, it needs to be emphasized, as Benenson does, that with respect to the apparently categorical probability claims we commonly make, there is not likely to be some simple, perfectly general rule for identifying the relevant body of evidence relative to which p is supposed to be probable. On the contrary, questions about the relevant body of evidence are likely to be questions that can be answered only contextually (taking into consideration whether the claim was made by, say, someone playing a game of chance or a scientist in his laboratory or someone in yet a different context).

33. There are three related notions that must be kept distinct here—the notion of an individual S believing a proposition p, the notion of S believing the proposition that p is likely (or probable) to a certain degree, and the notion of S believing with a certain degree of confidence that p is true. The notion of S believing a proposition p is relatively vague. Despite its vagueness it is a useful notion; it allows us to use a simple threefold classification (believing, disbelieving, and withholding judgment) to describe in a general way how S assesses p's chances of being true. The degree of confidence that S has in p is a much finer-grained notion; believing p is compatible with any number of degrees of confidence in p. The vague character of belief allows us only to say that believing p implies that one has a sufficiently high degree of confidence in p. (However, if we presuppose that we can understand the notion of S having a certain degree of confidence in a proposition without a prior understanding of belief simpliciter, we could stipulate, if we so wished, that S believes p only if he had X degree of confidence in p.) Related to both of these notions is the notion of S believing that a proposition p is likely (or probable) to a certain degree. It is frequently the case that when S believes p, he believes that p is highly probable. Indeed, at least one philosopher has claimed (seemingly risking a regress) that believing p is *equivalent* to believing that p is probable. See Richard Swinburne, *Faith and Reason* (Oxford: Clarendon, 1981), chap. 1. Also see Thomas Reid, who says, "nor is it in man's power to believe anything longer than he thinks he has

evidence" (Reid, *Essays on the Intellectual Powers,* chap. 10, sect. 1, in *The Philosophical Works of Thomas Reid,* ed. Sir William Hamilton [London; James Thin, 1895]). In any event, what is important for present purposes is that an individual *S* who believes *p* very often will believe (at least nonoccurrently) with an even greater degree of confidence a proposition about the probability of *p*— that it is probable, or that it is more probable than not, or some other such proposition. Moreover, even if *S*'s degree of confidence in *p* is sufficiently low to allow us to say that at best he withholds judgment on *p* (and at worst disbelieves *p*), he nonetheless may have a high degree of confidence in (and hence believe) the proposition that *p* has some significant (but low) probability.

34. Given this notion of "entails," we can say that *p* and *q* are identical propositions just if *p* entails *q* and *q* entails *p*. For a somewhat different distinction between implication and entailment, see Roderick Chisholm, *The First Person* (Minneapolis: University of Minnesota Press, 1981), 7.

35. Suppose the argument that threatens to make *p* controversial for *S*— the argument with premises e^1, e^2, . . . e^n—is defeated by *d* but that there is another proposition d^1 that defeats this defeater and that is believed by *S* as confidently as *d*. If all else is equal, will not the proposition *p* be controversial for *S* in such a situation? Yes, but the above conditions already imply this. In such a situation the proposition d^1 can itself be used to construct an undefeated argument with not*p* as its conclusion and with premises that *S* believes as confidently as *p*—for example, an argument with premises d^1, e^1, e^2, . . . e^n.

36. For the sake of simplicity, I assume here that were *S* to be ideally reflective, he would be able to determine what propositions he believes. (This is not to say that *S* now believes, even nonoccurrently, that he believes these propositions. See this chapter, note 25.) If this assumption is not made, then the way I have been intuitively characterizing uncontroversial propositions would have to be somewhat altered. Instead of saying that *p* is uncontroversial for *S* only if *S* would uncover no good reason to be suspicious of *p* were he to be ideally reflective (in the sense stipulated above—ideal reflection upon what he in fact believes and what arguments are likely to be truth preserving), we perhaps could say that *p* is uncontroversial for *S* only if *S* would uncover no reason to be suspicious of *p* were he to be ideally reflective about what arguments are likely to be truth preserving and were he given a list of what he currently believes.

37. Notice that the set of arguments that *S* on reflection would regard as sufficiently truth preserving were he to be ideally reflective does not merely constitute what *S*'s deepest epistemic standards would be were he to be ideally reflective; they constitute his current—that is, his actual—deepest epistemic standards. Remember that by hypothesis these arguments are ones that he would approve of given his current inclinations and dispositions; by hypothesis his opinions (on reflection) of these arguments would be self-generated. See section 1.3.

38. See section 1.6—especially the discussion near the end of how reasons for withholding on *p* might make *p* controversial for an individual.

39. However, presumably not every proposition that *S* believes is one about whose likelihood *S* also has a belief. Otherwise, there presumably would be difficulties with a regress.

40. I again assume that to believe that e^1 is highly probable is to believe

that e^1 is highly probable relative to some assumed body of evidence, say the body of total relevant available evidence. Notice also that this strategy of "prob-abilifying" the premises allows S's views (on reflection) about the strength of an argument (that is, about how likely the conclusion is given the truth of the premises) to play an important role in determining whether a proposition p is uncontroversial for him. For example, consider an argument with premises e^1 and e^2 and with not$p$ as its conclusion. Suppose S on reflection would regard this argument as sufficiently likely to be truth preserving. If he thinks this because he thinks that these premises imply not$p$, then the premises of this argument can be "probabilified" and the resulting argument—(e^1 is highly probable; e^2 is highly probable; thus, not$p$)—has a good chance of being one that S on reflection would regard as sufficiently likely to be truth preserving. Accordingly, even if S believes e^1 or e^2 with somewhat less confidence than p, the probabilized counterparts of these propositions stand a good chance of making p controversial for him. For there is a good chance that they, like e^1 and e^2, tend to make not$p$ epistemically rational for him but that they, unlike e^1 and e^2, are believed by him as confidently as p. On the other hand, if S on reflection would not think that e^1 and e^2 imply not$p$, the probabilized counterparts of these propositions do not stand as good a chance of making p controversial for him (even if he believes them as confidently as p), since the chances are not as good that an argument for not$p$ with these probabilized counterparts as premises would be regarded by S on reflection as sufficiently likely to be truth preserving.

41. For a related discussion, see my "Epistemic Conservatism," *Philosophical Studies* 43 (1983), 165–182. I there argue that a number of commonly endorsed philosophical positions, including standard versions of a coherence theory, presuppose a principle of epistemic conservatism, a principle that implies that believing a proposition always gives the believer some reason for thinking that the proposition is true. I also argue that such principles are implausible. See also chapter 7.

42. "You will find in a hundred places that the Scholastics have said that these propositions are evident, *ex terminis,* as soon as the terms are understood . . ." G. W. Leibniz, *New Essays Concerning Human Understanding,* bk. 4, chap. 7 (Chicago: University of Chicago Press, 1949).

43. This way of representing my claim was suggested to me by Aron Edidin.

44. Even so, such propositions can play an important, derivative role in arguments for other propositions. See the discussion of second-level arguments in section 2.5.

45. Notice that this explication of a defeater begging the question against another defeater parallels the explication given earlier (section 1.5) of a defeater begging the question against an argument that threatens to make p controversial.

46. Let d^1 be the proposition that S here has been given an antidote, and let d^2 be the proposition that S has been given an antidote for the antidote. Then, the proposition (d and d^2) will be a potential defeater of the argument (S believes p; thus, p), and moreover the proposition d^1 presumably will not defeat this proposition's defeater status.

47. Consider the following objection: "Although by hypothesis the premises of the argument in question here are believed by S as confidently as is p, none of these individual premises by itself is likely to be a potential defeater of the

argument (*S* believes *p;* thus, *p*). On the other hand, although the conjunction of these premises *is* likely to be a potential defeater, it may not be believed by *S* with anything like the confidence that he believes *p*." Yes, but even if *S* believes the conjunction with less confidence than *p*, he may very well believe with as much confidence as *p* a proposition about the likelihood of this conjunction. For example, he might believe with as much confidence as *p* the proposition that the conjunction has about a 50-50 chance of being true. Moreover, this proposition might very well be a potential defeater of the argument (*S* believes *p;* thus *p*). Think about the intuitive idea here in this way: Let *c* be the conjunction of the premises of the argument for not*p*. Construct a series of propositions that are the probabilized counterparts of *c*, in descending order of probability—for example, the series (*c; c* is highly probable; *c* is probable; *c* is about as probable as not; *c* has some significant but relatively low probability; and so on). The further one goes down this series, the more likely it is that one will find a proposition that *S* believes (at least nonoccurrently) with as much confidence as he believes *p*. On the other hand, the further one goes down this series, the less likely it is that one will find a proposition that is for *S* a potential defeater of the argument (*S* believes *p;* thus, *p*). So, whether the premises of the above argument make *p* controversial for *S* (despite the fact that they do not tend to make not*p* rational for him) is a function of how far one has to go down this series to find a proposition that *S* believes with as much confidence as *p*.

48. Note that the requirement here is that the conjunction be a potential defeater; the requirement is not that the conjunction be believed as confidently as *p*. As such, the requirement here is a relevancy requirement, a requirement indicating what kind of arguments for not*p* are eligible to make *p* controversial for *S*.

49. Suppose that *S* believes that he believes *p*. Then presumably there will be no problem here, since this proposition (the proposition that he believes *p*) is likely to be a convincing and non-question-begging defeater of the argument (*q, r;* thus, not*p*). Moreover, in many (and perhaps even most) situations in which *S* believes *p*, he will have this meta-belief, this belief that he believes *p*. However, there is no guarantee that this will be the case; and besides it does not seem as if the issue of whether or not *p* is uncontroversial for *S* here is one that is appropriately settled by whether or not *S* believes that he believes *p*. Accordingly, a requirement of the above sort is needed.

50. In order for there to be propositions that are epistemically rational for an individual *S*, it must be the case that *S* on reflection would have beliefs about how likely certain propositions are, given the truth of other propositions. Indeed, it must be the case that on reflection he would have second-order beliefs, beliefs about how likely certain propositions are, given that he believes them. This is a prerequisite of epistemic rationality; only of a being who is capable of having such beliefs can it be said that he believes (or fails to believe) what is epistemically rational for him. Accordingly, it presumably is the case that animals, severely retarded individuals, and young children are not capable of being epistemically rational (or epistemically irrational).

51. Is condition 2 redundant, given condition 3? After all, *if* propositions $e^1, e^2, \ldots e^n$ are believed by *S* as confidently as *p* and *if* they tend to make not*p* epistemically rational for *S* and *if* they are not defeated, cannot these propositions

be used to generate a convincing defeater of the argument (*S* believes *p;* thus, *p*)? Not necessarily. None of the individual propositions e^1, e^2, ... e^n need be even potential defeaters of this argument, and their conjunction need not be believed by *S* as confidently as *p*. Nevertheless, it frequently will be the case that some probabilized counterpart of the conjunction (for example, it is about as probable as not that the conjunction is true) will be believed by *S* as confidently as *p* and in addition will be a potential defeater. And accordingly, it frequently (but not necessarily) will be the case that if there are propositions that can be used to argue for not*p* in the way prohibited by condition 2, these same propositions can be used to generate a convincing defeater of the argument (*S* believes *p;* thus, *p*).

52. Do we not need to add to the above definition the qualification that there can be a defeater of (d^1 and d^2 ... and d^n) provided its defeater status is itself defeated? No, for if there are propositions c^1, c^2, ... c^n such that each is uncontroversial for *S* to assume and such that their conjunction defeats the defeater status of (d^1 and d^2 ... and d^n), then the above definition already implies that there are propositions that make *p* epistemically rational for *S*—the propositions (e^1, e^2, ... e^n, c^1, c^2, ... c^n).

2.   Subjective Foundationalism

1. For an extensive discussion of the kinds of privileged access an individual might have to the truth of a proposition, see William Alston, "Varieties of Privileged Access," *American Philosophical Quarterly* 8 (1971), 223–251. Also see Alston's "Self-Warrant: A Neglected Form of Privileged Access," *American Philosophical Quarterly* 13 (1976), 257–272.

2. Indeed, it is trivially the case that whenever we believe a proposition that is necessarily true, our belief is infallible (since it is impossible for our beliefs to be false). But even if we restrict ourselves to contingent propositions, there may be propositions about which, unbeknownst to us, our beliefs are infallible. Consider, for example, those characteristics that it is logically necessary for a thing to have if it is to have beliefs at all. Some of these characteristics may be such that we are not aware that they are prerequisites of belief. Thus, suppose for patently silly reasons (reasons we ourselves would regard as silly were we to be reflective) we believe we have characteristic *c*, where *c* unbeknownst to us is one of these prerequisites of belief. Then our belief in this proposition is infallible. But the proposition here need not be epistemically rational for us, much less properly basic for use.

3. I assume here that an agreement is likely to be truth preserving only if its conclusion would be true in most relevant close situations in which its premises are true.

4. Later in this section and in section 2.2 I examine in more detail the idea that we on reflection would think that such propositions are likely to be true when we believe them.

5. Roderick M. Chisholm, *Theory of Knowledge*, 2d ed. (Englewood Cliffs, N.J.: Prentice-Hall, 1977), 77–82. See also H. H. Price, *Perception* (New

York: Robert McBride, 1933), 185; Bertrand Russell, *An Inquiry into Meaning and Truth* (New York: W. H. Norton, 1940), 166 and 192–202; A. Meinong, "Toward an Epistemological Assessment of Memory," in *Empirical Knowledge: Readings from Contemporary Sources,* ed. R. M. Chisholm and R. J. Swartz (Englewood Cliffs, N.J.: Prentice-Hall, 1973), 253–270; C. I. Lewis, *An Analysis of Knowledge and Valuation* (La Salle, Ill.: Open Court, 1946), 334.

6. Is it possible for a proposition *p* (for example, that *S* sees a cat on the mat) to be properly basic for *S* and yet entail a proposition *q* (for example, that there is a cat on the mat) that is not even epistemically rational for *S*? Presumably not; it is plausible to think that the following is an acceptable principle of epistemic logic: Necessarily, if *p* is epistemically rational for *S* at *t* and if *p* entails *q*, then *q* is epistemically rational for *S* at *t*. This principle, however, must be distinguished from the following principle, which is not acceptable: Necessarily, if *p* is epistemically rational for *S* and if *p* *implies* *q*, then *q* is epistemically rational for *S*. This latter principle is not acceptable because *p* might imply *q* in a way that *S* even with ideal reflection would not recognize. However, when *p* entails *q*, the implication relation presumably is obvious enough that *S* on reflection would recognize that *p* implies *q*. (Remember that *S* cannot believe *p* if he does not understand *p*; remember also that *p* entails *q* only if necessarily *S* believes *q* when he believes *p* and *S* thinks (entertains) *q* when he thinks (entertains) *p*.)

7. To be sure, the explanation here *is* loose. Let *a* be the proposition that there is a cat on the mat and let *b* be the proposition that *S* is having a cat-on-the-mat kind of visual experience. From the fact, if it is one, that *b* is likely to be true when *S* believes *b* and that *(a* and *b)* is likely to be true when *b* is true and *S* believes *a*, it does not strictly *follow* that *(a* and *b)* is likely to be true when *S* believes *(a* and *b)*. A fortiori it does not follow that *S* on reflection would think this. Moreover, even if we waive this difficulty (assuming that even if it does not strictly follow from the considerations above that *(a* and *b)* is likely to be true when *S* believes it, these considerations do encourgage *S* on reflecion to think this), there may be a deeper explanation of why *S*'s believing *(a* and *b)* tends to make *(a* and *b)* epistemically rational for him. In particular, there may be conceptual explanations of why relatively normal people are likely to have the kind of epistemic standards that conditions (2) and (3) ascribe to *S*. There may be a conceptual explanation, in other words, of why a relatively normal person would be inclined to think on reflection that most relevant possible situations in which he believes that he is having a cat-on-the-mat kind of visual experience are situations in which this belief would be true, as well as a conceptual explanation of why a relatively normal person would be inclined to think on reflection that most relevant possible situations in which he has a cat-on-the-mat kind of visual experience and a belief that there is a cat on the mat are situations in which this belief would be true. See section 2.2.

8. Of course, such propositions may very well be epistemically rational for *S* even if they are not properly basic for him, since there may very well be propositions that are properly basic for him that can be used to argue for them in a way that is uncontroversial for him.

9. Notice that this does not altogether rule out the possibility of *S* on

reflection being mistaken in thinking this. Indeed, it does not altogether rule out the possibility that *S* on reflection might think of a necessary falsehood that his understanding it is enough to allow him to see why it cannot be false.

10. Notice, however, that *p* here is properly basic only if it is the case that simply by reflecting upon it *S* would become convinced (even though he is not now convinced) both that it is necessarily true and that understanding it is enough to provide him with an understanding of why it cannot be false. There presumably are propositions such that *S* could be taught that they are necessarily true even though he as he is now, with his present inclinations and dispositions, would not come to realize that this is so simply by reflecting upon them—that is, even though he would not on his own come to see that they are necessarily true. See section 1.3 for a discussion of the notion that an individual's deepest standards are a function of what he would believe on reflection, subject to the restriction that what he would believe on reflection is *self*-generated.

11. See section 4.3. See also the characterization of *evidential knowledge* in that section, which implies that *S* evidentially knows *p* only if his belief *p* is not just propositionally rational but also doxastically rational.

12. Compare: "If we do not take this view of probability; if we do not limit it in this way and make it, to this extent, relative to human powers, we are altogether adrift in the unknown; for we cannot ever know what degree of probability would be justified by the perception of logical relations which we are, and must always be, incapable of comprehending." John Maynard Keynes, *A Treatise On Probability* (London: Macmillan, 1921).

13. See, for example, Roderick Chisholm's notion of self-presenting states in "A Version of Foundationalism," in *Midwest Studies of Philosophy* 5, ed. P. French, T. Uehling, and H. Wettstein (Minneapolis: University of Minnesota Press, 1980), 543–564. He there says (roughly) that a state *a* is self-presenting for *S* just if necessarily *a* is such that if *S* has *a* and considers whether he has *a*, then *S* believes that he has *a*. For the exact definition, see page 549. Chisholm earlier (for example, in both editions of *Theory of Knowledge*) had defined the self-presenting in epistemic terms, as a state that is necessarily such that if *S* is in that state it is *evident* for him that he is in that state.

14. Of course, the state of, say, having a burned finger regularly prompts us in an indirect way to believe we are in pain; it does this by causing us to be in pain.

15. For a thorough discussion of views of this sort (as well as competing views), see Richard Fumerton, *Metaphysical and Epistemological Problems of Perception* (Lincoln: University of Nebraska Press, 1985).

16. One way of understanding the position of the phenomenalist is in terms of his beginning with the relatively uncontroversial claim that the more perceptual tests of there being a table that a chunk of space-time would pass the more likely it is that this chunk of space-time in fact has a table in it. The phenomenalist then extrapolates this claim into the much more controversial claim that necessarily a chunk of space-time that would pass all the perceptual tests of there being a table in it is a chunk of space-time that in fact has a table. Thus, according to a phenomenalist, with respect to the question of whether there is a table in front of me, there is no difference between a situation in which there in fact is a table in front of me and a situation in which an evil demon alters the situation

in front of me so that all the perceptual tests of there being a table in front of me would be passed. In other words, according to the phenomenalist, if the demon alters the situation in front of me so that I and every other perceiver would have tablelike perceptual experiences no matter what perceptual tests we performed, then ipso facto the demon has created a table in front of me. See Fumerton, especially pp. 160–161.

17. From the claim that we could not be in a situation in which there could not be physical objects it does not strictly follow that we could not lack bodies. All that strictly follows is that we can exist only in worlds in which it is possible, given the laws of nature, for us to have bodies. Notice, however, that if an individual *S* on reflection would believe that it is impossible for him (as well as other humans) to lack a body, he on reflection also would think that it is impossible (not just unlikely) for him to believe falsely that there are physical objects (since any situation with him in it must have at least one physical object). Accordingly, if *S* on reflection would believe this, it is easy to show that his belief that there are physical objects tends to be self-justifying for him (and hence to show also that the proposition that there are physical objects is likely to be properly basic for him).

18. But does not an appeal to how we conceive of ourselves just push the problem back a step, to the problem of knowing what kind of creatures we are? For suppose that unbeknownst to me the actual world is a world in which there cannot be physical objects. Then I must be wrong in thinking that my nature precludes my being in a world in which there cannot be physical objects. However, this does not affect the point. The point is not to vindicate our epistemic standards; it is not to prove that we are right in thinking (if we do think this) that we could not be in a world in which the laws of nature make it impossible for there to be physical objects, and it is not to prove that as a result we also are right in thinking that such worlds cannot be worlds in which our perceptual beliefs are radically false. Rather, the point is to try at least in a loose way to explain why we have the epistemic standards that I am assuming most of us do have, standards implying that most relevant possible situations in which we have simple perceptual beliefs are situations in which those beliefs are not mistaken.

19. Other kinds of views also might be used to help explain why our simple introspective beliefs, our simple perceptual beliefs, our simple memory beliefs, and so on, are likely to be self-justifying. For example, one such view appeals to the nature of belief. In particular, some philosophers have claimed that it is impossible for most of our simplest, most psychologically basic beliefs to be false—say, our simple introspective beliefs, our simple perceptual beliefs, our simple memory beliefs, and so on. This is thought to be impossible because in the simplest of cases the object of a belief just is the cause of the belief. But insofar as this is a conceptual truth about belief, there will be conceptual pressures upon us that will enourage us to think (at least on reflection) that most possible situations in which we have such beliefs are situations in which the beliefs are true. See, for example, Donald Davidson, "A Coherence Theory of Truth and Knowledge," in *The Philosophy of Donald Davidson: Perspectives on Truth and Interpretation,* ed. E. LePore (London: Basil Blackwell, 1986). Also see Hilary Putnam, *Reason, Truth, and History* (Cambridge: Cambridge University Press, 1981), chapter 1. For further discussion of such views, see section 3.2.

In a similar spirit, certain antirealistic positions also might be of some help in explaining why we have the epistemic standards we do. For insofar as the antirealist insists upon a tighter conceptual connection than does the realist between claims in a certain domain (such as claims about the past or claims about theoretical entities) being meaningful and our having "access" to their truth or falsity, he makes it more difficult to imagine situations in which the truth about such claims is systematically hidden from us. As a result, he also makes it more difficult to imagine situations in which our beliefs about such claims are radically and systematically false.

20. Nelson Goodman, *Fact, Fiction, and Forecast* (Cambridge: Harvard University Press, 1965), chap. 3 and 4.

21. This phrase is Keith Lehrer's. See his *Knowledge* (Oxford: Oxford University Press, 1974), 188.

22. See, for example, Donald Davidson, "A Coherence Theory of Truth and Knowledge." "What distinguishes a coherence theory is simply the claim that nothing can count as a reason for holding a belief except another belief. Its partisans reject as unintelligible the request for a grounding or source of justification of another ilk" (p. 320).

23. I assume here, as I did with traditionalist foundationalists, that coherentists are forwarding accounts of epistemic rationality. If coherentist accounts are best understood as accounts of a somewhat different notion (for a discussion of this issue see section 2.8) then coherentistism and subjective foundationalism are not competitors.

24. See, for example, Keith Lehrer, *Knowledge*; Gilbert Harman, *Thought* (Princeton: Princeton University Press, 1973); Nicholas Rescher, *The Coherence Theory of Truth* (Oxford: Oxford University Press, 1973); Laurence Bonjour, "The Coherence Theory of Empirical Knowledge," *Philosophical Studies* 30 (1976), 281–312.

25. Thus, according to a coherentist, every proposition that is epistemically rational for an individual S has *one* of the marks of properly basic propositions. Every such proposition is uncontroversial for S to assume as a premise—S properly can use any such proposition to argue for or against other propositions. Of course, there are other marks of properly basic propositions that these propositions lack, according to the coherentist—for example, an individual's beliefs in these propositions will not be self-justifying. However, in contrast to standard coherence theories, so-called negative coherence theories (for a discussion of this kind of coherentist account, see John Pollock, "A Plethora of Epistemological Theories," in *Justification and Knowledge,* ed. G. Pappas (Dordrecht: Reidel, 1979), 93–113) imply that *any* proposition believed by S is epistemically rational for him provided that the other propositions he believes do not support its negation. Such accounts might be as easily regarded as examples of an extreme foundationalism (albeit not traditional foundationalism) as of coherentism, since they in effect imply that every belief tends to be self-justifying. For a discussion of a closely related view, see chapter 7, especially section 7.3.

26. See section 6.5 for a further discussion of how a coherentist might understand mutual support.

27. Contrast with Lehrer, *Knowledge,* 202–204.

28. Accordingly, whatever exactly it is for propositions to be mutually sup-

portive, a necessary condition of mutual support cannot be that no proposition in the set is such that its negation is implied by the remaining members.

29. In chapter 6, the relationship between epistemic rationality and inconsistency (and near inconsistency) is discussed in more detail.

30. Suppose that $(e^1, e^2, \ldots e^n)$ is a set of propositions that are properly basic for S at t, and suppose at a slightly later time $t + n$ S comes to believe with as much confidence as some proposition in the original set that at least one member of this set is false. Then not all of the propositions in the original set can remain properly basic for him. In particular, if e^1 is the least confidently believed member, it cannot be properly basic for S, even if all of the other members of the original set still are. However, suppose e^1 and e^2 are tied for being least confidently believed—each being believed, let us say, with *exactly* the same confidence as the proposition that at least one member in the set $(e^1, e^2, \ldots e^n)$ is false. Then neither e^1 nor e^2 can be properly basic for S, since the negation of each proposition is implied (in an obvious way) by propositions that S believes as confidently as he does it. But what if S believes every proposition in the original set with exactly the same amount of confidence (with the same confidence that he believes that one of these propositions is false)? Does it then follow that *none* of these propositions are properly basic for S? Yes, strictly speaking, this does follow. However, although such a situation perhaps is theoretically possible, it is for all practical purposes impossible, since it is for all practical purposes impossible for each proposition in *any* relatively large set of propositions to be believed by an individual with *exactly* the same amount of confidence.

31. When I say that it is epistemically rational for S to believe *of* the set of propositions properly basic for him, where this is the set $(e^1, e^2, \ldots e^n)$, that it contains only truths, I mean only to say that it is epistemically rational for him to believe the proposition that the set $(e^1, e^2, \ldots e^n)$ contains only truths. On the other hand, I do not mean to say that it need be epistemically rational for him to believe the epistemic proposition that the set of propositions that are properly basic for him contains only truths.

32. I assume here (again) that a conjunctive argument with premises e^1, $e^2, \ldots e^n$ is not too complex for S to understand. For a related discussion, see section 7.1.

33. I again use "nature" loosely to refer to a deep-seated inclination or disposition. I do not mean to commit myself to the view that necessarily we have such inclinations.

34. What this implies, in turn, is that the relationship between epistemic irrationality and blameworthiness is less intimate than sometimes is thought. However, see section 5.5, where I introduce a notion that is very similar to the notion of epistemic irrationality but that is more closely linked with blameworthiness.

35. It is especially important to resist this temptation if one is interested, as I am, in defending a goal-oriented conception of rationality. See the discussion in section 1.1.

36. What is it to say that S has a good first-level argument for p in virtue of having a good first-level argument for the claim that his second-level argument for p is likely to have a true conclusion—or in virtue of his having a good first-level argument for the claim that R's testimony is reliable and R says that p? It

is to say that its being epistemically rational for him to believe *p* is *grounded* on this other claim. See section 4.3 for an explication of the grounding relation.

37. However, it need not be epistemically rational for *S* to believe of every such argument that its conclusion is likely to be true. It can be epistemically rational for *S* to believe both the proposition that the conclusion of an argument is highly likely to be true given that its premises are true, and the proposition that the conjunction of the argument's premises is highly likely to be true and yet not be epistemically rational for him to believe that the argument is highly likely to have a true conclusion. (Compare: By virtue of having an argument that gives the proposition (*R*'s testimony is accurate 75 percent of the time and *R* testifies *p* is true) a 75 percent chance of being true, *S* does not thereby have an argument that gives the proposition *p* itself a 75 percent chance of being true.)

38. There are two important points here. First, in our everyday lives the arguments we explicitly consider frequently are second-level arguments. Second, these second-level arguments can play a crucial role in making their conclusions epistemically rational for us. By contrast, the point here is not that our considering these arguments is itself always epistemically significant. Often, perhaps even usually, the conclusions of these second-level arguments would be epistemically rational for us even if we had not explicitly considered the arguments. As is the case with first-level arguments, it is enough that there be such an argument. Suppose, however, that *S* explicitly considers a second-level argument for *p* and that in the process of doing so he unsuccessfully tries to recall some information that would defeat the argument. Moreover, suppose that it is epistemically rational for *S* to believe that his failure to recall (even after careful reflection) any such defeating information is in itself a good indication that the argument is highly likely to have a true conclusion. In such a case, the fact that *S* has explicitly considered the argument and tried to defeat it is epistemically significant.

39. But might not there be another kind of incoherence in the account? Suppose, for example, that were *S* to be reflective he would think that he has a good argument for *p*. However, suppose he would also think that if he were to believe *p*, he would also come to believe some other proposition *q* for which he lacks a good argument. Acccordingly, might he not on reflection think that although he has a good argument for *p*, believing *p* is not likely to be an overall effective way of satisfying his epistemic goal? Or suppose that *S* on reflection would believe that although he has a good argument for *p*, if he were in fact to believe *p* an evil demon would alter the situation so as to make *p* false. Again, might not this prompt *S* to think that although he has a good argument for *p*, believing *p* is not likely to be an effective way of satisfying his epistemic goal? In such cases, it is necessary to distinguish between whether something Y is likely to satisfy a goal X, holding the present situation constant, and whether Y would be likely to satisfy goal X, taking into account any changes in the current situation that would be prompted by the occurrence of Y. More specifically, in the cases here it is necessary to distinguish between *S* on reflection thinking that his believing *p would* be likely to be an effective way of satisfying his epistemic goal, given that the premises of the argument in question are true, and his on reflection thinking that his believing *p is* likely to be an effective way of satisfying his epistemic goal, given that these premises are true. To determine whether his believing *p* would be likely to be effective, given the truth of these premises, it

is necessary for S to think about close possible worlds in which these premises are true *and* in which he believes p. And, as the above remarks suggest, these worlds might be ones in which S also believes q or worlds in which an evil demon conspires to make p false. But to determine whether his believing p is likely to be an effective way of satisfying his epistemic goal given the truth of these premises, it is not necessary for S to think about close possible worlds in which he believes p. All it is necessary to think about is whether p is true in most close worlds in which the premises are true. (Compare: It may be that the correct way for S to answer 13-across in the crossword puzzle on his desk *is* to write the letters a-a-r-d-v-a-r-k even if it also is the case that were S to begin writing these letters a demon would alter the puzzle in such a way as to make this answer incorrect.) This constitutes one of the ways in which the theory of epistemic rationality is an idealized theory, a theory that glides over various complications that are posed by beliefs in the actual world. For a related discussion, see section 1.1.

40. Notice that strictly speaking the epistemic goal is different at different times. For example, S's epistemic goal at time t is to have true beliefs and not to have false beliefs at that time t. By contrast, at a slightly later time t^1 his epistemic goal is to have true beliefs and not to have false beliefs at t^1.

41. For present purposes, the evidence that an individual S has can be thought of as those propositions that are properly basic for S as well as those propositions that are the premises of good second-level arguments. For a discussion of the latter kind of proposition, see section 2.5.

42. However, see section 2.8, where I introduce some non-Aristotelian conceptions of rationality, conceptions that might allow such evaluations to be construed as evaluations of the rationality of S's beliefs.

43. "Decision-theoretic" epistemologists often adopt a point of view closely associated with this goal. In particular, they often seek to describe the degree of confidence with which an individual S should believe a proposition given his evidence, where his evidence is roughly a function of what else he believes, the strength with which he believes it, and the probability calculus. So, this kind of decision-theoretic point of view evaluates how effectively a person pursues the goal of believing everything with an appropriate degree of confidence from a mixed perspective, a perspective that is in part radically subjective and in part radically objective. In particular, this kind of decision-theoretic point of view is radically subjective insofar as it implies that an individual believes what he does with an appropriate degree of confidence as long as these degrees of belief are not incoherent, where incoherence is defined in terms of the possibility of a Dutch Book being made against the individual. In effect, what this means is that his degrees of belief are "innocent until proven guilty"—unless there is a positive reason to be suspicious of them through the possibility of a Dutch Book being made against him. On the other hand, this decision-theoretic point of view is radically objective insofar as it implies that an individual's degrees of beliefs are coherent only if they in fact conform with the axioms of the probability calculus, thus precluding the possibility of a Dutch book being made against him; it is not enough that the individual believes (or that he on reflection would believe) that they so conform. Thus, for example, if p implies q, then given the axioms of the probability calculus, p on the evidence cannot have a higher probability than q on the evidence. Accordingly, the proponent of such a decision-theoretic

point of view must say that S cannot properly believe p with any more confidence than q. And this is so even if he and perhaps no one else realizes (or is even capable of realizing) that p implies q. For a clear statement of this kind of approach to epistemology and a recommendation for how one might try to develop it into an account of rational belief (as opposed to rational degrees of beliefs), see Mark Kaplan, "A Bayesian Theory of Rational Acceptance," *The Journal of Philosophy* 38 (1981), 305–330. See also Richard Jeffrey, *The Logic of Decision* (New York: McGraw-Hill, 1965); L. J. Savage, *The Foundations of Statistical Inference* (New York: Dover, 1962); and Ian Hacking, *The Logic of Statistical Inference* (Cambridge: Cambridge University Press, 1961), especially chap. 13.

44. Do we want also to be epistemically rational at future times? Presumably we do, but it is at least possible for the diachronic goal of being epistemically rational at future times and the diachronic goal of having true beliefs at future times to conflict, since it is possible that the most effective means to S's being epistemically rational in the future is a means that will put S in a worse position to believe truths. For example, if S does something that causes him to forget much of what he previously knew (and to forget that he has forgotten it), it perhaps will be easier for S in the future to be epistemically rational (since he will have less evidence with which to deal) but harder for him to believe truths (since what will be epistemically rational for him to believe might be less likely to be true—or at least it *now* might be epistemically rational for him to believe this). These two diachronic goals can be combined, as well, into the goal of being epistemically rational at future times while also being in a better position than now for believing truths. Indeed, perhaps for most of us this goal or at least something similar to it would be regarded as our fundamental diachronic intellectual goal. For a related discussion, see section 5.3.

45. After all, one might inquire why insofar as one is interested simply in now believing true theories and now not believing false theories we should prefer the simpler, or more fertile, of two theories. Is the world such that simpler, or more fertile, theories are more likely to be true? And even if (as is doubtful) the answer here is yes, one might still wonder whether simplicity and fertility are fundamental virtues of theories (that all else being equal we properly can use in any situation to help determine whether a theory is likely to be true) or whether they are derivative virtues, virtues "derived" from the fact (if it is one) that we have independent evidence (such as from the history of science) indicating that the simpler and more fertile of two theories is more likely to be true.

46. See, for example, Alvin Goldman, "What Is Justified Belief?" in Pappas, *Justification and Knowledge.*

47. See, for example, Ernest Sosa, "The Raft and the Pyramid," in French, Uehling, and Wettstein, *Midwest Studies in Philosophy* 5; and Sosa, "The Coherence of Virtue and the Virtue of Coherence," *Synthese* 64 (1985), 3–28.

48. In the discussion above, the notions of an internal and an external point of view do not closely correspond to the notions of internalism and externalism as these notions are standardly used in ethics and epistemology. In ethics, for example, "internalism" usually is used to pick out those views that make being motivated to do X (or wanting X) a necessary condition of having a reason to do X. See, for example, William Frankena, "Obligation and Motivation in Recent Moral Philosophy," in *Essays in Moral Philosophy,* ed. A. I. Melden (Seattle:

University of Washington Press, 1958). The notion of purely epistemic reasons to believe is not internalist in this sense; it can be epistemically rational for a person *S* to believe a proposition *p* even if he is not motivated to have true beliefs and not to have false beliefs (perhaps because he does not realize that this is one of his goals). In epistemology, on the other hand, "internalism" is often used to pick out positions that imply that a person can always tell (if he thinks carefully) whether it is rational for him to believe *p*. (See, for example, Alvin Goldman, "The Internalist Conception of Justification," in French, Uehling, and Wettstein, *Midwest Studies in Philosophy 5*. Subjective foundationalism is not an internalist position in this sense either; it is possible for a person to be mistaken in his epistemic judgments even if he deliberates as hard and as long as practical constraints allow. Subjective foundationalism, by way of contrast, is an internalist doctrine in the loose, intuitive sense that it makes the epistemic rationality of my beliefs a function exclusively of conditions that obtain "within me now." Thus, the epistemic rationality of my beliefs is a function of what I believe, the strength with which I believe what I do, and my dispositions to approve of various arguments on reflection, rather than a function of social conditions (say, what most people think) or the history of my beliefs (say, what caused me to believe what I do) or other such external factors. See also chapter 4.

49. Peter Klein in his *Certainty: A Refutation of Scepticism* (Minneapolis: University of Minnesota Press, 1981) indicates some sympathy for a view of this sort.

50. For a suggestion of this sort, see Stephen Stich, "Could Man be An Irrational Animal?" *Synthese* 64 (1985), 115–135. Stich says, "when we judge someone's inference to be normatively inappropriate, we are comparing it to (what we take to be) the applicable principles of inference sanctioned by expert reflective equilibrium." Before making this suggestion, Stich argues against more subjective views (for example, views that appeal to what the individual himself on reflection would think about one of his own inferences) and majoritarian views (for example, views that appeal to what most members of the community on reflection would think about the individual's inference) on the grounds that the individual himself as well as most members of his community might reflect wrongly. But of course, if this constitutes a good objection against subjective and majoritarian accounts, it also constitutes a good objection against Stich's "expert opinion" account (unless, of course, his account is trivialized by stipulating that no one who reasons wrongly can be recognized by the community as an expert).

51. For a helpful discussion of radically subjective views of rational belief, see Jonathan Kvanvig, "Subjective Justification," *Mind* (1984), 71–84.

52. See the discussion of "negative coherence" theories by John Pollock ("A Plethora of Epistemological Theories," in Pappas, *Justification and Knowledge*).

53. For further discussion of positions implying that *any* proposition that a person believes is thereby prima facie rational for him, see chapter 7.

54. It is important not to overemphasize the relativism implicit in the claim that there is no privileged perspective from which to make judgments about the rationality of an individual's beliefs and the intellectual practices, habits, and methods that led to these beliefs. In particular, the relativism here is not a vicious, paralyzing kind of relativism, which gives the individual a reason to be suspicious of his own decision-making processes. The relativism here attaches only to the

evaluation of an individual's beliefs as rational or irrational, the claim being that there is no single correct perspective from which to make these evaluations. For a related discussion, see section 2.10.

55. For example, it is closely related to the point of view adopted (implicitly) by those in the Cartesian tradition. Cartesians can be construed as being concerned with the epistemic goal (the goal of now believing those propositions that are true and not believing those propositions that are false) and with the perspective of the reflective individual himself (what the individual himself would take to be an effective means to his epistemic goal, were he to be sufficiently reflective). Of course, Cartesians also think that if an individual is sufficiently reflective, he will discover a means that is guaranteed to produce true beliefs and not to produce false beliefs—the means of believing only that which is clear and distinct. See also note 56.

56. On the other hand, Descartes as well as a number of other traditional foundationalists perhaps are best construed as trying to collapse the Aristotelian and objective conceptions into one another. Indeed, the implausibility of such accounts can be understood to be a natural consequence of this attempt to collapse the two conceptions. In particular, the implausibility of such accounts arises out of the suggestion that means to the epistemic goal that are guaranteed to be efective (that is, guaranteed to produce true beliefs and not to produce false beliefs) are introspectively available to every normal adult. Normal adults need only to reflect carefully enough to determine what these effective means are; if they reflect carefully enough, they will be able to identify propositions that are certain for them and to identify also how these propositions can be used to argue for other propositions in a way that is guaranteed to be truth preserving.

57. By way of contrast, one way of understanding pragmatist accounts of rational belief is to view them as denying that truth per se is ever an acceptable goal (and perhaps not even an understandable goal). Instead, a belief is rational only insofar as it in some way, perhaps an indirect way, helps secure our various practical goals. See, for example, William James, *Essays in Pragmatism* (New York: Hafner, 1948). Or, if a pragmatist is inclined toward a less objective conception of rationality, he might make an appeal to community standards, so that the rationality of any belief (as well as any inference, or the like) is ultimately to be judged in terms of what the community generally takes to be useful, as expressed, say, in its practices. Richard Rorty perhaps is suggesting a view of this kind in his *Philosophy and the Mirror of Nature* (Princeton: Princeton University Press, 1979).

58. For convenience, I assume in this section that traditional foundationalism and coherentism are accounts of epistemic rationality and hence are genuine rivals of subjective foundationalism. For the reasons discussed in section 2.8, such talk should be regarded as provisional. In any event, even if these accounts are accounts of some other notion of rationality, questions of the sort I discuss in this section will arise from them. For example, the question will arise as to how, given the theory, it can be rational (in the sense of rationality with which the theory is concerned) for an individual to accept the theory.

59. For a discussion of the relevance of this point for the problem of the Cartesian circle, see James Van Cleve, "Foundationalism, Epistemic Principles, and the Cartesian Circle," *The Philosophical Review* 88 (1979), 55–91.

60. See Alvin Plantinga, "Is Belief in God Rational?" in *Rationality and Religious Belief,* ed. C. F. Delaney (Notre Dame: University of Notre Dame Press, 1979), 7–27, who argues that traditional foundationalism *is* in this way self-referentially incoherent.

61. Once more, there are exceptions. The proposition that what coherentism recommends is likely to be true might be sufficiently supported by *S*'s evidence to make it epistemically rational for *S*, and the proposition that *p* coheres with the rest of his beliefs likewise might be sufficiently supported by *S*'s evidence to make it epistemically rational for *S*. Yet, *p* itself might not be sufficiently supported by his evidence to make it epistemically rational for him. Compare note 37.

62. Thomas S. Kuhn, *The Structure of Scientific Revolutions* (Chicago: University of Chicago Press, 1962); Paul Feyerabend, *Against Method* (London: New Left Books, 1975).

63. It is easy to exaggerate such differences. Whether we are engaged in a casual conversation or a serious study of other cultures, it is natural to emphasize the differences rather than the similarities between our culture and other cultures; it ordinarily seems more instructive as well as more entertaining to do so.

64. See, for example, Donald Davidson, "On the Very Idea of a Conceptual Scheme," *Proceedings and Addresses of the American Philosophical Association* 17 (1973–74), 5–20.

65. Analogously, it might be argued that given our current perspective we can see that human intellectual history has been largely a history of error. But if so, it might seem that we have inductive reasons to be suspicious even of those views and those arguments that we are most inclined to favor—reasons to suspect that they, like the views and arguments favored by our ancestors, are likely to be found lacking by future, better-informed generations. There is nothing in principle wrong with such a "meta-induction," even though it may undercut itself—even though it itself may provide us with a reason to be suspicious of it. For even if the meta-induction does undercut itself, it still might be capable of generating reasons for us to be suspicious of the arguments we now favor. Nevertheless, the skeptical consequences of this meta-induction can be avoided. They can be avoided because the situation that the meta-induction presupposes is not our situation. We do not have good reasons to believe that human intellectual history is largely a history of error. On the contrary, we have reasons to believe that most of what the ancients and the medievals believed about the world is true. For most of what they believed is what we believe.

66. There are those, of course, who argue that this is not possible. See Davidson, "On the Very Idea of a Conceptual Scheme." But for purposes of the discussion here, I will assume that this is possible. See also the discussion in section 3.2.

3.   Epistemic Rationality and Truth

1. Alvin Goldman, "What Is Justified Belief?" in *Justification and Knowledge,* ed. George Pappas (Dordrecht: Reidel, 1979), 1–23.

2. Marshall Swain, "Justification and the Basis of Belief," in *Justification and Knowledge,* 25–49.

3. Ernest Sosa, "The Raft and the Pyramid," in *Midwest Studies in Philosophy 5*, ed. P. French, T. Uehling, and H. Wettstein (Minneapolis: University of Minnesota Press, 1980), 3–25.

4. William Alston, "Self-Warrant: A Neglected form of Privileged Access," *American Philosophical Quarterly* 13 (1976), 257–272, especially p. 268.

5. For convenience, in this chapter I often drop the qualifier "epistemically" and talk simply of rational beliefs. But unless otherwise noted, what is being discussed is epistemic rationality. Similarly, for convenience I often will not explicitly mention the proviso that the set of propositions that are rational for an individual (or the set of his rational beliefs) be relatively large. But again, unless otherwise noted, I am assuming that this is so.

6. For the time being, I will assume that to rationally believe p in an epistemic sense is just to believe p when p is epistemically rational to believe. Later I will discuss a richer notion of epistemically rational belief. (See the discussion of propositionally rational and doxastically rational beliefs in section 4.2.) The points I am making in this chapter about rational belief also apply to the richer notion.

7. Hilary Putnam, "Realism and Reason," *Proceedings and Addresses of the American Philosophical Association* 50 (1977), 483–498; and Putnam, *Reason, Truth, and History* (Cambridge: Cambridge University Press, 1981), especially chap. 1; Donald Davidson, "On the Very Idea of a Conceptual Scheme," *Proceedings and Addresses of the American Philosophical Association* 17 (1973–74), 5–20; and Davidson, "A Coherence Theory of Truth and Knowledge," in *The Philosophy of Donald Davidson: Perspectives on Truth and Interpretation,* ed. E. LePore, (London: Basil Blackwell, 1986).

8. "What stands in the way of global skepticism of the senses is, in my view, the fact that we must, in the plainest and methodologically most basic cases, take the objects of a belief to be the causes of that belief." Davidson, "A Coherence Theory of Truth and Knowledge," pp. 317–318.

9. Putnam, *Reason, Truth, and History,* pp. 13–14.

10. For convenience, I assume in what follows not only that more of our simple beliefs must be true than false but also the stronger claim that more of our beliefs must be true than false. However, points analogous to the ones that follow could be made even if only the weaker assumption were made. In particular, the main point would be that, given this (weaker) assumption, there need be no incompatibility between subjective foundationalism and the (weaker) reliabilist thesis that more of our rational simple beliefs must be true than false.

11. Of course, this is not to say that subjective foundationalism is compatible with just any version of reliabilism—for example, a version that implies that a belief is rational just if it is the product of a belief acquisition process that over the long run will produce mostly true beliefs. It is only to say that, given the above assumptions about the nature of belief, even subjective foundationalism implies a version of reliabilism.

12. See, for example, John Pollock, "Reliability and Justified Belief," *Canadian Journal of Philosophy* (1984), 103–114, especially p. 105, fn. 4.

13. Indeed, I have suggested that the propositions that are the objects of our simple memory beliefs are often properly basic for us. See, for example, 2.1.

14. Alvin Goldman's reliabilist account of rational belief is just such an attempt. See Goldman, "What Is Justified Belief?" especially p.1.

15. See Alvin Plantinga, "Epistemic Justification," *Nous* 20 (1986), 3–19.

16. Namely, it is rational in the reflective subjective (or Aristotelian) sense. See section 2.8.

4.   Epistemic Luck

1. Or at least this is so unless some surprising thesis turns out to be true—such as a thesis that implies that our beliefs about the past (or certain kinds of them) are infallible. If such a thesis were true, it would not always be possible to imagine a situation that from the believer's perspective is indistinguishable from his present situation but in which his beliefs have a significantly different causal history. Some of his beliefs about the past might be beliefs about matters that were involved in causing him to have the beliefs he now has. (Analogously, subjective foundationalism allows the possibility that most epistemically rational beliefs might be false. Or at least it allows this possibility unless some surprising thesis turns out to be true—for example, a thesis that implies that most of our beliefs (whether rational or not) must be true. See section 3.2.)

2. Roderick Firth, "Are Epistemic Concepts Reducible to Ethical Ones?" in *Values and Morals,* ed. A. Goldman and J. Kim (Dordrecht: Reidel, 1978), 215–229.

3. John Pollock, "A Plethora of Epistemological Theories," in *Justification and Knowledge,* ed. G. Pappas (Dordrecht: Reidel, 1979), 93–113.

4. Marshall Swain, "Justification and the Basis of Belief," in Pappas, *Justification and Knowledge,* 25–49.

5. Hilary Kornblith, "Beyond Foundationalism and the Coherence Theory," *The Journal of Philosophy* 77 (1980), 597–611. Let us not worry about whether it is possible for a person who understands modus ponens to distrust it. Just assume that this is possible.

6. The problem here is analogous to the problem of wayward causation that has proved so difficult in action theory. See, for example, Roderick Chisholm, "The Descriptive Element in the Concept of Action," *The Journal of Philosophy* 61 (1964), 616; Donald Davidson, "Freedom to Act," in *Essays on Freedom of Action,* ed. T. Honderich (London: Routledge and Kegan Paul), 139–156; Richard Foley, "Deliberate Action," *The Philosophical Review* 86 (1977), 58–69; Irving Thalberg, *Perception, Emotion and Action* (New Haven: Yale University Press, 1977), chap. 4.

7. One of these details concerns how to deal with beliefs in propositions that are properly basic for S. What makes such beliefs doxastically rational? If for a proposition p that is not properly basic for S we say that S's belief p is doxastically rational just if (roughly) S believes p because he believes the premises of an argument that makes p rational for him, then perhaps for a proposition q that is properly basic a posteriori we could say that S's belief q is doxastically rational just if (again roughly) it is caused in an appropriately direct way by the fact that q. And perhaps for a proposition r that is properly basic a priori, we

could say that *S*'s belief *r* is doxastically rational just if it is caused in an appropriately direct way by his understanding *r*. Or perhaps there are other ways of capturing these doxastic senses. In any event, I will not dwell on this problem because, as I argue later, I do not think it necessary to introduce a causal-historical sense of rational belief.

8. See section 2.6 for a discussion of the distinction between first-level arguments and second-level arguments. It also is worth noting here that in requiring *S* to believe that he has a good argument for *p* if his belief *p* is to be doxastically rational, I am not requiring that *S* have a clear notion of what it is for something to be an argument. It is enough for him to have a rough, intuitive grasp of two claims being related in such a way that the second is true in most relevant possible situations in which the first is true. When he believes this of two claims, we can say that he believes the first can be used to argue for the second. For a related discussion, see section 1.2, including note 22.

9. Notice that all of these propositions might be (but need not be) properly basic for *S*—either properly basic a posteriori or properly basic a priori.

10. See section 4.3 for a discussion of evidential and nonevidential knowledge. Note also that even if an individual does not have evidential knowledge of a proposition *p* that is properly basic for him, he nonetheless might have nonevidential knowledge of it.

11. Or at least this is so providing (once again) that no surprising thesis turns out to be true—for instance, a thesis implying that (at least on careful reflection) an individual can always determine what causes his beliefs. See also note 1, this chapter.

12. One way in which a causal-historical requirement on rational belief might be trivial is by imposing causal-historical conditions on rational belief that necessarily a state must satisfy if it is to be a belief at all. Compare note 15.

13. Compare Keith Lehrer, *Knowledge* (Oxford: Oxford University Press, 1974), especially pp. 122–126. Also see Robert Audi, "The Causal Structure of Indirect Justification, *The Journal of Philosophy* (1983), 398–415, and Audi, "Foundationalism, Epistemic Dependence, and Defeasiblity," *Synthese* (1983), 119–134; George Pappas, "Basing Relations," in Pappas, *Justification and Knowledge*, 51–64; Ernest Sosa, "Epistemic Presupposition," in Pappas, *Justification and Knowledge*, 79–92, especially p. 88; and Peter Klein, "Real Knowledge," *Synthese* (1983), 143–164.

14. I ignore here the complication of probabilistic laws. However, even if there are irreducibly probabilistic laws, it presumably is the case that any true belief is the product of some reliable process—a process that is defined in such a situation-specific way that it is highly likely to generate true beliefs.

15. Donald Davidson in "A Coherence Theory of Truth and Knowledge" in *The Philosophy of Donald Davidson: Perspectives on Truth and Interpretation*, ed. E. LePore (London: Basil Blackwell, 1986) argues: "What stands in the way of global skepticism of the senses is, in my view, the fact that we must, in the plainest and methodologically most basic cases, take the objects of a belief to be the causes of that belief" (pp. 317–318). This view about the nature of belief might be thought to stand in the way not only of global skepticism but also in the way of there being an ideally veridical believer whose beliefs are not in general caused by what makes them true. Might, then, reliabilist accounts of knowledge,

or at least some sort of causal account of knowledge, be salvaged by appealing to a causal account of belief of at least roughly the sort that Davidson is proposing? It is hard to see how. First, nothing in Davidson's account of belief implies that most of an individual's beliefs that are not "methodologically basic" (for example, beliefs that are not straightforwardly caused by perception, memory, introspection and the like) must be caused by what makes them true. Second, even if Davidson's account did imply this, it could be used to salvage only a trivial causal account of knowledge. For, as is generally admitted today, an individual can know only that which he believes. (For a dissenting view, see Colin Radford, "Knowledge—By Examples," *Analysis* (1966), 1–11.) Thus, if the nature of belief requires that an individual's beliefs are ordinarily caused by what makes them true, on any account of knowledge it will follow that ordinarily if S is to know p his belief p must have been caused by p. In other words, if the notion of belief itself ordinarily involves causal conditions of the sort Davidson discusses, these same causal conditions cannot be used to distinguish knowledge from mere true belief. Of course, one might try proposing additional, nontrivial causal conditions of knowledge, conditions beyond those required for belief. However, any such additional conditions will be susceptible to the same kinds of problems that plague other causal conditions of knowledge. These problems can be illustrated by imagining a slightly less extreme case of an ideally veridical and epistemically perfect believer—for example, an individual who meets the causal conditions of belief and whose beliefs provide him with something like a perfect explanation of the world but whose beliefs do not meet the additional causal conditions of knowledge, whatever these are. Third, even if these two difficulties are somehow solved, causal accounts would still face a significant and heretofore unnoticed difficulty. It apparently would be the case that the only way to salvage a causal account of knowledge is by endorsing a controversial causal account of belief.

16. This is not to suggest, however, that being true and being the product of reliable (or properly functioning) faculties are together sufficient to make a belief an instance of knowledge. It is only to say that these conditions are the central conditions in a set of conditions sufficient for knowledge. Indeed, even reliabilists are generally not inclined to say that these conditions are themselves sufficient. See Alvin Goldman, "What Is Justified Belief?" in Pappas, *Justification and Knowledge,* 1–23. Also see Fred Dretske "Conclusive Reasons," in *Essays on Knowledge and Justification,* ed. G. Pappas and M. Swain (Ithaca: Cornell University Press, 1978), 41–60.

17. It is equally difficult, of course, to explicate with any kind of precision a causal-historical sense of knowledge. It is difficult, for example, to say what it is for an individual's faculties to be "appropriately reliable" or to be "properly functioning,"—to be reliable or to be functioning in a way that yields knowledge. For a discussion of some of these difficulties, see Richard Feldman, "Reliability and Justification," *The Monist* 68 (1985), 159–174.

18. Thus, Gilbert Harman in *Thought* (Princeton: Princeton University Press, 1973), says that S cannot know p if his reasoning essentially involves a falsehood; Keith Lehrer in *Knowledge* (Oxford: Oxford University Press, 1974), says that S cannot know p if his justification for p depends on a falsehood; and Roderick Chisholm, *Theory of Knowledge,* 2d ed. (Englewood Cliffs, N.J.: Prentice-Hall,

1977) says that S knows p only if p is nondefectively evident, where a necessary condition of p being nondefectively evident for S is there being some set of propositions that makes p evident for S and that contains no falsehood.

19. If p is properly basic for S, let us say that the argument (S believes p; thus, p) must in fact be likely to be truth preserving.

20. It is worth noting that these conditions seem not to be met in typical lottery cases. See section 6.3.

21. And perhaps some kind of social condition on knowledge is also needed—say, the condition that the individual not lack defeating information that is readily available in his community. For a defense of the need for some kind of social condition on knowledge as well as a thorough discussion of other approaches to knowledge, see Robert K. Shope, *The Analysis of Knowing* (Princeton: Princeton University Press, 1983).

22. In this way, the evaluation of beliefs is not fundamentally different from the evaluation of actions. Depending upon our interests and purposes, we can properly evaluate a person's action either by taking into account the character, habits, motives, and so on that prompted the action or by ignoring these "historical" considerations and instead concentrating upon whether the action was the "best" (in an appropriate sense of "best") of the relevant alternatives.

23. See Richard Foley and Richard Fumerton, "Epistemic Indolence," *Mind* 91 (1982), 38–56.

24. Compare Richard Feldman and Earl Conee, "Evidentialism," *Philosophical Studies* 48 (1985), 15–34.

25. For more on this notion of purely present states (and on the importance of this notion for certain metaphysical issues), see Alfred Freddoso, "Accidental Necessity and Logical Determinism," *The Journal of Philosophy* 80 (1983), 257–278.

5.   Nonepistemic Reasons for Believing

1. Indeed, if it is epistemically rational for S to believe that Y is an effective means to X, then all else being equal it is rational in a practical sense for S to bring about Y even if occurrences of its kind are hardly ever effective at securing S's or anyone else's practical goals. Thus, "practical reliabilism" is no more a necessary condition of this kind of practical rationality than epistemic reliabilism is of epistemic rationality.

2. In each of these cases, I simply am assuming that S's practical goals are similar to most other people's practical goals. Thus, in the first case mentioned above, I assume that one of S's practical goals is to be healthy; in the second case, I assume that being successful at his job is one of his goals; and in the third case, I assume that being wealthy is one of his goals.

3. Presumably, any such position presupposes an objective theory of goals. In particular, in presupposes that the relative values of an individual's goals are not determined (or at least not determined solely) by how much the individual cares about (wants or desires) them. For it is implausible to assume that any individual, much less *all* individuals, cares more about the epistemic goal than any combination of his other goals.

4. "It is wrong everywhere and for anyone to believe anything upon insufficient evidence." W. K. Clifford, "The Ethics of Belief," in Clifford, *Lectures and Essays* (London: Macmillan, 1879).

5. William James, "The Will to Believe," in James, *The Will to Believe and Other Essays in Popular Philosophy* (New York: David McKay, 1911).

6. In interpreting James to be proposing conditions sufficient but not necessary for it being rational to believe what is not epistemically rational (and this, I think, is not uncontroversial), I am giving James the benefit of the doubt. For if his conditions are both necessary and sufficient, James like the evidentialist would be commited to claiming that as long as *p* is an ordinary proposition that can be decided on "intellectual grounds," it cannot be rational all things considered for *S* to believe *p*—even if, say, the survival of the earth depended on his coming to believe *p*. And accordingly, James's position would be no more tenable than that of the evidentialist.

7. This same general point is made, explicitly or implicitly, by the following: Richard Gale, "William James and the Ethics of Belief," *American Philosophical Quarterly* 17 (1980), 1–14; Jack Meiland, "What Ought We to Believe? or the Ethics of Belief Revisited," *American Philosophical Quarterly* 17 (1980), 15–24; Ralph Barton Perry, "The Right to Believe," in Perry, *In the Spirit of William James* (Bloomington: Indiana University Press, 1958), 170–208; Roderick Firth, "Chisholm and the Ethics of Belief," *The Philosophical Review* 68 (1959), 493–506; and Nicholas Rescher, *Pascal's Wager* (Notre Dame: University of Notre Dame Press, 1984).

8. Thomas Reid seemed to hold an even stronger position, a position implying that it is impossible for *S* to believe *p* if he does not believe he has good evidence for *p*. That is, *S* must not only lack the belief that he has no evidence for *p*, he must also have the belief that he has good evidence for *p*: "nor is it in a man's power to believe anything longer than he thinks he has evidence." Thomas Reid, *Essays on the Intellectual Powers*, chap. 10, sec. 1, from *The Philosophical Work of Thomas Reid*, ed. Sir William Hamilton (London: James Thin, 1895).

9. This is Bernard Williams' phrase. See Williams, "Deciding to Believe," in his *Problems of the Self* (Cambridge: Cambridge University Press, 1973).

10. Notice that it can be epistemically rational for an individual *S* to believe *p* even though he does not have adequate evidence for *p* in this objective sense.

11. Or at least this is so for projects that involve a deliberate worsening of one's epistemic situation. This issue is discussed later in section 5.2

12. Contrast Hilary Kornblith, "Justified Belief and Epistemically Responsible Action," *The Philosophical Review* 93 (1984), 33–47.

13. This thesis needs to be distinguished from the thesis that the deductive consequences of any set of propositions that are epistemically rational for *S* are themselves epistemically rational for *S*. This latter thesis is implausible, because it commits one to a conjunctive rule of epistemic rationality, such that if *a* is epistemically rational for *S* and *b* is epistemically rational for *S*, then their conjunction also is epistemically rational for *S*. See chapter 6 and section 2.3.

14. Just as the evidentialist's claim that it is rational, all things considered, to believe (or to try to believe) *only* that which is epistemically rational is mistaken, so too the claim that it is rational, all things considered, to believe (or to try to believe) *all* that which is epistemically rational is mistaken.

15. No assumption is being made here, or in what follows, that an individual has direct control over what he believes. For present purposes, we can think of a person who tries as hard as he can to believe truths and not to believe falsehoods as a person who tries as hard as he can to gather evidence and to discern what this evidence implies or makes probable—the hope being that doing so will generate true beliefs and discourage false beliefs.

16. Compare Hilary Kornblith, "Justified Belief and Epistemically Responsible Action," who claims: "Justified belief is belief which is the product of epistemically responsible action; epistemically responsible action is action guided by a desire to have true beliefs."

17. However, he presumably could be faulted for not having done a good enough job of satisfying his nonepistemic goals, since it is almost never rational, all things considered, for an individual to try as hard as he possibly can to believe truths and not to believe falsehoods. See section 5.4.

18. Compare Roderick Chisholm, *Theory of Knowledge,* 2d ed. (Englewood Cliffs N. J.: Prentice-Hall, 1977), especially p. 17.

19. Many traditional foundationalist positions also guarantee this. Descartes plausibly can be interpreted as holding such a view and perhaps Bertrand Russell as well. See Bertrand Russell, *The Problem of Philosophy* (Oxford: Oxford University Press, 1912), especially chaps. 5, 6, and 7. See also Richard Fumerton, *Metaphysical and Epistemological Problems of Perception* (Lincoln: University of Nebraska Press, 1985), especially pp. 57–60, for a discussion of a related view, the view that whenever an individual is directly acquainted with some fact, he is directly acquainted with the fact that he is directly acquainted with the first fact. For criticisms of this kind of foundationalism, see William Alston, "Two Types of Foundationalism," *The Journal of Philosophy* (1976), 165–185.

20. Compare William Alston, "Level-Confusions in Epistemology," in *Midwest Studies in Philosophy 5*, ed. P. French, T. Uehling, and H. Wettstein (Minneapolis: University of Minnesota Press, 1980), 135–150.

21. If the conclusion of an argument is a proposition that S on reasonable reflection would regard as necessarily true, let us also insist that he on reasonable reflection would regard the premises as relevant to the conclusion.

22. And if q here is a proposition that S on reasonable reflection would regard as necessarily true, let us also insist that it must be the case that S on reasonable reflection would think that understanding p is enough to provide him with an understanding of why q cannot be false.

23. From what perspective is this claim of rationality to be made? It cannot be made from the nonidealized Aristotelian perspective that is at issue here (that would be circular). On the other hand, it might be made from an *idealized* Aristotelian perspective, so that the length of time it is rational for S to reflect is a function of what it is epistemically rational for S to believe about how his taking time to reflect on this argument is likely to affect his various goals (keeping in mind that the epistemic goal is his most important goal). Or it might be made from an *objective* perspective, so that the length of time it is rational for S to reflect is a function of how his taking time to reflect on this argument would in fact affect his various goals. Either way, the judgments of rationality made from this nonidealized Aristotelian perspective presuppose judgments of rationality made from some other perspective. Indeed, this should have been obvious from

the beginning, since the intuitive idea here is that it is rational in this nonidealized Aristotelian sense for *S* to believe *p* just if he has an uncontroversial argument for *p*, where an uncontroversial argument is one he would find unproblematic were he *reasonably* reflective.

24. In particular, perhaps for some philosophers the notion of what an individual is justified in believing is closely linked to the notion of what propositions an individual would be able to defend were he to be reasonably careful in studying the evidence available to him, where what counts as reasonably careful reflection is a function *not* of the individual's total constellation of concerns (this would allow the possibility that an individual's practical concerns influencing unduly what constitutes reasonably careful reflection and as a result influencing unduly what he is justified in believing); rather, it is a function of how carefully he should reflect were his epistemic goal his primary concern. This deemphasizes his practical concerns but does not altogether eliminate them; it does not imply, for example, that an individual should reflect until his opinions stabilize (even if this were to involve impractically lengthy reflection). Compare Hilary Kornblith, "Justified Belief and Epistemically Responsible Action"; Nicholas Wolterstorff, "Can Belief in God Be Rational if It Has No Foundations?" in *Faith and Rationality*, ed. A. Plantinga and N. Wolterstorff (Notre Dame: University of Notre Dame Press, 1982). Also see Roderick Chisholm, *Theory of Knowledge,* 2d ed., especially p. 7; and Roderick Chisholm, "A Version of Foundationalism," in French, Uehling, and Wettstein, *Midwest Studies in Philosophy 5*, especially p. 546. Each of these philosophers wants there to be a link between justified beliefs and epistemically responsible, or epistemically blameless, beliefs.

6.   *Consistency and Coherence*

1. For simplicity, I assume that the set here is not obviously inconsistent by virtue of *S* recognizing that one of its members—say, *p*—is necessarily false. If the set were obviously inconsistent in this way, then there need not be a proposition in the set whose negation the other propositions tend to make epistemically rational for *S*. Recall that propositions whose conjunction *S* on reflection would take to be necessarily false cannot tend to make epistemically rational for *S* any other proposition. See section 1.2. Recall also that the other propositions in the set tend to make epistemically rational not*p* for *S* only if *S* on reflection would take them to be relevant to not*p*. Again, see section 1.2. On the other hand, if the set of propositions were obviously inconsistent in this way, it still would follow that not all members of the set could be properly basic for *S*. In particular, *p* could not be properly basic for him.

2. I assume here that an argument with all these propositions as premises is not so complex that *S* even with ideal reflection could not understand it (and hence could neither believe that it is truth preserving nor believe that it is not truth preserving). Since the propositions here are limited to ones that are properly basic for *S*, this is a plausible assumption.

3. See, for example, Donald Davidson, "On the Very Idea of a Conceptual Scheme," *Proceedings and Addresses of the American Philosophical Association* 17 (1973–74), 5–20.

4. Keith Lehrer makes a claim similar to this in *Knowledge* (Oxford: Oxford University Press, 1974). In later works, he repudiates this view. See, for example, "Self-Profile," in *Keith Lehrer,* ed. R. Bogdan (Dordrecht: Reidel, 1980).

5. See section 4.3. Perhaps some of the reluctance of philosophers to admit that it can be epistemically rational for *S* to believe such a claim derives from the fact that *S* plausibly cannot be said to have evidential knowledge of it. But if so, their reluctance derives from a mistake, the mistake of conflating the conditions of knowledge with the conditions of epistemic rationality.

6. Marshall Swain makes a suggestion similar to this; see "The Consistency of Rational Belief," in *Induction, Acceptance and Rational Belief,* ed. M. Swain (Dordrecht: Reidel, 1970), 27–54.

7. However, there are those who find such "Dutch Book arguments" problematic. See, for instance, R. Kennedy and C. Chihara, "The Dutch Book Argument: Its Logical Flaws, Its Subjective Sources," *Philosophical Studies* 36 (1979), 19–33.

8. I assume here that coherentist accounts (or at least some of them) are accounts of *epistemic* rationality. See section 2.8 for a discussion that indicates that this may not be the most charitable way to interpret every coherentist account.

9. See, for example, F. H. Bradley, *Appearance and Reality* (London: George Allen and Unwin, 1897). Also see Brand Blanshard, *The Nature of Thought* 2 (London: Macmillan, 1939), especially chapters 25–27, and Bernard Bosanquet, *Implication and Linear Inference* (London: Macmillan, 1920).

10. See, for example, Wilfred Sellars, *Science, Perception, and Reality* (London: Routledge and Kegan Paul, 1963), especially 521–538; Gilbert Harman, *Thought* (Princeton: Princeton University Press, 1973); Lawrence Bonjour, "A Coherence Theory of Empirical Knowledge," *Philosophical Studies* 30 (1976), 281–312; Roderick Firth, "Coherence, Certainty, and Epistemic Priority," *The Journal of Philosophy* 61 (1964), 545-557.

11. See Lehrer, *Knowledge,* for a view similar to this.

12. See John Pollock, "A Plethora of Epistemological Theories," in *Justification and Knowledge,* ed. G. Pappas (Dordrecht: Reidel, 1979), 93–114; also see Nicholas Wolterstorff, "Can Belief in God Be Rational if It Has No Foundations?" in *Faith and Rationality,* ed. A. Plantinga and N. Wolterstorff (Notre Dame: University of Notre Dame Press, 1982). For a good discussion of the differences between foundationalism and coherentism, see Ernest Sosa, "The Raft and the Pyramid," in *Midwest Studies in Philosophy* 5, ed. P. French, T. Uehling, and H. Wettstein (Minneapolis: University of Minnesota Press, 1980), 3–25.

13. Lehrer, *Knowledge,* especially pp. 202–204.

14. Ibid., 203.

15. Roderick Chisholm, *Theory of Knowledge,* 2d ed. (Englewood Cliffs N.J.: Prentice-Hall, 1977), 82–84, and *The Foundations of Knowing* (Minneapolis: University of Minnesota Press, 1982), 33–42; C. I. Lewis, *An Analysis of Knowledge and Valuation* (LaSalle, Ill.: Open Court, 1946), 338–362; H. H. Price, *Perception* (New York: Robert M. McBride, 1933), 185; Roderick Firth, "Coherence, Certainty, and Epistemic Priority"; Bertrand Russell, *The Problems of Philosophy* (Oxford: Oxford University Press, 1959), 140.

16. In *Theory of Knowledge* Chisholm requires only that the members be

logically independent of one another, but in *The Foundations of Knowing* he in addition requires this kind of epistemic independence.

17. Nothing in subjective foundationalism implies that these propositions cannot be properly basic. So, nothing in subjective foundationalism implies that these propositions cannot be used as premises. However, for purposes of discussion, I will assume that these propositions are not properly basic for S.

18. There will still be a difference of opinion here, however. For Chisholm regards his principle of coherence, like his other epistemic principles, as being necessarily true, but nothing in subjective foundationalism implies that Chisholm's principle *necessarily* identifies propositions that are epistemically rational.

19. For closely related discussions, see the discussion of second-level arguments in sections 2.5 and 2.9.

7. Varieties of Epistemic Conservatism

1. Throughout this chapter I use the locution "S believes *of* set of propositions X that——" as shorthand for "S believes *that* the members of the set $(p, p^1, p^2, \ldots p^n)$ are——", where $(p, p^1, p^2, \ldots p^n)$ are the members of set X. So when I say it is epistemically rational for S to believe *of* the set of propositions properly basic for him that all are true, this means that it is epistemically rational for him to believe that the members of the set $(p, p^1, p^2, \ldots p^n)$ are all true, where this is the set of propositions properly basic for him.

2. However, this is not to say that, given subjective foundationalism, it must be epistemically rational for an individual S to believe the epistemic proposition that the conjunction of those propositions that are properly basic for him are true. It is only to say that where $(p, p^1, \ldots p^n)$ is the set of propositions properly basic for him, it is epistemically rational for him to believe the conjunction $(p$ and $p^1, \ldots$ and $p^n)$.

3. See the discussion in section 1.2 of situations that an individual S on reflection would regard as relevant for an assessment of an argument.

4. Analogously, if S believes with great confidence that there is about a 50–50 chance of one of the propositions in this set being false, then there may not be an argument for not*p* that keeps *p* from being properly basic for S. However, it is likely that this probabilistic proposition, perhaps along with the other more confidently believed propositions in the set, can be used to defeat the argument (S believes *p*; thus, *p*), preventing *p* from being properly basic for S. (See section 1.6.)

5. Unless otherwise noted, I will assume in the discussion that follows that we unproblematically can identify what we believe. If this assumption is not made, it will be even more difficult to argue for the versions of epistemic conservatism I discuss later.

6. Richard Fumerton provides an interesting twist on such considerations, suggesting in effect that those of us who are familiar with natural selection may have a good argument for the claim that although most beliefs of most people are true, it is *not* the case that most beliefs of most people (especially those not familiar with natural selection) are rational. Roughly, Fumerton's idea is that considerations of natural selection may indicate that we are "programmed" to

have true beliefs, such that we spontaneously form true beliefs in the presence of appropriate stimuli, even though the stimuli do not provide us with adequate evidence for these beliefs. The explanation for this, Fumerton suggests, might be that it is evolutionarily "dangerous to have to wait for evidence from which the belief could be rationally inferred." See Fumerton, *Metaphysical and Epistemological Problems of Perception* (Lincoln: University of Nebraska Press, 1985), 24–30. For further discussion of the relation between rationality and natural selection, see William Lycan, "Epistemic Value," *Synthese* (1985), 137–164; Stephen Stich, "Could Man Be an Irrational Animal?" *Synthese* (1985), 115–135; and Richard Feldman, "Rationality, Reliability, and Natural Selection," forthcoming in *Philosophy of Science*.

7. Nevertheless, some variations on claim (2) will be discussed in more detail in section 7.3

8. Donald Davidson perhaps has a metaphysical thesis of this sort in mind in his "A Coherence Theory of Knowledge and Truth," in *The Philosophy of Donald Davidson: Perspectives on Truth and Interpretation,* ed. E. LePore (London: Basil Blackwell, 1986).

9. Or at least, this is so subject to a couple of provisos. Roughly, the provisos are that the sets of epistemically rational propositions to which this rule is applied not be extremely large and that they not be extremely small. For if we allow the sets to be extremely small—so that they might consist of, say, only two members—the rule would imply a conjunctive rule, since the only way a set of two propositions can contain mostly truths is for both propositions to be true. But then, by taking propositions two at a time, it could be shown that it must be epistemically rational for a person to believe the conjunction of all the propositions that are epistemically rational for him. But this, as I have argued, is counterintuitive. See chapter 6, especially section 6.3. On the other hand, the sets of epistemically rational propositions to which the above rule applies cannot be enormously large either. For example, if $(p, p^1, p^2, \ldots p^n)$ is a set of propositions that are epistemically rational for S, but this set is so large that even with ideal reflection S could not understand the proposition that $(p, p^1, \ldots p^n)$ contains mostly truths, then it cannot be epistemically rational for him to believe of this set that it contains mostly truths. To simplify the following discussion, I will assume that the sets of epistemically rational propositions being discussed satisfy these provisos.

10. Roderick Chisholm, "A Version of Foundationalism," in *Midwest Studies in Philosophy* 5, ed. P. French, T. Uehling, and H. Wettstein (Minneapolis: University of Minnesota Press, 1980); reprinted with revisions in Roderick Chisholm, *The Foundations of Knowing* (Minneapolis: University of Minnesota Press, 1982).

11. Chisholm, "A Version of Foundationalism," 552.

12. I am here no longer assuming, as I did in the previous section, that a person knows what it is that he believes.

13. Notice that S can believe p here and that p can be explicitly contradicted (in Chisholm's sense) by the *set* of other propositions he believes without S having explicitly contradictory beliefs, say, without his believing not$p$ as well as p. For, p can be explicitly contradicted by the set (the conjunction) of other propositions he believes without S actually believing this conjunction.

14. In what follows I reserve the expression "epistemic conservatism" for fundamentalist versions of conservatism—to versions that imply that necessarily any believed proposition has some kind of favorable epistemic status.

15. Chisholm suggests something much stronger. He suggests that any believed proposition is rational for S provided that it is unsuspect for him. A proposition p is unsuspect, according to Chisholm, just if no other propositions with some presumption in their favor confirm not$p$. See "A Version of Foundationalism," 552–553. Accordingly, Chisholm seems to be suggesting not just that a believed proposition needs less additional support in order to be rational but also that any believed proposition is rational as long as there is no evidence against it (regardless of whether there is additional evidence for it).

16. Or at least, suppose there are minimal changes in what he believes. Given the nature of belief, it may not be possible for S to acquire the belief p without also acquiring (or perhaps losing) other beliefs as well. But even if this is so, it presumably is possible for there to be pairs of situations of the above sort where nothing that is relevant to the epistemic rationality of p changes except that S in the second situation comes to believe p and any proposition that p entails. Note again that I use entail in a special way. See section 1.5.

17. The qualification "ordinarily" is needed because (as I point out below) the fact that a person S believes p, where p is not a candidate to be properly basic, can prevent some other proposition q from being properly basic. But insofar as this is so, the fact that S believes p can also indirectly affect the rationality of p itself, since the rationality of p for S is a function of what is properly basic for S.

18. For a defense of the claim that any situation in which an individual at first glance might be thought to have explicitly contradictory beliefs can be plausibly construed in one of these ways, see Richard Foley, "Is It Possible to Have Contradictory Beliefs?" *Midwest Studies in Philosophy* 10, (Minneapolis: University of Minnesota Press, 1986).

INDEX

Aardvarks case, 26, 27
"All else being equal," 18, 296n12
Alston, William, 156, 306n1, 318n4, 324nn19,20
Anderson, A. R., 297n19
Antirealism, 309n19
Aquinas, St. Thomas, 1
Arguments: uncontroversial, 4–5, 9–14, 15–23, 28–33, 35–37, 39–40, 57–59, 297n15, 298n22; theory of persuasive, 4–5, 10; conclusions of good, 13, 76, 118–119, 181, 260–264; zero-premise, 56; second-level, 59, 114–117, 120, 148, 181, 193, 216, 304n44, 311n36, 312n38, 313n41, 320n8; first-level, 115–117, 148, 181, 192–194, 311n36, 312n38, 320n8
Aristotelian conception of rationality, 5–6, 66–67, 117, 121–122, 130–145, 209–210, 295n2, 316n56; nonidealized, 232–235, 324n23
Aristotle, 1
Astrologer case, 82
Audi, Robert, 320n13
Augustine, St., 1

Bank teller case, 176, 180, 184
Basicality, 56–59, 63; and subjective foundationalism, 68–83, 93, 94, 102–113, 114, 238–240, 263–264, 269–270; and traditional foundationalism, 69–70, 101
Beaker of water case, 110
Belief: acquisition of, 2, 10, 128–129, 133–134, 197–199, 266–267, 329n16; and understanding, 29–30, 32, 54, 80–82, 298n22, 307n9, 308n10; degrees

of, 41–42, 63–64, 126–127, 254–255, 301n28, 302n33, 311n30, 313n43; occurent, 41, 69, 270–271, 299n25; non-occurrent, 41, 47, 104, 108, 182, 269–271, 278, 299n25, 303n36; causal history of, 157, 171, 174–175, 177–180, 184–186, 187–191, 195, 197–199, 200, 202–203, 204–207, 319nn1,7, 320nn12,15; nature of, 164–165, 215, 218, 240, 275, 286, 288–291, 309n19, 320n15, 329n16; and knowledge, 186–197, 320n15, 321n16; evaluation of, 200–202, 204–205, 322n22
Belnap, N. D., Jr., 297n19
Benenson, F. C., 302n32
Berkeley, George, 1
Blame, 13, 231–235, 296n8, 311n34, 325n24
Blanshard, Brand, 326n9
Bonjour, Laurence, 310n24, 326n10
Bosanquet, Bernard, 326n9
Bradley, F. H., 1, 326n9
Brain-in-a-vat case, 89, 109, 111, 153, 162–164

Carnap, Rudolf, 1
Cape Cod beaches case, 49
Cat-on-the-mat case, 20–21, 26, 53, 74, 76–80, 90, 113, 182, 307n7
Causal history of belief. See Belief, causal history of
Causation, wayward, 178, 319n6
Chair-in-front-of-him case, 109–110, 113, 195, 267–268
Chicken-sexer case, 168–171, 187, 190, 195, 196
Chihara, C., 326n7